CANADIAN
INTERNET
HANDBOOK
1994 EDITION

$20 New User Discount

Valid to June 30, 1994

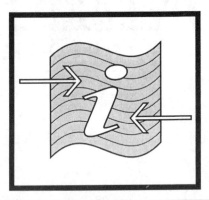

The *Canadian Internet Handbook* is pleased to announce that new users of the Internet can obtain a discount on their sign up to the Internet. The Internet Service Providers listed below will provide a discount of $20 off your first months usage, sign up fee, or some combination of both.

Participating Internet Service Providers

CAM	CCI Networks
Cyberstore	Data Tech
HookUp Communications	
Internex Online	Island Net
Login Informatique	MBNet
NSTN Inc.	SuperNet

CANADIAN
INTERNET
HANDBOOK

1994 EDITION

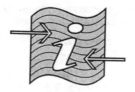

JIM CARROLL
RICK BROADHEAD

Prentice Hall Canada Inc.
Scarborough, Ontario

Canadian Cataloguing in Publication Data

Carroll, Jim, 1959-
    The Canadian Internet handbook
ISBN 0-13-304395-9

1. Internet (Computer network) - Handbooks, manuals,
etc. I. Broadhead, Rick. II. Title

TK5105.875.I57C37 1994 004.6'7 C94-930709-2

Prentice-Hall, Inc., Englewood Cliffs, New Jersey
Prentice-Hall International (UK) Limited, London
Prentice-Hall of Australia, Pty. Limited, Sydney
Prentice-Hall Hispanoamericana, S.A., Mexico City
Prentice-Hall of India Private Limited, New Delhi
Prentice-Hall of Japan, Inc., Tokyo
Simon & Schuster Asia Private Limited, Singapore
Editora Prentice-Hall do Brasil, Ltda., Rio de Janeiro

ISBN 0-13-304395-9

Production Editor: Kelly Dickson
Copy Editor: Dick Hemingway
Production Coordinator: Anita Boyle
Cover and Interior Design: Alex Li
Cover Image: Steven Hunt/The Image Bank

    4 5   98 97 96 95 94

Printed and bound in Canada.

Every reasonable effort has been made to obtain
permissions for all articles and data used in this
edition. If errors or omissions have occurred, they
will be corrected in future editions provided
written notification has been received by the publisher.

CONTENTS

....

3. THE INTERNET IN CANADA   37

4. INTERNET FUNDAMENTALS   59

FOREWORD

....

In an era where ideas leap across oceans and capital passes through time zones at the speed of light, in a world of vanishing borders and new communications frontiers, Internet is an idea whose time is now.

It is no exaggeration to say that Internet is the world's first virtual community, a global federation of 12,000 networks linking some 15 million people in 100 countries, its population estimated to be growing at one million users per month. At that rate, there'll be more Internet users than Canadians by 1995 and some experts predict more than 100 million people will be on "the Net" within five years.

No doubt many readers of this handbook are familiar with the fact that a number of Canadians are renowned internationally as commentators on the electronic media, including communications theorists such as Marshall McLuhan, George Grant, and Harold Innis. The "medium is the message" is obviously a world famous quote. But it was actually William Gibson, the science-fiction writer who lives in Vancouver, whose best-selling novels played a crucial role in popularizing the concept of "cyberspace" in recent years, sweeping it out from the hacker subculture into mainstream jargon and, in fact, making it the reigning definition for the world inside the Internet.

For Internet users in Canada, this handbook will serve as a useful and entirely appropriate tool because, as the cultural historian B.W. Powe writes, Canadians are "obsessed with methods of communications linkages." In a recent book, Powe presents a compelling case for Canada as the world's first "communications state" because our very existence, he observes, has always depended on our ability to communicate with each other across vast distances.

Powe explores this idea through achievements such as Alexander Graham Bell's invention of the telephone in 1876; the first intercontinental wireless message by Guglielmo Marconi on the coast of Newfoundland in 1901; and more recently, the rise on the Toronto skyline of the CN Tower, a mega-antenna to the world and a symbol for what Canada represents in the 1990s: "a paradigm for the electric city of the teleworld," Powe argues, a point confirmed by the fact that Canada has a state-of-the-art telecom network which today is about 95 percent digital.

It's relevant to note that the digital network now in place across Canada gives our country the advantage of an "information superhighway" — in every sense of the term. You want digital access? We have ISDN. You want intelligent networking services? Signaling System 7 is the foundation. You want video delivery? We have coax cable, fiber optics, and compression technology to deliver television signals over copper lines. You want broadband switching? Asynchronous transfer mode (ATM) is being introduced into the public network. These are the core elements of a so-called "super-network" that, in the years ahead, will connect Canadians to the opportunities of the Information Age and the global economy.

Long before the world ever heard about information superhighways, Northern Telecom had its own vision of the electronic community that we called The Intelligent Universe. And since introducing that vision over a decade ago, we've had thousands of people developing the technology and software that will make the electronic community a reality worth having. In the laboratories of Bell-Northern Research, our global R&D subsidiary with more than 9,000 employees worldwide, some of our advanced work in holograms, artificial intelligence, virtual reality and other fields will come along soon enough and change our lives. Change it again, that is, and faster than ever.

At the time we launched The Intelligent Universe, it was considered a visionary but far-off dream. Today, of course, little in communications and information technology surpasses the imagination, and anything that can be imagined is probably being developed. And we'll no doubt have innovations sooner than we think as demand increases from consumers, businesses, and other organizations for all types of interactive multimedia products and services.

With respect to the age of multimedia, when I was visiting the Western Cable Show in Anaheim, California at the end of

1993, I picked up an edition of *Multichannel News* that featured the headline: "If You Build It, Will They Come?" The question referred to the goal of building a national information infrastructure (NII) in the United States and whether, if created, there will be customers for the interactive multimedia services it delivers.

That exhibition in Anaheim hailed the coming convergence of the media, computer, and telecommunications industries. This convergence is not a futuristic prospect or a choice to be made among other choices: it's an onrushing train, and that's evident in the mega-mergers and cross-industry alliances we're seeing today, in all parts of the world, between telecom services providers and cable television companies.

As the speed of convergence accelerates, a new industry paradigm is emerging while the barriers crumble between computers, software, telephony, wireless and cable television. Furthermore, there's no precedent for the impending networked society arising from the convergence that is underway. This much is clear: the broadband digital networks we are putting in place today are not only the highways *to* the future, they are the multimedia superhighways to the 21st century.

The promised allures of multimedia superhighways — from video-on-demand movies, to checking out discount airfares on your living-room screen — may still be some time in the future. But there's no question we're rapidly entering a multimedia world where we will be able to communicate with just about anybody by sending them an electronic message; no matter where they are, the bundle of bits will find them. The knowledge of the world and the videos, too, will be just a point or click away. So will anyone we want to hear from.

It's not only the scope of change that's taking place in the world of communications, but also the speed at which it's happening. The making of the electronic community is a revolution in real time, something that's a constant source of amazement to even those of us directly involved.

But no less a source of amazement is that, without much notice, an information superhighway spanning the globe has already taken shape and yes, like flies to honey on a hot July day, millions of users have flocked to Internet.

In many ways, Internet is a prototype of the intelligent universe with its expanding range of information sources, its diversity of discussion groups that connect globally, its myriad communications pathways, and of course, its unique culture and codes of conduct for on-line socializing. As *The Financial Times* of London commented: "The Internet global network is leading the way down the information highway."

It's also evident that Internet and its administrators face significant challenges in the years ahead. Like any community contending with explosive growth, Internet must adapt to the stimulus provided by its newer participants, and conflicts have arisen about the purpose of the network and how it evolves. Privacy, information security, censorship, commercial content on the network are some of the big issues, along with ensuring that Internet embraces the developments we're seeing in broadband, multimedia, personal communications and advanced intelligent networking.

Jean C. Monty

President and Chief Executive Officer

Northern Telecom Limited

January 1994

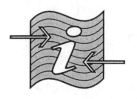

ACKNOWLEDGEMENTS

....

A number of people deserve special mention for their help with this book. Many thanks to our editor, Dick Hemingway, for his comments, his understanding, and his sheer tenacity in getting the job done. Ken Proctor and the staff at Prentice Hall Canada provided guidance and support when we needed it. Special thanks to Erich Volk for having the patience to coordinate our many postscript uploads; Kelly Dickson for just coordinating us; and special praise to Alex Li for his brilliant work on the book design — he is a true artist in every sense of the word!

This book would not have been complete without a detailed technical review of the manuscript by both Ed Hew of Xenitec Consulting and Mike Martineau of NSTN Inc. Our gratitude for their efforts in dealing with the tight deadlines we had to impose.

Additional thanks go to Rayan Zaccharissan and Tom Glinos at UUNet Canada for their technical advice and assistance, and to Lynn Fincham of UUNet Canada, for providing support when needed; to everyone at HookUp Communications, including Jason Mehring, Laurie Flood and Murray Kucherawy for technical guidance and assistance; to Ken Fockler of CA*net, Anton Aylward of UUNORTH, Greg Skafte at Alberta SuperNet, and Mike Patterson at BCNet, for answering our persistent questions; to the staff and representatives of the Internet Society, for providing statistical information; Bruce Becker, for giving us permission to reprint his comprehensive listing of Canadian USENET newsgroups; and to Ian Lumb and Allan Friedman of York University, for helping to fine-tune our questionnaires.

A separate and special thanks to HookUp Communications for providing an Internet account with which to "surf" the Internet.

We'd like to express our gratitude to Jean Monty for his inspiring foreword to the book.

We would also like to thank the Internet service providers, Gopher administrators, and librarians, who patiently answered our questions and put up with our constant deadlines and requests for clarification.

John Demco, the CA Domain Registrar, generously gave us permission to reprint his documents, including the listing of organizations in the Canadian Internet domain.

Rod Potter at York University kindly assisted us with screen captures of new Internet applications.

Infomart/Dialog Canada Inc. provided on-line research services, through their Infomart on-line research service.

A special word of thanks to all the people and organizations on the Internet who contributed information and provided ideas and suggestions for the book. We couldn't have done it without you.

Finally, the authors would like to thank their families, Christa and William Carroll, and Richard, Violet and Kristin Broadhead for their support and encouragement while the book was in progress.

Let's hope that Willie will one day "surf" the Internet at school and at work, as the network transforms itself into the information highway that we all dream about.

························

Contacting Us

We want to hear from you!

You can reach the authors by sending a message to jcarroll@jacc.com (for Jim Carroll), handbook@vm1.yorku.ca (for Rick Broadhead) or handbook@uunet.ca (to reach both of us.)

We welcome your comments, observations, suggestions and other information, as we begin to plan for the 1995 edition of the Canadian Internet Handbook.

ABOUT THE AUTHORS

....

Jim Carroll, C.A., is principal owner of J.A. Carroll Consulting, a Mississauga-based firm which assists organizations with telecommunications technology, with a primary focus in electronic mail and on-line information research systems. Mr. Carroll is a pioneer member of the Internet Society, and is a prolific writer with a regular monthly column on electronic mail in *Computing Canada* newspaper. As well, he is an Associate Editor of a new Canadian-based publication, *Information Highways*.

Rick Broadhead, B.B.A., is an MBA student in the Faculty of Administrative Studies at York University in Toronto. He is Executive Director of the Toronto Free-Net, a planned community computer system in Metropolitan Toronto that is soon to be connected to the Internet. In addition to being a pioneer member of the Internet Society, Mr. Broadhead has made contributions to *Internet: The Complete Reference* and *The Directory of Electronic Mail Addressing and Networks*.

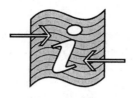

C H A P T E R   1

....

INFORMATION HIGHWAYS

You can't escape the fact that we are entering the information age — pick up any magazine or newspaper and you will likely read about it.

Watch the evening news, and you will probably see a report about some exciting new development with computers. Attend a conference, and you will hear someone giving a presentation about the information revolution. Watch a business report, and you will hear a story about the merger of a communications and entertainment company.

At the centre of these developments is the concept of the information highway.

Information highways are currently a very hot topic! Politicians, the media, and senior business executives are very excited about the concept of the information highway. We are told that the highway will offer everything from on-line shopping and banking at home services, to interactive television, video games and instant video libraries. Hotels, car rentals, and brokerage services will be just a keyboard command away. New "information appliances" will appear which will bring together televisions and computers. Telephone, cable and satellite networks will merge, creating huge pipelines through which all this information will flow.

It seems that everything from the future economic health of the country to the vitality of the Canadian nation is linked to the information highway. Companies from all industries are interested in the trend, that could result in the possible merger of entertainment, telephone, software and cable companies into new information highway media conglomerates. On Wall Street and Bay Street, financiers are keenly interested, anticipating the huge fees that will be generated by these deals. *Business Week*, in a feature article, asks, "Who Will Build the Information Highway?"

Grand pronouncements and vision statements and policy papers abound on why a *national information infrastructure* is critical to Canada's ability to compete. The need for public investment in the information highway is compared to the investment in Canadian railways over 100 years ago.

Undoubtedly, as the power of computers is married to global telephone and cable networks, we can expect some fascinating and wonderful new capabilities to emerge.

Yet, for many people, the information highway doesn't consist of home banking, electronic shopping or video on demand. The information age doesn't necessarily mean that everyone wants to play video games — nor do they want to passively watch new television capabilities or shop at home.

Instead, many people are indicating that they see a different vision of the information highway. Through the highway, they want to be able to communicate with people, to explore new electronic frontiers, to enhance their working and professional skills, to debate topics in global conferences or to seek information.

We might say that many people believe that the information highway will be used not just for passive entertainment, but for *knowledge networking*.

KNOWLEDGE NETWORKING

Knowledge networking is the ability to find information, when information is needed. It is the ability to send a question to thousands of people around the world who share an interest in a topic. It is the ability to send electronic mail messages to friends and business associates around the globe. It is the ability to work in an electronic "cocoon" at home, while still being able to provide work or professional services.

It is the ability to plug into the information highway and become a *knowledge worker*.

Forgotten in all the hype about the information highway is the simple fact that for many people, electronic communications are simply the ability to communicate with other people around the globe via computer systems.

Many people have discovered that this is already possible through a massive information network of breathtaking scope and wide diversity.

For many, the global information highway is already here in the form of the Internet.

ASK THE WORLD A QUESTION, AND YOU'LL GET AN ANSWER

Each time someone signs into the Internet, they are participating in a development that is so unique and far reaching, that many people believe it is a development in human communications equal to the invention of the printing press, the telephone and television.

The world has never seen anything develop as quickly, and on such a global scale, as the Internet. Quite simply, it's the world's largest network of networks. Over 15 million people are directly part of it, and perhaps an additional 25 million are accessible from it via electronic mail. It is used for education and research activities, for political purposes, for business activities, and for the simple fun of it.

Through the Internet people are exchanging electronic mail messages around the globe. It's not unusual nor is it difficult to communicate with people in Finland, New Zealand and the former Soviet Union, as quickly as you might communicate with a co-worker across the hall.

Users of the Internet are participating in global discussions on a variety of topics, ranging from computer technologies, to politics, to medical research to the band, Led Zeppelin. Individuals subscribe to a vast number of new electronic journals, on topics ranging from contemporary art, to space exploration, and to the evolution of democracy in Poland.

Elsewhere, people use the Internet to retrieve information: weather reports, academic research papers, recipes or scientific reports. Others use it to locate computer files and programs, or to retrieve the latest pictures from various NASA space probes, or to obtain the lyrics to songs from the band, Grateful Dead.

The Internet is a storehouse of global knowledge, accessible to anyone with a modem, personal computer or workstation, and a curiosity or need for information.

How Are People Using the Internet?

The number of ways that people are using the Internet is astounding. While in Chapter 2 we take a more in depth look at the way organizations and individuals are using the Internet, a few short examples indicate the diversity of use.

- Students use the Internet to gather information for research assignments and class projects.

  The River Oaks Public School in Oakville, Ontario has linked its students to the Internet, as part of an initiative to provide them with high tech skills.

  Most students at major universities, colleges and community colleges throughout Canada are provided with Internet access. In fact, use of the Internet has become almost as routine and mandatory as textbooks within some courses.

  An entire generation is growing up for which global electronic networking is a routine, everyday aspect of life.

- Computer specialists have discovered that the Internet is the place to be for computer and software support. It now seems that most major software and hardware companies are accessible via Internet electronic mail, and there are a dizzying number of areas in which particular products can be discussed.

  Hugh Fraser of Dofasco uses the Internet to contact a variety of computer system vendors, in order to arrange for support, to answer questions, and generally to ensure that the organization receives the highest possible degree of quality service from its networking systems.

- Journalists are finding the Internet to be an invaluable tool in their efforts.

  Mark Mietkiewicz, a producer for the national TV show CBC Midday, finds the Internet to be a useful resource in finding particular individuals for interviews. Mark says, "I've used the Internet to seek people with respect to a particular story. It's been very successful."

  For example, Mark recently circulated a request in several areas of the Internet, seeking people who were willing to comment on their memories of the Trudeau era, to tie into a show relating to the recent release of the Trudeau memoirs.

- Individuals are finding that the Internet can be used for just about anything.

  Loreen Gilmour, a part time teacher at Carleton University and a member of the Board of Directors of the Ontario Lottery Corporation, joined the National Capital Free-Net in Ottawa, after reading about it in a number of newspaper and magazine articles. The Free-Net is a grassroots community initiative with links to the global Internet.

  Loreen wanted to communicate with friends from Toronto and all over the world, which she can do through the links that the Free-Net has to the Internet.

  Today, she's using Free-Net for both personal and professional purposes. For example, she and her husband have used the Free-Net to scan restaurant reviews, as well as to locate a local curling club through the network. Since this information is also accessible via the Internet, such local community information concerning Ottawa is available to others around the globe.

  Professionally, Loreen has used the Internet to check government statistics, search for the location of library books and look for teaching tips.

- Politicians are looking to the Internet as a means of establishing contact with their constituency, and understand the significance of "plugging into" the global information highway.

  Premier Frank McKenna of New Brunswick uses Internet e-mail, as he believes that the use of telecommunications technology such as the Internet will play a significant role in positioning the New Brunswick labour force within the new global information economy.

  Premier McKenna can be reached via Internet e-mail at the address `premier@gov.nb.ca`.

This type of activity is not restricted to Canada or the United States; indeed, the range of the Internet is expanding daily to become a global phenomenon. Almost every country in the world is becoming involved in the Internet in some way.

WHY SHOULD YOU USE THE INTERNET?

Many people tend to be in awe of the Internet.

Given the level of hype occurring about the Internet, we have very high expectations of the network. But it is often difficult to cut through the technology to understand how using it might help us.

There are several reasons why you might want to use the Internet.

- You might be in an organization that has a desire to use Internet e-mail to establish a closer working relationship with customers, suppliers or business associates.

- You might want to use the Internet to obtain expert assistance and guidance in a variety of topic areas, whether this ranges from assistance with a particular piece of software or concerning a problem with your car.

- You might wish to become a knowledge worker, able to troll the globe at a moments notice, to find information relating to a particular problem or situation.

- You might just have a natural curiosity, and want to explore the outer limits of the network, to understand the impact that a global communication network has on society.

- You might just want to use it for fun.

Whatever your motivation, it is useful to understand that the Internet is not just a set of technologies: at its most basic level, it is a powerful new communications medium that provides its users with significant business or personal advantage.

It is also very much an on-line community (albeit a rather large one!), with its own unique culture, and its own unique spirit of co-operation. Understanding and respecting this unique culture is critical to your successful use of the network.

In this book, we will introduce you to terms like telnet, ftp, USENET, mailing lists, Gopher, Archie, WAIS and World Wide Web. In subsequent chapters, we will take a look at each of these technologies in greater depth — for understanding the technology is an important part of understanding how you can use the Internet.

E-MAIL — KEEPING IN CONTACT WITH THE WORLD

Electronic mail, known as e-mail, has proven to be one of the major success stories of the information age, and e-mail on the Internet has proven to be one of the most useful systems. Most people, once they begin using e-mail, wonder how they ever got along without it.

There is no doubt that use of e-mail within and outside of organizations is exploding. In fact, it is estimated that there will be over 5 million users of e-mail within Canada in a few years. In a significant trend, leading edge organizations are linking their e-mail systems to the Internet, providing them with powerful new communication capabilities.

Internet e-mail is becoming so pervasive, that an Internet e-mail address will likely be as mandatory in the future as the fax number is today. Estimates of the number of individuals reachable via Internet connected e-mail networks is now said to be surpassing 40 million.

It's astounding to see the ID's that appear on the Internet today; it's not uncommon to see the ID's of individuals from steel companies, oil firms, brokerage houses, insurance companies, software and hardware companies, and almost every other type of organization. Equally prevalent are the ID's of students, researchers, educators, scientists, journalists and politicians.

Many organizations are discovering that an Internet mailbox provides significant new capabilities that were not possible before.

KNOWLEDGE NETWORKING — ASK THE WORLD A QUESTION

It used to be, that if you had a question, you went to the library to find the answer.

Today, you can still go to the library, you can look up the answer in an on-line database or CD-ROM — or, you can ask the world.

Through areas of the Internet known as USENET newsgroups and electronic mailing lists, you can send questions to people with common areas of interest.[1] With USENET or mailing lists, you can participate in local or global "electronic conversations" over a period of days or weeks.

With literally thousands of topics available, you choose to belong only to those topics that interest you. You can knowledge network by sending a question to a particular group. You will find that you can usually receive an answer fairly quickly.

Many people use these Internet groups for *global knowledge networking*. By linking yourself to the globe, you establish a new method of obtaining knowledge: whether for your employer, your company, or your friends and associates.

How can you use the power of the Internet to answer a question? Quite simply, post a message to an Internet conference, known as USENET.

FINDING A VIDEO

In early November, *The Globe and Mail* published an article that described a hot, new childrens video that was selling like hotcakes in the U.S. One of the co-authors of this book thought it might be a good idea to buy a couple of copies to distribute as Christmas presents. Since it wasn't available locally, we decided to post a message to the Internet.

At 6:25AM on November 17, a message was sent to the USENET newsgroup `misc.kids`, an area in which people ask questions and exchange information about raising kids — a likely place to find an answer

By the next morning, several responses were received, including the following:

```
From:    sks@sharpe.com (Sharon Sharpe)
Date:    Wed, 17 Nov 1993 23:05:30 -0500
Message-Id: <qht6sAjGBh107h@sharpe.com>
Newsgroups: misc.kids
To:      jcarroll@jacc.com
References: <753535523.34snx@jacc.com>
Subject: Re: Video
Organization: Sharpe Engineering Services,
Loveland CO
X-Mailer: Helldiver 1.07 (Waffle 1.65)
Lines: 15

In <753535523.34snx@jacc.com>
jcarroll@jacc.com (Jim Carroll) writes:
>A recent issue of the San Francisco
Chronicle and New York Times, printed
>a story about a kids video that I am
trying to locate.

The video is called Road Construction
Ahead. You can order it by calling 1-800-
```

843-3686, or send $19.95 + $3.95 S/H to
Focus Video Dept. P14 138 Main Street
Montpelier, Vt. 05602.

I do not work for this company, I found
this ad in the local newspaper.

Sharon Sharpe - Sharpe Engineering Services

Date: Wed, 17 Nov 1993 11:36:59 -0500
From: Anne Paulson
<anne@quilty.Stanford.EDU>
Message-Id:
<9311171636.AA18657@quilty.Stanford.EDU>
To: jcarroll@jacc.com
In-Reply-To: jcarroll@jacc.com's message of
Wed, 17 Nov 93 11:25:23 GMT
Subject: Video

If you did track misc.kids, you would know
about:

Road Construction Ahead
Focus Video Productions
800-843-3686

Wonderful video. They have a new one out
on fire fighters.

-- Anne

Date: Wed, 17 Nov 1993 11:34:14 -0500
From: Debbie Leach
<debil@merlin.dev.cdx.mot.com>
Message-Id:<931634.4@laser.dev.cdx.mot.com>
To: jcarroll@jacc.com
Subject: Re: Video
Newsgroups: misc.kids
In-Reply-To: <753535523.34snx@jacc.com>
Organization: Motorola Codex, Canton, MA

Jim,

I'm sure you'll get a thousand replies but
here goes:

        Focus Productions Inc.
        138 Main St   Suite One
        Montpeiler, VT   05602
        (800) 843-3686
        $19.95 + $3.95 shipping

They are now selling a video about
firefighting as well. Some kids watch it
at least twice a day.

Debi
debil@merlin.dev.cdx.mot.com

Message-Id:<9311624.AA22386@iastate.edu>
To: jcarroll@jacc.com
Subject: Road Construction Ahead
Date: Wed, 17 Nov 1993 11:24:20 -0500
From: Karen Ann Smith
<kasmith@iastate.edu>

The video is Road Construction Ahead. It
is available from Chinaberry books
(sorry, I don't know the phone number), or
I can reprint another Misc.kids article for
you:

Content-Type: text/plain; charset="us-
ascii"
X-To: misc.kids.usenet
X-Mailer: <PC Eudora Version 2.0a10>
Lines: 34

I have received quite a few e-mail requests
for this info. and I have
responded to all I have received so far.
But for those who missed my original post
and would like to have the ordering
information, here it is.
This tape was produced by the same people
who made the Construction video discussed
here awhile back. I ordered Fire and
Rescue this morning so I have no idea yet
what it's like yet.

Promotional blurb:
Fire and Rescue - Kids can now go behind
the scenes and experience the thrills and
excitement of a day on the job with real
firefighters! Ride along as "Mike" the
friendly fire fighter takes you from the
fire training academy to the life and
action of a day at the fire house!

Hope your child(ren) enjoy.

I own Road Construction ahead, and it is
wonderful! I plan to buy the fire one
soon.

Karen Smith   kasmith@iastate.edu
Chemical Instrument Services (515) 294-4057
Iowa State University   Ames, IA 50011
      (Insert favorite quote here)

Through Internet mailing lists and USENET newsgroups, it is possible for people to communicate on a global basis with their peers — to network their knowledge, to share information, and to exchange answers to questions.

p.s. It's a great video.

KNOWLEDGE ACCESS

Often, you will have need to find information. Rather than trying to answer the question by knowledge networking, you might want to go out into the Internet to search for information.

The Internet is quickly becoming a repository for all types of information — whether it be documents, databases, computer files, weather reports, or even the full text of major books.

- Do you have a question about NAFTA?

  Through an Internet protocol known as Gopher, you can search a variety of database sites around the world for information on the trade agreement, including not only the original text of the agreement, but the official position papers of various social and policy groups in Canada.

  Browse through archives of mailing lists and newsgroups, and you can retrace the discussions that individuals have had through the Internet through the last several years concerning NAFTA. In doing so, you can locate experts who are familiar with the topic, to further extend your understanding of the issues surrounding NAFTA.

- Are you looking for a particular computer utility?

  Through a facility known as Archie, you can scan Internet systems worldwide looking for particular shareware and freeware computer files or documents, which you can try out without charge. You can then use an Internet utility known as FTP to sign onto remote computers to directly retrieve the file that you have located.

- Are you looking for information about the Internet?

  Using the facilities of Hytelnet, developed right here in Canada at the University of Saskatchewan, you can quickly search and review an up to date list of Internet resources of all types.

- Are you looking for support from the network vendor Novell?

  Using the World Wide Web protocol on the Internet, you can search the full text of Novell system manuals through a simple, easy to use interface.

These are but four examples of how Internet can be used to retrieve information. The scope of available information is vast. In fact, there is so much information that many people spend their time merely trying to catalogue various parts of the network or develop software to navigate through the network.

The key point is that the Internet is rapidly becoming a repository of interesting and useful information from around the world. Although at this time much of the available information is of an academic nature, it is becoming much broader in scope.

The implications of such a knowledge access tool is that the Internet will become as useful to you as the books on your shelf or as the encyclopedia at the library. (And in fact, there is one group of people who are promoting the "Interpedia": an Internet accessible encyclopedia).

EXCITEMENT AND FUN

Finally, the Internet is not all about knowledge networking and knowledge access.

In fact, some people find that the Internet is a fun place to be, merely as a means of communicating with electronic pen pals around the globe.

For others, exploring the Internet (known as "surfing the Internet") has become sport. The Internet is so large, with so many varied corners and interesting places to visit, that some people like to sign on and roam around, discovering fascinating locations and meeting interesting people with similar pursuits to themselves.

Elsewhere on the Internet, two rapidly emerging activities for more interactive enjoyment are MUDs (MultiUser Dungeons), a form of global adventure game, and Internet Relay Chat (IRC's), which permit you to carry on real-time conversations with other people on the Internet.

Regardless of what you do, the Internet is a new world to explore, and the mere thrill of exploration makes it a wonderful place to be.

One fact is clear: Internet traffic in Canada is growing — at substantial rates.

THE GROWTH OF THE INTERNET IN CANADA

Someone once joked that there are as many different estimates of the number of people on the Internet, as there are users of the network. Consider the press coverage.

- "In the electronic global village, the InterNet is the main street. As many as 17 million people use the InterNet, linked in roughly 14,000 computer networks. They're mostly at universities and government institutions, but some commercial firms have links as well. The number of computers with a direct link to the InterNet is estimated at 1.8 million worldwide, with about 1,000 new ones joining every day. More than half of the InterNet is in the U.S. but about 50 other countries have participating networks. Since 1988, its size has doubled every six to 15 months."

   The Toronto Star, Tue. 24, Aug. 93

- "The explosion of e-mail traffic on the Internet (the international electronic-mail network) represents the largest boom in letter writing since the 18th century."

   The Toronto Star, Sat. 29, May. 93

- "The Internet — the global network with more than a million separate computing locations in 75 countries — is growing so fast that no one knows for sure where the edges are. New machines are coming on line at the rate of 3,500 a day. No map can keep up."

   Sun (Vancouver), Fri. 11, Dec. 92

- "Still growing (by a staggering 25 per cent every three months), that cluster of networks is known now as the Internet — hundreds of regional computer networks that branch around the planet on dedicated data lines and satellite relays, completely independent of telephone company lines and equipment. Because there is no central authority, no one knows exactly how big the Internet is. A survey conducted this summer by the

Stanford Research Institute estimated there were just under one million network sites, or 'hosts,' with untold millions of individual users."

Sun (Vancouver), Fri. 04, Dec. 92

- "Internet is a vast network of networks that has become the foundation for what U.S. Vice- president Al Gore and others call the information superhighway of America's future. Internet's capacity is enormous, and connection costs are minimal."

Calgary Herald, Thu. 25, Feb. 93

- "The Internet is a loose-knit collection of an estimated 10,000 computer networks and 20 million users around the world. It links hundreds of databases and experts in countless fields."

The Edmonton Journal, Sat. 30, Oct. 93

- "The number of computers connected to Internet has grown from 30,000 in 1987 to 1.3 million in 170 countries at the end of 1992. Once an organization is connected to Internet — access for educational and re-search purposes is virtually free and unlimited — the number of individual users is hard to track. Some estimate that there are more than twenty million users of Internet today and that this will reach 100 million by the turn of the century."

The Globe and Mail, Tue. 28, Sep. 93

Thus, it would seem that most estimates of the size of the global Internet indicate that there are some 15-20 million people directly linked to the Internet, with some 20-30 million electronic mail users having access to Internet e-mail.

The network is growing at massive rates. Perhaps one of the most authoritative sources is *The Matrix*, a newsletter that reports on the global communications network. In their December 1993 issue, they indicated "By most those measures, Internet growth has been exponential for five years now. The measures differ, but it is probably not far wrong to say the Internet is doubling in size annually, or growing at 100 percent a year."[2]

In Canada, it is difficult to come across exact numbers concerning the size of the network. Some facts, however, indicate its rapid growth across the country:

- The volume of traffic sent to the National Science Foundation Network (NSFNet), the major U.S. Internet system, from Canadian networks increased at an average monthly growth rate of 1.6 to 2.8%, from September 1991 to October 1993. [3]

This means that traffic from Canada to the world is doubling every year.

- The number of networks registered in Canada with the NSFNet, has increased from 144 in September 1991 to 471 in October 1993, an increase of 227% in just two years.

- The volume of traffic sent from the NSFNet to Canadian networks during the same time period increased at rates of 3.9 to 5.1% per month, more than doubling each year.

- The number of organizations registered within what is known as the Canadian domain on the Internet, as seen in Figure 1.1, grew from 58 at the end of 1988 to 767 at the end of 1993, an increase of 1,222%.

FIGURE 1.1: NUMBER OF REGISTERED ORGANIZATIONS IN THE CANADIAN (.CA) DOMAIN, DECEMBER 1993

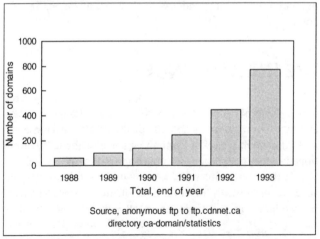

Source, anonymous ftp to ftp.cdnnet.ca
directory ca-domain/statistics

- CA*net, the major Internet system in Canada, saw Internet usage almost triple from March 1992 to November 1993, in terms of volume of information sent and received, as seen in Figure 1.2.

**FIGURE 1.2: TOTAL WEEKLY CA*NET TRAFFIC
MARCH 1992 TO NOVEMBER 1993**

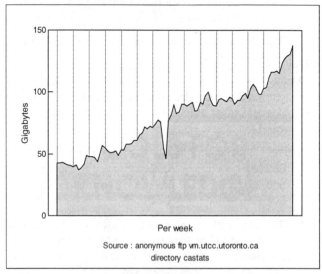

Per week

Source : anonymous ftp vm.utcc.utoronto.ca
directory castats

Canada's experience with rapid Internet growth is being encountered in other countries. Such growth means that the network is set to play a dominant role in any future computing initiative, in any country, in any organization, in any company.

THE INTERNET INDEX

While preparing this book, we came across the recently released "Internet Index," a compilation of Internet statistics and facts put together by an individual named Win Treese.

In this book, you will learn about some of the terms mentioned in the Index, such as Gopher and World Wide Web.

We thought the Internet Index might help to put into perspective the growth and evolution of the Internet. It is reprinted here with permission from the author.

```
The Internet Index
[format from "Harper's Index"]
Compiled by Win Treese
(treese@crl.dec.com), 7/8/93
Revised: 12/16/93

Annual rate of growth for Gopher traffic:
997%

Annual rate of growth for World Wide Web
traffic: 341,634%
```

Average time between new networks connecting to the Internet: 10 minutes

Number of newspaper and magazine articles about the Internet during the first nine months of 1993: over 2300

Number of on-line coffeehouses in San Francisco: 18

Cost for four minutes of Internet time at those coffeehouses: $0.25

Date of first known Internet mail message sent by a head of state: 2 March 1993 (Sent by Bill Clinton, President of the United States)

Date on which first Stephen King short story published via the Internet before print publication: 19 Sept 1993

Number of mail messages carried by IBM's Internet gateways in January, 1993: about 340,000

Number of mail messages carried by Digital's Internet gateways in June, 1993: over 700,000

Advertised network numbers in July, 1993: 13,293

Advertised network numbers in July, 1992: 5,739

Date after which more than half the registered networks were commercial: August, 1991

Number of Internet hosts in Norway, per 1000 population: 5

Number of Internet hosts in United States, per 1000 population: 4

Number of Internet hosts in July, 1993: 1,776,000

Round-trip time from Digital CRL to mcm-vax.mcmurdo.gov in McMurdo, Antartica: 640 milliseconds.

Number of hops: 18

Number of USENET articles posted on a typical day in February, 1993: 35,000

Number of megabytes posted: 44

Number of users posting: 80,000

Number of sites represented: 25,000

Number of Silicon Valley real estate agencies advertising with Internet mail addresses: 1

Terabytes carried by the NSFnet backbone in February, 1993: 5

Number of countries reachable by electronic mail: 137 (approx.)

Number of countries not reachable by electronic mail: 99 (approx.)

Number of countries on the Internet: 60

Amount of time it takes for Supreme Court decisions to become available on the Internet: less than one day.

Date of first National Public Radio program broadcast simultaneously on the Internet: 21 May 1993

Percent of Boardwatch Top 100 BBS systems with Internet Connectivity: 21

Number of people on the Internet who know you're a dog: 0

WHY DO YOU WANT TO BE PART OF THE INTERNET?

To put it simply, as the world enters the information age, and as we plunge into the 21st century, the Internet is emerging as the best way to get there.

In the next chapter, we will take a look at the way that a number of organizations and individuals are using the Internet to link themselves to what has become the world's first global knowledge network.

---

1 . As we will see in Chapter 7, USENET is not really part of the Internet, but makes use of the Internet. However, so many people now think of USENET as being part of the Internet, that the point is really quite academic.

2 . John S Quarterman and Gretchen Phillips, "Internet Growth," *Matrix News*, vol. 3, no. 12, pp. 4-5, MIDS, Austin, December 1993.

3 . Source: Tony Rutkowski, Internet Society

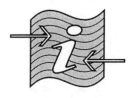

C H A P T E R   2

· ·

USING THE INTERNET IN CANADA

The Internet has become a powerful tool for many Canadian organizations and individuals. For years, it has been the exclusive domain of universities and research organizations but today, use has expanded well beyond these communities.

In this section we take a look at a broad section of Canadian society to understand how the Internet is being used on a day to day basis. Each example that follows involves use of the Internet from a different perspective.

Although some of the organizations discussed are not directly on the Internet, but have access to the Internet e-mail only, they are included in order to provide a complete picture of how this network is touching the lives of Canadians.[1]

The examples draw upon a number of Internet services, including e-mail, USENET newsgroups, Archie and file retrieval capabilities. In subsequent chapters, we will take a look at each of these Internet tools in greater depth.

The Canadian Forest Service, Petawawa, Ontario

The Canadian Forest Service is a sector of the new federal Department of Natural Resources Canada. The CFS is responsible for research and development into forestry management issues in Canada, and gets involved in policy aspects of international trade for forestry products.

At the Petawawa National Forestry Institute, one of seven regional offices of the Service, Internet e-mail is used by sixty scientists and support staff to communicate with universities and colleges in Canada, and with people around the world who share an interest in forestry and related topics. In addition, approximately 20 or 30 of those individuals participate in Internet newsgroups, and retrieve files and documents from around the globe.

Their activities include tracking information on the environment, computer vision, artificial intelligence tools, robotics projects and Geographical Information Systems (GIS). The CFS uses the Internet to stay informed about GIS developments from around the world, in order to determine the effect those developments might have on their own GIS projects.

The CFS also belongs to several specialized Internet mailing lists, including one that focuses on decision support systems for forest and ecosystem management. Through these lists the CFS can keep in touch with colleagues with similar areas of interest from around the world.

The CFS uses the Internet to locate public domain software that has been written by someone and released for use around the world with little restriction. Murray Strome, the Director of Forest Management Systems with the group, notes that "we use the Internet quite extensively to obtain documents and software pertaining to the systems that we use. We've found software related to artificial intelligence and neural networks, image analysis, GIS, and much more. We have found the quality of much of this software and its documentation to be of exceptionally high quality."

Murray also notes that their bio-technology group is starting to discover the Internet. Given the vast availability of bio-technology topics on the Internet, it is likely that bio-technology staff will soon discover the benefits of global knowledge networking.

The Canadian Forest Service is considering the establishment of an on-line Internet database, so that people from around the world can access information directly from the Canadian Forest Service.

Although the Canadian Forest Service began to use the Internet only about a year ago, it has already become indispensable to its activities.

Murray Strome of the Canadian Forest Service can be reached via Internet e-mail, **mstrome@pmfi.forestry.ca.**

Midland Walwyn Capital

Midland Walwyn Capital, one of Canada's largest stock brokerages, began to use the Internet this year in the same way that many organizations are starting to link to the network: through Internet electronic mail.

Currently, staff within the Information Technology group use Internet e-mail to communicate with major system vendors. Plans are to provide a seamless link between Internet e-mail and the cc:Mail local area network that the organization is implementing throughout the company.

Staff have discovered that a number of other financial firms on Bay Street and throughout Canada's financial community are linking to the Internet. "I'm aware of five other brokerages that are coming onto the Internet in Canada," notes Owen Stokes, UNIX System Administrator for the firm. "As well, development people at the Montreal and Toronto Stock Exchanges are on the Internet, and so we can exchange e-mail messages about new trading systems."

Internet e-mail is being used for system support. "Driving this link to the Internet is the implementation of UNIX systems in Canada's financial community. Most major UNIX system vendors have a heavy presence on the Internet, and thus it is the best route to get system support," indicates Owen.

Owen expects that usage will grow once the link to the cc:Mail network is put in place. Once anyone in the firm can easily send and receive e-mail to the Internet, there is a good likelihood that brokers and other professionals will begin to communicate throughout the Canadian financial community via the Internet.

Owen Stokes can be reached via Internet e-mail, **owen@midwal.ca**.

The Daily News, Halifax, Nova Scotia

The Daily News, one of two major daily newspapers in the provincial capital city of Halifax, joined the Internet early in 1993.

Today, it is using Internet e-mail to generate story leads, to contact experts, to keep in touch with its subscribers, and to provide for ongoing discussion of news topics.

Tom Regan, a columnist with the paper, uses his Internet mailbox to communicate with experts on particular topics around the world. "I regularly find bits of information that translate into stories, on every topic from the electronic highway, to freedom of speech, to overfishing by foreign fleets," Tom says.

He also uses Internet services to research topics. "I can sit at my desk, and locate an article or book in the local library, or at Dalhousie University."

As he and other reporters of the newspaper expand their use of the Internet, they have discovered that it provides a distinct competitive advantage — particularly as people begin to submit story leads via e-mail. "The Internet has become a source for tips. Several of the readers have sent me private e-mail messages about stories, that have paid off quite nicely," observes Tom.

The Daily News, through a joint pilot with their Internet service provider, NSTN Inc., encourages on-line discussion of specific columns. Tom is one of three columnists who have their own Internet "mailing list," which provides a place where subscribers and others can discuss topics within the paper. Tom notes that "the discussion group for my column has been the most interesting use of the Internet and the most rewarding. I very much enjoy the interaction with the people who read my column."

Not only that, but Tom finds that his Internet mailbox extends far beyond the local reader base. "It's strange to receive comments from Nova Scotians who live in far-flung places like Ottawa, or Vancouver, or Boston or Atlanta."

The Internet has become invaluable in his working life. "I can no longer conceive of doing my job without the 'Net." notes Tom.

Tom Regan can be reached on the Internet, **tregan@fox.nstn.ns.ca.**

Regina Public Library

The Regina Public Library established a link to the Internet, as the result of a decision by the board to support SaskNet, the regional Internet provider in Saskatchewan.

Although only the central library in Regina is on the network at this time, plans are to extend the reach of the Internet to nine other city locations over the next few years. "The public library in Saskatoon is also on the network, with similar usage at the central library. In addition, Saskatoon has a test underway at one branch," notes Russell Hawser, the Head of Computer Operations for the Regina Public Library.

Russell is extremely enthusiastic about the success that the Internet has enjoyed in the library. "Librarians at the head office are using the Internet for e-mail, and are participating in global mailing lists. The result has been fantastic," he notes.

Many of these individuals are participating in areas of the Internet that are of particular interest to them. "One individual, in charge of the Perry History Room at the main library, is involved in genealogical work. He's subscribed to numerous genealogy lists, and sometimes receives up to 20 megabytes of e-mail each weekend. This has helped in his efforts tremendously," Russell notes.

In addition, the Chief Librarian participates in a number of global public library discussion groups that address everything from technology, funding, skills and training. The Computer operations department of the library also uses USENET and mailing lists for system support.

Librarians are also starting to use tools such as Gopher and FTP, to retrieve documents from throughout the network.

A recent example shows the tremendous reach of the network. From an analysis of press reports, it's obvious that many libraries in Canada are considering whether making details available of the Karla Homolka trial, under a publication ban in the Province of Ontario, violates the spirit of the ban. Legal opinions have been obtained by some libraries to the effect that making information available in a library is not the same as "publishing." As the Regina Public Library analyzed its options, the Internet was used to retrieve details of major news stories, as well as to retrieve the transcripts of the news show "A Current Affair," which reported on the Homolka trial. In this way, the Internet was a primary method of obtaining information which might not otherwise be available — information which has now been made available to the public in a vertical file.

Libraries have a strong presence on the Internet, and in the case of the Regina public library, Internet e-mail is being used for communications to other libraries. In fact, Russell Hawser sees Internet e-mail emerging as the primary method of communications between public libraries in the province.

At this time, the library is only beginning to think about providing access to the Internet for the general public. "There has been some discussion about a Free-Net in this area, and we would likely get involved with that," says Russell.

Russell Hawser can be reached on the Internet, at **russ@rpl.regina.sk.ca**.

Foothills Hospital, Calgary, Alberta

The Foothills Hospital, southern Alberta's university hospital, and a regional referral, teaching and research centre, is located in the west end of Calgary. With over 6,300 employees, Foothills Hospital offers specialized care in trauma, burns, body and joint injuries/diseases, high-risk maternal and newborn care, cancer, acute stroke, heart disease and organ transplantation.

Within the Diagnostic Imaging group of the hospital, the Internet has become an indispensable tool.

Systems staff within the Diagnostics Imaging group use Internet e-mail and USENET conferences for systems support, to obtain help with respect to networking and system implementation issues, and to answer questions concerning specific software. The staff have begun to use Archie file retrieval capabilities to locate public domain software, which is used to assist in solving particular systems problems within the hospital.

In addition, physicists within the Nuclear Medicine Division of the Diagnostic Imaging group participate in a global mailing list on the topic of nuclear medicine, while the Magnetic Resource Imaging groups uses the Internet to obtain software support for a specialized research software product from the medical division of General Electric. Other physicists use Internet e-mail to communicate with their peers and experts around the world.

There has been some discussion within the group concerning the potential of telemedicine: that is, using Internet e-mail and other capabilities to transmit images of patients to specialists elsewhere in the world, or to receive patient images from other institutions in Alberta. However, the opportunity for telemedicine is still very much at the discussion stage, and certainly health funding cutbacks in the province are limiting the scope of initiatives in this area.

The Foothills Hospital has been linked to the Internet for a little over four years. However, according to Byron Draudson, Systems Manager of the Diagnostics Imaging group, the hospital has only just began to take advantage of the fantastic opportunities offered by the network.

"We're sort of on the tip of the iceberg," indicates Byron. "Two years from now, our Internet usage will have grown phenomenally."

Part of this growth will occur as other staff members, including physicians, radiologists and residents, discover the benefits of global knowledge networking. "Some radiologists are beginning to explore the Internet on their own," notes Byron, "and are gaining the ability to access information from other research and medical institutions across Canada and the United States."

Since the hospital has just linked the 800 users of the hospitals internal e-mail network to Internet e-mail, many now have the capability to participate in at least part of the Internet.

Byron can be reached via Internet e-mail, **byron.draudson@fhhosp.ab.ca**.

PEI Crafts Council, Charlottetown, PEI

For a province in which tourism is a primary source of revenue, a successful and healthy crafts industry in Prince Edward Island has a direct impact on the provincial economy.

The PEI Crafts Council, which has a mandate to help develop and support the crafts industry in PEI, is actively using the Internet in an effort to provide its members with new opportunities and easy access to hard-to-find information.

The PEI Crafts Council represents crafts producers such as weavers, glass producers, blacksmiths and other artisans. With over 150 members across the province, the Council provides a number of membership services, including organization of a Christmas craft fair, a newsletter, scholarships and sponsorship of the Island Craft Shop.

Peter Rukavina, the Information Manager of the PEI Crafts Council in Charlottetown, has been using the Internet to gather information useful to Council members. He does so by participating in a number of specialized Internet mailing lists focused on crafts, including one on quilting, one on clay art, and a general crafts mailing list. In addition, he is an active participant in several USENET newsgroups related to crafts, including those focusing on textiles, metalworking and woodworking.

A separate initiative of the Council has turned into a genuine Internet information retrieval service. Since PEI is a remote province, far removed from the major sources of craft supplies, it has often been difficult for producers in the province to locate particular products or supplies. The Crafts Council solved the problem by creating a database of crafts suppliers, which it now makes available to others on the Internet.

Peter notes "We offer solutions to crafts producers looking for information about sources of supplies, equipment, services and expertise. With a database of some 4,000 suppliers located across North America, we can provide references to crafts people looking for particular products (where can I buy a flexishaft in Manitoba?) or general supplier lists (who sells weaving supplies in Canada?). We also hold information about experts willing and able to offer training, education or advice."

The PEI Crafts Council has made this information available to anyone on the Internet, by supporting an e-mail query capability. At this time, it is receiving approximately 5 to 10 queries a week from around the world.

The Council is seeking to expand the service, on a cost-recovery basis, so that it can be used on a broader basis by the Internet community. In this way, the PEI Crafts Council could emerge as a global source for crafts related information.

There is growing interest concerning the Internet among crafts producers in the province. Although a few are actively participating at this time (for example, a blacksmith is active in the USENET metalworking conference), usage has been limited due to the lack of easy access within the province. Access will be made much easier when PEINet is deployed early in 1994.

There is now some interest within the Canadian Crafts Council concerning the PEI initiative, and there is a project underway to link each provincial crafts council, via Internet e-mail.

PEI might be a small province, but it is a major force in the Canadian crafts industry. As the Council continues to expand its use of the Internet, it also promises to become a force in the global crafts industry.

Peter Rukavina can be reached via Internet e-mail, **pete@crafts-council.pe.ca**. Further information concerning the Crafts Council database can be found in Appendix A, in the *Directory of Canadian Internet Resources*.

Shell Canada Ltd, Calgary, Alberta

With about 50 registered users, Shell Canada is starting to explore how it can use the Internet.

"We are just getting going," notes Ken Brausse, Staff Systems Analyst with Shell Canada in Calgary. "We are just exploring the possibilities out there, and are helping our people understand what they can use it for."

As in many other companies, Internet usage started as a result of a need for communications within the systems group. In the case of Shell Canada, the network is being used by systems staff to communicate with system vendors and other groups. In fact, Ken justified implementation of the Internet as a means of reducing telephone costs to major system vendors — which it has done.

Yet Ken believes that the Internet will be usable by many other people within Shell. "People are hearing about the Internet at conferences, and often return to ask if Shell has access," he notes. "People are starting to understand that the Internet has something for them."

In his own case, as a member of the customer advisory board of Cray Research, he often found that everyone else on the board was a member of the Internet. This drove his decision to bring an Internet link into the organization.

Recent new users within Shell include the Health and Environment department, which is participating in a number of environmental USENET newsgroups, as well as the law library.

Ken's attitude is that if someone within Shell needs access to the Internet, he'll provide it. "We want to put out the message that it is available — and if you have a good reason, we'll sign you up."

Ken Brausse can be reached via Internet e-mail, **brausse@shell.ca**.

Enterprise Network, Newfoundland

The Enterprise Network is an initiative in Newfoundland with the mission of providing electronic networking to rural and community development organizations in the province.

The Network currently serves more than 70, mostly volunteer, rural development agencies in the province. The Network provides business information (libraries, cd-rom products, customized databases, etc.) along with e-mail, file transfer and other data communications services.

The Network is also extending services to the general public. "We have established 6 rural Tele-Centres which offer electronic information services and business planning capabilities to rural business people and 'wannabe' entrepreneurs," says Richard Fuchs, CEO and Chair of the Enterprise Network.

The Internet solves the geographical problem of dispersed communities quite nicely. "We are trying to overcome the whole issue of geography and distance from markets by providing an easy to use network and, most importantly, by developing the skills of rural people so they can find ways to navigate the information economy," says Richard.

Theresa Pittman manages one of these Tele-Centres in Clarenville, a community of 5,000 people. "We help find information on particular types of businesses, including market trends," notes Theresa. "We are starting to use the Internet for that; for example, putting out queries for information and searching library indexes."

A new service of the Tele-Centre includes Internet training within a classroom. "We are trying to teach the students how to search for information, since that will be key to the information age," notes Theresa. Yet, the training courses will not be limited to a classroom setting: the organization is beginning to offer training to users via the Internet.

Theresa notes that "We have developed and started an Informatics two year diploma program to train people with skills needed for this new information driven economy. In January '94 we will be offering an Internet course. The 15 students currently enrolled attend classes at the college campus, however in January we are offering on a pilot basis an Internet course via distance (electronic) to 15 more students."

So far, it's been a useful experience for Theresa: "I have been working on developing the course so I have been spending a lot of time 'surfing' the Internet."

Internet access extends the reach of remote Newfoundland to the world, a point which Theresa stresses: "I think the rest of Canada, and probably the world, have the view that things in Newfoundland are very backward. However that is far from the truth. Newfoundland has about 700 communities and most of them are very small, population wise. Yet, we have computer links in many of these communities, and people in communities of over 100 are using e-mail, electronic libraries, and databases."

Richard Fuchs notes "Most of our users never touched a computer before we introduced them to the network, and most of them have never seen the inside of a university."

The Enterprise Network, using the Internet, is certainly out to change that fact.

Rich Fuchs can be reached via Internet e-mail **rfuchs@kean.ucs.mun.ca**. Theresa Pittman can be reached at **tpittman@mailer.entnet.nf.ca**.

Front Page Challenge, Vancouver, B.C.

If you watch the credits that appear on *Front Page Challenge*, you will see that the show now lists its Internet address: **front_page_challenge@mindlink.bc.ca**.

The show, on TV for a record 37 years, is the world's longest continuously running television panel show. With a new producer and an improvement in ratings, the show is experiencing a bit of a comeback.

Cameron Bell, the Executive Producer of the show, indicates that there are two reasons for obtaining an Internet address: "From a narrow focus, we want to solicit more contact from our audience. Currently, we might get 500 or more letters from people pertaining to guests on the show. We thought it important to encourage people to use fax or e-mail, and as a result, tagged our address onto the end of the show."

But more importantly, Cameron believes that a technology like the Internet leads to a form of interactive journalism: in which the viewer gets more involved with the show. Better communications will promote more interactivity — providing television more suited to the viewers needs.

The address has been shown only for a couple of months at this point. "Being as venerable as *Front Page Challenge* is, the audience is older, mainly over fifty. I don't think that there are many *Front Page Challenge* viewers who are on the Internet."

Yet, although Cameron hasn't received an overwhelming number of e-mail messages since the address was listed in the credits from late October, 1993, he isn't discouraged.

"We want to expand the audience," Cameron notes, indicating that there are longer term implications from getting involved with the Internet. "What is exciting to me is that broadcasters traditionally have few reliable methods of feedback for a particular show. You have to make a viewer really mad or really angry to get them to write a letter about how displeased they were with a show."

Cameron thinks that the Internet offers new methods to obtain this feedback: "I see the Internet potentially as one of the ways that there can be a large number of users responding to a broadcast. When that happens, broadcasting becomes communication."

In fact, Cameron believes that a technology like the Internet will have a profound impact on broadcast journalism — by turning it into more of a two way communication system, rather than merely a one-way show. "I don't believe that day is far off. It is definitely in the future. What we hope for is a genuinely significant amount of feedback and debate concerning the broadcast. That's the difference between publishing and communication."

Front Page Challenge can be reached by sending a message to **front_page_challenge@mindlink.bc.ca**.

Canadian Space Agency, Montreal, Quebec

The Canadian Space Agency supports, facilitates and coordinates space activities in Canada.

For example, it coordinates efforts by Canadian organizations booking experiments on NASA shuttle missions or on KC-135 weightless-simulation flights.

Based in Ottawa and Montreal, the organization has some 300 people linked to Internet e-mail. In addition, some scientists of the agency have been using the Internet for several years through their association with the National Research Council of Canada.

The space industry today is global — in a way that few other industries are. Since few countries have the resources to support solo space efforts, most space experiments are coordinated among scientists from around the world. Any particular mission, project or activity involves communications among people who are scattered across five continents.

As a result, the Internet has proven to be instrumental in the advancement of space science and space activities.

Some 80% of use of the Internet within the Canadian Space Agency is based on e-mail. The agency relies heavily on global Internet e-mail as a broadcast tool to disseminate information concerning projects and activities. "I can instantly send a message to people in different companies in Halifax, Florida, Toronto, Houston, Huntsville, and ten other locations," notes Ed Sloote, Program Manager, Space Station User Development Program.

This includes communications with NASA, the European Space Agency, the Japan Space Agency, and even the Russian Space Agency, as well as universities, research organizations and corporations around the world. Often, word processing documents are shared in collaborative projects, as team members on different continents work together as a single project group via e-mail. In fact, almost any global project or activity underway involves ongoing dialogue via e-mail.

Ed says that he regularly encourages other companies, businesses and organizations that he comes into contact with to make use of Internet e-mail.

Some individuals within the organization have begun to participate in a few specialized mailing lists. For example, Ed was recently participating in a mailing list that sent regular status reports concerning the Hubble mission.

The CSA is also a participant in the Canadian SchoolNet project, an effort to provide elementary and high-school students with global knowledge networking capabilities. Students participating in SchoolNet can send questions to the Canadian Space Agency. "A student might send in a question, stating that they are writing a paper on microgravity, and that they would like some help," notes Ed. The message is then directed to the appropriate expert on CSA staff for a response. This direct interaction between students and scientists implicitly encourages students in Canada to get more involved with science education.

Having access to global electronic mail via the Internet has been of tremendous help to the CSA. "It's made my business life a lot easier," says Ed. "Using it allows me to work more efficiently — and time zones are not a problem." He notes that he accesses his e-mail from wherever he is around the world.

In many ways, the CSA is only scratching the surface of the Internet. Given NASA's early involvement in the Internet, there is a massive base of information concerning astronomy and space related activities. This includes a number of specialized mailing lists focusing on space science, as well as USENET discussion groups. In addition, data archives on space and space activities abound on the Internet; for example, images from many NASA missions are available on-line within minutes of being received from space probes.

The CSA, while enjoying great success with Internet e-mail, is only beginning to discover other capabilities of the Internet. As it does so, it will no doubt find that the Internet is of even greater assistance in its mission to facilitate space activities within Canada.

Ed Sloote can be reached on Internet e-mail, **sloote@sp-agency.ca**.

Bank of Montreal, Toronto, Ontario

The Treasury department of the Bank of Montreal, located in the First Canadian Place building in downtown Toronto, has embarked on several projects involving sophisticated Unix networking systems.

Efforts to implement new applications involve coordination with external software vendors and system integration experts. This has led to a need for direct high level support from the vendors of the computer systems involved. To assist in the effort, the systems staff at the Treasury department are using the Internet extensively for day to day support activities.

The group uses the Internet to communicate via e-mail with system vendors, for the resolution of design issues and with respect to production problems. Often, this involves transferring error log reports to the database software vendors — who respond quickly with suggested solutions.

Guy W. Birkbeck, Database Specialist, Bank of Montreal Treasury, notes that the group uses the Internet to communicate with contacts elsewhere in the computer industry, concerning developments, trends, and changes and updates pertaining to particular products. "Information such as what people are saying about particular vendors, or tricks and tips with particular software, has proven to be invaluable in attempts to avoid problems at the bank," Guy observed.

Internet newsgroups have also proven to be useful with job placements. A recent posting to the Internet for a position within the Bank of Montreal generated at least 10-20 responses from across the country. "It's the cheapest advertising in town," notes Guy.

At this time, the systems group is accessing the Internet via a dial-out service only. "We are probably at the tip of the iceberg as far as use within the bank is concerned. But in the future, I see use of the Internet within the bank growing substantially," Guy observed.

Guy Birkbeck can be reached via Internet e-mail., **gbirkbec@bmo.com**.

Park View Education Centre, BridgeWater, Nova Scotia

Park View Education Centre (PVEC), with approximately 1000 students in grades 10 to 12, is a high school located in this rural Nova Scotia town.

In early 1990, an initiative known as "The Learning Connections" project, with the technical assistance of NSTN Inc., and funded by a joint agreement of the Atlantic Canada Opportunities Agency (ACOA), the Nova Scotia Department of Economic Development and the Social Sciences and Humanities Research Council of Canada, was established to link PVEC and a high school in Vancouver to the Internet.

The schools were the first in Canada to have an Internet address.

Students were provided their own Internet e-mail address, as well as given the capability to link remotely to other computers throughout the global Internet.

The objective of the Learning Connections project was to improve workplace skills, as well as to improve basic reading and writing literacy skills.

Students were linked with experts via e-mail, and were encouraged to query those experts with respect to class and individual projects. The results were remarkable; for example, a science class often found itself exchanging messages directly with scientists at NASA. Students in a World Problems course were able to communicate with people in the Eastern Bloc as part of their studies of the ongoing crisis in the ex-Soviet countries.

In addition, by linking remotely to other computer systems, the students gained invaluable insight into the skills necessary to search for information by computer.

Dr. Lorri Neilsen, the Director of Teacher Development at Mount Saint Vincent University, and the program coordinator for the Learning Connections project, noted that "the project changed their notion of where knowledge comes from — that knowledge doesn't just come from textbooks. The Internet encouraged them to do other things when looking for answers to questions. For example, in a project about Australia, the kids logged onto several systems in Australia in order to look further into particular questions."

Upon conclusion of the project, Lorri found that "all students showed a marked increase in literacy skills and technology skills; students with special needs and general students showed the most dramatic increase in literacy and communication skills."

These accomplishments resulted from an initiative which operated on a shoestring budget: the school had fewer than 10 computers, but up to 500 children accessed the network through these systems.

Although the Learning Connections initiative is over, the spirit of the project lives on in SchoolNet, a major initiative underway in Canada which has the intent of linking elementary and high schools across the country to the Internet.[2]

Dr. Lorri Neilsen can be reached by Internet e-mail at **lneilsen@linden.msvu.ca**.

The Polar Bear Heaven BBS, Rankin Inlet, North West Territories

Imagine dialing into a bulletin board computer system that has the working slogan, "Bringing the Internet to the Arctic!"

The Polar Bear Heaven BBS, located in Rankin Inlet, North West Territories is that system.

Located some 1000 miles from the North Pole, the system probably deserves recognition as one of the most interesting Internet sites in Canada.

Chris O'Neill, the fellow responsible for the system, notes that "the Polar Bear Heaven BBS was the was the first Internet node in the NWT domain and, as far as I'm aware, the most northerly Internet node in Canada. I won't claim to be the most northerly node in the world as there may be some U.S. sites in Alaska that are closer to the North Pole than I."

Although small, with about two dozen members, what the Polar Bear Heaven lacks in numbers it makes up for in enthusiasm. In addition to other services, users of the system have access to a range of Internet services, including Internet e-mail, access to about a dozen USENET dozen newsgroups, and a daily NWT weather forecast from the University of Michigan Weather Underground system.

Not only that, but the Polar Bear Heaven system is "home" to the Foxpro-L mailing list, a global Internet mailing list for the discussion of issues pertaining to the full suite of Foxpro database development tools from Microsoft Corporation. With approximately 500 members from around the world, the list supports from 10-15 messages per day — which goes to prove that Internet resources can be established anywhere there is a computer system. Members of the list probably don't give a second thought that any questions they send to the list are routed through the Canadian High Arctic on their way to the rest of the world.

Chris believes that the Internet is useful in dealing with the obvious isolation felt by those who live in the north. "I enjoy having Internet access because it gives me a sense of being connected with the rest of the world. As you can imagine, the North is rather remote and isolated. Although we get television and radio from the South, it's easy to be overcome with a sense of isolation, particularly during the long winter months. As an active Internet user, I am able to keep in touch with many people around the globe, both on a social and professional level."

Chris, in his day job, is the Director of Finance & Administration for the Keewatin Regional Health Board, the Crown Agency of the Government of the North West Territories that is responsible for the delivery of all health services to the Keewatin Region of the NWT. Operating some eight health centres spanning to Repulse Bay in the north, and south to Sanikiluaq in the Belcher Islands, the agency provides full emergency evacuation, dental, optimetric, and specialist services.

Chris believes that the Internet has a real role to play in the North. Already, the Government of the Northwest Territories is installing an Internet site to link the Department of Education to the network. Use is expected to expand to other government departments as employees come on-line.

Chris believes that such networking can only benefit the delivery of health services in the North. "I see such a service as being a very viable way to provide distance education, peer support, research and even distance medicine services that are currently not available due to our geographic isolation and the costs involved in transportation," Chris told us.

Dealing with Chris, you can't help but notice his sheer enthusiasm with his use of the Internet. Our first message from him read like this:

```
From:   coneill@polarbear.rankin-inlet.nt.ca
(Chris O'Neill)
Date:   Wed, 15 Dec 1993 23:22:16
Message-Id: <Y4h@polarbear.rankin-
inlet.nt.ca>
Reply-To: coneill@polarbear.rankin-
inlet.nt.ca
To:     HANDBOOK@VM1.YorkU.CA
Cc:     jcarroll@jacc.com
References:
<199312132007.AA27806@hustle.rahul.net>
Subject: Re: New Internet Book
Organization: Polar Bear Heaven BBS -
Rankin Inlet, NWT Canada
X-Mailer: Helldiver 1.07 (Waffle 1.65)
Lines: 248
```

```
Gentlemen:

Happy Holidays from the Canadian Arctic,
Santa's backyard! ;-)
I hear that Toronto is facing the distinct
possibility of having a "Brown Christmas."
If you'd like, I can probably arrange for a
plane load of the white stuff for you,
since we actually experienced a "White La-
bour Day" up here! ;-)

Seasons Greetings to you and yours...

Chris O'Neill
System Administrator
Polar Bear Heaven BBS
Rankin Inlet, NWT

-----------------------------------------
Chris O'Neill, System Administrator    Po-
lar Bear Heaven BBS
coneill@polarbear.rankin-inlet.nt.ca
Rankin Inlet, NWT, Canada
Bringing the Internet to the Arctic!
BBS/Fax: (819) 645-2015
```

With such enthusiasm, it's likely that Chris will see his dream become reality over time.

Chris O'Neill can be reached via Internet e-mail, **coneill@polarbear.rankin-inlet.nt.ca**.

Summary

As can be seen in the examples we have considered, the Internet is starting to play a role in business, research, entertainment, government and health care organizations in Canada.

As we begin to explore the Internet, keep in mind the many ways that these organizations are using the Internet to their advantage, and think how you might begin using it within your own organization.

---

1 . As will become apparent in later chapters, there is some debate over whether organizations that only have access to Internet e-mail should be considered to be on the Internet. For purposes of describing how the network is being used, all organizations are considered in this section.

2 . Further information concerning SchoolNet can be found in Appendix C.

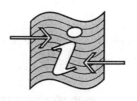

....

THE INTERNET IN CANADA

In this chapter, we will examine the Internet in Canada in order to understand how it can be used by individuals or organizations.

This chapter explores the organizations that make up the Internet in Canada. By the end of this chapter, you will have an understanding of:

- CA*net

- regional providers

- commercial Internet providers

- acceptable use policies and commercial use of the network

- future trends with the Internet in Canada

INTERNET MYTHS

If you talk to some people about the Internet, you might have heard that:

- It's a network that can be used only for academic and research purposes

- It's funded by the government

- It's free

None of these assertions are true, and in fact, each is incorrect in a unique way.

THE HISTORY OF THE INTERNET

The history of the Internet has been told countless times, in many magazine articles and books, so we don't want to repeat it here in detail.

The basic facts are that the Internet began as an initiative in 1969 by the U.S. Department of Defense to establish a reliable communications network. The result was an effort to link the military establishment, universities and defense contractors by computer, into a network known as the ARPANET.

The ARPANET was based upon a common set of communication protocols, known as TCP/IP.

In the mid-1980s, the National Science Foundation began to provide funding for the establishment of research and academic networks throughout the U.S., and began to link those networks into a high speed network known as the NSFNet. NSFNet was based upon the TCP/IP protocols originally established in ARPANET.

As the NSFNet evolved in the United States, the national research and academic networks, NetNorth and CDNNet, emerged in Canada. Although not based on Internet protocols, these two networks provided a starting point for the establishment of a Canadian Internet network, which eventually emerged in CA*net.

Elsewhere around the world, a similar pattern of smaller networks linked into country networks occurred. Eventually, networks from each country were linked to each other, primarily through the NSFNet.

In this way the Internet was created.

Acceptable Use Policies

Most regional and national networks were created and funded by governmental agencies for the specific purpose of linking educational and research institutions. Their mandate was clear: networking should occur in order to enhance local, regional and national research and development (R&D).

In effect, most networks placed a restriction on what the network could be used for. The network could be used for education, research or development activities. The network could not be used to make money, nor could it be used to support profit-oriented activities. These restrictions came to be known as "Acceptable Use Policies," or AUP's.

As the primary U.S. national academic and research oriented Internet network, the NSFNet put in place a very restrictive AUP that limited the type of information that could be transmitted across the network. For example, the NSFNet AUP specifically prohibits "use for for-profit activities (consulting for pay, sales or administration of campus stores, sales of tickets to sports events, and so on) or use by for-profit institutions...." and prohibits "extensive use for private or personal business."

However, because the AUP did not specifically prohibit use by commercial organizations, a number of commercial companies, primarily computer system vendors, began to use the Internet to provide technical support to organizations involved in research and development — which clearly was not a ban of the AUP. In addition, many defence contractors began to communicate with the ARPANET because they were doing work for the Department of Defense, providing further momentum to TCP/IP based networks.

Yet, because of these two "loopholes" in the AUP, and because of abuse of the "educational" provisions of the AUP, network usage grew.

It was clear that there was potential for profit-oriented companies to provide Internet networking capabilities, and it was also clear that in many cases, the NSFNet AUP was being abused or ignored.

This situation led to the arrival of a number of "commercial Internet providers" in the late 1980s — companies in the business of selling access to the Internet for a profit, to companies that wanted to use the Internet in their profit directed activities.

As the number of commercial Internet providers grew, they established a Commercial Internet Exchange (or CIX). The creation of CIX permitted these commercial Internet providers to exchange Internet traffic among themselves without ever touching networks with Acceptable Use Policies — thus permitting broad use of the Internet for any purpose whatsoever.

THE INTERNET IN CANADA

The arrival of commercial Internet providers resulted in an explosion of Internet traffic, from 1989 to the current date, and a rapid shift in the type of traffic found on the global Internet.

As the network evolved elsewhere, Canada played a major role.

"Canada has the 2nd largest Internet infrastructure in the world," says Tony Rutkowski, the Vice President of Publications for the Internet Society, an organization founded to promote the growth of the Internet.

Certainly, Canada has enjoyed a very successful implementation of Internet capabilities across the country. Although exact numbers are hard to come by, estimates of the number of individuals who have Internet access in Canada today range from 500,000 to 1 million people.[1] Yet, many of them might not be aware that they have such access.[2]

The major Internet system in Canada today is CA*net[3], established in the late eighties to provide global networking capabilities to Canada's education and research communities. CA*nets role is equivalent to the role of the NSFNet.

Even though CA*net is the national network, it really is a coordinating body for some 10 regional (or provincial) networks — each of which has its own particular name. Originally, these systems were the only way to get onto the Internet in Canada.

Yet, since some of these networks had restrictive Acceptable Use Policies (not all of them did), you couldn't get access to the Internet via these networks if you weren't affiliated with a research or educational institution.

REGIONAL NETWORKS IN CANADA

Alberta	ARNET
British Columbia	BCNET
Manitoba	MBNet
New Brunswick	NB*Net
Newfoundland	NLnet
Nova Scotia	NSTN (Nova Scotia Technical Network)
Ontario	ONet
Prince Edward Island	PEINet
Quebec	RISQ (Reseau Interordinateurs Scientifique Quebecois)
Saskatchewan	SASK#net

Today, however, access to the Internet within Canada is not restricted to this backbone system.

The arrival of a number of Canadian based commercial Internet providers has meant anyone with a PC, a modem and money to spend can join the Internet. In some locations, you don't even have to pay to join the network: for example, in Ottawa and Victoria, community initiatives known as Free-Net's provide free access to some (not all) Internet services. MANs — Municipal Area Internet Networks, are also starting to appear in a number of communities, providing low cost, at-cost Internet connectivity. As well, a number of local bulletin board systems[4] are providing Internet access as part of their service offerings.

The proximity of Canada to the U.S. results in additional Internet access methods. Major U.S. communication services such as Delphi and BIX offer full Internet capabilities, with access via a local telephone call in major Canadian cities.

In Appendix A, *The Directory of Canadian Internet Service Providers* details the various methods by which you can link into the Internet in Canada. This includes Canadian regional networks and commercial providers, Canadian commercial Internet providers and U.S. providers.

The Internet originally began as a network that was to be used strictly for research and academic purposes — a role that is rapidly changing. Since there are a number of methods that can be followed to join the Internet in Canada, and given that a number of these methods might still have restrictions on how you can use the network, it is important to understand the history of the Canadian Internet environment.

CA*net — The National Coordinating Body for Research Networks

CA*net was created in 1989 to establish a new national research and development network as the result of an initiative by the provincial networks that existed at that time, and through the involvement of people from NetNorth, a Canadian networking initiative that had provided (and still provides) some connectivity to educational institutions in Canada.

The establishment of CA*net was funded by the National Research Council. Today, CA*net connects ten regional networks, each originally established to provide networking capabilities to the academic and research communities in their respective province — mostly among universities and colleges.

**FIGURE 3.1: COMPARATIVE NETWORKING SPEEDS
9600BPS, 56KBPS AND T1**

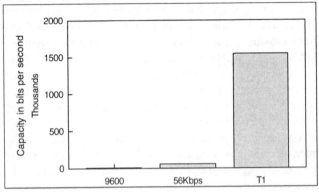

Today, CA*net, through the organization CA*net Networking Inc., links these networks via a mixture of 56Kbps lines, up to the equivalent of T1 (1.5Mbps) data speeds[5] CA*net officials expect to complete a migration to T1 capability throughout the country by the end of 1994.

To put the impact of this upgrade into perspective, consider Figure 3.1, which displays the comparative speeds of a 9,600 baud modem, a 56Kbps line, and a T1 line. Note that access by a 9600 baud modem barely makes the graph compared to the other two communication lines.

The upgrade to faster speeds throughout the entire CA*net network promises users of these systems broader Internet capabilities, particularly as some newer Internet technologies emerge.[6]

CA*net is linked to the major American research network, NSFNet (the National Science Foundation network) via high speed links to three U.S. universities (Cornell, Princeton and the University of Washington). Through these links, it provides the ten regional Canadian networks with access to the rest of the global Internet.

At this time, CA*net is funded by member fees paid by the ten regional networks, as well as through an operating grant from the National Research Council. CA*net is also represented on the Board of Directors of CANARIE Inc., a new initiative with the mission "to support the development of a communications infrastructure for a knowledge based

Canada." CANARIE is discussed near the end of this chapter.

In return, CA*net is responsible for coordinating the provision of networking services to these regional networks — in effect, combining the purchasing power of the ten provinces to obtain lower cost network services.

CA*net also provides national network maintenance and administrative services over the CA*net network, through a joint venture of IBM, the University of Toronto and Integrated Network Services Inc.

An important aspect of CA*net is that it provides a Canadian presence in the international networking community. Although many of the regional networks could likely get cheaper Internet access by going directly to the U.S., by working together the regional networks can promote the Canadian networking environment and associated industries.

Regional Networks

Although they are referred to as the "regional networks," they are simply each province's own network — all 10 of them.

Each regional network in Canada is now taking a different approach with respect to its role in the Canadian Internet networking scene. While some believe that they should continue to support only academic and research use of the network, others have become particularly aggressive in providing networking services to the commercial sector. Some might even be considered to be in the category of "commercial Internet providers," discussed in the next section.

Two networks that couldn't be more different in their approach are ONet in Ontario, and the Nova Scotia Technology Network (NSTN Inc.).

ONET

ONet is a not-for-profit organization that provides networking services to some 87 organizations in the province of Ontario in support of their research and education activities.

At this time, ONet provides Internet networking services to most Ontario universities and community colleges, including such organizations as the University of Toronto, the University of Western Ontario, Humber College and Seneca College.

As well, ONet provides Internet access to the Ontario government and to several commercial organizations, including Gandalf Canada (an Ottawa based manufacturer of data communications and information network software and hardware), Newbridge Networks Corporation (also based in Ottawa, it manufactures digital networking products) and Bell Northern Research (the research and development arm of Bell Canada and Northern Telecom).

Finally, a number of federal government organizations, including Statistics Canada, the National Research Council and Atomic Energy of Canada Limited, receive their Internet access through ONet.

Each participating organization pays a membership fee based upon their annual research and development (R&D) budget and upon the speed of the data link provided to them. In this way, ONet is completely supported by the funding of its member organizations.

ONet is not in the business of providing access to any organization for unrestricted use of the Internet; in fact, it has an "Acceptable Use Policy" (AUP) which restricts use of the network to educational and R&D activities. All of the institutions participating in ONet have agreed to the terms of the AUP.

In general, the AUP states that use of the network for "instruction, research, development and technology transfer at not-for-profit organizations," or use "by for-profit organizations in support of research, development and technology transfer" is acceptable.

Blatant commercial use of ONet, such as for the "unsolicited distribution of advertising material" is unacceptable.

Through its AUP, ONet is restricting usage of the Internet to those with research and academic activities. As a result, unless you are a member of an institution linked to ONet, or qualify under the AUP, you can't get access to the Internet through ONet.

ONet, as the largest component of the Canadian Internet, has done a remarkable job in building a strong networking infrastructure among the educational and research communities in Ontario.

Yet, organizations such as ONet find themselves under increasing pressure, both as the result of the ongoing growth of the Internet, and as the result of the changing role of the Internet.

While an Acceptable Use Policy is in place, ONet likely finds itself with a growing volume of commercial traffic — and is trying to reconcile its research mandate to the reality of network use by its customer base, and the contradiction between an AUP and a desire by corporations, the government and media for an "information superhighway."

NSTN Inc.

One organization that has discovered that it can provide both R&D and commercially oriented networking services is the Nova Scotia Technology Network (NSTN Inc.)

NSTN Inc., an incorporated company, is quickly evolving to become more than a provider of Internet services to the education/research marketplace.

Originally established in the late 1980s, it initially provided Internet access, with the help of its sub-contractor, Dalhousie University, to seven Nova Scotia universities and a handful of local research institutions, such as the Bedford Institute of Oceanography.

Today, operating out of storefront offices on a busy main street in an industrial park in Metro Halifax, NSTN is aggressively selling Internet services across the province of Nova Scotia. Given the impact of globalization on the Nova Scotia economy, NSTN Inc. views its mandate to be one of providing global knowledge networking capabilities to the people of the province of Nova Scotia.

Internet services are sold by a full time sales staff of four, as well as through a variety of sales agents across the province. The company has established access points in nine major cities and towns. Customers include newspapers, bookstores, individuals, corporations and the provincial government.

NSTN Inc. is enjoying respectable growth: it has gone from one new account per day to over 100 new accounts per month. In a province the size of Nova Scotia, this is a remarkable accomplishment.

NSTN Inc. views the provision of Internet networking to be the entrant point to other services, including training, consulting and systems integration services. The company will provide more than just a network link: for example, if an organization wants to set up an Internet database but doesn't have the equipment or infrastructure to support it, NSTN Inc. will do it for you.

With a simple $35 signup, and simple Internet dialup rates as low as $5 an hour during the day and $1 an hour at night, NSTN Inc. effectively sells access to the world to the average Nova Scotian. When one considers that the Canadian economy needs all the help it can get to respond to changes in the global economy, NSTN Inc. can be said to be playing a key role in the upgrading of skills of people within the province.

Yet, NSTN Inc. does not view that its market is restricted to the Province of Nova Scotia. In fact, it has plans to open an Internet node in Ottawa early in 1994, and plans to expand to Toronto shortly after that.

Commercial Networks in Canada

The Internet networking scene in Canada is quickly changing as the result of the arrival of a number of commercial Internet service providers.

"Commercial Internet providers" is the phrase that is used to describe those for-profit companies which sell Internet access to the general public, organizations and corporations. Under this definition, a few of the regional networks (such as NSTN Inc.) could also be classified as commercial Internet service providers.

Commercial Internet providers in Canada are not very large organizations — to put into perspective the marketplace that Internet services can be purchased from, it is useful to take a look at two organizations active in the marketplace, UUNet Canada and HookUp Communications.

UUNET CANADA

UUNet Canada, a private company established in Toronto in 1991, provides Internet capabilities to a number of commercial organizations in Canada, as well as directly to individuals. In addition, it sells Internet service to networking organizations that want to provide their members with Internet access: a number of major bulletin boards in effect resell UUNet services, providing their members with Internet access.

UUNet Canada is affiliated with UUNet Technologies of Falls Church, Virginia, the largest commercial provider of Internet networking services in the world. As such, UUNet Canada ends up servicing a number of Canadian subsidiaries of global organizations, which have contracted for network services through UUNet Technologies. Through its relationship with UUNet Technologies, UUNet Canada has access to the technical and engineering expertise of this large U.S. concern.

UUNet Canada provides a suite of services, from simple dialup access to Internet mail and newsgroups, to dedicated access lines. With presence in such cities as Toronto, Montreal, Vancouver and Calgary, and some 600 customers, UUNet is the first commercial provider to have expanded direct coverage to major locations across Canada. Rates range from $6 an hour for simple dialup, to a flat fee of $1,200 for dedicated 56Kbps access.

HOOKUP COMMUNICATIONS

Ontario based HookUp Communications provides local dialup and direct connection to the Internet for corporations, organizations and individuals. Founded at the beginning of 1993, HookUp currently has local dial up service in Ontario extending from Scarborough in the east to Waterloo in the west, Markham in the north to Stoney Creek in the south. Service is scheduled to begin in Ottawa in February 1994 and to other major Canadian cities before the end of 1994. As well, through HookUp's 1-800 service, any organization or individual across the country can be connected to the Internet through HookUp.

HookUp provides a number of innovative plans for corporations or individuals to subscribe to the Internet. Each plan is based on either a monthly or annual subscription fee, which provides a certain minimum number of hours. If usage exceeds the minimum number of hours, an hourly rate is charged, ranging from $0.50 to $3.00, for each hour over and above the minimum.

In this way, an organization will know with a fair degree of predictability what it must pay each month for Internet services.

The pricing model used by HookUp is used by a number of other Internet providers across the country, and it is gaining a high degree of acceptance. It is likely that this pricing model will continue to evolve as the standard within the industry.

The company has a client base that is doubling in size each month. With a network of sales agent organizations, HookUp expects to see a tripling of staff in 1994.

U.S. Commercial Networks

Even organizations without a physical office in Canada are selling Internet access to Canadians. Delphi, a large-scale communication service based in the U.S., provides full Internet access to several hundred thousand subscribers around the globe. Since Delphi is accessible via a local phone call to a data network in most Canadian cities, it has effectively become an Internet provider in Canada.

We can expect to see many more services like Delphi offering Internet access. The giant CompuServe information service, with well over 1,000,000 subscribers around the globe, is rumored to be close to providing full Internet capability. (It can currently be used to send and receive Internet e-mail.) CompuServe is widely used across Canada and will become a major player in providing access to this vital global resource.

The result of all of these organizations getting involved in the commercial Internet provider business is an increasing number of methods by which someone can join the Internet in Canada, as well as a wide variation in the cost to access and use the Internet.

The *Directory of Canadian Internet Service Providers* in Appendix A, includes a detailed overview of current commercial Internet providers in Canada.

COMMERCIAL USE OF THE INTERNET

Given the increasing number of methods by which you can access the Internet in Canada, the important question that needs to be asked is "can you use it for commercial purposes, or is it a restricted network?"

According to Tony Rutkowski of the Internet Society, "it's a non-issue. It's already been commercialized."

The topic of commercialization of the Internet raises the ire of many people on the network. Yet, it really has become an academic question, of interest only to those who like to debate the issue *ad nauseam*.

The Internet is used for commercial purposes worldwide, and enforcing existing Acceptable Use Policies today is like trying to scoop water with a sieve.

While it is true that the Internet began as a network to support the exchange of information for academic and research purposes, today the Internet has evolved into a global network that is increasingly used by business for commercial purposes. The Internet Society reports that, as of March 4, 1993, 51% of the registrants on the Internet were commercial, and only 29% were research oriented.

Corporate organizations have realized the significance of the world's largest network by linking themselves to it. IBM linked their internal e-mail system to the Internet in May of 1990. Today, there are more than 200,000 users sending more than 350,000 messages through the IBM Internet gateway each month. In a recent survey of 1,300 of those users, 56% indicated that they used the Internet to send electronic mail to customers, peers and government agencies.

In Canada, we are seeing an increasingly substantial number of corporate organizations obtain their own Internet network addresses, as indicated in Figure 3.2.[7]

FIGURE 3.2: NETWORK REGISTRATIONS IN THE CANADIAN (.CA) DOMAIN

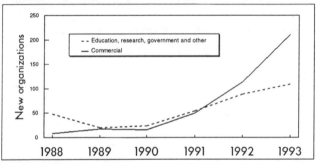

The number of registrations is increasing for a variety of reasons. In some cases, registration has been the result of a conscious decision by an organization to make use of the Internet, while in other cases alert technical staff realize that they had better register the organization name and obtain sufficient networking addresses while there is still time.[8]

Organizations in Canada that have registered on the Internet include organizations as diverse as Canada Post, the Toronto Stock Exchange and the Hospital for Sick Children in Toronto. A full list of Canadian organizations with registered Internet domains is included in Appendix A, *Organizations Registered in the Canadian (.ca) Domain.*

The Impact of Commercialization

The result of the increasing commercialization of the Internet is a quagmire of Acceptable Use Policies, resulting in a massive and wonderful state of confusion.

The best advice is to understand the AUP of the organization that provides you with Internet service, and do your best to respect it, while understanding that the concept of AUP's is rapidly evolving.

MESSAGE ROUTING

Perhaps the easiest way to understand the state of the Internet in Canada, given the proliferation of different usage policies and the number of players involved, is to understand how e-mail messages are routed.

The impact of differing acceptable use policies from some of the regional networks in Canada, is that simple e-mail messages often travel bizarre routes on their way to a final destination.

For example, a message between the two authors of this book travelled the route indicated in Figure 3.3.[9]

FIGURE 3.3: MESSAGE ROUTING

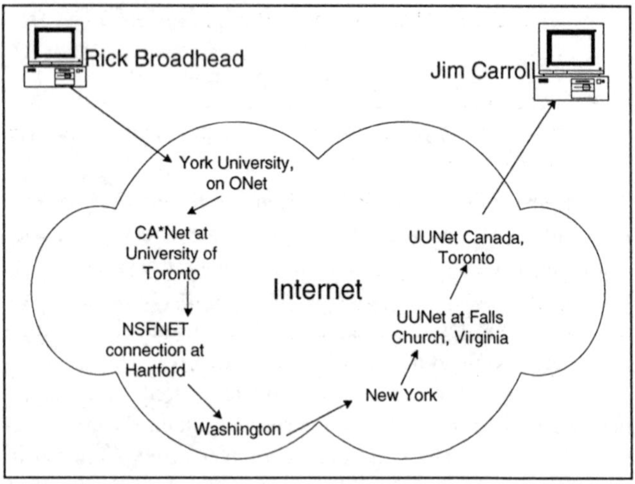

Although such routing does not result in any incremental cost for a particular message, it does result in additional network complexity, and over time, higher costs overall for organizations participating in the Internet in Canada. In addition, as use of the Internet grows, it has a profound performance impact particularly when it involves the transfer of large files.

It is not just e-mail that is affected by this routing, but any Internet application.

If UUNet Canada and ONet could agree on how to exchange information directly, such a long and complicated route would not be necessary. We should expect (and hope) to see such network rationalization occur over time.

WHO PAYS FOR THE INTERNET?

This brings us to the final issue. Who pays for the Internet?

There is a simple answer. Everyone does — one way or another.

- There is some modest government funding for CA*net. Of the current $7 1/2 million dollar budget, approximately 2/3 comes from a federal government grant, through the CANARIE initiative.

- Regional networks such as ONet are fully funded by their member organizations.

  For example, the University of Western Ontario pays a fee to ONet to gain access to the Internet. To staff and students of UWO, the Internet might appear to be free — yet, their institution is paying for access directly.

- Commercial Internet providers in Canada obtain their link to the Internet either via a regional network, via another Canadian commercial Internet provider, or via a a U.S. based commercial Internet service providers.

  For example, the commercial Internet provider Mindlink in British Columbia purchases their Internet link from the regional BCNet network. Internex Online in Ontario purchases their link from UUNet Canada, while HookUp Communications purchases their link directly from Sprint, a U.S. telecommunications company.

  Each of these companies is paying for their link into the Internet, and then charges a fee to their users for access to the network.

- Given the number of commercial Internet networks, a growing number of people are using the Internet on a pay per use basis.

There is a perception among some users that the Internet is free. As can be seen above, this is not the case.

Obviously, students and members of research institutions do not see a bill for their use of the network, but the institution to which they belong is clearly paying for the network.

Elsewhere, a growing number of people and organizations are paying directly for access to the Internet through a commercial Internet provider.

WHERE IS THE INTERNET GOING IN CANADA?

The Internet in Canada is at a point of transformation and is faced with a number of significant issues.

First and foremost, the AUP's are clearly under attack as the network continues to expand at alarming rates. Secondly, involvement from major telecommunications companies could cause a change in the "culture" of the network away from an informal group of networks. And most of all, the CANARIE initiative presents an opportunity for Canada to continue with successful evolution of the network in Canada.

An Evolution in Acceptable Use Policies

Between the two extremes of ONet and NSTN Inc. are eight other regional networks, each with different policies and mandates.

NSTN Inc. is not unique among the regional/provincial Internet networks in Canada in providing commercial access to the Internet. For example, BCNet is aggressively selling Internet networking services to companies and individuals in British Columbia.

Yet, in some other provinces, regional networks continue to restrict their activities to the provision of services to academic and research communities. That's not to say that there is something wrong with this approach ; many people would argue that by focusing on empowering our R&D sector, the Canadian economy gets the greatest benefit.

The future evolution of each regional/provincial network is the topic of a major debate in Canada, and will continue to be so for some time. For example, ONet is currently debating its AUP.

It is a typically Canadian reality that a simple issue can become so complex. What it does mean in the interim is a typical Canadian hodgepodge of methods for accessing Internet services from these regional providers.

If you are in Nova Scotia, you can purchase Internet services from NSTN Inc., regardless of who you are. If you are in Ontario, you can't buy service from ONet unless you are an academic or research based organization, but soon, you can buy it from NSTN Inc. in Ottawa and Toronto.

Or you can access from any one of the Internet providers in the province. See Appendix A for a complete list of Internet providers province by province.

Corporate Involvement

One of the most astonishing things about the Internet is that it took the corporate world, and particularly, the well-established global communications companies, completely by surprise. It is only in the last year or two that major organizations have begun to take notice of the network.

The signs of awareness are already there, indicating more corporate involvement. Two major cable companies in the United States now offer access to the Internet via cable TV wires; Northern Telecom has invested $5million in Advanced Network Services Inc. (ANS), the group responsible for managing the NSFNet, AT&T has taken on responsibility for establishing a centralized directory of Internet services — and so on. Major communication organizations around the world are examining the Internet, trying to determine what it will mean to their business.

In Canada, even some of the regional networks are being "privatized," with recent involve by telephone companies in the regional networks in PEI and New Brunswick.

The simple fact of the matter is that the Internet became, almost overnight, a significant and far-reaching global network, and became the *de-facto* information highway around the world, and indeed, in Canada. The Internet promises to play a major role in the continued evolution of the information highway.

Larger Network Capacities

The communications technology that supports the Internet continues to get faster, permitting the transmission of even greater volumes of information via the network. The impact of higher capacities throughout the Internet will lead to even greater use, and even more innovative and exciting applications.

To put into perspective where the Internet is headed, it is important to note that the major U.S. network, NSFNet, has just completed an upgrading to T3 speeds, a significant increase of magnitude in networking capacity. Figure 3.4 demonstrates the significant increase in networking capacity that such an upgrade provides.

FIGURE 3.4: COMPARATIVE NETWORKING CAPACITIES T1 AND T3

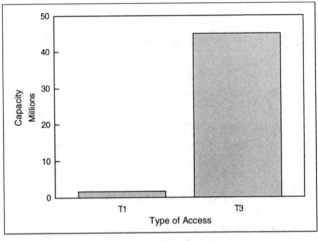

Yet, capacity increases don't stop there. In the U.S., the federal government is supporting an initiative to replace the NSFNet. Although still very much in the discussion stage, the initiative, known as the National Research and Education Network (NREN), indicates that networking technology involving "gigabit speeds" might be involved.

The often quoted example is that the NREN would permit the entire Encyclopedia Britannica to be transmitted from coast to coast in seconds. To put this type of network into perspective, consider Figure 3.5, which compares the current T1 and T3 network implementations to the proposed NREN network. In this case, T1 capacity doesn't even register on the graph.

As Canada upgrades its major Internet CA*net network to T1 capacities, the United States is in the final stages of completing an upgrade to a network that is approximately 30 times larger in magnitude, and the next step beyond that is also under consideration. Although it is not fair to compare these capacities, given the differences in population between the two countries, it is apparent that Canada is in danger of having inadequate Internet networking capacities compared to the U.S.

FIGURE 3.5: COMPARATIVE NETWORKING CAPACITIES T1, T3 AND PROPOSED NREN

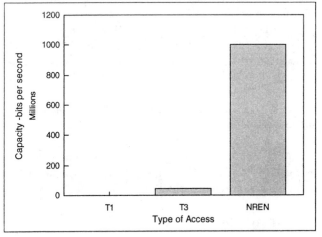

As Jean Monty indicated in his forward to this book, Canada has the technology, the knowledge, and the wherewithal to approach the issue of the information highway. What is required is a national will and a national vision, driven by commercial, government and educational interests.

The current state of the planned upgrade makes one wonder if Canada is building a dirt road while our neighbors to the south build an information highway.

CANARIE

This brings us to consideration of CANARIE.

CANARIE (Canadian Network for the Advancement of Research, Industry and Education), an initiative funded by industry and government, is Canada's effort to build an "information highway" in Canada. Funded with some $26 million in its first phase, CANARIE includes representatives of CA*net, the federal government and other organizations.

Although CANARIE's mission is "to support the development of the communications infrastructure for a knowledge-based Canada, and thereby contribute to Canadian competitiveness in all sectors of the economy, to prosperity, to job creation and to our quality of life," it is becoming obvious that it will play a major role in what the Internet is to become in Canada.

In many ways, CANARIE is only just beginning to deal with the challenge it faces. As the phrase "information highway" enters popular culture, CANARIE has begun to realize that perhaps its mandate extends beyond a mere upgrade of an existing network.

As of December 1993, CANARIE had begun to sponsor a number of focus groups with interested parties across Canada to determine the future of the electronic highway in Canada. Current plans include an effort by CANARIE to continue upgrading of CA*net.

Yet CANARIE could be doing much more than merely supporting the upgrading of the existing academic/research Internet in Canada.

CANARIE should not represent just the current Internet networking interests in Canada, but must represent all sectors of the networking community.

A MANDATE FOR CANARIE

If "information highway" is becoming a catch-phrase for the new economy, it is also becoming a bandwagon that everyone is jumping on.

Yet, for all intensive purposes, many of the people who will talk of the significance of the "information highway" in the time to come, will have little practical knowledge of the Internet, and will not appreciate the significance of this global knowledge network to the future evolution of the information highway in Canada.

Pundits, executives, special interest groups, corporations and politicians will talk about the information highway, in terms that will make it appear that it will magically cure all of Canada's economic ills.

Yet, few of these people will have learned how to leverage the global knowledge found within the Internet.

Few of them will understand what the highway is or can be, while purporting to represent us in its development. The result would be a mis-investment by Canada in a significant strategic resource.

We need to ensure that, in Canada, the investment in the information highway does not turn Canadians into a nation of "couch-potatoes" — a nation of people using the information highway solely to play video games, watch TV and become passive participants in an entertainment network.

CANARIE, through an expanded mandate, should ensure that the information highway provides to Canadians the global knowledge networking capabilities that will be critical to participation in tomorrow's global economy.

Anything less will mean an important opportunity lost for all Canadians.

EVOLUTION OF THE NETWORK

Where should Canada go with the Internet?

In many ways, this question often answers itself, as the organizations who participate in the Internet choose how it should evolve.

As we have seen, many of the participating organizations in Canada are continuing to debate acceptable use policies, use by the commercial sector, and government funding of Internet networks.

Like all other issues in Canada, however, we could end up debating the future, while the future walks right over us. It is important to keep in mind that even as Canada debates the future evolution of the Internet, any organization or individual can establish themselves on the Internet by purchasing cheap, inexpensive Internet access from any number of large U.S. based Internet providers.

It is important for Canadian organizations and governments to consider whether they should invest in evolution of the Internet knowledge network, and to determine what level of funding should be required. It is important that this occur soon.

There is nothing sadder than reading extracts from an on-line debate in March/April 1993, in which a small group of companies in an industry identified as a "growth sector" in our "new economy," attempted to get Internet network access through a regional service provider.

Days of delay occurred as the provider debated whether it should respond and provide network services, and debated its own AUP. What made it ironic was that even as this was occurring, the provincial government was announcing that the particular network involved was a fundamental component of the province's move to the "new economy."

If our current networking organizations cannot support the evolution of global knowledge networking to Canadian organizations, it is time for them to move out of the way and leave responsibility to those with the energy and vision to prepare Canada for the information superhighway.

One would hope that everyone would recognize the opportunity for a made-in-Canada strategy — if affected participants choose to develop such a strategy.

Such a strategy would recognize the Internet as an academic/research network, as a commercial network, and as a recreational network. It would recognize the Internet as the foundation to the information highway for Canada.

Such a strategy would recognize reality.

---

1 . This estimate is based on discussions with representatives of UUNet Canada, BCNet, and NSTN Inc. Exact estimates are impossible to come by, given the fact that any particular Internet site might link one person or several thousands of people to the Internet. The publication Electronic Mail and Micro Systems estimated 600,000 Internet users in Canada as of October 1993, in their January 1, 1994 issue.

2 . Throughout corporate Canada, for example, many information technology professionals are linking their organizational networks to the Internet, in order to gain technical support from major system vendors. Yet, use of the network has not been extended to the balance of staff throughout the organization, due to the lack of understanding of the strategic benefit of the Internet.

If you are wondering if your organization already has access, ask your computer department: you might be pleasantly surprised.

3 . The proper title for the organization is CA*net Networking Inc. For purposes of brevity, CA*net is used throughout the book.

4 . Bulletin board system, or BBS, are computer networks accessible by modem. Usually established by hobbyists, they provide access to computer files, games, electronic mail, discussion groups, and other services.

5 . 56Kbps and T1 are the standard names applied to dedicated line capabilities that can be used for voice and data. The graphs that follow put into perspective the capacities of these lines, compared to popular 9600 baud modems.

6 . For example, "radio" broadcasts are now being transmitted through the Internet. Known as Internet Talk Radio, the service, originating in the U.S., features such programs as "Geek of the Week," in which prominent Internet networking personalities are interviewed. Individuals with high speed Internet links and the proper software can hear the interview, received via the Internet, through their computer system. Some CBC Radio shows are now also available via the Internet, using similiar technology.

7 . This chart is for those organizations in the Canadian domain, and is from information maintained by CA*net. In Chapter 4, we review the "domain naming" system in further depth. It should be noted that organizations registering in the Canadian (.ca) domain are not the only organizations in Canada using the Internet.

8 . As previously mentioned, the Internet is based upon TCP/IP networking protocols. These protocols include the use of "IP addresses", which are addresses of four sets of numbers, separated by periods, i.e. 121.2.11.5. IP addressing is discussed in greater depth in Chapter 4, including discussion of the fact that there is an upper limit on the number of available IP addresses.

9 . A key reason for the success of the Internet is that information is easily re-routed through the network, thus making the Internet literally failure proof. For example, if any system in the example were unavailable, an alternate route would be automatically found.

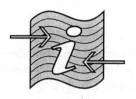

....

INTERNET FUNDAMENTALS

I n this chapter, we will examine the fundamental protocol of the Internet, TCP/IP, including an overview of the Internet Domain Name System. We will also examine the "client/server" model of computing.

It is important to understand Internet fundamentals, and in particular the Internet Domain Name System, for it will have an impact on every Internet tool that you might use, from Internet e-mail, to systems like Archie, Gopher and WAIS.

Understanding the client/server model as it affects the Internet will help you to understand the reasons for some of the limitations that might exist on your use of the Internet.

INTERNET ORGANIZATIONS

In order to understand the fundamentals of Internet operation, it is necessary to know about some of the organizations involved in the network.

As we have indicated, no one runs or owns the Internet — it is a global network supported by many thousands of participating networks.

However, any cooperative effort of this scope requires a high degree of coordination, standardization and registration. There are a number of organizations responsible for these activities, including the following:

- Internet Society — an organization dedicated to promote the growth of the Internet. The key mission of the Society is "to provide assistance and support to groups involved in the use, operation and evolution of the Internet."

  An application form to join the Internet Society is included in Appendix B. For a small fee, you will receive a quarterly newsletter reporting on Internet issues, and can participate in an on-line mailing list to which Internet news and developments are posted.

- Internet Architecture Board — an organization which coordinates research and development into Internet related issues, and standard setting for Internet activities. The IAB, as it is known, is responsible for the technical evolution of the network.

- Internet Engineering Task Force — A component of the IAB, it develops Internet standards for review by the Internet Architecture Board.

- InterNIC — The Internet Network Information Centre (InterNIC) run by AT&T, General Atomics and Network Solutions, Inc. InterNIC serves as a registrar for Internet domain names and network numbers (as described in the next section), and provides information and directory services concerning the Internet.

- Commercial Internet Exchange (CIX) — CIX is responsible for exchanging Internet traffic directly between commercial Internet providers, thus avoiding any restrictive acceptable use policies. CIX also gets involved in issues having to do with the ongoing commercialization of the Internet.

In Canada, national organizations such as CA*net, regional providers such as BCNet and ONet, the CA*net Registry and commercial organizations such as UUNet Canada, are involved in specific Canadian Internet issues.

In particular, as we begin to examine the Canadian Domain Name system, we will take a look at how both CA*net and the InterNIC get involved.

TCP/IP BASICS

The Internet is based upon a computer networking protocol known as TCP/IP (Transmission Control Protocol/Internet Protocol), developed as part of the original ARPANET initiative described in the previous chapter.

The TCP/IP protocol includes the use of IP addresses and Domain Names. An example of an IP address is `131.162.2.77`. An example of a name under the Domain Name system is `vml.yorku.ca`.

The IP address and Domain Name system form the heart of the global Internet.

Why Is This Important?

As you travel the Internet, you will often see phrases such as `Telnet to 131.162.2.77` or `ftp to ftp.cdnnet.ca.` This means that you will use either the numeric IP address or domain name when you establish a link to another computer on the Internet. Specific Internet applications that you might use, including e-mail, FTP or Telnet, will use IP addresses and Domain Names. This requires that you have some understanding of the IP addressing and Domain Name scheme.

IP Addresses

An IP address is a fundamental component of the TCP/IP networking protocol.

IP addresses consist of four sets of numbers separated by periods. For example, Acadia University in Nova Scotia has the IP address 131.162.2.77. The address is unique throughout the Internet world, and will be used by individuals and by Internet applications to reach Acadia University.

The IP address is used most often with the `telnet` command (discussed in Chapter 6), to reach a particular computer on the network.

Think of an IP address as being the Internet equivalent to a telephone number.

The current IP numbering scheme allows for what are known as Class A, B and C addresses. Class A addresses are allocated only to the largest organizations or networks, while at the other end of the spectrum, Class C addresses are used by smaller or medium sized organizations or networks.

In many cases, multiple Class C addresses are used by one organization. This is particularly true as the Internet continues to grow. Under the current IP address protocol, there is an upper limit on the number of potential A,B and C addresses. Although the reason for the upper limit is far too technical a discussion for this book, and although solutions are in the works, the best advice is — if your organization does not yet have a registered IP address, get one!

Although an organization with a private TCP/IP network can use any set of numbers it wishes, those that participate in the global Internet must obtain a unique IP address from the InterNIC.[1]

Organizations in Canada desiring an IP address must obtain it from the CA*net IP Registry, which has been allocated a set of numbers, by the InterNIC, for use within Canada. At this time, only Class C addresses are available for use in Canada.

Appendix B contains the form *Canadian Internet Protocol Network Number Application for Class C Network Number(s)*, which should be used by Canadian organizations wishing to obtain an IP address.

Internet Domain Names

Since people often remember names better than they do numbers, the people involved in the Internet came up with the Domain Name System. This permits each computer (referred to as a "host") on the Internet to be reached by a simple name, rather than just IP addresses.

Internet applications such as Telnet, FTP, and gopher can be used with either an IP address or a host name, based upon the Domain Name system, to reach a particular computer. Common practice is to use the host name, as it is more descriptive and easier to remember.

There are a number of components to the Domain Name System, including *top level domains* and *subdomains*, which in Canada include *provincial* and *municipal* domains. A *company* or *organization* name is also included.

The Domain Name System

Figures 4.1 and 4.2 give some examples of the registered names for several Canadian organizations.

FIGURE 4.1: ORGANIZATIONS IN THE "CANADIAN .CA DOMAIN"

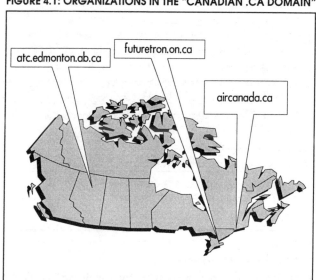

FIGURE 4.2: ORGANIZATIONS IN THE TOP LEVEL "ZONE NAMES"

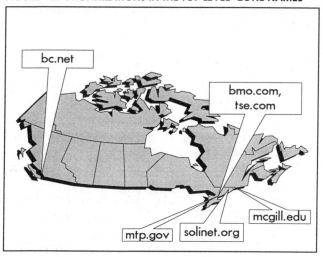

TOP LEVEL DOMAINS

As can be seen in Figures 4.1 and 4.2, at the right most portion of every Internet host name is a top level domain, which is either:

- a country code.

    Country codes are two character codes, as defined by the International Standards Organization. The country code for Canada is **.ca.**

or

- a descriptive zone name.

  These descriptive zone names include the following categories:

.com	Commercial organizations
.edu	Educational institutions or sites
.gov	Government institutions or sites
.mil	Military sites
.net	Network organizations; often used by organizations reselling Internet services
.org	Other organizations

SUBDOMAINS IN CANADA

In Figure 4.1, the names used by two of the organizations include *subdomains*.

In Canada, under the .ca domain, a geographically oriented *subdomain* hierarchy is used.

The scope of presence within Canada determines where an organization is registered within that hierarchy. Subdomains, when used, include:

- a provincial code, i.e., **.ab** for Alberta in the example in Figure 4.1.

- a city or municipality name, i.e., **edmonton** for the example in Figure 4.1.

The registrar of the Canadian domain provides the following rules of guidance to determine what type of subdomain name an organization can obtain in Canada:

- if the organization is national in scope, i.e., has presence in more than one province, or is incorporated or chartered nationally, the name of the company is used with the .ca domain name, i.e., **aircanada.ca.**

- if the organization is based in only one province, but has multiple locations in the province, the province name is included, i.e., **futuretron.on.ca.**

- if the organization is small and based in only one jurisdiction, the municipality name is included in the subdomain name, i.e., **atc.edmonton.ab.ca.**

The following provincial codes are used within Canadian subdomains.

PROVINCIAL CODE	FOR ORGANIZATIONS REGISTERED IN:
.ab	Alberta
.bc	British Columbia
.mb	Manitoba
.nb	New Brunswick
.nf	Newfoundland
.ns	Nova Scotia
.nt	North West Territories
.on	Ontario
.pe	Prince Edward Island
.qc	Quebec
.sk	Saskatchewan
.yk	Yukon

Registering Domain Names

Organizations in Canada have the choice of either registering within the Canadian (.ca) domain or registering within one of the three character zone names, as discussed above.

The choice will depend on several factors, mostly having to do with the image the organization wishes to create with respect to its Internet domain name.

An organization should register with the Canadian Domain Registry if it wants a .ca domain name. It should register with the InterNIC directly if it wants to be within the .com, .mil, .net or other top level domains.

Some organizations have expressed frustration with the Canadian domain name system, and it is always the subject of ongoing debate within the Internet community.

In particular, smaller organizations, which are required to use provincial and municipal subdomains, often do not like the complex names that might arise, for example, **prince-rupert.bc.ca.** As a result, some organizations turn to the InterNIC to register directly within a .com or .org domain.

The decision on where to register and what type of domain name to obtain is very much related to image. As Rayan Zacharriason of UUNet Canada indicates: "It's a 'corporate image' thing. If you don't want to be perceived as different from most U.S. companies, you register in .com. If your organization is international, or mobile, or vague, you register in .org."

REGISTERING UNDER THE .CA CANADIAN DOMAIN

Registration under the Canadian (.ca) domain is coordinated by CA*net, and is currently overseen by:

```
CA Domain Registrar
c/o John Demco
Department of Computer Science
University of British Columbia
Vancouver, British Columbia
V6T 1Z2
E-mail: ca-registrar@CDNnet.CA
```

Appendix B includes the document *CA Subdomain Application Instructions*, which provides full details for registering with the Canadian .ca domain.

You should not send a registration application directly to the CA Domain Registrar. Instead, you should submit the application through one of the Committee Members as listed within the document *CA Subdomain Application Instructions*.

REGISTERING DIRECTLY WITH THE INTERNIC

Organizations which do not wish to register in the Canadian (.ca) domain, but wish to register within one of the descriptive zone names, should arrange for this through their Internet service provider, or contact the InterNIC directly.

OTHER ISSUES RELATED TO DOMAIN NAMES

There are two other issues related to the Domain Name system.

- There are many organizations which are not yet directly on the Internet, i.e., they do not have a computer which is directly connected to the Internet and hence, cannot be directly reached via the Internet.[2]

  Yet, these organizations might desire to link their internal e-mail system into the Internet. In order to do this, they must have a name registered on the Internet.

  To get around this dilemma, the concept of an MX (Message Exchange) record was introduced, which allows an organization to obtain and use a name for purposes of e-mail.

Accordingly, as we examine the domain name scheme, keep in mind that any organization, even if it is not directly linked to the Internet, can participate in the Internet Domain Name System.

- There is nothing to prevent an organization from registering within multiple domains. For example, the University of Toronto can be found with the subdomain names `utoronto.ca` and `toronto.edu`.

CLIENT/SERVER AND THE INTERNET

In the chapters that follow, we will take a look at major Internet applications:

- Chapter 5: Internet electronic mail (e-mail)

- Chapter 6: knowledge networking, using applications such as Internet mailing lists and USENET

- Chapter 7: remote access applications, such as Telnet and FTP

- Chapter 8: knowledge retrieval applications, such as Gopher, WAIS, Hytelnet, Archie and World Wide Web

If you read computer magazines or work in the industry, you will be inundated with articles that mention client/server computing.

To understand how you might make use of the these applications in different software environments, it is important to understand the client/server model of computing.

A Technical Definition of Client/Server Computing

In the client/server computing model, a client computer runs a program that acts on behalf of a user, to access data located on a server computer.

The client computer contains the intelligence to formulate a query or run a program, while the server contains the horsepower and capability to store the data and access it quickly.

A client can be used to access any number of server applications, resulting in more flexible application design capabilities. Likewise, a single server can service a number of clients.

A Practical Definition

A client is a computer program that asks questions, to find information within data located on a server.

FIGURE 4.3: CLIENT/SERVER MODEL

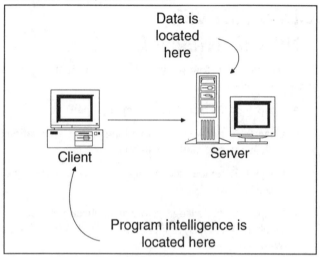

The Impact of Client/Server on the Internet

When you are using the Internet, the location of the client that you use has a direct effect on:

- how an Internet application is used
- how easy it is to use
- what the application looks like as you use it
- the speed with which the application runs

The client that you use might be located:

- somewhere out on the Internet
- on your own system

    or

- on the system of your Internet service provider

DIRECT CONNECTIONS TO THE INTERNET

Where the client is located depends on whether you are directly connected to the Internet or not.

In Chapter 9, we take a look at methods by which an individual or organization can establish a link to the Internet.

FIGURE 4.4: METHODS OF LINKING TO THE INTERNET

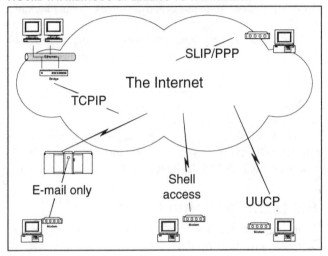

In a nutshell, individuals on networks which have a "hardwired" (i.e., permanent) TCP/IP network connection to the Internet, are considered to be directly on the Internet. As well, individuals or networks with SLIP or PPP access via a dialup modem are also considered to be directly on the Internet.

Those who use "shell access" or UUCP are not directly connected to the Internet. Those who only send and receive e-mail to the Internet are not directly connected to the Internet.[3]

Those with only an e-mail link to the Internet can do little else besides sending and receiving e-mail, while users of UUCP cannot use much more than Internet e-mail and USENET newsgroups.[4]

Individuals with shell account access encounter limitations in the sophistication of the programs that they can use on the Internet.

Individuals with direct connectivity to the Internet using TCP/IP (either hardwired or using SLIP/PPP) can use many of the more sophisticated and useful versions of client software when interacting with the Internet, and hence, will enjoy greater ease of use with the network.

Shell Account Limitations

Users with shell access to the Internet can use most major Internet applications, including Gopher, WAIS and Archie. However, there are limitations imposed as a result of using "communications software" which involves "terminal emulation."

When linked to the Internet service provider, the individual with shell access must use communications software that "pretends" to be a terminal on the system of the Internet service provider. This is known as terminal emulation.

Yet, even the best terminal emulation software is subject to limitations in what it can do.

For all practical purposes, if you are linked to the Internet via terminal emulation you can in no way consider your system to be "directly" on the Internet.

The Location of the Client

Terminal emulation results in substantial limitations for shell account users, in terms of what they can do with the Internet, and the degree of sophistication of the applications they can run.

The impact of the limitations mean that the "clients" you use on the Internet are not located on your own system, but are located somewhere else. This makes the Internet a little more difficult to use.

To put this into perspective, let us examine three different situations involving the location of the client.

In these examples, the client is located:

- on some remote computer, somewhere in the Internet

- on the computer of your Internet service provider

  or

- on your own computer or local network

CLIENT LOCATED ON A REMOTE SERVER

The first case, seen in Figure 4.5, is usually found in the situation where an individual accesses an Internet service provider via a shell account connection. The individual is not directly connected to the Internet.

FIGURE 4.5: CLIENT LOCATED ON A REMOTE SERVER

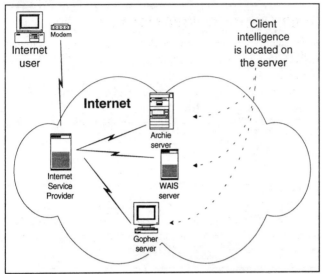

Once linked to the Internet service provider, a user establishes a link out to various computers on the Internet to run clients such as Archie, WAIS, or Gopher.

In this case, the client (Archie, WAIS or Gopher) runs on a remote system located somewhere on the Internet, which also happens to be the server.

The individual is limited to using the application as a "terminal" user, which limits the "friendliness" of the application, and the speed with which it operates.

In Figure 4.5, the client (intelligence) and server (data) are located on the same system.[5]

CLIENT INTELLIGENCE LOCATED ON INTERNET SERVICE PROVIDER

In the second case, seen in Figure 4.6, the client is located on the system of the Internet service provider, and is accessed via a shell account.

For example, with some Internet service providers in Canada, programs such as Gopher and Archie can be run directly on the host within your Internet service providers network, rather than on a computer located somewhere else on the

Internet. The result is improved speed of the application, and in some cases, an easier to use application.

FIGURE 4.6: CLIENT LOCATED ON INTERNET SERVICE PROVIDER[6]

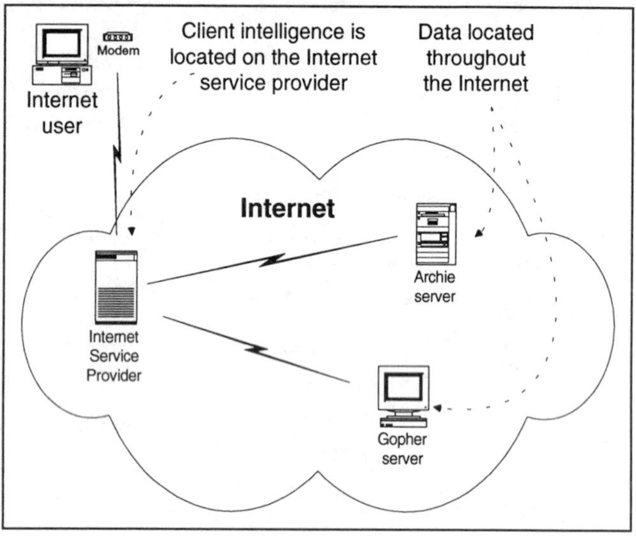

However, even running such an application on a host at your Internet service provider will not permit you to run programs of the degree of sophistication found in the next example, for those who are directly connected to the Internet.

CLIENT LOCATED ON YOUR OWN COMPUTER OR NETWORK

Figure 4.7 presents an example of those who are "connected directly to the Internet" via a hardwired TCP/IP connection or by using SLIP/PPP.

In this case, the client intelligence is located on their own computer system, i.e., the application, which might be WAIS, Archie or Gopher, runs on their own system or network, even if it is accessing data contained on servers located somewhere else on the Internet.

Since the application is local, it runs much quicker, and since it will use TCP/IP protocols directly, it is friendlier and easier to use. In this case, the individual is not subject to the restrictions imposed by running the application as a "terminal" user.

FIGURE 4.7: CLIENT LOCATED ON LOCAL COMPUTER

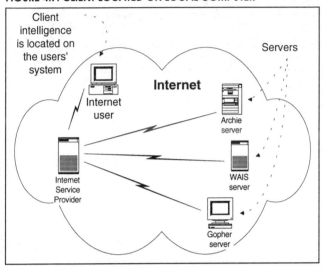

In fact, it is within this mode of use that many of the exciting, new developments in the Internet are occurring, as we will see in Chapter 8.

The Impact of the Location of the Client

Methods of establishing connectivity to the Internet will be addressed in Chapter 9.

For now, however, keep in mind that the applications presented in the following chapters, and in particular Chapter 8, are presented from the perspective of a terminal user accessing the Internet via a shell account.

In the latter part of Chapter 8, we take a look at some of the more sophisticated applications for those directly connected to the Internet using TCP/IP, including those with SLIP/PPP connections.

---

1 . There have been a number of organizations with private TCP/IP networks that encountered substantial difficulty when they tried to join the Internet, since they had not obtained registered IP addresses from the InterNIC or its predecessors.

2 . Even so, these organizations might have obtained an IP address from InterNIC or the CA*net Domain Registry, to prepare themselves for eventual direct connectivity to the Internet.

3 . These methods are explained in greater depth in Chapter 9. For now, keep in mind that the method you use to link to the Internet, might mean that you are not directly on the Internet.

4 . As will be seen in Chapter 6, however, it is possible for e-mail users to receive Intenet files from FTP sites, using a file retrieval-by-e-mail feature.

5 . As we will see in Chapter 8, with programs like Gopher and WAIS, there are multiple server locations involved. Programs like WAIS and Gopher end up accessing
data from throughout the Internet. Hence, you could be using the client on a remote
server, while the data is located on multiple different servers throughout the Internet.

6 . WAIS is not shown in this diagram, as there are few WAIS clients throughout the
Internet.

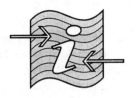

. . . .

CHAPTER 5

INTERNET ELECTRONIC MAIL

When people and organizations talk about the "information highway," there is a great deal of emphasis on multimedia and video applications.

Electronic mail, or e-mail, is often viewed as "pedestrian" and "old-fashioned." Yet, Internet e-mail is probably one of the most popular Internet applications.

E-mail is the only application that extends well beyond the boundaries of the real Internet, involving many other e-mail systems and many different technologies.

Due to the trend to list Internet addresses on business cards, in magazines, newspapers and even television shows, Internet e-mail is beginning to achieve a very high public profile.

Internet e-mail addresses are based upon the Internet Domain Name System described in the previous chapter, which provides for standard format addresses to be used throughout the network.

An address in the form of, for example, **jcarroll@ jacc.com**, is becoming as essential for some business and personal relationships, as the fax number was in the mid-eighties. When people begin to list their Internet e-mail addresses on their business cards, you know that the address style has gained mass acceptance.

There are two reasons for this:

- the growing number of e-mail systems which now have links to the Internet

This includes corporate and organizational systems linked directly to the Internet, as well as many other e-mail systems such as MCIMail, CompuServe and Delphi.

- the easy to understand style of Internet e-mail address

  Addresses like **billg@microsoft.com** or **president@whitehouse.gov**, the Internet addresses of Bill Gates and Bill Clinton, are easily recognizable as Internet addresses.

It is this easy recognition that is key to the dominance of Internet e-mail for communication between people on different computer systems

A Global Standard for E-Mail

There is a global standard for e-mail. It's called X.400.

Fortunately, Internet e-mail has nothing to do with it.

X.400 is a standard adopted by an international standards body (CCITT) defining how e-mail should be exchanged among different e-mail systems.

X.400 works well at a technical level, but fails miserably as a simple, easy to use method of sending and receiving e-mail.

For example, one of the authors of this book has the following X.400 addresses on three different commercial e-mail systems.

```
C=CA;A=TELECOM.CANADA;DD=ID=JA.CARROLL;F=JIM
   ;S=CARROLL
C=GB;A=TELEMAIL;P=LANGATE;O=TMCA.UNI;OU1=155
   7TOUC;G=JIM;S=CARROLL
C=US;A=MCIMAIL;DD=ID=;F=JIM;S=CARROLL
```

His Internet address is jcarroll@jacc.com.

Which would you prefer?

You will find a lot of business cards with Internet addresses appearing on them. You won't find many listing X.400 addresses.

The world is quickly accepting the use of Internet e-mail addresses, because they are easy to understand and easy to use. It would appear that X.400 addresses are being rejected out of hand, because they are confusing, complex, and are not easy to use or remember.

Quite frankly, the standard is not gaining wide acceptance — another reason why you should want to get going on Internet e-mail.

WHAT IS INTERNET E-MAIL?

A strict definition of Internet e-mail is that it consists of e-mail sent and received from computers which are directly connected to the Internet.

However, such a definition is unworkable today, given the number of other systems that are connecting to the Internet.

The simple fact of the matter is that Internet e-mail, because of its easily recognized address, is increasingly used for inter-organizational communications, and is rapidly emerging as the backbone of a globally linked e-mail network.

Many different types of e-mail technologies are now being linked to the Internet. These systems include:

FIGURE 5.1: E-MAIL SYSTEMS CONNECTED TO THE INTERNET

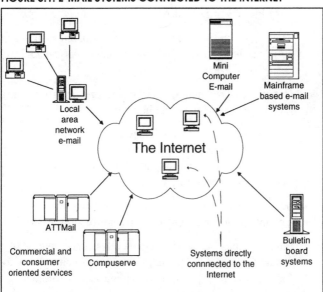

- local area network, or LAN, based e-mail systems.

  Many organizations are actively implementing LAN based e-mail systems, such as Microsoft MSMail, Lotus cc:Mail, Lotus Notes and WordPerfect Office, to support the exchange of e-mail within the company.

  The number of LAN based e-mail users in corporate organizations is expected to grow to some 40 million in North America by 1995.

Organizations with advanced LAN e-mail strategies involving these technologies are actively implementing software that permits people to send and receive messages from the Internet.

As a result, many people within organizations implementing cc:Mail, MSMail or other similar LAN e-mail systems are finding that they have the capability to reach individuals on the Internet.[1]

For example, Lotus Corporation, which uses cc:Mail and Lotus Notes throughout its worldwide organization, is reachable via the Internet, with the registered Internet domain, `lotus.com.`

- in-house mainframe and minicomputer systems, such as IBM PROFS or Digital All-in-1.

  These systems, the predecessor to LAN based e-mail, are still in wide use throughout many organizations, particularly *Fortune* 1000 companies.

  Companies are linking their mainframe and minicomputer e-mail systems to the Internet.

  For example, the Ontario government, which uses a number of these systems as well as LAN based e-mail systems, is linked to the Internet through the sub-domain, `epo.gov.on.ca.`

- bulletin board systems (BBS), which range in size from a couple of dozen people to thousands of subscribers.

  For example, Canada Remote Systems, historically Canada's largest BBS, has linked its e-mail system to Internet e-mail (as well as providing access to other Internet services), thus providing their customers with access to the world.

- commercial e-mail systems, such as AT&TMail and MCIMail, and in Canada, TheNet:Mail (formerly Envoy 100) and Immedia.

  Organizations which do not run e-mail on their own LAN's, minicomputers or mainframes, often end up buying e-mail on commercial e-mail systems. In addition, some *Fortune* 500 companies have adopted commercial e-mail systems for their communications to external companies.

Yet, even as these systems encountered growth in the 1980s, they now find their business base under attack by the attractiveness and low cost of Internet e-mail. These systems have responded by providing direct links to Internet e-mail.

At the Information Technology Association of Canada (ITAC), an internal cc:Mail network is linked to Immedia, a commercial e-mail provider based in Montreal. Since Immedia is linked to the Internet, ITAC essentially has access to Internet e-mail — through the Internet domain, `immedia.ca.`

- consumer based communication services which include e-mail capabilities.

Systems such as CompuServe, BIX, Prodigy and GENIE have several million users scattered throughout the world. Subscribers use these services to participate in on-line conversations, access software and technical support, and perform other on-line activities.

These systems have been very aggressive in linking their e-mail to Internet e-mail, and have effectively become part of the global Internet e-mail system.

E-Mail Client Software

In addition to these many different e-mail systems with indirect connectivity to the Internet, there are many companies with a more direct connection to Internet e-mail.

These organizations use a variety of client e-mail software systems like elm, Pine, Eudora, Pegasus, and Z-Mail within UNIX, DOS or other operating platforms. Many of these systems provide an excellent, simple to use interface to e-mail.

When dealing with Internet e-mail, you must realize that everyone you deal with might read, send, and work with Internet e-mail in a way that is completely different from the way that you work with it. With so many different systems linked to Internet e-mail, there is a wide variety of Internet e-mail clients in use.

Some will find it easy to send and receive e-mail because they have access to simple, straightforward client software, while for others, e-mail will be difficult because the client they use is less straightforward. According to Mike Martineau of NSTN, Inc., "I think we need to remember that people's view of the Internet is significantly coloured by the client software they use."

How Many E-Mail Users Are There?

In December 1993, *The Matrix*, a newsletter which reviews Internet developments, estimated that anywhere from 34.5 million to 69.1 million people around the world were using e-mail systems that were somehow linked to the Internet.[2]

Even though many of these people would not be aware that they have such a link to the Internet, a lot of organizations are beginning to exploit the connectivity that they already have, as we saw in Chapter 2.[3]

The result is an ever increasing use of Internet e-mail for all kinds of business, social, personal and organizational communications.

Creating Internet E-Mail Messages

As mentioned, the number of different software packages that someone might use to create or receive an Internet e-mail message is almost as diverse as the Internet itself.

For example, the authors of this book each use e-mail in two distinctly different ways:

- one accesses a mainframe account at a large university and creates and receives message while on-line;

- the other has a program, called UUPC, that periodically "polls" (calls) an Internet service provider throughout the day, to send and retrieve e-mail. E-mail is actually composed and read off-line on his own computer, with an easy to use Windows software program.

Chapter 9 includes a discussion of some of the technical issues related to methods to link yourself or your organization to the Internet. This includes discussion of linking to Internet e-mail.

Given the wide number of possible methods by which people can access and use the Internet, it's not possible within this book to detail all the steps involved in dealing with your own Internet e-mail. For that, we suggest you refer to the manual of the particular client software you use, and discuss with your Internet service provider any special technical considerations.

THE STRUCTURE OF AN INTERNET E-MAIL MESSAGE

An Internet e-mail message has several distinct parts.

Although any particular message might be more or less complex, a sample Internet message looks like this: [4]

```
Date:    Fri, 16 Jul 1993 18:43:35 -0400
From:    Jack Churchill
<Jack.Churchill@syd.deg.csiro.au>
Subject: Re: Need info on MIME-capable news
servers/readers
To:      Jim Carroll <jcarroll@jacc.com>
Cc:      info-metamail@thumper.bellcore.com
In-Reply-To: <31-PCNews-124beta@jacc.com>
Message-Id: <Pine.3.07.9307170831.A962-
b100000@digi.syd.deg.csiro.au>
Mime-Version: 1.0
Content-Type: TEXT/PLAIN; charset=US-ASCII


On 16 Jul 1993, Jim Carroll wrote:

> On the other hand, I understand that the
MSMail to SMTP gateway
> is the biggest selling gateway that MS
has.....showing that while
> organizations are beating the X.400 drum,
they are demanding and
> getting connectivity to the Internet.
>
> 51% of the entities now registered on the
Internet are >commercial in nature.

That doesn't surprise me.  In fact our site
already has 2 of these
gateways - one for a Novell network.  I'm
pushing for another one for my department
for the masses of Windows for Workgroups
users that keep popping up requesting a
better mailer than say WInqvt for sending
documents, etc.  I keep telling them that
winqvt is going to mime, pc-Eudora will too
but they're more interested in MS-mail.

        Jack N. Churchill
        Jack.Churchill@dem.csiro.au
        CSIRO  Division of Exploration and
        Mining
        churchill@decus.com.au
        PO Box 136  North Ryde  NSW  2113
        Phone:  +61 2 887 8884
        Australia
        Fax:    +61 2 887 8921
```

Take a moment and examine the message. You will note that it includes the following components, or fields:

- `Date:`

    The date/time the message was created by the sender.

- `From:`

    The name of the sender, and the full Internet address of the sender.

- `Subject:`

    In this case, the mail program inserted a RE: in the subject field, to indicate that this is in response to a prior message.

- `To:`

    The intended recipient of the message.

    In this case, the message is being sent to Jim Carroll, whose Internet address is jcarroll@jacc.com.

- `Cc:`

    A copy of the message has also been sent to a mailing list called info-metamail@thumper.bellcore.com

    It is likely that this message went to several thousand people around the world through this mailing list.

    Messages can also include a Cc:, or carbon copy field.

- `In-Reply-to:`

    In the case of the message above, Jack was answering a message which the author had sent earlier. This is used by many e-mail systems to cross reference messages.

- `Message-Id:`

    A unique message address, generated by the e-mail system of the sender.

- `Mime-Version:` and `Content-Type`

    The sender of this message is working with the newest evolution of Internet e-mail, known as MIME (Multipurpose Internet Multimedia Extensions), which provides interesting new e-mail capabilities.

The rest of the message contains the text of the message, as well as the *signature* of the creator of the message.

Internet messages also often include an X-mailer: field, which indicates the e-mail client software used to create the message.

In addition, a bcc: (blind carbon copy) field might be found within some messages.

The sample message is actually a response to an earlier message from Jim Carroll.

Answering Messages

Once you are on the Internet you might find that you receive a lot of e-mail each and every day.

To help you remember what a particular message is about, many of the e-mail systems used with the Internet quote the original message text in the response. "Quoting" the original message is optional.

For example, in the sample message, a special marker has been placed by the software in front of the text of Jim Carroll's original message — using a } symbol. (Many different types of markers are used.)

The software has also made reference to the fact that the text is from a message that Jim Carroll wrote on Sep. 30.

```
On 16 Jul 1993, Jim Carroll wrote:

> On the other hand, I understand that the
MSMail to SMTP gateway
> is the biggest selling gateway that MS
has.....showing that while
> organizations are beating the X.400 drum,
they are demanding and
> getting connectivity to the Internet.
>
> 51% of the entities now registered on the
Internet are >commercial in nature.
```

Jack Churchill was then able to type his message to Jim Carroll, with easy reference to the original message in his response.

Use of such a feature is a courtesy that will be very much appreciated by those you communicate with.

An E-Mail Signature

The sample message includes an e-mail signature which provides further information concerning the sender.

In the case of the sample message, the signature includes the name of the author, the title, company address, and fax and telephone numbers. As well, it includes reference to a couple of Internet e-mail addresses that the sender has.

Most Internet e-mail systems automatically append "signatures" to the end of messages. Other systems connected to the Internet, such as CompuServe; accordingly, you shouldn't always expect to see them in every Internet message.

In general, signatures should be concise, and should not be overdone. In a document released on USENET called "A Primer on How to Work With the USENET Community," by Chuq Von Rospac, guidance is given with respect to how to structure signatures. Although the document is specifically with regard to use of the USENET news system, the guidance is equally applicable to e-mail signatures.

> "Signatures are nice.... Don't overdo it.
> Signatures can tell the world something
> about you, but keep them short. A signature
> that is longer than the message itself is
> considered to be in bad taste. The main
> purpose of a signature is to help people
> locate you, not to tell your life story.
> Every signature should include at least your
> return address relative to a major, known
> site on the network and a proper domain-
> format address. Your system administrator
> can give this to you. Some news posters
> attempt to enforce a 4 line limit on
> signature files -- an amount that should be
> more than sufficient to provide a return
> address and attribution."

What Do Canadian E-Mail Addresses Look Like?

Internet e-mail uses the domain-name style of addressing, based upon the Domain Name System.

An Internet e-mail address usually consists of a name or some identifier, followed by an @ symbol, followed by the Domain Name. For example, `jcarroll@jacc.com` contains the user name (jcarroll) and the domain name (jacc.com).

As seen in Chapter 4, the Internet Domain Name System results in e-mail addresses in Canada that:

- Uses a .ca extension, if registered within the Canadian domain.

  The address might include a city/jurisdiction name and province, depending on the size of the organization, and the location of that organization within Canada.

Within the Canadian domain, some Internet addresses in Canada would appear with names such as `Pete_Smith@mediumcorp.ab.ca`, for an organization in Alberta, `TJones@smallco.ns.ca`, for a company in Nova Scotia, or `Al_Stevens@big company.ca,` if the company is national in scope.

- Other Internet addresses, within organizations that are not part of the Canadian domain but are registered directly with the Internet InterNIC, might have Internet addresses that end in .com, .edu, .gov, or other extensions.

  Such an address will usually include the name of the organization next to the extension, i.e., `TJones@ Bigco.com`.

E-Mail Styles

It is important to note that the information that appears in front of the @ symbol in an e-mail address will vary, depending on the particular e-mail system used, the Internet vendor, and the way that names are used within the organizational e-mail system.

- Some addresses will use some combination of the first name and last name i.e., Pete_Smith or PSmith. Since spaces are not allowed, the first and last name are separated, usually by a _ character or dot.

- Other addresses might use alpha-numerical characters, i.e., 76467.3502 for CompuServe, 384-9385 for an address on MCIMail, or aa1234 for an address on a Free-Net.

- Other addresses might use nicknames or nonsense names.

In other words, there are no rules on what must be used in front of the @ symbol. Some sites will let you choose your own address.

The result is an incredible diversity of addresses throughout the Internet.

Other E-Mail Systems

One reason for the explosion in the use of Internet e-mail is the fact that the domain method is, compared to the alternatives, easy to use and easy to understand.

As indicated, many other e-mail systems are linking to the Internet, in order to provide their users with expanded e-mail connectivity.

The following section describes how to send messages to these other e-mail systems.

CONSUMER ORIENTED SYSTEMS

A number of large, consumer-oriented on-line systems with close to 5 million users have linked themselves to the Internet. Using a few simple rules, you can reach people on the following systems:

NAME OF SERVICE	MAIL EXTENSION	ADDRESSING DETAILS
America Online	aol.com	userid@aol.com
BIX	bix.com	userid@bix.com
CompuServe	compuserve. com	user #@compuserve. com. CompuServe addresses consist of a nine digit number, separated by a comma, i.e., 76467,3502. Remember to substitute a . for the , in the CompuServe address, i.e., 76467,3502, becomes 76467.3502@compuserve .com when sent e-mail to from the Internet.
Delphi	delphi.com	userid@delphi.com
GEnie	genie.com	userid@genie.geis.com
Prodigy	prodigy.com	userid@prodigy.com. Recipient must be registered with Prodigy to receive mail.

Individuals of these networks can be reached by combining their on-line user address with the extension listed above.

For example, to reach someone on CompuServe, send a message to their userID, followed by @compuserve.com. To reach the CompuServe address of one of the authors, send a message to 76467.3502@compuserve.com.

COMMERCIAL E-MAIL SYSTEMS

Individuals using commercial e-mail vendors are also reachable from the Internet, using the following syntax.

NAME OF SYSTEM	MAIL EXTENSION	ADDRESSING DETAILS
AT&TMail	att.com	userid@attmail.com
GEIS (GE Quikcom)	ge.com	userid@org.geis.com. Only reachable if the organization has agreed to accept external e-mail from the Internet.
Immedia	immedia.ca	userid@immedia.ca
MCIMail	mcimail.com	user#@mcimail.com. User# is an eight digit number, separated by a dash.

Other alternatives are possible, depending on the e-mail system you are trying to reach.

What About Envoy 100?

Next to the Internet, Envoy 100/iNet 2000 is probably the best known public e-mail system in Canada.

With many subscribers in government and industry, Envoy 100/iNet 2000 enjoyed a substantial presence in the Canadian e-mail marketplace through the 1980s. With approximately 70,000 users across the country, it is still well recognized, particularly within the federal government.

Now renamed TheNet:Mail, the service is managed by Worldlinx, a subsidiary of Bell Canada.

For some time, Envoy did not have a link to the Internet, although a number of "back-doors" were available. However, early in 1994, Worldlinx is making Internet e-mail available to users of TheNet:Mail. E-mail can be sent to, and received from, Internet users, through this new gateway.

For an Internet user to send to someone on TheNet, either the address or "registered name" must be known. The addressing involves a mixture of X.400 and Internet formats.

A sample message, from the Internet to the Envoy/TheNet:Mail address JA.CARROLL, would be sent as follows:

```
/c=ca/a=telecom.canada/s=carroll/dd.id=ja.ca
   rroll/@resonet.com
```

A sample message, from the Internet to the Envoy/TheNet:Mail address pete.smith, a member of the organization "e100.sprt," would be sent to:

```
/c=ca/a=telecom.canada/o=e100.sprt/dd.id=pet
   e.smith/@resonet.com
```

If you only know the userid of the X.400 recipient, then an organization or surname must also be provided, as has been done in the example above.

Worldlinx, the Bell subsidiary now responsible for TheNet:Mail, notes that some of the addressing as shown in the examples below will be simplified early in 1994 to make it much more "Internet-like" formats. For example, you should soon be able to reach Worldlinx directly by sending to name@worldlinx.com.

Since the gateway uses X.400 addresses, the examples can get exceedingly complex, very quickly. As a result, for more information on this new gateway, contact TheNet:Mail Customer Assistance Centre, by sending an Internet message to helpdesk@resonet.com.

How Complex Can Internet Addressing Get?

E-mail addressing can get very complex, very quickly — particularly if you are trying to reach people on the e-mail system of an organization that is not directly connected to the Internet, but is connected through one of the commercial e-mail vendors such as AT&TMail or MCIMail.

For example, many organizations are linking their in-house e-mail systems to commercial e-mail vendors. Some of the vendors have done a good job in developing Internet gateways, others have not.

The particular blend of software in use at an organization will directly impact how easy it is to reach a particular person within a particular company.

For example, staff at Ernst & Young in Canada make use of MSMail on their in-house Macintosh-based local area network. Their MSMail system is also linked into the commercial service GE Quikcom, so staff at E&Y are reachable by sending to **username@ey.geis.com**. This is a relatively simple, Internet address.

On the other hand, the Corporate Office of George Weston Ltd. has linked an internal Microsoft MSMail system to AT&TMail. Because AT&TMail has done a rather poor job of building its Internet e-mail gateway, staff at Weston's are reachable by sending to an Internet address in the form **gwl!gwl!gwlid@gweston.attmail.com** — not the easiest type of e-mail address to use (gwl stands for George Weston Limited).

One would hope that AT&TMail would invest in its gateway product to correct such a deficiency, permitting an address that would be simpler and more straightforward, i.e., something like userid@gweston.attmail.com.[5]

E-MAIL ETIQUETTE

When sending and receiving e-mail on the Internet, you should keep in mind this simple rule:

What you type and what you say in your e-mail messages could one day come back to haunt you. Be careful.

The use of Internet e-mail (or any e-mail system) requires an on-line etiquette, or a set of manners, that you should keep in mind when using Internet e-mail.

E-Mail Is Different

There are several characteristics about e-mail that should make you cautious in the way you use it.

- E-mail is fast.

  In the "good old days," before the arrival of computer technology, people were careful with paper letters. A response took time to prepare, was well thought out, and was probably reviewed a few times before being sent. There was no room for error on paper correspondence.

  That's not the case with e-mail. Within seconds of receiving a message, you can respond — often, without thinking about what you have typed.

  Do you really want people to receive messages that you haven't carefully thought about?

- E-mail is wide reaching.

Within seconds, you can create a message or response to a message that will reach one person, twenty people or thousands of people (particularly if you are responding to a mailing list posting. If the mailing list is linked to a USENET newsgroup, your message will reach an even larger audience.)

If you write an e-mail message in anger, you might say something that you regret. Do you really want to send copies to a lot of people to your message?

- E-mail is easily saved.

Computer technology permits people to easily store the e-mail messages they send or receive. [6]

What this means is that any e-mail message you send to someone could end up in their personal data archive, or even in an organizational archive. If you are posting to an Internet mailing list, your message could end up in several archives around the world that are open to public viewing.

If you write something controversial or stupid, do you want to risk having your words come back to haunt you at some future point?

- E-mail is easily forwarded.

E-mail technology promotes the easy distribution of information. What you write and send to someone, can be easily forwarded by them to someone else, or posted to a global mailing list or USENET newsgroup. They might not realize that you intended the message to be for limited distribution. Before you know it, your message could be sent all over the world.

Do you really want a message that you intended for just one person, to be forwarded to a number of people?

- E-mail is easily mis-interpreted.

The person reading your e-mail message can't see your body language. They can't see if you are smiling, frowning or crying as you write it. It is more difficult for them to interpret what you have written.

Often this leads to mis-interpretation — what they think you mean, is often not what you really mean.

Do you want to run the risk of having someone misunderstand your message?

Flaming

The on-line world has come up with a term to describe what happens to people who ignore these risks, and who write an e-mail message while their emotions are not in check.

It's called flaming.

Flaming is the tendency for people to quickly type out an e-mail message in anger, without thinking the message through.

Remember this warning.

At some time, you will regret sending an e-mail message.

You will regret it a lot.

If you are ever angry and begin to respond to a message — stop, and think for a moment. Do you really want to send an angry response? Knowing that the other person might keep your message for a long time? Or might forward the message to a lot of other people? Or might be extremely insulted by what you type?

E-Mail Guidance

A few simple suggestions might make it easier for you to avoid problems in sending e-mail messages.

- Don't use just capitals in your messages. This is called shouting. Imagine receiving a message that looks like this:

  ```
  GREG. WE NEED TO UNDERSTAND HOW TO REOR-
  GANIZE FOR THE JUNE 5TH MEETING. IT'S IM-
  PORTANT THAT WE GET TOGETHER NOW. CALL ME
  SOON
  ```

  Such messages are difficult to read, and cause others to get frustrated with the messages that you send them. Always be careful to type in upper and lower case.

- Use a meaningful subject line. Remember that the person you are sending the message to might receive tens or hundreds of messages each day. To make it easier for them to deal with your message, provide a subject line that is meaningful and to the point.

- Take your time in thinking about a response to a message. Particularly if the message makes you mad. The best advice is to get up, and go for a glass of water or cup of coffee. Or take a walk. Go shopping. Watch TV, or read a book. Don't ever, ever, ever, respond to a message when you are mad!

- Don't send a carbon copy of your message to the rest of the world, unless you have to. When sending an e-mail message, it is easy to send copies to a lot of people, including people who might have no particular interest in your message. Be judicious with respect to the people who get a copy of the message.

- Summarize what you are responding to. If you are lucky, you are using an Internet e-mail software package that quotes the original message text in your response, as we saw in the section "Answering Messages" above. Be sure to use this feature to make it easier for the recipient to remember what the message was about. Edit it down so that you are leaving in only the relevant text. There's nothing worse than getting three pages of an original message, with a few words in response at the end.

- Use special characters to label your emotion. For example, to *highlight* a point, consider using >>>>>special<<<<<< characters to emphasize certain words or phrases. For example, rather than typing in a message that looks like this:

```
It is important that we meet as soon
as possible.
```

you might type

```
It is !!!!!!important!!!!!! that we
meet as soon as possible.
```

This will help to get across the urgency of the situation.

As you use the Internet, you will discover that people use all kinds of neat tricks to help them emphasize points within their messages. Carefully observe, and in time, you will come up with your own distinctive Internet writing style.

Smileys

The e-mail world has come up with an ingenious way of expressing emotion within a message by the use of special characters that some call *emoticons*. Others call them smileys.

A smiley is a set of symbols that, when turned on its side, represents some type of character. For example, a (-: is really a sideways smiley face; a (-; is a sideways smiley face winking, while)-: is a sad face with a frown.

A :-) is often used in a message to indicate that the preceding remark was made in jest. Smileys are important so that people don't misinterpret what you type.

These characters can be used within e-mail messages to add additional emphasis. For example.

```
Pete,
Your summary was interesting(-;.
Have a good day.
John
```

or another message

```
Pete,
I didn't get the report finished.   )-:
Call me.
John
```

There are so many possible smileys, that a book has been written about them.

As you use the Internet, you will see a lot of smileys in use within messages. Begin to accumulate your own special list of them. If you are looking for more, you can find a number of sites on the Internet that keep lists of smileys.

HOW DO I LOCATE AN INTERNET E-MAIL ADDRESS?

At some point you will want to determine how to obtain the e-mail address of a particular person or organization.

Invariably, as you use various parts of the Internet, you will come across a message from someone that reads as follows:

```
I am looking for Bob Smith in New York
City. Does anyone know his Internet address?
```

Such a question is silly, since there is no easy answer. Most important, Bob Smith might not have an Internet address!

The Internet does not have any central storage location that lists all possible users of the network. Although there are a variety of services located throughout the Internet that let you find addresses of various people, these services are not comprehensive, and are not really a good solution to your dilemma.

Fortunately, many people are starting to list their Internet addresses on their business cards, and addresses are beginning to gain as much acceptance on business cards and correspondence as fax numbers did in the mid-70s.

Simple Solutions

The easiest way to find out the Internet address of particular people is probably simply to ask. Pick up the phone and call them. Maybe they know. If they know they are on the Internet, and know how to send a message, but don't know what their address is, ask them to send a message to your Internet address.

You will see what their address is, and can respond to them in the future.

WHOIS

If this doesn't work, and you must begin exploring the world of the Internet to try to locate an address, take a deep breath. There are a lot of resources on-line to look into.

Many of these resources are known as WHOIS servers, simple programs that let you query for the name of an organization or individual.

One of the most popular is the WHOIS database, located at the resource services department of the Internet Network Information Centre (InterNIC).

Although the database is not comprehensive, it is a useful starting point. To access the database, Telnet to **rs.internic.net,** and type **whois** at the InterNIC prompt, as seen on the following screen.

```
                                     E:94% VT100 ‡  00:03:16  4:12p
                                    CML 205-876-5618 (DSN)746
Carroll Auto Sales (NET-C105571)C105571                 198.249.80.0
Carroll College (CARROLL)        CARROLL1.CC.EDU        140.104.1.1
Carroll College (NET-CARROLLNET)CARROLLNET              140.104.0.0
Carroll College (NETBLK-CRRLLCLG) NETBLK-CRRLLCLG  199.5.171.0 - 199.5.172.0
There are 16 more matches.  Show them? y
Carroll College (CC-DOM)                                CC.EDU
Carroll County General Hospital (NET-CCGH-1) CCGH-1     198.51.120.0
Carroll County General Hospital (NET-CCGH-2) CCGH-2     198.51.121.0
Carroll Pont./Bui/GMC (NET-C104612) C104612             192.224.208.0
Carroll, Eric M. (EC43)        eric@UTCS.UTORONTO.CA    (416) 978 3328
Carroll, Gary (GC248)                                  +43 662 46 911 420
Carroll, James (JC198)         4carroll_j@SPCVXA.SPC.EDU   201-843-1970
Carroll, Jim (JC718)           jcarroll@jacc.com        +1 416 274 5605
Carroll, Jim (JC33)            carroll@WM-MERCER.CA     416-868-7013
Carroll, Jim (JC443)           jcarroll@SCOTIA-MCLEOD.COM  416 862 3904
Carroll, Jim (JC69)            jimc@JTS.COM             (416) 512 8910
Carroll, Johnny (JC579)        CARROLL@DEPT.CSCI.UNT.EDU   (817) 565-2279
Carroll, Leo (LC1)         (301) 862-8744 862-8764 (DSN) 326-3512 ext 8744
Carroll, Michael [Sgt] (MC475)  lowry@LWR3B201.AF.MIL
                                    (303) 676-5121 (DSN) 926-5121
Carroll, Russ (RC502)          RUSSC@RWC.COM            (619)689-2321
Carroll, Thomas R. (TRC7)      tcarroll@SNOW.NOHRSC.NWS.GOV  (612) 725-3039
Whois:
```

Ninety-nine percent of the people on the Internet are not listed on WHOIS, which is what makes it such a limited tool.

As a result, a tool like the InterNIC WHOIS should only be used to look up organizations, or contacts for particular companies.

POSTMASTER

When it's really important, you can usually send a message to the postmaster at a particular location, to ask how you might get in touch with someone at their organization. Most locations on the Internet have a postmaster account for their organization, i.e., **postmaster@epo.gov.on.ca.**

Obviously, this won't work if you try to ask the question of a postmaster at an extremely large organization or commercial on-line e-mail system, i.e., **postmaster@ibm.com** or **postmaster@compuserve.com.**

Use such queries with discretion, since you should remember that there is an individual at the other end of the system who might be swamped with such requests.

Periodic Postings

A good starting point to the techniques used to try to locate a particular e-mail address is the document *How to find people's E-mail addresses* by Jonathon Kames.

The document is posted on a regular basis to several USENET newsgroups, such as news.answers. As well, it can be obtained via FTP. from the site ftrm.mit.edu, in the directory **pub/usenet-by-group/news.answers.**

From that directory, obtain the document finding-addresses. Chapter 6 describes how documents can be retrieved using FTP.

You can also obtain the document, by creating an Internet message to **mail-server@rtfm.mit.edu.** In the text of the message, type the line

```
send usenet/news.answers/finding-addresses.
```

Within a few hours, you should receive the document back within an e-mail message. This uses a capability of Internet e-mail known as "query by mail" or "file-retrieval by e-mail" which is also discussed in Chapter 6.

1 . It should be noted that organizations which want to implement gateways from their LAN based e-mail systems to the Internet, should appreciate the technical complexity of the project. Many of the current Internet gateways for popular LAN based e-mail systems do not function well unless set up correctly, and to set them up correctly, you must have a good working knowledge of the Internet, and in particular, Internet messaging.

2 . *Matrix News*, December 1993. Volume 3, No. 12.

3 . For example, an organization that has linked its LAN e-mail system to the Internet might not have told everyone that it can send and receive e-mail to the Internet.

4 . Note that the actual appearance of the message will depend on the type of computer you are using, the e-mail software found on that computer, the type of link that you have to the Internet, and the type of Internet service provider that you use. The definitive work that discusses the components of an Internet e-mail message is *The Internet Message*, by Marshall T. Rose (Prentice-Hall, 1993), which takes an in-depth look at the message from a detailed technical perspective.

5 . This issue also has much to do with what you should consider when purchasing various e-mail gateways. Any gateway should be examined closely to determine the impact that it will have on simple, straightforward addressing.

6 .One of the authors has on file about 60 megabytes of messages, representing e-mail messages sent/received since October 1985.

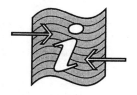

C H A P T E R   6

....

REMOTE ACCESS APPLICATIONS FTP AND TELNET

Telnet and FTP are two Internet resources, similar in concept but different in function.

Both let you sign on to other computers on the Internet; but while Telnet lets you run programs on the other computer, FTP permits you to retrieve files from the remote computer system.

TELNET AND FTP CLIENTS

The examples shown in this chapter demonstrate the most basic use of Telnet and FTP.

In this simplest form of usage, commands are typed in order to connect to a location, to run an application, or to retrieve a file.

Yet, the methods seen in this chapter are most often used when accessing the Internet through a dialup "shell account," as discussed in Chapter 9. Keep in mind that the particular method by which you might use FTP and Telnet could differ, depending on the Internet service provider that you use, and depending on the type of client software that you have available.

Through a number of Internet service providers, it is becoming possible to use Windows, Macintosh or other graphical operating platforms (in particular, for graphical UNIX platforms), permitting you to easily navigate to Telnet and FTP sites, and to "point-and-click" to retrieve files or access specific Telnet resources.

Such programs can be run by those with a direct TCP/IP connection to the Internet. In addition, several Internet service providers are extending the full power of the Internet to casual dialup users, through the use of connections based upon the SLIP/PPP protocols, as discussed in greater depth in Chapter 9.

As a result, as you review this chapter, keep in mind that not all people will use FTP and Telnet in this way and indeed, it might be possible for you to use these applications in a better, friendlier fashion

TELNET

Telnet opens your world to other Internet resources by providing you with the capability to run programs on other computers on the Internet. There are a number of locations throughout the Internet which you can Telnet to, and use without charge.

The Directory of Canadian Internet Resources in Appendix A includes a listing of other resources on the Internet that you can Telnet to, including access to:

- information search programs such as Gopher, Mosaic or WAIS;

- the on-line catalogues of various libraries, such as the Vancouver Public Library, in order to search for particular books or other materials. A complete listing of libraries in Canada which you can access through the Internet, can be found in Appendix A, in the *Directory of Internet-Accessible OPACs in Canada*;

- Free-Net's (currently established in Victoria and Ottawa), to access local community information;

- other information resources, ranging from baseball scores, on-line games, and local weather.

As well, you can reach any other Telnet resource worldwide from your Canadian Internet account (if your account provides Telnet service), such as the "Weather Underground" system at the University of Michigan, which includes details on Canadian weather.[1]

Keep in mind that with some of the "knowledge retrieval" tools discussed in Chapter 8, including Gopher and World Wide Web, it is much easier to "tour" the Internet with these tools than it is by using Telnet.

Telnet Command

The Telnet program is accessed from your Internet host by typing telnet. Once you have accessed the Telnet command, you will see the prompt TELNET> on the screen.

Once at that prompt, you can use the **open** command with an Internet address to establish a link to a particular Internet resource, or you can use other Telnet commands to change your terminal type or perform other activities.

However, it is not often that you will need to go into the Telnet program directly like this. More often, you will type the Telnet command with the address of the resource you are trying to reach. The address that you type is either the domain name or domain address.

For example, to reach the library of the University of Saskatchewan, you would type the following at the main prompt of your Internet service provider:

- the domain name, i.e by typing **telnet
  sklib.usask.ca**

or

- the domain address, i.e by typing **telnet
  128.233.1.20**

On occasion, you will be advised to use the domain name with a particular "port." This is required when you are accessing a system on the Internet in which the port directs you to a particular application. You are usually told when a particular port address is required. Type the port number after the Telnet address, when a port number is required.

A Sample Telnet Session

The following session details the steps taken to Telnet to the Vancouver Public Library, which has made its on-line catalogue available to the Internet.

The session uses a login ID of **netpac,** and a password of **netpac1**. These are provided by the library as the general IDs for public access, as detailed within the listing of *Directory of Internet-Accessible OPACs in Canada* in Appendix A of this book.

```
                                      E:94% VT100 ‡  00:00:53  7:57a
$ telnet
telnet> open vpl.vancouver.bc.ca
Trying 134.87.100.1...
Connected to vpl.vancouver.bc.ca.
Escape character is '^]'.
Sequoia Telnet Server Ver 3.5
login: netpac
Password:
Copyright (c) 1989 Sequoia (All Rights Reserved)
******************************************************************************
*              Welcome to the Sequoia at Vancouver Public Library!          *
******************************************************************************
NETPAC,NETPAC1
```

Note that you could also, at the Unix $ prompt, just type
`telnet  vpl.vancouver.bc.ca,` rather than typing
`telnet,` waiting for the prompt, and then typing the address.

Once attached to the library, you are prompted for the
type of terminal that you are using:

```
                                      E:94% VT100 ‡  00:00:56  7:57a




Please indicate which terminal you are using.

  1. ANSI Emulation
  2. ADDS Viewpoint emulation
  3. ADDS Viewpoint 60 Emulation
  4. VT52 Emulation
  5. VT100 Emulation
  6. Wyse 30
  7. Wyse 50
  8. Wyse 50 Terminal, ADDS VP Enhanced Mode
  9. Wyse 60
 10. Wyse 75
 11. Wyse 150
 12. ADDS Regent 25
 13. Quit (Logoff)

   Enter Selection>
```

Once you have indicated your terminal type, you see some
copyright information, and are then presented with the main
menu of the Vancouver Public Library system.

```
                                          E:94% VT100 #  00:01:24  7:58a
 17 JAN 94            Dial-in Public Access Catalog            05:03AM
                            ONLINE CATALOGUE
                    Choose one of the following searches:

  1.  Title                          10.  Community Organization Directory
  2.  Title--Keyword                 11.  Consumer Index
  3.  Author                         12.  Community Events Calendar
  4.  Author--Keyword                13.  Quick Reference File
  5.  Subject                        14.  City Council Minutes Index
  6.  Subject--Keyword               15.  Not Available
  7.  Format                         16.  Not Available
  8.  Call Number                    17.  Logoff
  9.  Borrower Record Inquiry




  Enter your selection(s) and press <Return> :
 Commands: ?=Help, BB=Bulletin Board
```

Special Notes About Telnet

When using Telnet, as seen in the example above, you should keep in mind that:

- Some applications that you access will ask you to specify the terminal type that you are using.

  Be sure that you understand the type of terminal that your communications software supports.

  Most services will support, at a bare minimum, the popular terminal type VT-100.

- Remember the "escape character" for your particular Internet provider.

  The session above, once it began to connect to the Vancouver Public Library, noted that the `'Escape character is '^]'`. That means to press the ctrl key and] together on your computer.

  The escape character permits you to exit from a particular Telnet session in case the service you have linked into doesn't make it obvious how to exit, or if your current session seems to "hang" or "freeze."

Seeking Help

Keeping in mind that the particular operation of Telnet might vary depending on the particular UNIX host or Internet service provider you use, you can usually obtain help on Telnet commands, by typing help at the Telnet prompt.

```
                                          E:94% VT100 ‡   00:01:51  7:58a
$ telnet
telnet> help
Commands may be abbreviated.  Commands are:

close         close current connection
logout        forcibly logout remote user and close the connection
display       display operating parameters
mode          try to enter line or character mode ('mode ?' for more)
open          connect to a site
quit          exit telnet
send          transmit special characters ('send ?' for more)
set           set operating parameters ('set ?' for more)
unset         unset operating parameters ('unset ?' for more)
status        print status information
toggle        toggle operating parameters ('toggle ?' for more)
slc           change state of special charaters ('slc ?' for more)
z             suspend telnet
!             invoke a subshell
environ       change environment variables ('environ ?' for more)
?             print help information
telnet>
```

These commands permit you to change your terminal type,
set special characteristics for particular services, or display
your current status.

In normal circumstances, you will use few of these commands.

Telnet Resources

A number of Canadian based Telnet accessible resources are
included in Appendix A, in the *Directory of Canadian Internet Resources*.

Additional resources can be found throughout the Internet,
with new ones commonly added. Subscribing to particular
USENET newsgroups, or to specialized mailing lists, will
help to guide you to other resources on the network.

The Internet contains a treasure trove of computer programs, documents and images you can retrieve for your own
use.

FTP

Many of these items are available through file servers located
throughout the Internet, using FTP (file transfer protocol).
The types of resources that you can retrieve include:

- public domain and shareware software, i.e., software
  written by people and released for general use by anybody. In some cases, a fee or donation is required in
  order to comply with the terms provided with the
  software.

- documents discussing the Internet or virtually any topic imaginable, in text form or specialized word processor form. In other cases, documents are available in "Postscript" format, which requires a printer with Postscript capability.

- images from NASA and other organizations in a variety of formats. You will need a file viewer compatible with the particular file type in order to view the image.

- sound files, i.e., CBC radio programs are now available via the Internet. You will need sound capability on your system in order to deal with the file.

Using FTP

As you start to use the Internet, you will often see reference to documents or other information available by FTP.

For example, you might come across a phrase, "To obtain a copy of the document robo.txt, use anonymous FTP to access 'sushi.pic.alx.ca' and look in the directory pub/survey."

Translated, this means that you should:

- use FTP to access the system `sushi.pic.alx.ca`

- once there, log in to the system with the user ID `anonymous`

- once logged in, move to the directory `pub/survey,` which contains the document `robo.txt`

Once there, you use the FTP `get` command to retrieve the file.

FTP Basics

There are a few things to remember when using FTP on the Internet:

- many services permit "anonymous" logins; that is, they allow anyone on the Internet to access them, by providing a user ID of `anonymous`.

  When you use the anonymous ID, you are asked for a password. As a courtesy, you should send your own e-mail address as the password. In some cases, the FTP server will only permit a connection if you do identify yourself in this way. Some even validate what you supply.

- most of the services you will access with FTP on the Internet are UNIX based, and will be running software that is case sensitive. In other cases, you might be ftp'ing from a non-UNIX machine, with file names in upper case. In that instance, filenames are not case sensitive.

  File names must usually match the case exactly as seen within the directory or as specified in the note that you read about the file.

- many of the domain names that you will use with FTP are preceded by the word FTP or some other unique name, i.e., the FTP site at the domain **dal.ca**, will actually be **ftp.dal.ca**.

- if you are retrieving anything other than a text file, you must use the **binary** command, to ensure that the file is sent to you in the proper format. You do this by typing **binary** once you have reached at FTP site.

- if you are using an Internet service provider by a dialup modem as a "shell account" user (i.e., you are not directly connected to the Internet), your retrieval of any file by FTP might be a two step process, as seen in Figure 6.1

  In the first step, you use FTP to retrieve a particular file from a remote system on the Internet. This transfers the file back to the system of your Internet service provider.

  In the second step, you invoke a process to transfer the file from your Internet service provider to your own computer.

  Because the second step will vary depending on the Internet service provider used, this book can describe only the first step. Be sure to check with your Internet service provider to make sure that you understand the second step.

  It should also be noted that this second step might not be required with some Internet service providers: the file transfer might occur directly to your own computer when you type the **get** command.

FIGURE 6.1: TWO STEP FILE RETRIEVAL

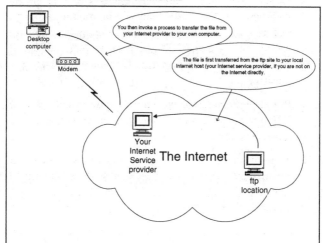

Like Telnet, the FTP command can be issued by itself to enter the FTP program, or it can be used with an address to directly access a computer on the Internet.

More often than not, you will type the command **ftp** followed by the address of the particular Internet site; for example, **ftp ftp.usask.ca**.

A Sample FTP Session

Once you are linked to another computer, you can use the **get** command to retrieve particular files, the **dir** command to look at file directories, and the **cd** command to change directories. Other commands are available, as detailed below.

In this sample FTP session, we take the following steps:

- we link to the site **ftp.cdnnet.ca**, using the command **ftp ftp.cdnnet.ca.**

- once there, a login name of **anonymous** is used, and a password is entered (matching the e-mail address of the user). The password is usually not echoed (i.e., shown on the screen) as it is typed.

- once logged in, at the **ftp** prompt, the command **cd ca-domain** is typed to move to the **ca-domain** directory. Once there, a directory is requested by typing **dir**.

- the command **get application-form** is then typed to retrieve that particular file.

  Upon completion, the FTP session indicates that the file was successfully transferred. (If you are directly on the Internet, this will have transferred the file to your own computer system; if not, this indicates that the file has been copied to the file of your Internet service provider.)

- once the file is successfully transferred, the **quit** command is entered to return to your local Internet host.

In the second screen of the example below, since the session occurred on a system that was not directly attached to the Internet, two more procedures are necessary:

```
                                          E:94% VT100 ‡  00:02:28  7:59a
$ ftp ftp.cdnnet.ca
Connected to relay.cdnnet.ca.
220 relay.cdnnet.ca FTP server (Version 2.1WU(2) Sat May 15 15:39:16 PDT 1993) r
eady.
Name (ftp.cdnnet.ca:jcarroll): anonymous
331 Guest login ok, send your complete e-mail address as password.
Password:
230-
230-Welcome to the anonymous FTP archives at CDNnet Headquarters.
230-
230-This is an experimental FTP server.  If your FTP client crashes or
230-hangs shortly after login please try using a dash (-) as the first
230-character of your password.  This will turn off the informational
230-messages that may be confusing your FTP client.
230-
230-You can get in touch with the maintainers of this archive by sending
230-a message to HQ@CDNnet.CA.
230-
230-The local time is Mon Jan 17 05:05:37 1994.
230-
230 Guest login ok, access restrictions apply.
Remote system type is UNIX.
Using binary mode to transfer files.
ftp>
```

```
                                          E:94% VT100 ‡  00:04:16  8:01a
total 198
-rw-rw-r--  1 2009     2000          21845 Jan 15 22:50 application-form
lrwxrwxrwx  1 2009     103              26 Jul 12  1993 ca -> registrations-hierar
hical
-rw-rw-r--  1 2009     103            4142 Dec 29 00:19 committee-members
-rw-rw-r--  1 2009     103           40510 Jan  2 20:34 graph.ps
-rw-rw-r--  1 2009     103            1603 Jan 16 22:05 index
-rw-rw-r--  1 2009     103           54206 Jan 16 22:05 index-by-organization
-rw-rw-r--  1 2009     103           40921 Jan 16 22:05 index-by-subdomain
-rw-rw-r--  1 2009     2000           8685 Feb  2  1993 introduction
drwxrwxr-x  2 2009     103           18432 Jan 16 22:02 registrations-flat
drwxrwxr-x 14 2009     103            5120 Jan 16 21:35 registrations-hierarchical
-rw-rw-r--  1 2009     103            2258 Jan 16 22:05 statistics
226 Transfer complete.
ftp> get application-form
local: application-form remote: application-form
200 PORT command successful.
150 Opening BINARY mode data connection for application-form (21845 bytes).
226 Transfer complete.
21845 bytes received in 4.6 seconds (4.6 Kbytes/s)
ftp> quit
221 Goodbye.
$ mv application-form app.txt
$ sz app.txt
```

- in order that the file can be saved to a DOS machine, the file **application-form** is renamed **app.txt**, using syntax specific to the local UNIX host (**mv application-form app.txt**)

- the command **sz app.txt** is then typed to transfer the file from the system of the Internet service provider to a local PC, using the Zmodem protocol.[2]

FTP Directories

To use FTP, you must learn to work with and understand standard UNIX directories.

UNIX directories, as seen in the example session above, include information on the type of file, the status of the file, and information concerning the "owner" of the file.

For the uninitiated, these directories can seem a little bit overwhelming at first, unless you remember a couple of key pointers:

- Entries that begin with a **d** are directories. The DOS user can think of them as subdirectories beneath the directory currently shown.

- Entries beginning with anything else are usually files.

Consider the following two directory listings taken from an experimental CBC FTP site within the Department of Communications, available at **debra.dgbt.doc.ca**.

First, a command is issued to switch to the directory pub/cbc, where the directory is then listed.

```
                                        E:94% VT100 ‡  00:00:55  8:02a
250 CWD command successful.
ftp> dir
200 PORT command successful.
150 Opening ASCII mode data connection for /bin/ls.
total 4396
drwxr-xr-x  2 114      114           512 Jan 13 15:55 .cap
-rw-r--r--  1 114      1            1523 Jan  6 16:59 README
drwxr-xr-x  3 114      114          1024 Dec 23 17:55 basic-black
drwxr-xr-x  3 114      114           512 Dec 23 17:55 canada
-rw-r--r--  1 114      1            1402 Jan 12 23:10 cbc.html
drwxr-xr-x  3 114      114           512 Jan  5 20:29 front-porch
-rw-r--r--  1 114      114           369 Jan 12 23:04 more-info.html
-rw-r--r--  1 114      114       4457122 Jan 12 23:08 ottawa-story.au
drwxr-xr-x  2 114      1            1024 Jan 13 23:08 pix
-rw-r--r--  1 114      114          3494 Dec 23 23:17 press-release
-rw-r--r--  1 114      1            6361 Jan 14 21:13 product-list
drwxr-xr-x  3 114      1             512 Dec 23 16:26 quirks-and-quarks
-rw-r--r--  1 114      1            1616 Jan 13 23:01 radio.html
-rw-r--r--  1 114      114           424 Dec 17 00:13 sounds.by.gopher
drwxr-xr-x  6 114      114           512 Dec 23 17:55 sunday-morning
drwxr-xr-x  2 114      114           512 Dec 30 16:00 tools
drwxr-xr-x  3 114      1             512 Jan 14 21:16 transcripts
226 Transfer complete.
ftp>
```

The listing above shows a number of directories (preceded with the letter d), as well as a number of files (without a d). This includes the directories **fireside** and **quirks-and-quarks,** as well as the files **press-release** and **product-list**.

The command to switch to the directory **canada** is then typed, and a listing of the **canada** directory is requested.

```
                                              E:94% VT100 ‡   00:01:18  8:03a
250-  it was last modified on Thu Dec  9 20:38:18 1993 - 39 days ago
250 CWD command successful.
ftp> dir
200 PORT command successful.
150 Opening ASCII mode data connection for /bin/ls.
total 16932
drwxr-xr-x  2 114       114           512 Dec  9 23:08 .cap
-rw-r--r--  1 114       114          3262 Dec  9 20:38 README
-rw-r--r--  1 114       114        930021 Dec  9 19:06 all.that.freedom.au
-rw-r--r--  1 114       1            78007 Dec 23 15:29 canada.gif
-rw-r--r--  1 114       1             1370 Dec 23 16:31 canada.html
-rw-r--r--  1 114       1            11274 Dec 23 15:29 canada.small.gif
-rw-r--r--  1 114       1             3387 Dec 23 15:29 canada.tiny.gif
-rw-r--r--  1 114       114       2319631 Dec  9 19:06 counterpoint.au
-rw-r--r--  1 114       114       3215717 Dec  9 19:07 je.suis.moitie.moitie.au
-rw-r--r--  1 114       114       3604605 Dec  9 19:07 my.canada.au
-rw-r--r--  1 114       114       1242175 Dec  9 19:08 northern.reflections.au
-rw-r--r--  1 114       114       3058919 Dec  9 19:08 quebec.poetry.and.protest.
u
-rw-r--r--  1 114       114        934202 Dec  9 19:09 speak.english.speak.french
au
-rw-r--r--  1 114       114       1819780 Dec  9 19:09 stories.that.bind.au
226 Transfer complete.
ftp>
```

This directory shows a number of files, such as **ca-nada.gif** and **je.suis.moitie.moitie.au,** as well a directory named **.cap.** The files in the directory are quite large, ranging up to 3.6 megabytes in size (3,604,605 bytes, for the file **my.canada.au**).[3]

Basic FTP Commands

As with any resource on the Internet, there are several commands that you can use at the FTP prompt. The most often used commands to retrieve files and view directories are as follows:

COMMAND	MEANING	EXAMPLES
cd	change directory	**cd public**, to switch to the directory public
		cd /, to return to the top directory
dir	list the directory	**dir**, for a basic directory listing. Can also use ls on most systems.

get	retrieve a file	**get filename**, to retrieve a particular file
mget	get multiple files	**mget new*.***, to get any files beginning with the letters new
quit	leave the FTP site	

If you have the right to leave files at a particular Internet site, you can use the put and mput commands to transfer files to that server.

More information on the above, and other FTP commands, can be obtained by typing **help** at the FTP prompt.

Other FTP Issues

There are two other issues that you will have to deal when you begin retrieving files using FTP.

FILE TYPES — FORMAT

Obviously, to use particular files that you obtain on the Internet, you must have a program capable of dealing with the format of the retrieved file.

You can't load a WordPerfect document from a PC into a Macintosh unless you have a program that will convert it to the format of your Mac word processor. You can't deal with a Postscript file unless you have a Postscript printer, or you have a program that can view or convert a Postscript file. You can't run a compiled UNIX program on an MSDOS computer — and so on.

Since the topic of file format and file types is far beyond the topic of this book, keep in mind that while the Internet might make available a lot of files, you must have appropriate programs to deal with them.

FILE TYPES — COMPRESSION

In order to speed up the file transfer process, many of the files throughout the Internet have been compressed or combined.

Files with the extensions .zip, .arc, .Z or .z, .tar, .lzh, .sit or cpt are compressed or combined or both. You will need appropriate software to uncompress or uncombine the file that you retrieve.

The most common type of file extension is .Z, indicating a file that has been compressed using the UNIX program

compress. Many FTP sites on the Internet include an un-compress program to return the file to its original state, if you don't have one already available on your Internet service provider.

Make sure that you have appropriate tools to uncompress or uncombine files that you might retrieve.

File Retrieval Via E-Mail

It is possible to retrieve many of the files that are available via FTP, via e-mail instead.

This is done by sending an e-mail message to a specific address at the FTP site which has been set up to permit e-mail queries. Not all sites offer this service.

In your message, you type a specified phrase, indicating that you want to retrieve a file, and indicating file name (with directory) that you are trying to retrieve.

One of the most popular of these sites is a server at the Massachusetts Institute of Technology (MIT), which has an FTP site containing information about the Internet.

For example, to retrieve a document from this site that details how to use the ftp-by-mail service:

- create a message to mail-server@rtfm.mit.edu.

- in the text of the message, you type a command that will send a help file, or will retrieve specific files that might otherwise have been available via FTP.

For example, to obtain help, send an e-mail message as follows:

```
Date: Thu, 30 Dec 1993 08:41:24 est
Reply-To: jcarroll@jacc.com
From: jcarroll@jacc.com (Jim Carroll)
To: mail-server@rtfm.mit.edu
Cc:

help
```

To obtain actual files, use the send command within the body of the message, i.e.:

```
Date: Thu, 30 Dec 1993 08:43:06 est
Reply-To: jcarroll@jacc.com
From: jcarroll@jacc.com (Jim Carroll)
To: mail-server@rtfm.mit.edu
Cc:
```

```
send /pub/usenet/news.answers/mail/mailing-
  lists/part1
send /pub/usenet/news.answers/mail/mailing-
  lists/part2
send /pub/usenet/news.answers/mail/mailing-
  lists/part3
send /pub/usenet/news.answers/mail/mailing-
  lists/part4
send /pub/usenet/news.answers/mail/mailing-
  lists/part5
send /pub/usenet/news.answers/mail/mailing-
  lists/part6
```

There are quite a number of sites throughout the Internet that permit file retrieval via e-mail. Although there might be minor variations in the method, the concept is consistent from location to location.

---

1 . This includes on-line database retrieval systems which charge for usage, such as Dialog and Nexis. Often, accessing these services via the Internet is less expensive than accessing them via regular data services like Datapac or Tymnet.

2 . These two steps, and the commands used, are specific to the Internet service provider used in this example — the procedure used on your particular provider will vary.

3 . Any file with an **.au** extension are audio or voice files. The files in this particular example are actual audio files of various CBC radio programs. Refer to the Internet Resources list for more information on this particular ftp site.

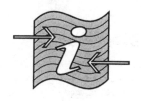

C H A P T E R 7

· ·

TOOLS FOR KNOWLEDGE NETWORKING

Internet mailing lists and USENET are the two primary methods by which you can "knowledge network" through the Internet.

A Quick Definition

A mailing list is a collection of e-mail addresses. Any message sent to the address of the mailing list is automatically sent to the address of every member of the mailing list.

Information that you receive from mailing lists comes in with your regular Internet e-mail — no special software is required to read a message sent to a mailing list, although special software is used to manage the mailing list itself.

USENET is a global system for the exchange of information on thousands of topics, referred to as "newsgroups." Individuals can choose to subscribe to any particular newsgroup, read information sent to the newsgroup, and add or "post" information to the newsgroup. Each posting is referred to as a "news article."

USENET is like a massive global bulletin board with thousands of different information resources.

You read the USENET newsgroups that you belong to with "newsreader" software, which also permits you to post messages to USENET.

What's the Difference?

Although the mechanics of a mailing list and USENET differ, both permit you to join a particular group and receive information or converse with people concerning the topic within the group.

Anyone with an Internet e-mail address can choose to join any number of mailing lists: your only constraint will be the volume of information that you can read during the day.[1]

And, since you can obtain USENET news through most Internet service providers, you can choose to subscribe to the "newsgroups" which interest you. Given that current estimates are that some 100 megabytes of information is posted to USENET each day, you will have to be selective with respect to which newsgroups you subscribe to.

USENET newsgroups are not much different in concept from mailing lists. The major differences are that:

- USENET information is more structured, with individual postings filed into particular newsgroups. In contrast, e-mail messages from mailing lists are part of your general e-mailbox, unless you have some type of special filtering software.

- Most USENET newsgroups undergo a series of steps of approval, before they become widely distributed through the USENET system. Anyone can start a mailing list if they have the right software.

- USENET has a culture that frowns upon networking for commercial purposes. Mailing lists can be used for anything.

- USENET news articles have a limited life span. Because of the large number of USENET messages, many sites will delete messages beyond a certain date (usually two weeks, and sometimes much less). Messages sent to mailing lists will last as long as messages last in your mailbox.

- USENET news articles are not sent to personal mailboxes, but are sent to sites for review by a number of people.

- USENET was designed as a mechanism to permit the re-broadcasting of information on a very wide basis. Any USENET article goes out to all the Internet hosts on the planet that wish to receive that specific newsgroup, or that don't refuse that newsgroup. E-mail, on the other hand, was designed as a point-to-point method of communicating, and even with mailing lists, suffers from some problems in trying to be a broadcast tool.

Other than this, USENET is similar to mailing lists, permitting people to participate in knowledge networking with others from around the globe on a variety of topics.

To make matters more complex, there are also some "bi-directionally gated newsgroups" within USENET. Any news article sent to such a newsgroup is also distributed automatically to others via a mailing list.

MAILING LISTS

With thousands of different mailing lists on the Internet, you can choose to join any particular mailing list. Once you have joined, you will receive any message sent to the list.

Simply put, an Internet mailing list operates as shown in Figure 7.1.

FIGURE 7.1: INTERNET MAILING LISTS

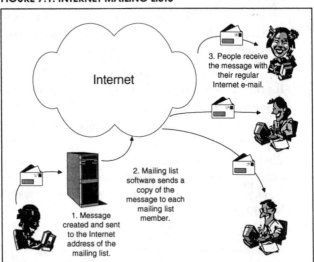

With the growing number of e-mail systems that have the capability to send messages to and receive messages from the Internet, it is no surprise that there are thousands of Internet mailing lists on virtually every topic imaginable.

Internet mailing lists are a convenient method for people on different computer systems to discuss particular topics or share information concerning specific issues.

Mailing lists have emerged as a new method of publishing, with a number of journals, newsletters and other information summaries available to anyone with Internet e-mail access.

Once you join a mailing list you will receive a copy of any message sent to the list. A mailing list might consist of as few as two people, or it might contain several thousand.

Types of Lists

Mailing lists on the Internet differ by their purpose; some are used for discussion, while others are used for newsletters, and yet others are used to summarize information that has appeared in other lists or in USENET newsgroups.

An example of the types of mailing lists throughout the Internet would include those that are:

- moderated

    In a moderated list, any message sent by you goes to the moderator, who determines if it should be redistributed to the list.

    Lists are moderated in order to ensure that messages sent to the list are tightly focused on the list topic.

    Moderated lists are managed by an individual who takes on responsibility for sending messages to the list. The moderator takes on an active role in determining what should be sent to the list, ensuring that only those messages relevant to the topic of the list are received by subscribers.

    Although anyone can join and receive messages that have been sent to a moderated list, only certain people are allowed to send to the moderated list—usually, the moderator.

    Moderated lists are often used for newsletter and journals, as well as for lists that summarize messages received from people concerning the list topic. In the latter case, the list becomes a forum for discussion, yet is tightly focused on the particular topic due to the involvement of the moderator in determining what should and should not be sent.

- unmoderated

  In an unmoderated list, any message sent by you immediately goes to everyone on the list.

  An unmoderated list might permit anyone to send to it, or it might be restricted, permitting only members to send to it.

- closed

  The Internet is a very diverse place; this results in some lists that are not open to everyone.

  You must meet some type of qualification to join the list — even to receive messages sent to the list.

Using Lists — The Mechanics

The mechanics of Internet mailing lists are quite straight-forward.

You subscribe or join an Internet mailing list by sending an e-mail message to an Internet address established for the purposes of list maintenance.

Once your message has been received at the destination, your request to be added to or deleted from a list is:

- processed manually by the list owner,

  or

- processed by a specialized piece of software, which automatically makes the change to the appropriate list.

For example, the following message is a copy of an original request to subscribe to a mailing list called **net-happenings**, a list which summarizes new Internet announcements.

```
Date: Thu, 09 Sep 1993 07:22:52 edt
Reply-To: jcarroll@jacc.com
From: jcarroll@jacc.com (Jim Carroll)
To: listserv@is.internic.net
Cc:

subscribe net-happenings Jim Carroll
```

When this message was received at **listserv@is.internic.net**, a program called **LISTSERV** processed the details of the message, and the Internet e-mail address **jcarroll@jacc.com** was added to the list.

LISTSERV AND OTHER METHODS

Many Internet mailing lists are based on **LISTSERV**, a program developed over the years which manages the process of list administration. **LISTSERV** is but one type of mailing list manager — although it is very popular, there are others.

When **LISTSERV** is used for list management, most of the process of adding and deleting users is automatic, requiring little human intervention. For these lists, requests to be added to or deleted from a particular list are sent to an Internet e-mail address of the form **LIST-SERV@whatever**.

In other cases, when **LISTSERV** is not used to manage the list, requests are usually sent to an address of the form **listname-request@whatever**, i.e., by sending a message to the name of the list, followed by **-request**. Sometimes, this syntax is not used, and you might be required to send your request to a regular Internet address.

An important point to remember is that you should never try to join or leave a list by sending a message to the list itself — you will only end up aggravating all the members of the list, since they all receive a copy of your request!

Examples – Joining, Sending, Leaving

Details concerning how to join a particular list are found within announcements of new lists, or are found within documents which describe Internet mailing lists.

Always be sure to keep the details about a new list when you join — since you might need that information when you want to leave the list.

JOINING A LIST

You can join a mailing list by sending a message to **LISTSERV@wherever**, if the list is based upon **LISTSERV**.

If **LISTSERV** is not used to maintain the list you are trying to join, your message might go to an address of the form **listname-request@wherever**, or might go to a simple Internet address.

If **LISTSERV** is used, in the text of the message you type **SUBSCRIBE LISTNAME FIRST LAST**, substituting the name of the list you want to join, and typing your first and last name (separated by a space).

For other list managers or for manual lists, you might be required to type something different in the text of the message.

Your message will be intercepted by the **LISTSERV** or other program, and the process of being added to the list will begin.

Sometimes, you will receive a message back with separate steps to follow to continue the process of joining. Eventually, you will receive a message notifying you that you have been added to the list.

Two examples highlight the possible methods of joining a mailing list.

- Consider a mailing list which discusses the Toronto Blue Jays. To join the list, you send a message to **jays-request@hivnet.ubc.ca**.

  In this case, **LISTSERV** is not used to manage the list, and the list request is probably handled manually.

- On the other hand, **Canada-L**, a mailing list for the discussion of political, social, cultural and economic issues in Canada, is managed with **LISTSERV**.

  To subscribe to the list, you send a message to **LIST-SERV@VM1.MCGILL.CA**, and in the text of the message, you type the command **SUB CANADA-L yourfirstname yourlastname**.

SENDING TO A LIST

Once you have joined the mailing list, you can send a message to everyone on the list, by sending to the address for that list.

Software at the receiving system (i.e., **LISTSERV**) will take the message and send a copy to each member of the mailing list.

- for example, to send a message to the Blue Jays list, you send a message to **jays@hivnet.ubc.ca**, and to send a message to the **Canada-L** list mentioned above, send a message to **CANADA-L@VM1.MCGILL.CA**.

LEAVING A LIST

You can leave the mailing list through the same process as joining the list, by sending a message to **listname-**

request@whereever, and typing SIGNOFF LIST-
NAME FIRST LAST.

Starting Your Own List

The greatest benefit of the Internet comes through the fact
that anyone can establish their own Internet mailing list.

Your Internet service provider might be able to provide
you with your own Internet mailing lists. If so, you can establish a mailing list on a particular topic, and invite your
friends and peers to join the list. Over time, you might find
that the list begins to gain recognition throughout the
Internet.

Many Internet lists began informally, yet have emerged to
become the global "home" for a particular topic. Given the
power of global knowledge networking, establishing your
own mailing list on a topic of importance to you could
become one of your most useful Internet resources.

Information on Lists

The obvious question is "how do I find a particular list?"

Often, you will hear about a mailing list by word of
mouth, or it will be mentioned in some Internet resource that
you track. In particular, a few USENET newsgroups as
discussed within the next section, are often used to announce
new lists.

There are a number of resources available on the Internet
which provide details on mailing lists. A sample entry, from
the document: *Publicly Accessible Mailing Lists,* described
below, details information for the mailing list concerning
Canada's favorite baseball team:

```
Toronto Blue Jays
Contact: stlouis@unixg.ubc.ca  (Phill St-
Louis)
Purpose: Discussion of the Toronto Blue
Jays Baseball Club including player
transactions, predictions, game commentary,
etc.  Everyone welcome!
```

The same list is described in the *List of Interest Groups*
document described below:

```
jays@hivnet.ubc.ca
[Last Updated 9/92]
```

This is a mailing list for fans of the
Toronto Blue Jays baseballteam. Scores and
highlights of games, player transactions,
draft picks, and status of rival teams will
be discussed on this group.
This list is not archived.
To join:
Please send all requests to jays-
request@hivnet.ubc.ca or to
phill@hivnet.ubc.ca
Coordinator: Phill St-Louis
(phill@hivnet.ubc.ca or
stlouis@unixg.ubc.ca)

MAJOR SOURCES

You can retrieve several definitive summaries of available
mailing lists on the Internet, including from the sources detailed below.[2]

If retrieving these documents by e-mail, keep in mind that
these documents are quite large — for example, the List of
Interest Groups described below is over 1.2 megabytes in
size. If you are using a commercial e-mail provider which
charges on a per character basis, be prepared for a rather ex-
treme bill!

None of these sources is comprehensive — since new lists
are being added throughout the Internet on a regular basis,
these summaries are a good starting point to get an idea of
the lists that are out there.

BITNET LISTS

BITNET is a global network that is separate from the
Internet, yet it links academic institutions and research
organizations worldwide. It is fair to say that, although
BITNET is not disappearing, it is rapidly merging into
and becoming part of the Internet.

BITNET provides global electronic mail and mailing
list capabilities (and in fact, is where the **LISTSERV**
program originated). It is home to some of the most
diverse and interesting mailing lists available. Internet
users can join any of these mailing lists.

The document "*List of all LISTSERV lists known to
LISTSERV@BITNIC*" provides a comprehensive
summary of over 4,000 special interest lists.

To obtain this document, send a message to **list-
serv@bitnic.bitnet** or **listserv@bitnic.**

`educom.edu.` In the body of the message, type `list global.`

PUBLICLY ACCESSIBLE MAILING LISTS

(Currently maintained by Stephanie da Silva.)

This is the definitive summary of Internet lists. Revised monthly, the list contains a detailed description of each list, as well as information on how to subscribe.

To obtain a copy of the list via e-mail, send a message to `mail-server@rtfm.mit.edu.` In the text of the message, type:

```
send
/pub/usenet/news.answers/mail/mailing-
lists/part1
  send
/pub/usenet/news.answers/mail/mailing-
lists/part2
  send
/pub/usenet/news.answers/mail/mailing-
lists/part3
  send
/pub/usenet/news.answers/mail/mailing-
lists/part4
  send
/pub/usenet/news.answers/mail/mailing-
lists/part5
  send
/pub/usenet/news.answers/mail/mailing-
lists/part6
```

each on a separate line. (Additional parts might be added in the future — check for details.)

The document is also available by anonymous FTP at `rtfm.mit.edu`, in the directory `/pub/usenet/news.answers/mail`, under the file name `mailing-lists`.

DIRECTORY OF ELECTRONIC JOURNALS AND NEWSLETTERS

(By Michael Strangelove of Ottawa.)

The directory details a number of journals and news-letters which you can subscribe to via e-mail. Although heavily academic and research oriented, it does give an excellent overview of the wide diversity of topics that you can subscribe to via mailing lists.

To obtain the document, send an e-mail message to `listserv@acadvm1.uottawa.ca`. In the body of the message, type

```
get ejournl1 directry
get ejournl2 directry
```

each on a separate line within the message.

LIST OF INTEREST GROUPS.

This document refers to itself as the "List of lists" — a listing of special interest group mailing lists available on the Internet.

To obtain the listing, send a message to `mail-server@nisc.sri.com`. In the text of the message, type `send netinfo/interest-groups`.

NEW-LIST MAILING LIST

This is a mailing list for announcements of new mailing lists, primarily for those based upon the `LISTSERV` software.

To join the list, send a message to `LIST-SERV@VM1.NODak.EDU`. In the text of your message type the command: `SUB NEW-LIST firstname lastname`.

NET-HAPPENINGS LIST

If you really want to track what is going on with the Internet, you should join the `net-happenings` list.

To join the list, send a message to `list-serv@is.internic.net`. In the text of the message, type `subscribe net-happenings first last`, substituting your first and last name for `first` and `last` in the command.

This list has about 15-20 messages per day, including announcements concerning new mailing lists and other Internet resources are sent to this list on a regular basis throughout the day. As well, information that even remotely impacts the Internet, such as initiatives relating to the "information highway" or "national information infrastructure," are often sent to the list.

The result is a continuous stream of messages that are wide ranging and varied, but somehow relate to the Internet.

You should only join this list if you have a desire to receive a lot of e-mail, and you want to track what is going on with the Internet. *This list is for hard core Internet junkies only.*

USENET

USENET is described by many people as the "world's largest bulletin board system," even though it is definitely not a Bulletin Board System.

USENET consists of several thousand topic areas known as newsgroups, with topics ranging from locksmithing to pyrotechnics to religion to C++ computer programming.

As a user of the Internet, you can choose to subscribe to any of the USENET newsgroups that your Internet service provider carries. Not all providers carry all newsgroups.

Some USENET newsgroups are moderated in ways similar to mailing lists. However, since most USENET newsgroups are unmoderated, you can send (referred to as "posting") to any newsgroup as well.

Newsgroup Categories

Newsgroups within USENET belong to a series of categories.

The major (global) newsgroup categories are:

CATEGORY	TOPIC
biz.	Business oriented topics
comp.	Computer oriented topics
misc.	Stuff that doesn't fit elsewhere
news.	News and information concerning the Internet or USENET
rec.	Recreational activities, i.e., bowling, skiing, chess, etc.
sci.	Scientific topics
soc.	Sociological issues
talk.	Debate oriented topics

There is also an alt. group. What can you find in alt. groups? You name it; alt. groups likely discuss it. Anyone can start an alt. group without approval, but not all sites carry all alt. groups. The result is a somewhat free-wheeling atmosphere, with some of the most controversial newsgroups being located in the alt. category.

SubTopics

Each category consists of several hundred or thousand topics, organized into sub-categories.

For example, the newsgroup category rec. (recreation topics), includes the sub-categories:

- rec.arts
- rec.audio
- rec.music

and below this, a further categorization can be found, for example:

- rec.arts.poems
- rec.arts.misc
- rec.arts.bonsai.

For very popular topics, another level of categorization might be found. For example, because of the popularity of science fiction within the Internet, there are several science fiction newsgroups within the rec.arts.sf category, including:

- rec.arts.sf.misc
- rec.arts.sf.movies
- rec.arts.sf.science

An individual could choose to subscribe to all the rec.arts.sf groups (getting all three above as well as others), or could choose to subscribe to only the rec.arts.sf.movies group.

CANADIAN NEWSGROUP CATEGORIES

Bruce Becker (`news@gts.org`) maintains a list of Canadian news groups. The categories within his list, for major locations (excluding specific university categories) include:

CATEGORIES	TOPICS	CATEGORIES	TOPICS
ab	Alberta	mtl	Montreal
atl	Atlantic	nf	Newfoundland

bc	British Columbia	ns	Nova Scotia
calgary	Calgary	**ont**	Ontario
can	Canadian	**ott**	Ottawa
edm	Edmonton	**qc**	Quebec
hfx	Halifax	**tor**	Toronto
kingston	Kingston	**van**	Vancouver
kw	Kitchener/ Waterloo	**wpg**	Winnipeg
man	Manitoba		

MAJOR CANADIAN NEWSGROUPS

Some of the more popular Canadian newsgroups include:

- `can.general`. Discussion of general Canadian issues. A wide ranging number of topics.

- `can.jobs`. A surprising number of job postings are made to this group; perhaps 20 a week. Most are for computer expertise, with a particular emphasis on UNIX systems.

- `can.politics`. Deficits, governments, and all the related topics are discussed in here. A very busy newsgroup. Be prepared to argue.

- `ont.general`. Discussion of topics relevant to Ontario. For example, there has been much discussion recently of the Karla Homolka/Paul Teale trial ban, with banned articles concerning the trial often being posted here.

- `can.domain`. Discussion of policies and procedures relevant to registration under the .ca domain, and technologies and other issues affecting domain registration in Canada. A good place to track Internet issues in Canada.

As well, several communities in Canada are very active with their local Internet newsgroups, including those within the kw. (Kitchener Waterloo), ott. (Ottawa) and tor. (Toronto) newsgroups.

A Sample USENET Message

A USENET message looks like an e-mail message, with some subtle differences. The primary difference is that a newsgroup message includes reference to the newsgroups the information was posted to, within the Newsgroups: line.

For example, the following message was posted to the newsgroups ba.internet,alt.bbs.internet,alt.internet.services:

```
Xref: uunet.ca alt.bbs.internet:13081
alt.internet.services:14563
ba.internet:1759
Newsgroups:
ba.internet,alt.bbs.internet,alt.internet.s
ervices
Path:
jacc!uunet.ca!uunet.ca!uunet!tadpole.com!ne
ws.dell.com!swrinde!elroy.jpl.nasa.gov!usc!
howland.reston.ans.net!agate!ames!decwrl!de
cwrl!netcomsv!netcom.com!mspace
From: mspace@netcom.com (Brian Hall)
Subject: Product Support via the Net
Message-ID: <mspaceCIvEo0.3D5@netcom.com>
Organization: Mark/Space Softworks
References: <terryCIu4AI.BoM@netcom.com>
<CIurtz.8sw@world.std.com>
<tMn8jK5QQFlTyarn@crl.com>
Date: Thu, 30 Dec 1993 23:02:23 GMT
Lines: 19

lchiu@crl.com (Laurence Chiu) writes:

>What I am hoping for is that one day
manufacturers provide support
>via the Internet in the same way as they
do in CIS forums. Perhaps
>via moderated usenet groups? It's really
annoying to find that
>support files, tech support and some good
discussion on many topics
>can only be found on CIS and to get it you
have to pay $8/hr or $17
>for 9600 access!

Many already do (take a look at my .sig).
The internet is a great way to
keep in touch with customers.  Of course
this makes the most sense for
companies/products that are comm related
(at the moment), but I suspect that
will change.

--
```

Brian Hall
Internet: mspace@netcom.com
Mark/Space Softworks
AppleLink, AOL: MARKSPACE
Macintosh connectivity software.   info via
anon ftp netcom.com:pub/mspace
            >>>> Stop by and say hello -
MacWorld, Booth 4374. <<<<

How Does USENET Work?

To understand what USENET is and how it works, consider the newsgroup `rec.sport.football.canadian`.

Formed a number of years ago, it was established to provide a convenient discussion forum for the Canadian version of the sport.

CREATING A NEWSGROUP

The process through which `rec.sport.football.canadian` was created sheds some light on how USENET operates currently. Note that this process applies for the "big-7 hierarchy," i.e., for the .`comp`, .`rec`, .`sci`, .`news`, .`soc`, .`talk` and .`misc` newsgroups. Procedures for other hierarchies might vary.

- The individual who wanted to start the newsgroup sent a message to the moderator of the USENET newsgroup, `news.announce.newgroups`, as well as to several other newsgroups, indicating why such a newsgroup should be formed. The message contained a "charter" for the group; that is, the reasons for the group, and an overview of what the group would be used for (the discussion of Canadian football). The message was posted to `news.announce.new-groups` by the moderator of that group.

- A period of discussion concerning the merits of having a special group devoted to Canadian football took place within the newsgroup `news.groups` for a month or so. Any one could have participated in this discussion.

- Once the period of discussion was complete, a "call-for-votes" went out, for people to vote on whether the group should be created. A designated period of time was set aside for voting, and an individual volunteered to be the official vote-taker. Anyone is permitted to vote.

- Once the period of time was up (usually 21-30 days), the votes were tabulated, and the group was found to have met the standard USENET acceptance criteria (the standard rule is that there are at least 100 more yes votes than no votes; and at least 2/3 of the votes have voted yes).

- Since the group "passed," a "newsgroup control message" was sent out by David Lawrence,[3] the moderator of the **news.announce.newgroups** newsgroup, advising all USENET sites that **rec.sport.canadian.football** was now considered an "official" USENET list. The "newsgroup control message" provides the group with "official status."

- Had **rec.sport.canadian.football** had not passed the vote, a newsgroup control message to create the group would not have been sent out by David Lawrence, and the group would not be an official group. The result would have been that most USENET locations would refuse to carry the group, since it hadn't passed the vote. (And in fact, it could even end up on a list of invalid newsgroups).

  Those who ignore the guidance over how to establish a new newsgroup will almost certainly fail in their attempt.[4]

- One other factor is that even though it is now an official newsgroup, any USENET site has the choice as to whether it will or will not carry the **rec.sport.football.canadian** newsgroup.

It is this global co-operative effort concerning the establishment of new newsgroups that is at the heart of USENET.[5]

READING NEWS

Once the newsgroup **rec.sport.football.canadian** was approved, people could subscribe to the newsgroup and could begin posting information to it.[6]

Hence, upon approval:

- Messages posted to **rec.sport.canadian.football** are now transmitted throughout the USENET system.

- Individual users of USENET choose what newsgroups they want to belong to. Those with an interest in the CFL, choose to belong to the `rec.sport.ca-nadian.football` list.

- Each user then reads their USENET groups using newsreader software.

NEWSREADER SOFTWARE

Some individuals read USENET "on-line," i.e., while linked to the computer of their Internet service provider by modem or some other link.

Others read if "off-line," i.e., all USENET articles for groups they belong to are transferred to their computer or local network, and are read locally while not linked to another computer.

Newsreader software differs depending on the Internet service provider and the method used to retrieve USENET news, and on whether you are reading it on-line or off-line.

Newsreader software organizes each newsgroup into listing by newsgroup topic. For examples, within the DOS program SNEWS (an off-line reader for PC's), the newsgroups subscribed to by one of the authors appears as follows:

```
 Select Newsgroup   (Simple NEWS 1.91)   [499k]

 >    1. alt.internet.services              12 (74)
      2. can.jobs                              (1)
      3. comp.groupware                        (1)
      4. comp.infosystems                      (1)
      5. comp.internet.library                 (0)
      6. comp.mail                             (0)
      7. comp.mail.mime                      2 (3)
      8. comp.mail.misc                      4 (16)
      9. comp.mail.multi-media                 (1)
     10. comp.mail.sendmail                  1 (17)
     11. comp.mail.uucp                      1 (5)
     12. comp.protocols.iso.x400              (3)
     13. comp.risks                           (0)
     14. comp.security.misc                   (0)
     15. junk                                  (5)
     16. news.announce.newgroups              (0)
     17. news.announce.newusers               (0)
     18. news.sysadmin                        (0)
     19. ont.general                         (23)

 ESC=quit   TAB=next unread group   ENTER=read group   F1=help
```

Within each topic, individual postings are listed.

For example, within the `ont.general` newsgroup on December 30, 1993, the following articles appeared.:

```
      Select Thread  (Simple NEWS 1.91)  [496k]
Group: ont.general                                    23 articles
                                                       0 unread
    1.        1 MAGIC BBS may close due to Homolka BAN
    2.        1 World's Longest Ski Tour: 28th Canadian Ski Marathon
    3.        1 Hey folks!  Try banning THIS!
    4.        1 Canada's Federal Income Tax is unconstitutional
   ` 5.        2 UseNet -- Let the Censorship Begin ......
    6.        2 Freedom FROM the press?  (was Let us stop and think...)
    7.        1 A List of Quotable Quotes from 'Dr.' Joe Baptista...
    8.        1 Q: PST and GST on photogr
 >  9.        1 Photo-radar
   10.        1 ccs.carleton.ca dial in data numbers anyone?
   11.        2 H RAP BROWN AT U OF TORONTO
   12.        1 Let us stop and think for a minute
   13.        3 Freedom FROM the press? (was Let us stop and think...)
   14.        1 canadian law and just
   15.        1 Photo Radar - tips?
   16.        1 Photo-radar (how to beat
   17.        1 What is *with* you people?  (was Freedom FROM the press?
   18.        1 Need Ride To/From Toronto This Weekend?

   ESC-select group   TAB-next unread   ENTER-next article   F1-help
```

Of course, users of other newsreader software will likely see
a completely different presentation of USENET.

USENET- What It's Not!

There are some things that you should know about USENET:

- It isn't the Internet.

  USENET happens to be carried over the Internet, as
  well as other networks.

  Yet, it has come to be so closely identified as an
  "Internet resource," that most people think of USENET
  as being a fundamental part of the Internet.[7]

- It isn't owned by anyone, nor is there one central
  authority that runs it.

  USENET exists because of the co-operative efforts of
  thousands of people around the globe: first and foremost, the thousands of UNIX system and news administrators of subscribing systems from around the world;
  and secondly, through the efforts of a wide number of
  volunteers who catalogue USENET resources, conduct
  votes, post information and participate in countless
  other ways.

  The result is an on-line system which is managed
  through the co-operative effort of literally thousands of
  people from around the globe. Some call it organized
  or cooperative anarchy.

- It isn't for commercial use

  There is no surer way to receive streams of on-line
  abuse, than by abusing USENET for what is clearly a
  profit-oriented activity.

USENET was developed to support the exchange of knowledge and information. There are thousands of topics — yet with all the millions of news articles posted to USENET, it maintains a certain culture. Even as the Internet becomes more commercialized, USENET seems to be maintaining its status as a system not to be blatantly used for commercial purposes, even though there are some buy-and-sell newsgroups.

- It is used to a limited extent for commercial purposes

  Even though USENET isn't for commercial use, there are some newsgroups that exist for distribution of information concerning certain products, and for service announcements from system vendors.

What does this mean? You might use USENET with regard to your business "I am trying to get my computer to do this; does anyone have any hints," but you certainly shouldn't use USENET to try to drum up business. "Hey, I've started a consulting firm. Call me if you need help — my rates are $120 an hour."

Network Etiquette

The most important things you can learn about USENET is that:

- it has a unique on-line culture;

- those who do not respect this culture do so at their own peril.

The culture includes procedures and guidance concerning topics such as newsgroup creation (as described above); what the network can be used for (i.e., non-commercial activity); how to post news articles; newsgroup names; official vs. non-official newsgroups; chain letters; inappropriate postings; and hundreds of other issues of etiquette.

The easiest way to learn about USENET culture is to:

- Join several newsgroups and watch how they work for some time.

  In particular, if you are interested in how USENET newsgroups are established, subscribe to the groups **news.announce.newgroups** and **news. groups.**

`News.announce.newgroups` is the place where proposals for new groups are posted. `News.groups` is the place where these proposals are debated.

Be prepared to be shocked by what you might see in a debate: sometimes simple proposals for a new newsgroup degenerate into raging debates, with emotions getting out of hand and insults and accusations flying with fury. Why? It's the culture of USENET.

There is no better way to understand the culture of USENET than to belong to `news.groups` for a few months.

- Documents such as *A Primer on How to Work with the USENET Community* and *Rules for Posting to USENET* are posted regularly to the groups `news.newusers.questions` and `news. answers`, and can also be retrieved from a number of FTP locations.

Using USENET

The method that you use to subscribe to and read news articles will depend on how you access the Internet; there are far too many methods to describe here.

You should seek instructions from your service provider on the specific steps you should follow.

However, there are several things to keep in mind regardless of how you access USENET:

- If you respond to a posting within a USENET newsgroup, you can choose to post a follow-up message that goes to the newsgroup, or you can choose to send an e-mail message to the original poster.

- You should have some type of method of saving an article to your own computer.

- If you encounter a message that looks like gibberish, it might be a uuencoded file. If it isn't, it could be a ROT-13 message. ROT-13 is a simple method of changing characters in a message (A turns into N, B turns into O, etc.), and is used for controversial postings, offensive jokes, or other postings that skirt the line.

- People ROT-13 a message, to warn you that it might be of questionable taste. Your news software likely has a method to de-ROT-13 the posting.

- Many USENET newsgroups periodically post an FAQ, or Frequently Asked Question list. The purpose is two fold: to help out new users, but also to avoid the situation where new users continually post the same question over and over again and again every time they subscribe to a group.

  FAQ's are archived in many locations, and are available via FTP. The best source is `rtfm.mit.edu`, in the directory `pub/usenet/news.answers`.

  For example, an FAQ, prepared in conjunction with the newsgroup `rec.sport.football.canadian`, describes many of the special aspects of Canadian football. It can be found in the document `canadian-football` at the FTP site above.

A complete list of Canadian newsgroups as of December 1993 is provided in Appendix A, in the document *Directory of Canadian USENET Newsgroups*, reprinted with the permission of Bruce Becker. Bruce posts the message on a regular basis to a number of Canadian newsgroups, including `can.general`. Corrections and updates concerning Canadian newsgroups can be sent to Bruce at `news@gts.org`.

Lists of Newsgroups

Listings of USENET newsgroups in the major categories above can be found within the document List of Active Newsgroups, posted to the groups `news.announce.newusers` on a frequent basis.

You should also check with your Internet service provider to obtain a list of the newsgroups they provide. Not all providers distribute all newsgroups.

---

1 . Individuals on commercial and consumer oriented services that have links to the Internet (i.e., Compuserve, ATTMail, etc), should be careful in subscribing to mailing lists. These services, which charge either on a per character basis or time basis, might result in substantial charges to receive messages from mailing lists with a large number of messages.

2 . References to file locations and information retrieval on the Internet sometimes changes, as systems shut down and as new organizations take on efforts previously undertaken by someone else. The Internet is a constantly evolving place: as a result, these instructions, while current as of December 1993, are not guaranteed to always work.

3 . In this role, David Lawrence comes the closest to being a central authority for
USENET. He maintains his position as the result of having built up a large amount of
trust and respect from all members of the USENET community through the years.

4 . One of the authors knows this is true, from personal experience.

5 . The process of newsgroup creation in Canada is not as formal. According to Bruce
Becker, "No formal process exists - can.general, ont.general, tor.general or tor.news
is where such things are usually discussed, although some newgroups have been
issued without prior discussion. These are viewed differently at various sites - either
they are ignored, created, or aliased to existing groups." Ed Hew notes "It is
generally good practice to post your proposal in the 'general' newsgroup for the
hierarchy you wish to expand, and to enlist the support and agreement of the site
administrators who will be carrying the traffic for your new newsgroup. The more
regional the hierarchy, the more important this may be.For example, there is no point
in creating a kw.<something> if no one will propagate it."

6 . If their Internet service provider provides USENET service and if the provider chose
to carry that particular newsgroup.

7 . In fact, you can probably join a USENET newsgroup in which you could debate
whether USENET is really part of the Internet or not. The discussion has gone on in
some groups for months and years....

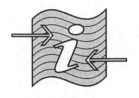

C H A P T E R   8

· ·

TOOLS FOR KNOWLEDGE RETRIEVAL

I n this chapter, we take a look at some of the tools that can be used for information retrieval on the Internet — ways of extending your capabilities to locate and retrieve knowledge on particular topics.

Even though tools like Telnet and FTP are at your disposal, they aren't the easiest systems by which to discover Internet resources. With FTP and Telnet you must refer to books or documents which describe FTP or Telnet sites. Since the Internet is changing so quickly, such documents are often out of date as soon as they are available.

Programs like Gopher, Hytelnet, WAIS, World Wide Web and Archie solve this problem nicely, and are on the cutting edge of information retrieval. These tools provide you with new ways of searching, browsing, and reviewing information from around the world. Using them, you can discover niches of information that might be relevant to your particular needs.

Two of these tools, Hytelnet and Archie, were developed in Canada, and have gained worldwide recognition as major Internet tools!

In this chapter, in order to describe these tools to you, we explore the network very much as a tourist with a camera, and show you some of the pictures that we have taken. Keep in mind that the examples shown are using a simple terminal dialup to the Internet.

As you will see at the conclusion of this chapter, a number of very sophisticated tools are emerging that make it very easy to explore the Internet with a point-and-a-click of your mouse. These new tools promise to take Internet information retrieval into yet another dimension.

LIMITATIONS OF INTERNET INFORMATION SOURCES

Internet is not a solution to all your information needs.

If you have come to the Internet to look for market research reports, or to be able to perform in depth research on particular topics based on major industry magazines or publications, or to find financial statements or other corporate information, you've come to the wrong place.[1]

Using the tools described in this chapter can often be frustrating and difficult.

In many situations, you will become frustrated because you cannot find the information that you are looking for.

You must remember that the Internet had its roots in research and academic communities. As a result, a lot of the available Internet information sources tend to be from those communities, and are not the types of information that you are seeking.

Although the range and breadth of information available on the Internet is constantly growing, you should keep in mind that it is not a solution to all of your information needs. There are other solutions, which might more adequately target your particular information needs.

COMMERCIAL INFORMATION SERVICES

There are many other research tools available through networked systems, including those that you pay a usage for over and above any Internet access charge.

These include systems like Dow Jones News Retrieval, Dialog and Nexis, massive warehouses of information. For example, Dialog and Nexis each contain up to fifteen years worth of the full text of major magazines and newspapers from around the world. Search rates range from $50 to several hundred dollars per hour. These services are all accessible from the Internet, although you must separately arrange for a user ID and password on each system, and must make appropriate billing arrangements.

In Canada, major on-line research systems include Infoglobe and Infomart, which carry the full text of such publications as *the Globe and Mail*, *Financial Post*, *The Ottawa Citizen* and other major daily newspapers. In addition, these services carry corporate profiles, market research reports, stock prices (delayed) and other types of information. At this time, neither Infoglobe or Infomart are accessible via the Internet. Rates for usage of these databases also varies, but is usually in the range of $100/hr and up.

MULTIPLE SOURCES OF INFORMATION

When it comes to information, there is a simple rule that you must remember — you get what you pay for.

The limited range of Internet databases is but one type of available on-line information. If information research is key to your activities, consider examining the alternatives available in commercial on-line databases as described above, but keep in mind that you must be willing to pay for that information.

GOPHER

If you read various computer magazines, you might come across the term "net-surfing."

Gopher could be best described as a surf-board for the Internet.

Gopher solves the problem of resource discovery by providing an easier method to explore the Internet. Developed at the University of Minnesota, it provides a menu-based view of Internet resources, guiding you to a variety of locations on the Internet and permitting you to view and retrieve documents or files.

P. Copley, Ph.D., a founder of The Electronic University in San Francisco (ror@netcom.com), had this to say about Gopher in a posting he recently made to the network (reprinted with permission).

```
The Internet gopher is the express elevator
of  the  Internet,  capable  of cutting
through layer upon layer of information
quickly.  It permits you to traverse the
world's data banks.  You can be viewing a
color photograph  of an  ancient  Chinese
```

vase stored on a computer in Taiwan and, on
a moment's notice, "be" in the UK,
downloading a database of historical
names and dates. It enables you to
easily retrieve all sorts of information
and to connect to many other services.
Invented at the University of Minnesota,
home of the "Golden Gophers" sports
teams (hence the name), the gopher program
connects many of the major Internet
computers together into one unified
information service or "gopher space."

In a matter of little more than two and one half years, gopher has sprung up from one installation on the University of
Minnesota campus to well over one thousand around the
world. One key to gopher's success has been that it is not
overly complicated. It is easy to use, and, moreover, makes
an orderly, logical presentation out of dissimilar and scattered "chunks" of information from all over the Internet.

Given the size and range of the Internet, Gopher is also
proving to be a wonderful way to get yourself lost on the
Internet.

A Sample Gopher Session

The easiest way to understand Gopher is to review a couple
of Gopher sessions.

In this first example, we are looking for a weather report
for Nova Scotia.[2]

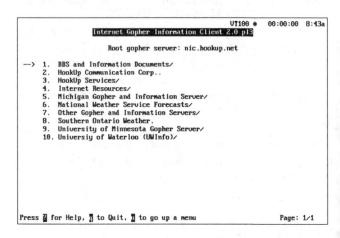

Using HookUp Communications, a Canadian Internet service
provider, we access Gopher by typing **gopher** at the $

prompt. This presents us with the main Gopher menu for HookUp. [3]

Not every Internet service provider will provide a Gopher client. Referring back to our discussion of "client/server" and the Internet in Chapter 4, you will remember that when running an Internet utility such as Gopher, you are running it either on:

- your own PC or network

- on your Internet service provider

  or

- on some remote system on the Internet which you establish a Telnet session to.

If your Internet service provider has not installed a local Gopher client, typing Gopher at the prompt will not work.

In addition, the Gopher menu of any particular Internet service provider or Internet host will be different, and will change over time. The prompts used within the Gopher session on your Internet provider might differ from the prompts used in this example.

As a result, the sample menu above is not exactly what you would see on any other provider or Gopher site.

Notice as well that the prompt --> is placed at the first entry on the screen. To choose an item, you type its corresponding number or move the prompt with your cursor keys.

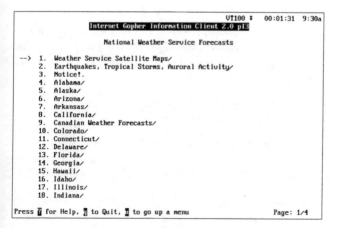

We start our journey by choosing menu item **6. National Weather Service,** which presented the screen shown above.

Menu item 9. Canadian Weather Forecasts, provides a list of locations by province (not shown). Eventually, we see a weather forecast for the province of Nova Scotia.

```
                                              VT100 *  00:00:00  8:41a
Forecasts for southern ontario issued by the ontario weather centre
Of environment Canada at 5.00 am est Tuesday 4 january 1994 for today
And Wednesday.
The next scheduled forecast will be issued at 11.00 am today.

Synopsis.
  a wintry blast heading our way..
  a winter storm will give eastern ontario a significant snow fall of
15 centimetres with higher amounts locally and the same in the
Niagara peninsula.  this storm will whip up north to northeasterly
Winds gusting to 60 km/h.  the combination of these winds and
Temperatures today barely rising above minus 10 will make it feel as
Cold as minus 20 to minus 30 degrees in most places.  the storm will
Pull into new england tonight bringing the snow to an end.
Wednesday will see the return to more sunshine but at the expense of
Colder temperatures with windchill values diminishing.
Eastern districts however will experience high windchill values.

Metro toronto.
Today..windy and cold with periods of snow ending by evening.
  snow accumulation 2 to 5 cm.  Northeast wind gusting to 60 km/h
  giving blowing snow and high windchill values.  High near minus 7.
--More--(12%)[Hit space to continue, Del to abort]
```

Using Gopher

What could be easier?

Gopher helps you to discover many resources on the Internet that you might not be readily aware of, or that might have been difficult to find using Telnet and FTP. For example, Gopher will assist you in finding:

- information on Internet resources

- Many Gopher sites will point you to resources which help to locate USENET FAQ's (Frequently Asked Questions) and other documents about various Internet services

- complete guides to the Internet, and documents on how to use various Internet services

- particular mailing lists or USENET newsgroups, by allowing you to search some of the documents mentioned in the chapter on mailing lists and USENET

- locations of software within particular FTP sites (although Archie, described below, is the industrial strength file finder of the Internet world)

Gopher Jewels

The massive growth in the number of Gopher sites and services brought together a group of people who believed that they should index some of the more interesting sites on the Internet.

The result was Gopher Jewels, a service accessible from many Gopher services. Information within Gopher Jewels is categorized by topic.

Your Internet service provider might or might not provide access to Gopher Jewels. If access is provided, the location within the menu could be different for each service provider. The easiest way to find out if you have access to Gopher Jewels on your local client is to look around through the menus; and if you cannot find it, ask your Internet service provider for help.

For example, accessing a Gopher Jewels menu item shows the current level of categorization, as seen within the next two screens.

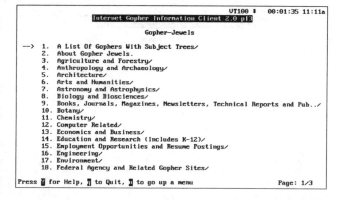

```
                                    UT100 ‡    00:01:35 11:11a
                  Internet Gopher Information Client 2.0 p13

                           Gopher-Jewels

   -->  1.  A List Of Gophers With Subject Trees/
        2.  About Gopher Jewels.
        3.  Agriculture and Forestry/
        4.  Anthropology and Archaeology/
        5.  Architecture/
        6.  Arts and Humanities/
        7.  Astronomy and Astrophysics/
        8.  Biology and Biosciences/
        9.  Books, Journals, Magazines, Newsletters, Technical Reports and Pub../
       10.  Botany/
       11.  Chemistry/
       12.  Computer Related/
       13.  Economics and Business/
       14.  Education and Research (Includes K-12)/
       15.  Employment Opportunities and Resume Postings/
       16.  Engineering/
       17.  Environment/
       18.  Federal Agency and Related Gopher Sites/

  Press ? for Help, q to Quit, u to go up a menu           Page: 1/3
```

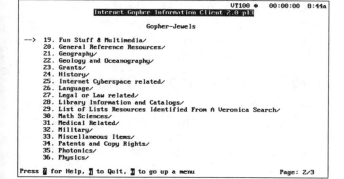

```
                                    UT100 *    00:00:00  8:44a
                  Internet Gopher Information Client 2.0 p13

                           Gopher-Jewels

   -->  19.  Fun Stuff & Multimedia/
        20.  General Reference Resources/
        21.  Geography/
        22.  Geology and Oceanography/
        23.  Grants/
        24.  History/
        25.  Internet Cyberspace related/
        26.  Language/
        27.  Legal or Law related/
        28.  Library Information and Catalogs/
        29.  List of Lists Resources Identified From A Veronica Search/
        30.  Math Sciences/
        31.  Medical Related/
        32.  Military/
        33.  Miscellaneous Items/
        34.  Patents and Copy Rights/
        35.  Photonics/
        36.  Physics/

  Press ? for Help, q to Quit, u to go up a menu           Page: 2/3
```

If we choose the menu item **19. Fun Stuff** we see the following screen:

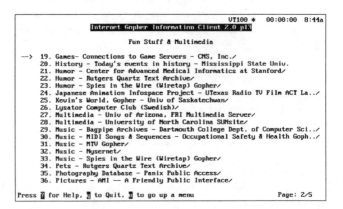

By choosing the MTV gopher, we make our way to a listing of MTV (U.S. music video channel) resources on the Internet.[4]

Choosing any of these topics leads us further into the Gopher service of MTV, permitting us to retrieve record and video reviews, concert listings and other information.

Using Gopher to Find an Organization

In another example, we will use Gopher to find out if a particular organization (in our example, Esso Canada) has registered with the Canadian .ca Internet domain.

We know that the Gopher at the Nova Scotia Technology Network includes a "White Pages" service, which permits you to look up entries in the Canadian domain listing.

Through our main Gopher menu, we choose the item "Other Gopher and Information Servers."

From there, we narrow in on North America, to Canada, where we see a listing of Canadian Gopher servers. The second page of the listing (accessed by typing +), shows the following:

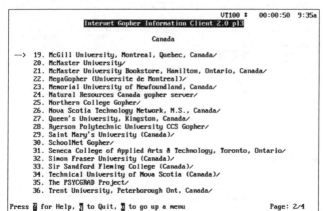

Menu item 26 takes us to the NSTN menu:

Menu item 16., **White Pages**, presents us with a query; in this case, the organization to look for:

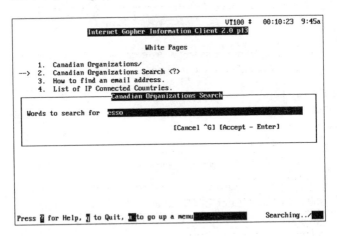

and we see the details on Esso Canada.

```
                                            VT100 ‡   00:10:47  9:45a
Subdomain:       ESSO.CA
Date-Received:   1991/03/18
Date-Approved:   1991/06/02
Date-Modified:   1993/06/09
Organization:    ESSO Chemical Canada
Type:            For-Profit Corporation
Description:     ESSO Chemical Canada is a Canada wide national oil company.
Admin-Name:      Peter Graw
Admin-Title:     System Administrator
Admin-Postal:    ESSO Chemical Alberta Limited
                 PO Box 28000
                 Edmonton, Alberta
                 T5J 4R4
Admin-Phone:     +1 403 998 6870
Admin-Mailbox:   admin@IOL.CA
Tech-Name:       Ken Gehring
Tech-Title:      End User Computing Support
Tech-Postal:     ESSO Chemical Alberta Limited
                 PO Box 28000
                 Edmonton, Alberta
                 T5J 4R4
Tech-Phone:      +1 403 998 6068
--More--(72%)[Hit space to continue, Del to abort]
```

Mailing a Gopher Document

A nice feature of most Gopher systems is the ability to:

- download the document immediately to your own computer. You can only do this if the technical setup of your service provider, gopher site and personal computer software support this (working in unison);

- transfer the file to your Internet service provider, to save it for downloading later (the method you would use if you couldn't use the download method above);

or

- have a document that you are viewing sent to you via e-mail (if neither of the methods above work).

For example, in our weather forecast example, we see a prompt on the last page of the display.

```
                                           VT100 ‡   00:02:06  9:31a
Extended forecasts for Thursday Friday and Saturday for Nova Scotia
And prince Edward Island issued by environment Canada at 5.00 am
Ast Tuesday 04 january 1994.

Nova Scotia
Prince Edward Island.
Thursday.. Windy. Variable cloudiness with chance of flurries.
 lows near minus 10. Highs near minus 3.
Friday.. Variable cloudiness with chance of flurries. Lows near
 minus 12. Highs near minus 2.
Saturday.. Periods of rain or snow. Lows near minus 6. Highs near
 plus 3.
Probability of precipitation in percent.
 30 Thursday 40 Friday and 100 Saturday.
Normals for the period... Lows near minus 7. Highs near zero.

End/jbm



Press <RETURN> to continue,
   <m> to mail, <D> to download, <s> to save, or <p> to print:
```

Choosing **(m) to mail**, we are prompted for the Internet e-mail address that we want to send the document to.

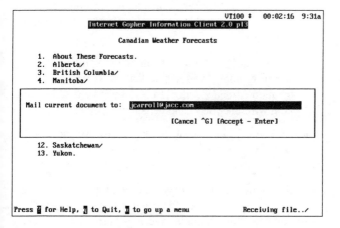

```
                                           VT100 ‡   00:02:16  9:31a
         Internet Gopher Information Client 2.0 p13

                   Canadian Weather Forecasts

    1. About These Forecasts.
    2. Alberta/
    3. British Columbia/
    4. Manitoba/

 Mail current document to:  jcarroll@jacc.com

                            [Cancel ^G] [Accept - Enter]

   12. Saskatchewan/
   13. Yukon.



Press ? for Help, q to Quit, u to go up a menu        Receiving file../
```

Gopher Bookmarks

One of the most useful aspects of Gopher is the ability to use bookmarks.

When you have used Gopher to locate a particular Internet resource, and you want to go back to access it again, you might find that you have a difficult time finding it. Remembering which menus you worked your way through is not the easiest thing to do.

Gopher bookmarks permit you to keep track of particular Gopher resources, and access them through your own personal Gopher menu. There are four basic bookmark commands:

a	add an item to your bookmark list
A	add the current search to the bookmark list. For example, you might have run a search within Gopher and retrieved a list of documents. Typing A will save the search to your personal Gopher menu so that you can quickly return there.
v	view your current bookmark list
d	delete a bookmark

Other Gopher Information

When using Gopher, there are other things to keep in mind:

- Gopher menus show symbols to indicate what you will find behind a particular menu item.

  As usual, these symbols could be different from the example, depending upon your Internet service provider.

  These include ? for a menu item that will lead you to a search prompt; / to indicate that the menu is followed by another menu; and <TEL> to indicate that the menu item will link you to another site via Telnet.

- As you explore Gopher, look for **Veronica**, a utility which permits you to search Gopher resources through a keyword search.

- If you are directly connected to the Internet, you might be able to use one of the newly emerging "clients" for Gopher. For example, recently introduced software which runs within Microsoft Windows or on an Apple Macintosh, provide a GUI (graphical user interface) view of Gopher information, making it even easier to navigate throughout the system

The Growth of Gopher

By one estimate, the number of Gopher servers on the Internet is increasing at an annual rate of 997%.[5]

One of the primary reasons why the number of Gopher servers is increasing at a dramatic rate, is that any institution connected to the Internet can establish its own Gopher server, mount information on it, and make it accessible to anyone else in the world with Gopher.

Many organizations on the Internet are actively encouraging the use of Gopher. For example, York University encourages student groups to put information on Gopher and make it available to the rest of the campus and around the world.

As a result, Gopher is rapidly becoming an important information dissemination tool throughout the Internet.

HYTELNET

Hytelnet is a Canadian program, originally written by Peter Scott of the University of Saskatchewan Libraries, with assistance from Earl Fogel of the same institution.

Hytelnet summarizes information available on Internet resources worldwide.

Although you can use a Telnet session to a site that has Hytelnet (for example, Telnet to access.usask.ca to run it the Hytelnet client at that location), it is far more convenient to run it on your own computer. Versions of Hytelnet are available for Amiga, MSDOS, Macintosh, UNIX and VMS systems.

To obtain Hytelnet for PC's, ftp to ftp.usask.ca. You will find the file HYTELN66.ZIP in the directory pub/hytelnet/pc. Other versions are also available on that system.

The following screens provide a brief tour of Hytelnet, as run on an MSDOS system.

Sample Hytelnet Session

The introductory screen indicates the types of information that are available. The two key entries are "**Library catalogs**" and "**Other Resources.**"

```
                  Welcome to HYTELNET version 6.6
                          October 10, 1993

                What is HYTELNET?          <WHATIS>
                Library catalogs           <SITES1>
                Other resources            <SITES2>
                Help files for catalogs    <OP000>
                Catalog interfaces         <SYS000>
                Internet Glossary          <GLOSSARY>
                Telnet tips                <TELNET>
                Telnet/TN3270 escape keys  <ESCAPE.KEY>
                Key-stroke commands        <HELP.TXT>
.........................................................................
Up/Down arrows MOVE      Left/Right arrows SELECT    F1 for HELP anytime

                  CONTROL/HOME returns here   ALT-T quits
.........................................................................
                HYTELNET 6.6 was written by Peter Scott
                E-mail address: aa375@freenet.carleton.ca


 Screen 1 of 1  FILE: START.TXT                              F1=HELP
```

By moving to **<SITES2>** with the cursor key and pressing
return, we see a menu of various resources available by Telnet.

```
                  Other Telnet-accessible resources

            <ARC000>  Archie: Archive Server Listing Service
            <CWI000>  Campus-wide Information systems
            <FUL000>  Databases and bibliographies

            <DIS000>  Distributed File Servers (Gopher/WAIS/WWW)
            <BOOKS>   Electronic books
            <FEE000>  Fee-Based Services

            <FRE000>  FREE-NETs & Community Computing Systems
            <BBS000>  General Bulletin Boards
            <HYT000>  HYTELNET On-line versions

            <NAS000>  NASA databases
            <NET000>  Network Information Services
            <DIR000>  Whois/White Pages/Directory Services

            <OTH000>  Miscellaneous resources



 Screen 1 of 1  FILE: SITES2                                 F1=HELP
```

Choosing the **Databases and bibliographies**
entry shows the following screen:

```
                  Databases and Bibliographies

<FUL035> AAtDB: An Arabidopsis thaliana Data Base
<FUL041> ABSEES: American Bibliography of Slavic & East European Studies
<FUL043> Arizona State Economic Development Database
<FUL031> Bank of England Quarterly Bulletin Time Series Data
<FUL001> BLAISE-LINE (British Library's On-Line Service)
<FUL002> British Library Document Supply Centre
<FUL055> CARL System Database Gateway
<FUL029> Central Statistical Office Macro-Economic Time Series Data
<FUL046> Coalition for Networked Information Server
<FUL004> CONSER database (journal/serial/periodical indexes)
<FUL005> Constitutional Documents (USA)
<FUL006> Court of Appeals of Ohio, Eighth District, County of Cuyahoga
<FUL007> Dartmouth Dante Project
<FUL024> Earth Images Catalogue LEDA
<FUL025> Earth observation satellite data inventory service
<FUL033> Einstein On-Line Service
<FUL049> Electronic Periodic Table of the Elements
<FUL008> Environmental Education Database
<FUL009> ERIC (Educational Resources Information Center Documents)
<FUL048> Eureka Example screens (Research Libraries Group)
<FUL044> EX-USSR data files
<FUL010> General Accounting Office Documents
 ↕↕  Screen 1 of 3  FILE: FUL000                            F1=HELP
```

Choosing the entry `<FUL055>` provides details concerning how to Telnet to the **CARL** service.

```
                         CARL System Database Gateway

TELNET DATABASE.CARL.ORG or 192.54.81.76
Select 5 for vt100

                   WELCOME TO THE CARL SYSTEM DATABASE GATEWAY

CARL Systems, Inc. is proud to present our Shopping List of Databases.
Many of the databases included require a password.  If you would like to
look at one of these restricted databases, please contact CARL Systems,
Inc. at database@carl.org or 303/758-3030.  If you have already been
given a password to a database, please enter your password when
prompted.  There are a number of library catalogs and free databases
available, please feel free to look around.

   1.  UnCover
       (Article Access and Delivery)
   2.  Information Access Company Databases
       (including Business Index, Magazine Index and others)
   3.  Grolier's Academic American Encyclopedia
   4.  Facts on File
   5.  H.W. Wilson Databases
       (including Library Literature)
   6.  Other Information and Article Databases
  ██  Screen 1 of 2  FILE: FUL055                             F1=HELP
```

Hytelnet was originally written for use by librarians, and hence includes a separate section on library resources. Examining the entry for Canada (several levels down from the `<SITES1>` entry on the starting point above), we see a listing of these libraries.

```
<CA040> Ottawa Public Library
<CA001> Queen's University
<CA016> Saint Mary's University
<CA049> Saskatoon Public Library
<CA029> Simon Fraser University
<CA024> St. Boniface General Hospital Library
<CA017> Technical University of Nova Scotia
<CA027> Trent University
<CA045> Universite de Moncton - Bibliotheque Champlain
<CA037> Universite de Sherbrooke
<CA019> University College of Cape Breton
<CA051> University of Alberta
<CA022> University of British Columbia
<CA003> University of Calgary
<CA052> University of Guelph
<CA020> University of Kings College
<CA034> University of Lethbridge
<CA023> University of Manitoba Libraries
<CA002> University of New Brunswick
<CA047> University of Ottawa
<CA012> University of Prince Edward Island
<CA008> University of Saskatchewan
<CA005> University of Toronto
<CA035> University of Victoria
  ██  Screen 2 of 3  FILE: CA000                      F1=HELP
```

Choosing **Saskatoon Public Library**, we are provided a screen which details the Telnet address and other information necessary to sign into the library service.

```
                      Saskatoon Public Library
TELNET CHARLY.PUBLIB.SASKATOON.SK.CA or 192.197.206.1
Username: PUBLIC
At the PAC >>> prompt, type  pac

OPAC = DRA <OP004>

To exit, type EXIT
At the PAC >>> prompt, type  quit




Screen 1 of 1  FILE: CA049                              F1=HELP
```

Hytelnet is a simple, effective, and quick way to track Internet resources.

Since updates are released fairly regularly, it is highly recommended.

WAIS

WAIS (Wide Area Information Server) is another tool used to locate information throughout the Internet.

WAIS runs on everything from a supercomputer at its developer, Thinking Machines, to many other types of computers throughout the Internet. It is not as widely deployed as Gopher, however.

WAIS is very different from Gopher; rather than searching for information through a series of menus, as you do in Gopher, WAIS searches a number of global Internet resources by permitting you to specify the word or phrases you are looking for.

If you are familiar with commercial full text database systems like Dialog, Nexis, Dow Jones News Retrieval, Infoglobe or Infomart, WAIS will be the closest counterpart, given its reliance on full-text searching.

Yet, because it can query computers located in many different locations around the Internet, it is also very different in scope from these services.

When using WAIS, you specify the words that you are searching for, and WAIS performs the search. Once complete, it provides a listing of "hits," describing databases or documents that match your search term. It does this by ranking the relevance of retrieved items and giving them a "score" that approximates how closely the retrieved items match your search request.

When searching a specific database or group of databases, WAIS runs the search on databases scattered throughout the Internet, as seen in the following figure:

FIGURE 8-1: WAIS IN OPERATION

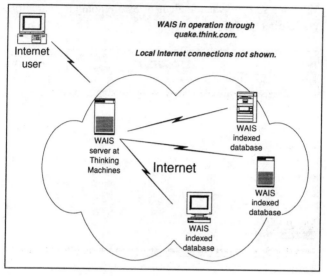

In this example, an Internet user is linked to the WAIS server located at Thinking Machines. When a variety of databases are selected from this WAIS server, WAIS actually sends queries to these databases, which could be scattered throughout the Internet around the world. The results are then retrieved and displayed to the user, within seconds.

In this way, WAIS lives up to its name: Wide-Area Information Servers.

Sample WAIS session

In this sample WAIS session, we Telnet to quake.think.com.
Through Thinking Machines, we will:

- first query a "directory-of-servers."

  This will query descriptions of approximately 500 WAIS servers that are linked to the Thinking Machines WAIS system, and will return a list of databases that contain the search term in the description.

- select one of the databases, and query it further for particular information.

When you Telnet to `quake.think.com`, you will be prompted to "login." Type **WAIS**, and type your Internet address when asked.

Once your connection is established, you will see the following screen, which indicates you are going to search the WAIS directory-of-servers:

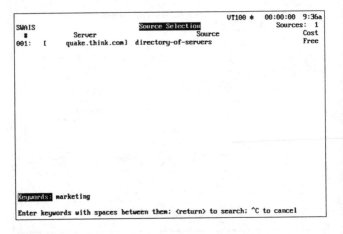

Typing **w** permits us to enter a word to search for; we type `marketing`.

This presents a list of two databases that contain the word `marketing` in their description, below.

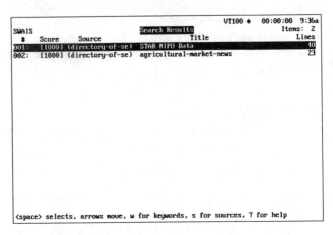

Displaying the second of the two items, we note that it does include reference to "marketing" information.

```
                                                    UT100 *   00:00:00  9:38a
SWAIS                           Document Display                    Page:  1
(:source
  :version  3
  :ip-address "128.193.124.4"
  :ip-name "nostromo.oes.orst.edu"
  :tcp-port 210
  :database-name "agricultural-market-news"
  :cost 0.00
  :cost-unit :free
  :maintainer "wais@nostromo.oes.orst.edu"
  :subjects "business marketing commodities agriculture agricultural"
  :description "Server created with WAIS release 8 b3.1 on Oct  5 22:40:47 199
1 by wais@nostromo.oes.orst.edu

This server contains the agricultural commodity market reports compiled
by the Agricultural Market News Service of the United States Department
of Agriculture. There are approximately 1200 reports from all over the
United States. Most of these reports are updated daily. Try searching for
'portland grain.'

For more information contact: wais@oes.orst.edu
"
Press any key to continue, 'q' to quit.
```

With a couple more steps, we can search this database and retrieve actual documents.

Searching this database for the word barley, for example, results in the following:

```
                                                    UT100 *   00:00:00  9:40a
SWAIS                           Search Results              Items: 31
  #     Score      Source                    Title                    Lines
001:  [1000] (agricultural-ma)  Re:   RH GR110,                         124
002:  [ 778] (agricultural-ma)  Re:   RH GR112                           82
003:  [ 778] (agricultural-ma)  Re:   WA CB121                         2462
004:  [ 611] (agricultural-ma)  Re:   FZ GR115                           53
005:  [ 611] (agricultural-ma)  Re:   JO GR110,PMGRAIN                  116
006:  [ 611] (agricultural-ma)  Re:   WA CB351 PROSPECTIVE PLANTINGS    954
007:  [ 556] (agricultural-ma)  Re:   JO GR211,WEEKLYFEED               130
008:  [ 556] (agricultural-ma)  Re:   MS GR115 WKLYGRM                   65
009:  [ 500] (agricultural-ma)  Re:   RH GR111                           58
010:  [ 500] (agricultural-ma)  Re:   SJ GR051 NAT. GRAIN SUMMARY        86
011:  [ 500] (agricultural-ma)  Re:   WA GR101 GRAIN INSPECTIONS        232
012:  [ 444] (agricultural-ma)  Re:   BL GR110 MT DAILY GRAIN            52
013:  [ 444] (agricultural-ma)  Re:   BL GR115 MT WEEKLY GRAIN           52
014:  [ 444] (agricultural-ma)  Re:   HC GR115 SO CALIF WKLY CASH GRAIN  72
015:  [ 444] (agricultural-ma)  Re:   JO GR116,ADD WEEKLY                87
016:  [ 444] (agricultural-ma)  Re:   SV GR110                           94
017:  [ 444] (agricultural-ma)  Re:   WA CB101 CROP PRODUCTION          373
018:  [ 444] (agricultural-ma)  Re:   WA CB301 GRAIN STOCKS             184

<space> selects, arrows move, w for keywords, s for sources, ? for help
```

Displaying the first document on the list, we see a commodities report.

```
                                                    UT100 *   00:00:00  9:40a
SWAIS                           Document Display                    Page:  1
Subject:   RH GR110
Date: Tue, 04 Jan 94 01:23:12 PM


RH GR110
RICHMOND VA FED STATE JANUARY 4, 1994


VIRGINIA GRAIN


TRENDS FOR RICHMOND AND PETERSBURG

WHEAT     -  UP 3-8    NEW CROP DOWN 2
CORN      -  NO QUOTE  NEW CROP STEADY
SOYBEANS  -  DOWN 16   NEW CROP UP 1
BARLEY    -  STEADY
MILO      -  STEADY
Press any key to continue, 'q' to quit.
```

WAIS Searches

WAIS is an interesting and powerful technology, and to many people, it represents the future of information searching and knowledge retrieval on the Internet.

Yet, WAIS can be frustrating.

- One of the main reasons for this has to do with the quality of information on the Internet itself, and the way information is indexed.

  Looking for information on market research, for example, turned up only two references within the WAIS search above.

  Yet, the WAIS server above includes several databases which might obviously contain market research references, including one called online@uunet.ca. This database, an index of discussions for those involved in information brokerage and on-line research, includes several references to market research reports. Yet, because the WAIS description for this database does not allude to that fact, the database is overlooked through a standard WAIS search of the "directory-of-servers." You would have to know that online@uunet.ca exists, and choose to query it directly.

- Novice users often retrieve documents that, upon examination, are irrelevant.

  Full text retrieval is an art in itself, and takes time and effort to learn. Experts at full text retrieval often command premium prices in the marketplace, as it is a skill which is not easily learned. Do not expect fabulous results during your first attempts.

Using WAIS is a little like being able to open the door to a vault, but being frustrated because you are not sure which key opens each safety deposit box.

WORLD WIDE WEB

World Wide Web, developed in Europe at CERN, the European Laboratory for Particle Physics, is another Internet initiative which promises much easier browsing of Internet resources.

Like WAIS, World Wide Web servers link to information from throughout the Internet.

Rather than providing full text search of these resources, WWW (as it is known) provides a unique, "hypertext" method of accessing information. That is to say, each WWW screen, identifying resources or other information, includes pointers to other WWW screens, with some pointers eventually leading you to specific bits of information and knowledge.

Using WWW is a little like following a maze; you can take a lot of different turns, and each time you are not sure where you are going to end up.

WWW, like gopher, is an excellent tool to discover the full diversity of the Internet.

Sample WWW Session

To try out a World Wide Web server, we Telnet to **info.cern.ch**. No additional login is required.

After navigating a couple of screens that detail where to find more information about WWW, we are presented with an introductory screen.

```
                                        VT100 ‡   00:01:11 11:14a
                                                  Overview of the Web
                      GENERAL OVERVIEW OF THE WEB

     There is no "top" to the World-Wide Web. You can look at it from many points
     of view. Here are some places to start.

   by Subject[1]          The Virtual Library organises information by subject
                          matter.

   List of servers[2]     All registered HTTP servers by country

   by Service Type[3]     The Web includes data accessible by many other
                          protocols. The lists by access protocol may help if
                          you know what kind of service you are looking for.

     If you find a useful starting point for you personally, you can configure
     your WWW browser to start there by default.

     See also: About the W3 project[4] .
       [End]

   1-4, Back, Up, Quit, or Help:
```

Note that the WWW screen includes numbers next to each item. As you dig further into WWW, you will find that complete sentences contain a variety of numbers, each of which points to a different Internet resource.

In effect, information within WWW is cross-linked to other information sources, using what is called Hypertext technology. If we take a look at the following screen (from somewhere within WWW), we can see that there are a variety of references within a single sentence to different resources.

```
                                     VT100 ‡   00:03:05 11:31a
                      Sources of Data Potentially Available via WWW (45/138)
Mailing lists          Why not archive a mailing list, index it, deduce the
                      links between messages, and put it up using WWW? Many
                      groups are coordinated using mailing lists, which lack
                      an easy access to back-issues. Some mail servers
                      archive the stuff anyway, and so would be the natural
                      site for an archive server. An important aspect is the
                      generation of links between related articles. See
                      mailing list handlers MAILBASE[13]  and the Mailbase
                      data [14]and LISTSERV[15] Italian LISTSERV[16] , and
                      the WWW mailing lists[17] for example, and Ed V's
                      index of public mailing lists[18] .

Journals[19]           Electronic journals are mostly distributed by mail or
                      or using BITNET. (Because if they are on the Internet
                      news schemes suffice?). VOICE[20] is an exception, as
                      well as some journals whose back-issues are available
                      (often compressed) by anonymous FTP (often from IBM
                      machines).

Library systems.       See the hytelnet[21] database of telnet sites etc.
                      and other lists[22] .  Examples of systems coming on
                      the web include all sites running Aleph (TM)
1-38, Back, Up, <RETURN> for more, Quit, or Help:
```

Organization of WWW Information

From our "entry point" into WWW, we can choose to view by topic area:

```
                                     VT100 ‡   00:01:11 11:16a
                      The World-Wide Web Virtual Library: Subject Catalogue
                          THE WWW VIRTUAL LIBRARY

This is a distributed subject catalogue. See also arrangement  by  service
type[1] ., and other subject catalogues of network information[2] .

Mail www-request@info.cern.ch to add pointers to this list, or if you would
like to contibute to administration of a subject area.

Aeronautics            Mailing list archive index[3] . See also NASA LaRC[4]

Agriculture[5]         Separate list, see also Almanac mail servers[6] ; the
                      Agricultural Genome[7] (National Agricultural Library,
                      part of the U.S. Department of Agriculture)

Archaeology            Classics and Mediterranean Archaeology[8]

Astronomy and Astrophysics[9]
                       Separate list.

Bio Sciences[10]       Separate list .

Chemistry              Department of Chemistry[11] at the University of
1-108, Back, Up, <RETURN> for more, Quit, or Help:
```

or by service type (i.e., FTP, WAIS, etc.):

```
                                     VT100 ‡   00:03:16 11:23a
                      Data sources classified by access protocol
                      RESOURCES CLASSIFIED BY TYPE OF SERVICE

See also categorization exist by subject[1] .  If you know what sort of a
service you are looking for, look here:

World-Wide Web servers[2]
                       List of W3 native "HTTP" servers. These are generally
                      the most friendly. See also: about the WWW
                      initiative[3] .

WAIS servers[4]        Find WAIS index servers using the directory of
                      servers[5] , or lists by name[6] or domain[7] . See
                      also: about WAIS[8] .

Network News[9]        Available directly in all www browsers. See also this
                      list of FAQs[10] .

Gopher[11]             Campus-wide information systems, etc, listed
                      geographically. See also: about Gopher[12] .

Telnet access[13]      Hypertext  catalogues by Peter Scott. See also: list
                      by Scott Yanoff[14] . Also, Art St George's index[15]
1-28, Back, Up, <RETURN> for more, Quit, or Help:
```

The examples above show World Wide Web in its most basic form, when accessed from a simple terminal program. Programs are already available on a number of platforms which present a more friendlier way to view WWW resources, as discussed at the conclusion to this chapter.

World Wide Web is another example of how Internet resources and the Internet itself will continue to evolve, making it easier for participants to locate information scattered throughout the world.

ARCHIE

Archie, a program developed in Canada at McGill University and now marketed and supported worldwide by a Canadian company, Bunyip Information Systems, permits you to search file archives around the Internet by file name.

Like many Internet resource programs, you can run Archie:

- directly on your Internet linked system, if Archie is one of the service offerings;

  or

- by Telnet to an archie site. Some of the more popular sites include:

```
archie.rutgers.edu    128.6.18.15
   (Rutgers University)
archie.unl.edu        129.93.1.14
   (University of Nebraska in Lincoln)
archie.sura.net       128.167.254.179
   (SURAnet archie server)
archie.ans.net        147.225.1.2
   (ANS archie server)
archie.au             139.130.4.6
   (Australian server)
archie.funet.fi       128.214.6.100
   (European server in Finland)
archie.doc.ic.ac.uk   146.169.11.3
   (UK/England server)
archie.cs.huji.ac.il  132.65.6.15
   (Israel server)
archie.wide.ad.jp     133.4.3.6
   (Japanese server)
```

Sample Archie Session

In the following example, Archie is run on an Internet service provider, which has been accessed using a dialup connection.

First, we establish whether we can run archie on this system by typing **archie**. Archie responds with details on how it can be used.

```
                                    E:94% VT100 *   00:00:00  9:39a
$ archie
Usage: archie [-acelorstuLV] [-m hits] [-N level] string
            -a : list matches as Alex filenames
            -c : case sensitive substring search
            -e : exact string match (default)
            -r : regular expression search
            -s : case insensitive substring search
            -l : list one match per line
            -t : sort inverted by date
        -m hits : specifies maximum number of hits to return (default 95)
    -o filename : specifies file to store results in
         -h host : specifies server host
            -L : list known servers and current default
       -N level : specifies query niceness level (0-35765)
$
```

Typing **archie -L** gives us a listing of the archie servers that are available worldwide, and indicates that our archie queries will use the server at **archie.sura.net**.

```
                                    E:94% VT100 *   00:00:00  9:39a
$ archie -L
Known archie servers:
        archie.ans.net (USA [NY])
        archie.rutgers.edu (USA [NJ])
        archie.sura.net (USA [MD])
        archie.unl.edu (USA [NE])
        archie.mcgill.ca (Canada)
        archie.funet.fi (Finland/Mainland Europe)
        archie.au (Australia)
        archie.doc.ic.ac.uk (Great Britain/Ireland)
        archie.wide.ad.jp (Japan)
        archie.ncu.edu.tw (Taiwan)
* archie.sura.net is the default Archie server.
* For the most up-to-date list, write to an Archie server and give it
  the command `servers'.
$
```

Finally, we run an archie query to look for any programs containing the phrase uupc (in this case, looking for the program UUPC, which is a popular off-line method of using e-mail and USENET for MSDOS computers).

We do so by typing **archie -r uupc**. Archie responds with a listing of sites and filenames, as seen below.

```
                                    E:94% Pause!!    00:00:00  9:49a
$ archie -r uupc

Host swdsrv.eduz.univie.ac.at

    Location: /novell/pegasus/misc
         FILE -r--r--r--     214425   Sep  9 15:41   uupc11xd.zip
         FILE -r--r--r--      54399   Sep  9 15:41   uupc11zn.zip
         FILE -r--r--r--     204283   Sep  9 15:42   uupc11zo.zip
         FILE -r--r--r--     173696   Sep  9 15:43   uupc11zr.zip
    Location: /os2/hobbes/all/comm
         FILE -r--r--r--     214425   Sep 13 07:23   uupc11xd.zip
         FILE -r--r--r--     177679   Sep 13 07:23   uupc11z2.zip
         FILE -r--r--r--     187602   Sep 13 07:23   uupc11z3.zip
         FILE -r--r--r--      55313   Sep 13 07:22   uupc11z4.zip
         FILE -r--r--r--     309935   Sep 13 07:22   uupc11za.zip
         FILE -r--r--r--     374904   Sep 13 07:22   uupc11zb.zip
         FILE -r--r--r--     112300   Sep 13 07:22   uupc11zc.zip
```

We can then choose to use anonymous FTP to these sites to retrieve any of these program files.

IRC

Internet Relay Chat is a relatively new application on the Internet, but one which is gaining an increasing amount of attention.

IRC is best described as a "CB radio" for the Internet. Using IRC, you can participate in on-line discussions in real-time with other Internet users. Discussions are either open or private.

To use IRC, you must have either:

- a direct connection to the Internet and have the IRC client software on your own system

    or

- use a version located on your Internet service provider.

In both cases, you will also need an IRC server location to access. Your Internet service provider might automatically link to a site. The major Canadian location is at ug.cs.dal.ca

To check if you have IRC access, type IRC at your Internet service provider prompt.

A listing of IRC servers in Canada can be found in Appendix A, in the document *Directory of IRC Servers in Canada*.

FINGER

Finger is a utility originally used in the UNIX world to list users on a local system, or to list users located at another location on the Internet.

Users of UNIX systems can list information about themselves which can be accessed via Finger. For example, typing:

```
finger franklin@ug.cs.dal.ca
```

is an interesting example of the use of Finger.

Some locations on the Internet are now using Finger as a simple method of making information available . For example, to obtain recent information on auroral (Northern Lights) activity in Canada, type

```
finger aurora@xi.uleth.ca
```

THE FUTURE OF INFORMATION RETRIEVAL

New Internet tools are rapidly emerging — systems like Mosaic, for example, which provide a graphical front end to information in WAIS, World Wide Web or Gopher servers.

These applications permit an individual to access any of the Internet resources simply by double-clicking with a mouse on a menu choice or search result.

In order to give us a flavor of the type of application that is emerging, Rod Potter, at York University in Toronto (**rodp @ender.ccs.yorku.ca**), provided us with these sample images of the way that he uses the Internet.

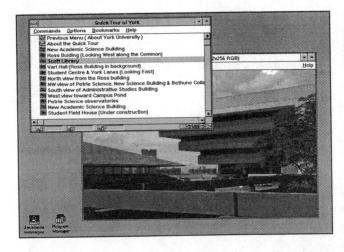

In this first screen, HGopher for Windows displays a menu providing a "Quick Tour of York." Choosing a particular menu item displays the image associated with the choice -- demonstrating how these tools are resulting in a tight link between information browsing and image display.

The tools result in a more graphical representation of methods of accessing information. Rather than a dull, dreary series of menu choices, a Gopher menu at York might be displayed like this:

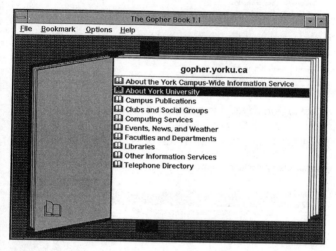

Accessing the CBC radio files mentioned previously, using the product NCSA Mosaic for Windows, results in the following type of screens.

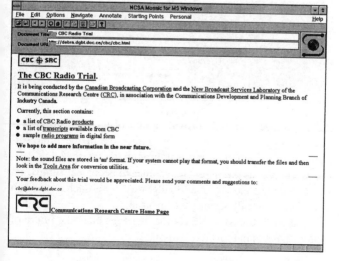

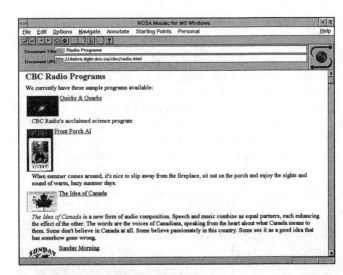

Clicking on any of the highlighted items results in a display of information for that choice.

A WAIS query within WAIS for Windows looks like this:

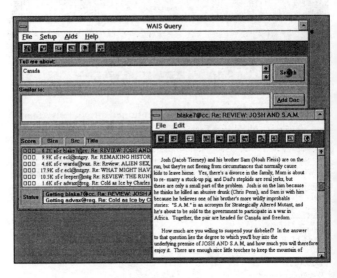

These images can only provide a hint of how the Internet is becoming easier to use, and are indicative of the future direction of information retrieval through the Internet.

Certainly, as the Internet continues to become a significant component of the information highway, tools such as seen on these screens will become indispensable.

Mike Martineau of NSTN Inc. believes that "the future of the Internet is in tools like Mosaic."

Mike indicates that these tools will launch the Internet into organizations in a way that has not been seen before. "I truly believe that WWW, with Mosaic-like viewers, will be the 'killer' application that catches many people's imaginations. WWW is not just hypertext, but hypermedia. That is, it supports information retrieval in multiple formats using hypertext technology."

The sophistication of Mosaic can be astounding, says Mike. "I have seen information services which use a map as the main presentation screen. Clicking on different areas of the map bring up information related to that area of that map — weather, for example."

Certainly, Mosaic is gaining attention. "Many companies are stepping up to WWW as THE technology with which to present info on the Internet — companies like Novell, Quarterdeck and QMS," says Mike.

"Telnet and FTP are, in my opinion, dying applications. They are hard to use and understand," Mike comments, when asked about the future of information retrieval on the Internet. "WWW can fully replace Telnet, FTP, Gopher and WAIS. It handles information in a variety of forms and is capable of being the only information retrieval system that people need use. Mosaic is available today, for Windows, MACs and Unix systems."

---

1 . In a significant development, the U.S. government has decided to make available information filed with the Securities and Exchange Commission via the Internet, rather than via a pay-per-use on-line commercial database. This occurred after an intense grassroots campaign by Internet supporters that such information should be publicly available.

2 . The National Weather Service data is made available courtesy of the National Science Foundation-funded UNIDATA Project and the University of Michigan.

3 . Through a Gopher client, you can also connect directly to a Gopher server without going through all the menus. For example, you could have typed GOPHER NSTN.NS.CA to link directly to a Gopher server at the Nova Scotia Technology Network.

4 . MuchMusic, Canada's equivalent, hasn't discovered the Internet yet.

5 . The Internet Index, compiled by Win Treese (treese@crl.dec.com), 7/8/93, revised: 12/16/93

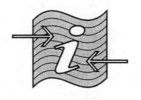

C H A P T E R   9

....

CONNECTING TO THE INTERNET

In Chapter 4, we discussed the client/server model of computing, and indicated how this might affect the way that you use the Internet. In particular, we noted that if you were "directly connected" to the Internet, your use of the system will differ from those who are not.

In this chapter, we examine some of the technical methods by which you might link yourself to the Internet:

- electronic mail only

- e-mail and USENET

- access via a "shell" account

- direct connection via TCP/IP

- direct connection via modem, using SLIP/PPP

The possible connections are shown in Figure 9.1.
Appendix A includes the *Directory of Canadian Internet Service Providers,* and details the range of services offered by companies to access the Internet from within Canada.

Some of these providers provide UUCP, shell, TCP/IP and SLIP/PPP access to the network; others provide only one or two of these options; and still others provide only e-mail access to the Internet.

What is appropriate in your circumstances depends upon

- your particular communication needs

- the technical effort that you are willing to put in to participate in the network

FIGURE 9.1: INTERNET CONNECTIVITY

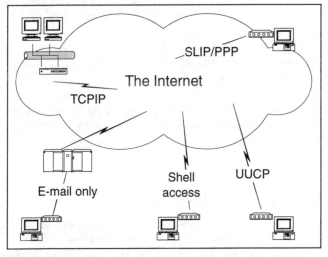

- the amount of money that you have available to spend

- the hardware and operating system platform in which you operate

ELECTRONIC MAIL ACCESS ONLY

With the popularity of the domain style method of addressing e-mail, as found on the Internet, it is evident that many people and organizations want to have an "Internet address."

In some cases, an individual might like to be able to send and receive Internet e-mail from home or from the office.

In other cases, an organization might desire a link to the Internet in order to communicate with trading partners, computer system vendors, suppliers and customers. Since the organization might have an e-mail system in use within the company, it wants to link the internal e-mail system to the Internet, permitting anyone in the organization to send and receive Internet e-mail.

To establish e-mail-only access to the Internet, you can subscribe as an individual to a commercial electronic mail or to an on-line service that has a link to Internet e-mail.

Or, you could choose to link a corporate or organizational local area network or other internal e-mail system to one of these services. (As we will see in the next section, you could also choose to establish a UUCP connection to an Internet service provider, to use only for the purpose of Internet e-mail.)

The *Directory of Canadian Internet Service Providers* includes reference to a number of commercial e-mail and on-line services which have established links to Internet e-mail. These systems include U.S. based services such as CompuServe, GEnie, ATTMail, and MCIMail. In addition, users of TheNet:Mail (formerly Envoy 100/iNet 2000) will be able to send and receive messages from the Internet early in 1994.

Access as an Individual

As an individual, you can choose to subscribe to one of the services just mentioned. Many of these services come with, or make available, special communications software which makes it easy to send and receive e-mail messages.

FIGURE 9.2: SIMPLE E-MAIL ACCESS VIA A THIRD PARTY

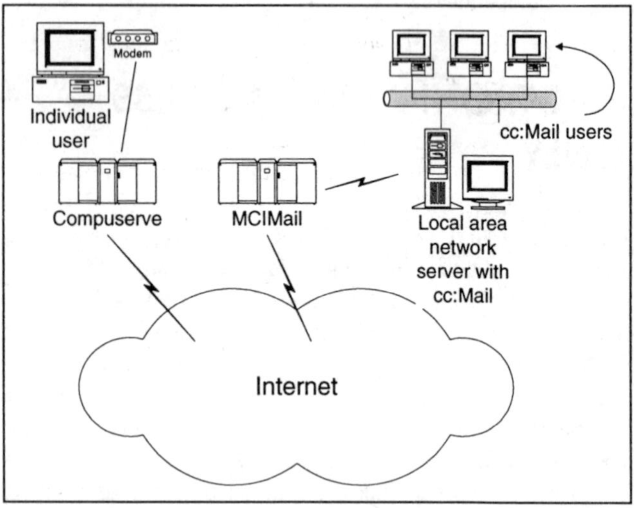

Using a service such as CompuServe or MCIMail provides you with your own unique Internet address, which can be used to receive Internet messages, and provides you the capability to send e-mail to anyone with an Internet e-mail address.

For example, in Figure 9.2, an individual accesses CompuServe, and since CompuServe has a link to Internet e-mail, the individual can send and receive Internet e-mail messages.

Access from a Corporate E-Mail System

It is also possible to link a local area network based e-mail system or other corporate or organizational e-mail system to a commercial e-mail system or on-line service, and from there, communicate with people on the Internet.[1]

For example, in Figure 9.2, a corporate local area network e-mail system, cc:Mail, has been linked to a commercial e-mail service, MCIMail. Since MCIMail has connectivity to and from Internet e-mail, individuals on the cc:Mail network are effectively linked to Internet e-mail.

Many organizations already linked to a major commercial e-mail service might be pleased to discover that they already have access to and from Internet e-mail.

The method of establishing such a link range from the technically simple to the technically complex. The method chosen by your particular organization will have much to do with how complex your Internet e-mail address becomes:

- For example, if you have linked your local area network e-mail system to CompuServe, your Internet address might be in the form: `name@company.compuserve.com`, which is nice and straightforward, and is recognizable to the Internet community.

- Other services do not provide as simple a form of addressing. For example, an Internet address for a LAN e-mail system linked AT&TMail looks like `org!org!name@attmail.com`, which is rather ugly, difficult to remember, and certainly not straightforward! Not only that, it violates the basic structure of Internet e-mail, as specified in several Internet standards documents.

- If your link to a commercial e-mail provider involves X.400, your Internet address will likely consist of a combination of X.400 and Internet addressing. Since few people on the Internet accept X.400 style addressing, you will likely find that this is not a workable solution.

An example of how not to link a commercial e-mail service to the Internet is found with the service from SprintMail, one of the largest commercial e-mail providers in the U.S.

An example of an Internet address through SprintMail using X.400 addressing is:

```
pn=jim.carroll/ou=1557touc/o=tmca.uni/prm
d=langate/admd=telemail/c=gb/@sprint.com
```

With this type of alphabet soup address, you can see why it is important to carefully consider your options!

VIA UUCP

The second method of establishing a link to the Internet is to use the "UUCP" protocol.

Using UUCP, you can participate in Internet e-mail and USENET newsgroups.

Strictly speaking, since you are not directly connected to the Internet, and do not have an IP address, you are not "on" the Internet.

UUCP Explained

Many Internet services providers provide UUCP service; that is, they permit users to send and receive Internet e-mail and USENET news using the UUCP protocol.

UUCP stands for Unix-to-Unix Copy Protocol, which is a "store-and-forward" basic file transfer utility found within most UNIX systems. UUCP takes on responsibility for copying e-mail and USENET postings to and from your Internet service provider. Using UUCP, you are only intermittently connected to your Internet service provider.

In order to use UUCP, you will need:

- a UUCP program for your system;

  and

- an e-mail program and newsreader software that work with your version of UUCP. This often comes with the UUCP program that you are using.

There are a number of ways in which UUCP can be used:

- as an individual, i.e., you use UUCP on your own to send and receive Internet e-mail and USENET news;

- from a LAN, i.e., UUCP is used to link several individuals on a LAN to Internet e-mail and USENET news (not shown in Figure 9.3);

  or

- from an e-mail system, i.e., UUCP is used to link an internal e-mail system to Internet e-mail.

FIGURE 9.3: E-MAIL ONLY ACCESS VIA UUCP

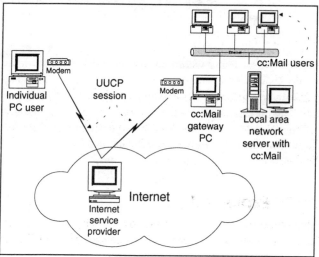

How Does UUCP Work?

UUCP is a *batch oriented system* — that is to say that:

- any messages that you create are not sent to your Internet service provider immediately, but are sent the next time you make a UUCP call to your provider;

- any messages sent to you are only received by you when you make a UUCP call to provider;

- USENET news is delivered to you, for the groups that you choose to belong to, when you make a UUCP call to your provider.

UUCP Software

There are many implementations of UUCP for popular operating systems.

LINKING INDIVIDUAL USERS VIA UUCP

For example, UUPC for MSDOS (do not confuse UUPC with UUCP) comes with a simple program that permits you to send and receive Internet e-mail, and has the capability to receive USENET news. However, it does not have a newsreader: a program that permits you to read the USENET news you receive. In this case, you need newsreader software, such as SNEWS, in addition to your UUPC software.

You will also find programs throughout the Internet that can enhance your basic UUCP software. For example, the e-mail programs found within UUPC and Waffle work within DOS. Using HellDiver, written by Rhys Weatherley, and EZMail, from Cinetic Systems, you can choose to read, answer, and create e-mail within a friendly Windows program, while still using UUPC or Waffle as your main UUCP program. In addition, HellDiver can be used to read your USENET news within Microsoft Windows.

A sample configuration might be UUPC to manage the transfer of e-mail and USENET news to and from your Internet service provider, EZMail to read and send e-mail, and SNEWS to read USENET news.

It's obvious that mixing and matching seems to be the name of the game!

LINKING LAN E-MAIL SYSTEMS VIA UUCP

A number of e-mail "gateways" are available, which permit a link from an internal LAN based e-mail system to an Internet service provider via UUCP. These gateways, which are specialized computer programs, extend the reach of an organizational e-mail system, and are an alternative to using a commercial e-mail system as described above.

These alternatives usually do not include provision for USENET news.

One popular alternative in the Internet world is a freeware package called Pegasus, which provides e-mail to users on a Novell network. Since Pegasus will work with the Waffle program mentioned above, it can be used in a scenario in which Waffle performs the basic UUCP mail transfer function and Pegasus is used as the e-mail client.

Another product, Lotus cc:Mail UUCPLINK, provides a link between cc:Mail and an Internet service provider via UUCP. The product provides a straightforward connection between cc:Mail and Internet e-mail. A number of UUCP style connectivity products like UUCPLINK are starting to emerge for popular LAN based e-mail systems.

When examining a UUCP solution like this, keep in mind that the product might provide you with e-mail only; i.e., UUCPLINK does not provide for USENET news. The current implementation of UUCPLINK, version 2.0, has a number of weaknesses that make it difficult to use with certain Internet service providers. However, these products seem to be evolving, so improvements could be on the way.

Technical complexity is a watchword when considering this type of alternative.

Finally, locations with a UNIX host will have a wealth of public domain and shareware UUCP alternatives at their disposal, which provide e-mail and USENET news client software and UUCP transport. In this scenario, users of a DOS or Macintosh local area network access the UNIX host as a terminal, and run the e-mail and USENET news clients as terminal users.

ACCESS VIA A SHELL ACCOUNT

"Shell account" access is available through either a Canadian Internet provider, or through one of the major commercial on-line services based in the U.S.

Since a great number of Internet service providers offer shell access, and since it can be the easiest method from a technical perspective to access the Internet, shell access is recommended for most individuals who are curious about the Internet and want to explore what it offers.

You access a shell account like you would any other on-line service. Using communications software, you dial your Internet service provider, and sign in to an account with your user ID and password. You are then presented with a menu from which to choose Internet services, or are presented directly with a prompt from which you can access Internet services.

When using a shell account, keep in mind that you are using terminal emulation which, as discussed in Chapter 4, results in a number of limitations on how you can use the Internet.

Through a Canadian Internet Provider

Many of the Internet service providers in Canada offer shell access. There is also a derivative of shell access, known as TAC, that provides access to some but not all of the Internet services accessible through shell access.

FIGURE 9.4: SHELL ACCESS VIA CANADIAN INTERNET SERVICE PROVIDERS

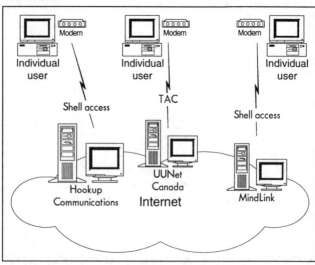

For example, HookUp Communications, which provides access in Toronto, Kitchener and other major centres, as well as 1-800 access, allows you to dial in to its system and directly access Internet services via a shell account.

```
                                      E:97% VT100 ‡   00:00:54  9:49a
nic
Welcome to HookUp Communications.


nic!login: jcarroll
Password:
Last   successful login for jcarroll: Wed Jan 12 16:30:25 EST 1994 on ttyA04
Last unsuccessful login for jcarroll: Fri Dec 31 06:27:56 EST 1993 on ttyA03
SCO UNIX System V/386 Release 3.2
Copyright (C) 1976-1990 UNIX System Laboratories, Inc.
Copyright (C) 1980-1989 Microsoft Corporation
Copyright (C) 1983-1993 The Santa Cruz Operation, Inc.
All Rights Reserved
nic


                     HookUp Communication Corporation

Mon Jan 10 03:40
 Please read hookup.announce for important announcements.

TERM = (dialup) vt100
Terminal type is vt100
$
```

When you dial in, you are prompted to enter your login name, password, and terminal type (usually vt-100, if your communications software supports this).

At the $ prompt at the bottom of the screen, you can use Telnet or FTP. In addition, since Gopher and Archie are resident on the HookUp system, using these two applications is faster than using them via Telnet to some other computer on the Internet.

Via a Commercial On-Line Service

Several major commercial on-line services that provide on-line conferences, games, research libraries and other services, also provide full or partial access to the Internet.

FIGURE 9.5: INTERNET VIA COMMERCIAL ON-LINE SERVICES

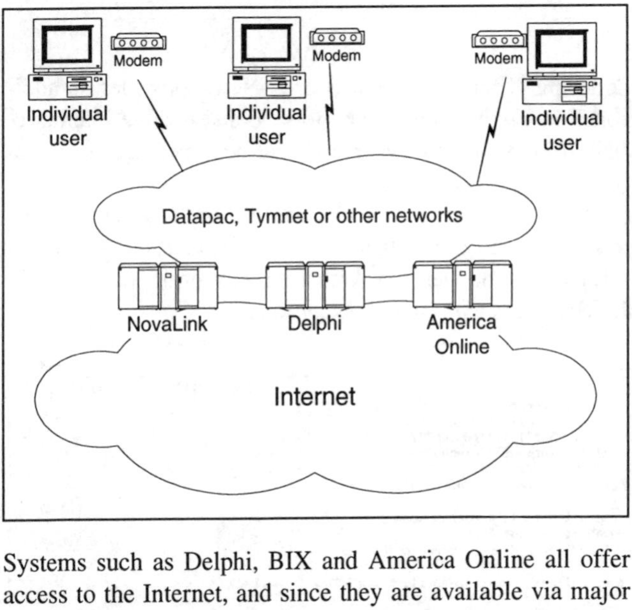

Systems such as Delphi, BIX and America Online all offer access to the Internet, and since they are available via major communication networks such as Datapac, SprintNet and Tymnet, they are often accessible via a local telephone call within Canadian cities and towns.

An example of such a service is NovaLink, based out of Shrewsbury, Massachusetts. NovaLink is accessible via a local call in Toronto, Vancouver, Ottawa, Montreal and Calgary (via the CompuServe data network), and provides access to Internet e-mail, USENET news, FTP and Telnet, in addition to other services.

When you dial into Novalink and access Internet from the main menu, you will see the following:

```
                                        E:94% VT100 *  00:00:00  2:35p
Menu choice (or 'X' for previous): i

9/27/93  NovaLink has just installed a QWK mail program.  Please be
advised that until this message disappears, this feature is in beta,
_use_at_your_own_risk_.  If you have any problems, questions or remarks
please email Bulloney.

Please see the Internet Help Desk topic message #90 in the Internet
Bulletin Board for a note on QWK mail reader compatability.

Email Clufkin for Internet and UNIX help!

Page: INTERNET
14:39:28 EST, 10-JAN-94

     A ... About the Internet Connection
     B ... Internet Bulletin Board
     F ... Feedback to Internet/Unix Admn
     L ... Library of Internet Help Files
     N ... Netmail & UseNet News
     S ... Shell (Telnet, FTP, etc.)
     T ... Internet Teleconference

Menu choice (or 'X' for previous):
```

Choosing N for Netmail & UseNet News, provides an additional menu, that permits you to send and receive Internet e-mail, join and read newsgroups, and post messages to newsgroups.

Another menu choice leads you to shell access, which permits you to use Telnet and FTP. In addition, since NovaLink runs Gopher and Archie directly on its own system, these services are fast and responsive.

```
                                        E:94% VT100 *  00:00:00  2:35p
     L ... Library of Internet Help Files
     N ... Netmail & UseNet News
     S ... Shell (Telnet, FTP, etc.)
     T ... Internet Teleconference

Menu choice (or 'X' for previous): n

Internet Netmail & UseNet News
NovaMail Version 2.00
(C)1993 Inner Circle Technologies, Inc.

Your mailbox: explorer@novalink.com <Rick Broadhead>

J ... Join Newsgroup
P ... Post News
Q ... QWK-Mail Transfer
R ... Read private NetMail
S ... Scan Newsgroups
U ... Unjoin Newsgroup
W ... Write private NetMail
Z ... Special features
X ... Exit

Option:
```

Access via systems like NovaLink, Delphi or America Online is often an easy way to access Internet services, and works well for those who don't have inexpensive access through a local Internet service provider. In addition, the range of other on-line services available, such as forums, games, and on-line research libraries makes them an attractive alternative for your communication needs.

However, since you are using services based in the U.S., you do end up paying a bit of a premium to use the Internet in this way. With the growing number of Canadian Internet providers providing 1-800 access, there is even less incentive to use a U.S. based service.

DIRECT CONNECTIONS TO THE INTERNET

Direct connections to the Internet are supported by the use of the TCP/IP protocol.

Systems directly on the Internet are usually linked via an Ethernet network connection through a device known as a "router," or use PPP (Point-to-Point Protocol) via serial lines. In addition, dialup users accessing the Internet via a modem can make use of either SLIP (Serial Line Interface Protocol) or PPP to provide full TCP/IP capabilities, and in effect be directly connected to the Internet.

Networks directly linked to the Internet have a registered Internet IP address, and are able to link directly to any other computer on the Internet.

Benefits of a Direct Connection

Individuals with a direct connection to the Internet are directly using the TCP/IP protocol stack. The result is that the applications they run interact much more closely with other computers throughout the Internet, without the limitations imposed by terminal emulation.

The result is that these individuals can take advantage of the wealth of new software emerging for Internet applications, such as the Mosaic and GUI versions of WAIS and Gopher as seen in Chapter 8.

This results in a substantial lessening in complexity of the Internet, and a significant increase in the usefulness of the network.

Nature of the Connection

When Ethernet or PPP is in use for a permanent, full time connection to an Internet service provider, computers are considered to be "hardwired" to the network. Use of SLIP/PPP via a modem is considered to be a casual Internet connection.[2]

HARDWIRED CONNECTION

A hardwired connection to the Internet is usually through a dedicated communications line of speeds from 19,200bps, 56Kbps, up to T1 and T3 speeds, using Ethernet or PPP.

Let us consider a portion of ONet, the research and academic Internet network in Ontario.

Figure 9.6, which presents but a small part of ONet, indicates that networks at the University of Western Ontario, Sheridan College, the National Research Council and the University of Waterloo are directly connected to the Internet, using a variety of permanent communication lines (T1 lines, and 56K/128K). In addition, a dedicated link to NSFNET via CA*net exists.

FIGURE 9.6: PART OF ONET

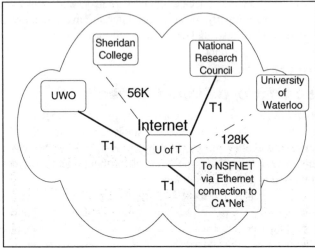

Computers at these locations are considered to be permanently attached to the Internet. Individuals on networks at these locations are considered to be directly connected to the Internet.

Establishing a hardwired connection to the Internet is not necessarily a trivial undertaking. For example, within the DOS environment, each PC on the network must load software which provides the PC with the ability to "talk TCP/IP" (referred to as the TCP/IP protocol stack); the network must be linked into the Internet service provider, usually via a device known as a router or network bridge; dedicated lines must be brought into the organization to support the connection; and many other details must be pursued. The scope of establishing TCP/IP connectivity directly to the Internet is far beyond the capabilities of this book. Many excellent sources and reference guides exist.

A number of Internet service providers take on an active role in assisting an organization to establish a direct, hard-wired or permanent connection to the Internet.

SLIP/PPP FOR CASUAL MODEM CONNECTION

As discussed, SLIP and PPP are an increasingly attractive and inexpensive option used to provide full TCP/IP connectivity via a dialup modem as an alternative to a shell account.

Dialup modem connections via SLIP/PPP usually involves speeds of 14,400 baud (14.4kb) or 19.2kb.

There are a number of implementations of SLIP and PPP available for most operating system platforms. If you plan to implement such a package, be prepared for a bit of a technical journey, as you will be required to gain a bit more familiarity with TCP/IP issues.

BUNDLED SOFTWARE

Some vendors are providing "bundled" software to casual dialup users, to make it easier to use the Internet using SLIP/PPP.

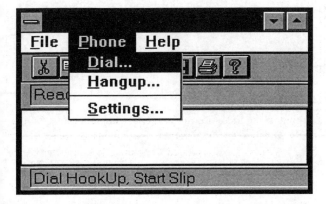

HookUp Communications, for example, provides users with "HookUp Dialer for Windows," a program which will provide a simple SLIP connection to their service. Establishing the SLIP connection is as simple as choosing a menu item.

HookUp also provides access to several other Internet tools, making them available from within Microsoft Windows.

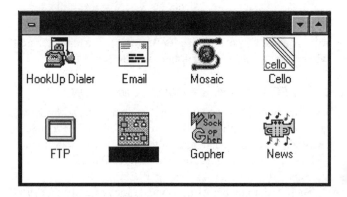

Using these tools provides you access to some of the more sophisticated Internet software packages. One of the most popular is Eudora, seen here in its PC version.

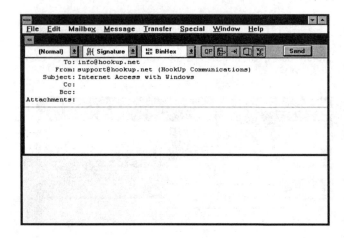

Direct Connections to the Internet and E-mail

Many organizations with a direct connection to the Internet do so via a UNIX system. In those cases, SMTP is usually involved as the primary e-mail server software that communicates with the rest of the Internet. SMTP stands for Simple Mail Transport Protocol, and is the e-mail system at the heart of many UNIX operating systems.

These companies use clients on UNIX workstations with SMTP as the e-mail server. If other e-mail systems are used in the organization on non-UNIX systems, it becomes necessary to put in place a gateway to SMTP, to permit these users to reach the rest of the Internet.

This is not a trivial undertaking.

Organizations which desire to link systems such as MSMail or cc:Mail to SMTP, must appreciate the complexity of such an undertaking. SMTP is recognized throughout the Internet world as one of the most demanding software programs ever developed.

Accordingly, should you wish to establish this type of e-mail connectivity, be sure that you obtain adequate technical advice or resources.

SUMMARY

Each method discussed in this chapter differs in complexity, cost, functionality, and ease of use. What is appropriate for you depends on your own particular circumstances.

If you merely want the ability to send and receive Internet e-mail messages, examine the alternatives to establish e-mail only access, either as an individual or by linking the e-mail system of your organization to the network.

If you are interested in exploring the Internet, a dialup shell account is one method of establishing access quickly and easily. Yet, recognize that there will be limitations on how you can navigate the Internet as a result of your use of terminal emulation.

Using SLIP/PPP via a dialup connection is increasingly attractive, particularly as organizations begin to bundle such software into nice, simple solutions.

Finally, if you discover that the Internet is right for you, establishing a permanent or hardwired connection for your organization could be the next step.

As Ed Hew, of Xenitec Consulting, notes about Internet connectivity, "just like with RAM and with disk space, you never have enough. You always discover that you need more connectivity to accommodate what you didn't know you could do yesterday."

Keep in mind as you explore your options, that Canada is witnessing the birth of an active and thriving market of Internet service providers, detailed in Appendix A in the *Directory of Canadian Internet Service Providers*, each of which have a number of attractive service options.

You will find that many of the organizations listed in this book are enthusiastic and willing to help you solve your Internet connectivity challenge.

---

1 . It is also possible to link an internal e-mail system to the Internet using smtp. Since this is the method used by companies which have a direct connection to the Internet, we do not review that method until later in this chapter.

2 . A SLIP/PPP connection might be temporary, used only during a particular dialup session, or it might be in place on a permanent basis, giving the appearance of direct, permanent connectivity to the Internet. However, for purposes of this discussion, we are trying to differentiate between those who have a full time connection to the Internet from their local area network, and those who casually access a direct connection to the Internet as a dialup user.

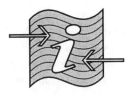

CHAPTER 10

PUTTING THE INTER- NET INTO PERSPEC- TIVE

The Internet has been described by some people as a development in human communication that ranks in importance with the development of the printing press, the telephone or television.

Certainly, the Internet is an important system. As we have seen throughout this book, it is providing new and innovative ways for individuals and organizations to communicate.

There is no doubt that it has become a force in global politics and is beginning to have a profound effect on world issues.

During the Russian revolution in 1990, Internet connected networks were used as a means of rapidly distributing information coming from President Boris Yeltsin's office in the Russian White House. In 1989, Chinese students used the Internet to distribute information globally during the Tianneman Square crisis. It has emerged as one of the major communication systems in Eastern Europe. Vice-President Al Gore is a major supporter of it. Scientists active in planetary exploration now acknowledge that the Internet is a faster vehicle for the distribution of knowledge and updates in their field than any other medium. The map of the Human Genome, when finalized by the French in late December 1993, was first made available on the Internet.

To be part of the Internet is to participate in a unique development in human history.

Yet, we need to keep the Internet in perspective.

Like any emerging technology, the Internet comes straight at you, warts and all.

WHAT'S WRONG WITH THE INTERNET?

There are two truisms about the Internet:

- Understanding the Internet is like trying to comprehend Rubik's Cube.

- Navigating the Internet is like trying to navigate the dark side of the moon without a a map or flashlight.

Is It Too Difficult to Use?

In an article titled "Lost in Cyberspace" in the Saturday, December 18 issue of the *Vancouver Sun*, writer Robert Neville stated that

```
"The Internet is a hostile world for the
novice — To put it bluntly, on the Internet
only the very tenacious survive."
```

In more ways than one, Robert Neville is correct.

The Internet is a massive, complex system. It is difficult to understand, and many times, even more difficult to use. It can be particularly trying for the new user. If you can't use some of the new software that is emerging to browse the Internet because you aren't directly connected to the network, it is frustrating. If you are Macintosh or Windows enthusiast, it can be infuriating.

To use the Internet is to be willing to be challenged.

As Robert Neville indicates in his article:

```
"What happens is that every single intui-
tion they have developed about how computer
systems operate is promptly vio-
lated.....Like my friend and me, they find
themselves logged on to distant computers,
computers wholly different from any they
have encountered, computers that moreover
seem devoted to the bizarre and awkward."
```

It's Difficult to Find Information

The Internet is an access method to knowledge and information scattered around the globe.

The information that you need might be found in a USENET newsgroup, in a mailing list, FTP site, gopher server, WAIS server or in a Telnet-accessible database.

If you have mastered the art of finding a needle in a haystack, you will still find the Internet to be a challenge. A master directory to Internet resources doesn't exist: that is why there are books that detail such information. That is why tools that let you "surf" the network are gaining in popularity.

Discovering the information that you need isn't a simple, straightforward undertaking when it comes to the Internet.

There Is Too Much Information

In some ways, there is too much information on the Internet. As more people are attracted to the Internet, the volume of information will continue to explode.

In an article titled "How the Net Caught Science," published in the June 16, 1993 issue of *The Globe and Mail,* author William Broad addressed the issue of too much information.

```
"Dealing with the Internet is like dealing
with a fire hose," said Susan Kubany,
president of Omnet Inc."Much of the beauty
and wonder of Internet and its resources,
if you look on the horizon, could become a
horrific problem. Systems and people will
shut down. I know people who have stopped
using Internet because they get 500 mes-
sages a day."
```

As the number of Internet users increases, many people are concerned that the quality of available information will see a corresponding decrease. In the same article, William Broad noted:

```
"So many people are now putting so much ma-
terial on the networks that data overload
and psychological burnout have become hot
topics."
```

Quite simply, at some point you will sit back and ask yourself how you will ever possibly deal with all the information that you discover on the Internet.

The problem of too much information, much of it irrelevant, is particularly acute in USENET and within some electronic mailing lists.

Internet Is Subject to Abuse

The key thing about the Internet is that in many areas, particularly USENET and mailing lists, anyone can post a message.

This often leads to abuse, and messages and information that you, and probably 99% of the other people on the network, do not want to read.

Out of the blue, a disgruntled person will appear in a USENET conference and begin posting streams of garbage, quickly turning what was once a pleasant discussion area into a place you would rather not be. Other times, chain letters appear, people hawk the latest pyramid sales scheme, or the hottest networked marketing scam is posted throughout the network. People intent on righting some perceived historical wrong suddenly appear in a conference, dumping waves of information dredged up from some obscure book or magazine.

It is inevitable in human communication that some people try to take advantage of a communications medium. The Internet, through its unique on-line culture, often manages to squelch such activities, for a time. But inevitably, they come back again, and again, and again.

It Suffers From Too Much Hype

In the final days leading up to the conclusion of writing this book, the level of Internet hype within the media seemed to reach a feverish pitch.

The Internet was featured in *MacLean's* magazine, *Canadian Business Magazine*, *The Toronto Star* and other newspapers. Interviews with Internet personalities began to appear on mainstream radio shows. The NBC television network featured the network for a period of three nights in its evening newscasts.

Listening to the hype, it would appear that the Internet is a magical solution that will instantaneously help you to easily focus in on the critical information that you need to find.

There is no doubt that the Internet is a powerful and useful tool. Yet, the Internet is not the solution to all of your information needs.

Yes, there is a lot of information available on the Internet, but there is also a lot of information that is not available. There is some excellent information on the Internet, but there is also a lot of useless information.

Do not look to the Internet as a magical solution. Instead, view it as a powerful and far-reaching global information tool to put in your toolbox. But remember that you have a lot of other tools at your disposal.

Its Culture Is Changing

The Internet has been built as the result of a cooperative effort that really has no equal in human history. There is a definite spirit on-line, and a culture that thrives upon grassroots participation.

Yet, as the Internet begins to attract more interest, more commercial participation, and more users, its culture will undoubtedly begin to change. The Internet tomorrow will probably be different from the Internet of today.

To some, this is a good thing, and to others, this is a very negative evolution. Regardless of what the change means, the Internet will begin to change.

The result? Who knows. But one thing is sure: the Internet today will probably be different from the Internet of tomorrow.

Its Competitive Advantage Might Be Fleeting?

Some people will tell you that the Internet is a tool that will give your organization significant competitive advantage.

To be realistic about it, the Internet does offer *some* competitive advantage to organizations and individuals. Right now, the advantage can be significant for organizations that learn to effectively knowledge network with the Internet.

Yet, the ironic thing about competitive advantage is that once everyone seizes it, it stops being an advantage.

As more and more organizations sign onto the Internet, we must begin wonder whether some of the competitive advantage that it currently provides, will begin to disappear.

WILL THE INTERNET BE EASIER TO USE?

In his "Lost in Cyberspace" article, Robert Neville concludes that the Internet needs to be much easier to use.

"Anyone who can use a straightforward piece of microcomputer software should be able to access information on the Internet. If they cannot, it is too hard. And if it is too hard, we should all be asking loudly for it to be made easier. Information is for everybody."

The Internet is evolving on a regular basis. Applications like Gopher make it easier to "surf the 'Net." Newer applications such as Mosaic provide a GUI-front end to the network, making it even easier to use.

We will continue to see dramatic leaps forward in usability of the network.

In Canada, leading edge organizations such as HookUp Communications and the Nova Scotia Technology Network are working with software in the Windows, Macintosh and other environments, to provide simple dial-up-and-click access to the Internet, and to make it easy to use many of the emerging Internet tools. As the Internet gains more attention, we will see similar initiatives from many other service providers.

In many ways, the Internet is in a period of transition, changing from an informal network to a network that is being packaged for particular types of users. Given the growing corporate interest in the Internet, it won't be long before you can buy access to the Internet as easily as you buy computer software: in a box in a store.

BE A PIONEER

As you approach the Internet, treat it with some awe, apprehension., respect, but approach it. It's too valuable a resource to ignore.

Yet, as you begin to work with the Internet, recognize it for what it is: a new territory.

Treat the Internet as though you are a pioneer, because if you begin using it now, you are.

Today, the Internet is a vast unexplored territory. There are only crude maps and few signposts, and those that do exist are quickly replaced by others. If you manage to carve out a place for yourself in this new and strange land, you must be prepared for some frustration along the way.

Understand that you are going to have to put in some effort to access the Internet, to explore it, and to learn how to use it to your benefit.

TELL US ABOUT IT

When you finish your explorations of the Internet, send us (the authors) an e-mail message at **handbook@ uunet.ca.** Since that address is an electronic mailing list, your message will reach both of the authors.

We'll be working away on the 1995 edition of the *Canadian Internet Handbook*.

Perhaps you have a good story, useful advice, or tips or strategies to tell us about. We'd like to pass them on so that others might learn and benefit from your experience. The Internet, like all communities, is dependent upon the cooperation and participation of all its members — and we can all work together to improve the way the Internet works.

A P P E N D I X A
D I R E C T O R I E S

··································

THE DIRECTORY OF CANADIAN INTERNET SERVICE PROVIDERS

This is a comprehensive directory of over 45 organizations that provide Internet services in Canada In this directory, we cover the entire spectrum of Internet service providers, from those offering only dial-up mail services, to those offering high-speed dedicated connections. Whether you are looking for a connection for yourself or a connection for your business, this directory will help you locate a suitable Internet Service Provider in your local calling area.

Internet Service Providers that are not listed in this directory, and wish to be added, are invited to contact the authors at **handbook@uunet.ca** so that they can be included in the next edition of this book.

The directory is organized into three sections. The first section lists those Internet Service Providers with operations in a single province. The second section is an alphabetical list of Internet Service Providers that operate in more than one province. The third and last section is a list of American Internet providers that have local access numbers in Canada.

Each entry in this directory is structured like this:

Name of the organization or service
Town or city where the organization is located.

The organization's Internet domain.

Mailing address and telephone number of the Internet Service Provider. If the organization has a fax number and/or an Internet address for general queries, this information will be listed here.

Brief description of the organization or service. Most of the descriptions were provided by the Internet Service Providers. They should not be taken as an endorsement of the organization or service by the authors.

Service Area:	Indicates locations where the customers can access the service with a local telephone call.
1-800 Service:	Indicates whether customers can access the service using a 1-800 data number.
PDN Service:	Indicates whether customers can access the service using a public data network. Public data networks allow you to access computers in another city with a local telephone call. For example, CompuServe, a commercial online service located in Ohio, has local telephone numbers in several Canadian cities. When you call these numbers, your call is routed through a public data network to CompuServe's computers in Ohio. Public data networks can be cheaper than making a long distance call, but they can still be expensive. Public data networks in Canada include BT TYMNET and Datapac.
Connection Via:	Indicates who the Internet Service Provider buys their Internet connection from.
Leased Line Service:	Indicates whether the Internet Service Provider offers leased line service. Leased lines are used when an organization requires a dedicated (i.e. 24 hour, 7 day-a-week) connection to the Internet.
Dedicated Dial-Up Service:	Indicates whether the Internet Service Provider offers "dedicated dial-up" service. This is an arrangement where the customer has access to a telephone and modem for his/her exclusive use. A dedicated dial-up connection can be used on a casual dialup basis, or the connection can be held open 24 hours a day.
Dedicated Line Speeds Supported:	Indicates the dedicated line speeds that the Internet Service Provider supports.
SLIP/PPP Service:	Indicates whether the Internet Service Provider offers SLIP and/or PPP service.
UUCP Service:	Indicates whether the Internet Service Provider offers UUCP service. We tell you

if the Internet Service Provider provides only mail feeds, only USENET feeds, or both mail and USENET feeds. We also indicate how USENET subscriptions are handled. On some systems, you can modify your own newsgroup subscriptions. On other systems, an administrator has to make the changes for you.

Interactive Accounts:	Indicates whether the Internet Service Provider offers dial-up (terminal emulation) accounts on a host that is either directly or indirectly connected to the Internet. If interactive accounts are available, we list which Internet services are supported, and provide additional information about the accounts. Some Internet Service Providers give you a choice between a **menu-driven interface** (where you select Internet services off a menu) and **shell access** (where you have access to a UNIX command prompt). On some systems, off-line mail readers are supported, allowing you to read your Internet mail off-line on your own computer.
Maximum Casual Dial-Up Speed:	Indicates the maximum modem speed that the Internet Service Provider supports for casual dial-up connections.
USENET News:	Indicates whether the Internet Service Provider offers USENET News. If the Internet Service Provider offers Clarinet news, it will be noted.
Local File Archives:	Indicates whether the Internet Service Provider maintains local file archives.
Domain Registration Service:	Indicates whether the Internet Service Provider offers "full" or "limited" domain registration service. "Full service" means that the Internet Service Provider will help customers with the registration paperwork *and* submit the registration form on the customer's behalf. "Limited service" means that the Internet Service Provider will only help customers with the registration paperwork (the customer has to submit his/her own registration). There may be an extra fee for domain registration service. Check with the Internet Service Provider to see if they charge for this service.
Domain Park Service:	Indicates whether the Internet Service Provider operates a **Domain Park**. This means that the Internet Service Provider will allow you to become a subdomain under their domain. For example, let's suppose you want to call your computer **zzzz**. If your Internet Service Provider's

	domain is **north.net**, your system could become **zzzz.north.net**. This is an alternative to registering your own domain.
Consulting Services:	Indicates whether the Internet Service Provider offers consulting services. Areas of specialization are listed.
DNS Service:	Indicates whether the Internet Service Provider supplies primary and/or secondary nameservers for a customer's domain. In order to register an Internet domain, you must have two independent domain nameservers. Domain nameservers are machines on the Internet that can answer queries from other domain nameservers about your domain.
Commercial Traffic:	Indicates whether the Internet Service Provider allows message traffic that is not in support of research or education. Many Internet Service Providers have **Acceptable Use Policies** (AUPs) which prohibit certain types of message traffic on their system. Check with each Internet Service Provider for specific guidelines.

HOW TO SIGN UP

If the Internet Service Provider allows "on-line" registration (i.e. you can sign up using your computer and your modem), instructions will be provided under this heading. This includes registration over the Internet, if such capability exists. If the Internet Service provider does not permit on-line registration, you will be told to contact the organization for registration instructions. If you already have Internet access, the Internet Service Provider may be able to send you a registration form by electronic mail.

Rates

Prices for a selection of the Internet Provider's services will be listed under this heading. Rates may have certain conditions attached. Furthermore, rates are subject to change without notice. The authors assume no responsibility for errors or omissions. Contact the Internet Service Provider directly for complete pricing information.

FOR MORE INFORMATION

If the Internet Provider distributes service and/or pricing information by FTP, Gopher, or Telnet, it will be noted under this heading.

PART 1:
DOMESTIC PROVIDERS OPERATING IN A SINGLE PROVINCE

BRITISH COLUMBIA

The Almanac Users Group
Ladysmith, British Columbia
almanac.bc.ca

RR#2 - 233 Dogwood Drive
Ladysmith, British Columbia
VOR 2EO
Voice: (604) 245-3214
Internet: kmcvay@oneb.almanac.bc.ca (Ken McVay)

*The Almanac Users Group provides low-cost UUCP/News services to the
central Vancouver Island area.*

Service Area:	Central Vancouver Island, including Ladysmith, Nanaimo, Lantzville, Chemainus.
1-800 Service:	No.
PDN Service:	No.
Connection Via:	Malaspina College.
Leased Line Service:	No.
Dedicated Dial-Up Service:	No.
Dedicated Line Speeds Supported:	N/A.
SLIP/PPP Service:	No.
UUCP Service:	Yes. Mail and news feeds. Waffle available at no charge to non-commercial users. $100 fee if installation required. Newsgroup changes must go through a service person.
Interactive Accounts:	Yes. Gateway connection to the Internet. Internet mail. Permanent disk space. Shell access.
Maximum Casual Dial-Up Speed:	14,400 bps.
USENET News:	Yes. 2400+ newsgroups.
Local File Archives:	Yes. Text documents.
Domain Registration Service:	No.
Domain Park Service:	Yes.

Consulting Services:	No.
DNS Service:	No.
Commercial Traffic:	Yes.

HOW TO SIGN UP

Call or send electronic mail for information.

Rates
UUCP/USENET Accounts:
$50 one-time setup fee. $10 monthly domain access/maintenance fee.
Shell Accounts:
$50 one-time setup fee. $10 monthly domain access/maintenance fee.

BCnet
Vancouver, British Columbia
BC.net

BCnet Headquarters
515 West Hastings Street
Vancouver, British Columbia
V6B 5K3
Voice: (604) 291-5209
Fax: (604) 291-5022
Internet: Mike@BC.net (Mike Patterson)

BCnet is a wide-area data communications network (WAN) that interconnects local-area networks (LANs) in British Columbia. It interconnects the organization-wide LANs of all the provinces, universities, the majority of its community colleges, most of its major research labratories, and many schools, government offices, non-profit organizations, research-oriented organizations, and commercial companies. In addition, BCnet provides these organizations with access to the world-wide Internet.

Service Area:	Vancouver, Victoria, Nanaimo, Courtenay, Kelowna, Kamloops, Trail.
1-800 Service:	No.
PDN Service:	No.
Connection Via:	CA*net.
Leased Line Service:	Yes.
Dedicated Dial-Up Service:	Yes.
Dedicated Line Speeds Supported:	2400 bps-10 Mbps.
SLIP/PPP Service:	Yes. SLIP and PPP. Dedicated service only.
UUCP Service:	No.
Interactive Accounts:	No.
Maximum Casual Dial-Up Speed:	No casual dial-up services.
USENET News:	No. Planned.

Local File Archives:	Yes. BCnet information.
Domain Registration Service:	Yes. Full service.
Domain Park Service:	No.
Consulting Services:	Yes.
DNS Service:	Yes. Primary and secondary nameservers.
Commercial Traffic:	Yes.

HOW TO SIGN UP

Call or send electronic mail for information.

Rates
One-time connection fee of $500.
Monthly fees ranging from $137.50 (link of less than 9.6Kbps) to $4,125 (link of 1,344Kbps).
Cost of routers and modems, data line, and maintenance/upgrates, must be provided for by the connecting organization.

Cyberstore Systems Inc.
New Westminster, British Columbia
cyberstore.ca

#320 - 720 Sixth Street
New Westminster, British Columbia
V3L 3C5
Voice: (604) 526-3373
Fax: (604) 526-0607
Internet: info@cyberstore.ca

Cyberstore is an Internet public access provider, featuring a variety of value-added services, including: a UNIX-based BBS with a Graphical User Interface, dedicated and dial-up SLIP or PPP, a dial-up SMTP gateway for a variety of DOS/Novell based e-mail packages, and consultant services and software for organizations seeking to deliver products and services using the Internet.

Service Area:	Greater Vancouver. Expansion is planned to Victoria, Seattle, Edmonton, Calgary, Toronto, and Ottawa.
1-800 Service:	No.
PDN Service:	No.
Connection Via:	BCnet and ANS.
Leased Line Service:	Yes.
Dedicated Dial-Up Service:	Yes.
Dedicated Line Speeds Supported:	14.4-56 Kbps.
SLIP/PPP Service:	Yes. SLIP and PPP.
UUCP Service:	Yes. Mail and news feeds. Newsgroup changes must go through a service person.

Interactive Accounts:	Yes. Direct connection to the Internet. 1 MB permanent storage/user. Telnet, FTP, Gopher, WAIS, WWW, IRC. Shell access not currently available, but planned in 1994.
Maximum Casual Dial-Up Speed:	14,400 bps.
USENET News:	Yes. 3,600+ newsgroups, including Clarinet News.
Local File Archives:	Yes. Shareware.
Domain Registration Service:	Yes. Limited service.
Domain Park Service:	No.
Consulting Services:	Yes. Information services delivery. On-line order-entry systems.
DNS Service:	Yes. Primary and secondary nameservers.
Commercial Traffic:	Yes.

HOW TO SIGN UP
Internet:
*Telnet to cyberstore.ca, login as **guest**. No password required.*
Modem:
*(604) 526-3676, V.32bis, login as **guest**. No password required.*

Rates
Standard Dial-Up Account:
$20 setup fee plus $89/year. 75 minutes/day. Internet mail, USENET, IRC.
Premier Dial-Up Account:
$20 setup fee plus $129/year. 75 minutes/day. Internet mail, USENET, IRC, Telnet, FTP, Gopher.
Premier Plus Dial-Up Account:
$20 setup fee plus $249/year. 150 minutes/day. Internet mail, USENET, IRC, Telnet, FTP, Gopher.
Dial-Up SLIP/PPP:
(i) 14.4 Kbps
$75.00 setup fee. $1.75/hour. Minimum $60.00/month, maximum $450.00/ month.
(ii) 56 Kbps
$155.00 setup fee. $3.25/hour. Minimum $180.00/month, maximum $900.00/month.
Dedicated SLIP/PPP:
(i) 14.4 Kbps
$75.00 setup fee. $300/month. No hourly charge.
(ii) 56 Kbps
$155.00 setup fee. $650/month. No hourly charge.

For More Information
FTP:	Telnet:	Gopher:
cyberstore.ca	*cyberstore.ca* *login: **guest***	*cyberstore.ca*

DataFlux Systems Limited
Victoria, British Columbia

dataflux.bc.ca

1281 Lonsdale Place
Victoria, British Columbia
V8P 5L3
Voice: (604) 744-4553
Fax: (604) 480-0899
Internet: info@dataflux.bc.ca

*DataFlux Systems provides dial-up and dedicated access to the Internet
as well as consulting and network services.*

Service Area:	Greater Victoria area. Plans to expand to the rest of the Island, Vancouver, and interior British Columbia.
1-800 Service:	No.
PDN Service:	No.
Connection Via:	BCnet.
Leased Line Service:	Yes.
Dedicated Dial-Up Service:	Yes.
Dedicated Line Speeds Supported:	14,400 bps.
SLIP/PPP Service:	Yes. SLIP and PPP.
UUCP Service:	Yes. Mail and news services. Newsgroup changes must go through a service person.
Interactive Accounts:	Yes. Direct connection to the Internet. 2.5MB permanent storage/individual user. 5MB permanent storage/commercial account. Extra storage is free upon approval. Telnet, FTP, Gopher, WAIS, WWW, IRC, Hytelnet. Shell access.
Maximum Casual Dial-Up Speed:	14,400 bps.
USENET News:	Yes. Approximately 1500 newsgroups.
Local File Archives:	Yes. SUN system patches. Macintosh archive.
Domain Registration Service:	Yes. Full service.
Domain Park Service:	Yes.
Consulting Services:	Yes. Network design, installation, setup, and administration. Communications consulting.
DNS Service:	Yes. Primary and secondary nameservers.
Commercial Traffic:	Yes.

HOW TO SIGN UP
Call or send electronic mail for information.

Rates
Personal Account:
$19.95/month includes 3 hours of connect time during non-peak hours. Additional hours are $3/hour during peak hours and $6/hour during peak hours.
Commercial Account:
$39.95/month includes 3 hours of connect time. Additional hours are $4/hour.

Helix Internet
Vancouver, British Columbia
helix.net

Helix Exploration Ltd.
#902-900 West Hastings Street
Vancouver, British Columbia
V6C 1E6
Voice: (604) 689-8544
Fax: (604) 732-0131
Internet: info@helix.net

Helix is a BBS that provides users with full Internet access. Users log into a UNIX system with all the popular Internet utilities and services available.

Service Area:	Vancouver region.
1-800 Service:	No.
PDN Service:	No.
Connection Via:	BCnet.
Leased Line Service:	No.
Dedicated Dial-Up Service:	No.
Dedicated Line Speeds Supported	N/A.
SLIP/PPP Service:	Yes. SLIP only.
UUCP Service:	No.
Interactive Accounts:	Yes. Direct connection to the Internet. 2-3 MB permanent storage/user. Telnet, FTP, Gopher, IRC. Menu-driven system with shell access available.
Maximum Casual Dial-Up Speed:	14,400 bps.
USENET News:	Yes. Approximately 500 newsgroups.
Local File Archives:	Yes. Shareware for Macintosh and IBM.
Domain Registration Service:	No.
Domain Park Service:	No.
Consulting Services:	Yes. Macintosh. Internet connectivity.
DNS Service:	No.
Commercial Traffic:	No.

HOW TO SIGN UP
Modem:
*(604) 689-8577, V.32bis, login as **new**, password is **new**.*

Rates
$12/month and up.

InterLink On-Line Services Inc.

Victoria, British Columbia
interlink.bc.ca

4252 Commerce Circle
Victoria, British Columbia
V8Z 4M2
Voice: (604) 385-4302
Fax: (604) 727-6418
Internet: queries@interlink.bc.ca

InterLink provides turn-key value-added Internet services, via low-cost leased lines, for organizations that do not have, or wish to operate, their own server.

Service Area:	Victoria. Expansion is planned to other cities with point-of-presence provided by BCnet or another mid-level or regional network.
1-800 Service:	No.
PDN Service:	No.
Connection Via:	BCnet.
Leased Line Service:	Yes.
Dedicated Dial-Up Service:	Yes.
Dedicated Line Speeds Supported:	300-14,400 bps over a voice grade line. Higher speeds available on request.
SLIP/PPP Service:	Yes. SLIP and PPP. Dedicated service only.
UUCP Service:	No.
Interactive Accounts:	No.
Maximum Casual Dial-Up Speed:	N/A.
USENET News:	Yes. Full feed.
Local File Archives:	No.
Domain Registration Service:	Yes. Full service.
Domain Park Service:	Yes.
Consulting Services:	Yes. Turn-key solutions to inter-networking.
DNS Service:	Yes. Primary and secondary nameservers.
Commercial Traffic:	Yes.

HOW TO SIGN UP

Call or send electronic mail for information.

Rates

Call or send electronic mail for information.

ISLAND NET

Victoria, British Columbia
amtsgi.bc.ca

AMT Solutions Group Inc.
P.O. Box 6201, Depot 1
Victoria, British Columbia
V8P 5L5
Voice: (604) 721-6030
Internet: mark@amtsgi.bc.ca (Mark Morley)

Island Net's goal is to provide a full spectrum of Internet and other BBS services to the general public at very reasonable prices. The other BBS services we offer include local file areas, CD ROMs, special interest groups, and vendor BBSs. We emphasize a colorful, easy-to-use interface so that members do not have to be Internet or UNIX wizards. The software that drives the system was developed in-house.

Service Area:	Victoria, Western Communities, Sooke, Sidney, Gulf Islands. Possible expansion to Nanaimo and Vancouver.
1-800 Service:	No.
PDN Service:	No.
Connection Via:	BCnet.
Leased Line Service:	No.
Dedicated Dial-Up Service:	Yes. Schools and organizations only.
SLIP/PPP Service:	No.
UUCP Service:	Yes. Mail and news feeds. Software not supplied, but assistance is provided with location of software, installation and configuration. Newsgroup changes must go through a service person.
Interactive Accounts:	Yes. Direct connection to the Internet. Telnet, FTP, WAIS, WWW, IRC, Archie, Talk, custom FTP. Shell access not currently available, but planned in 1994. QWK-compatible readers supported (e.g. SLMR). Freeware/shareware off-line readers available.
Maximum Casual Dial-Up Speed:	14,400 bps.
USENET News:	Yes. Approximately 2500 groups.
Local File Archives:	Yes. Shareware, games, documents, pictures.
Domain Registration Service:	Yes. Full service.

Domain Park Service:	No.
Consulting Services:	Yes. Internet usage. UNIX training and administration. Network design, installation and training. Custom software design and implementation. Mechanical design and Autocad work.
DNS Service:	Yes. Primary and secondary nameservers.
Commercial Traffic:	Yes.

HOW TO SIGN UP
Internet:
*Telnet to island.amtsgi.bc.ca, login as **new**. No password required.*
Modem:
*(604) 477-5163,V.32bis, V.42bis, login as **new**. No password required*

Rates
Billing Method #1: $2.50/hour prepaid. No time limits. No other charges.
Billing Method #2 : $20/month for 1 hour/day.

For More information
Telnet:
island.amtsgi.bc.ca
*login: **guest***

Mind Link! Communications Corporation
Langley, British Columbia
mindlink.bc.ca

105 - 20381 62nd Avenue
Langley, British Columbia
V3A 5E6
Voice: (604) 534-5663
Fax: (604) 534-7473
Internet: info@mindlink.bc.ca

Mind Link's mission is to provide high-quality access to on-line communications, at a price affordable to the general public.

Service Area:	Lower mainland of British Columbia. Aldergrove, Bowen Island, Cloverdale, Fort Langley, Haney, Ladner, Langley, Mission, Newton, New Westminster, North Vancouver, Pitt Meadows, Port Coquitlam, Port Moody, Richmond, Vancouver, West Vancouver, Whalley, White Rock, Whonnock, Vancouver East, West, North, South.
1-800 Service:	No.
PDN Service:	No.
Connection Via:	BCnet.
Leased Line Service:	No.
Dedicated Dial-Up Service:	No.

Dedicated Dial-Up Speeds Supported:	N/A.
SLIP/PPP Service:	Planned for 3rd quarter, 1994.
UUCP Service:	Planned for 3rd quarter, 1994. Both mail and news feeds.
Interactive Accounts:	Yes. Direct connection to the Internet. Telnet, FTP, IRC, Archie. Gopher planned for 1st quarter, 1994. Permanent storage. Menu-driven with shell access available. Custom off-line mail reader. International e-mail-to-fax gateway.
Maximum Casual Dial-Up Speed:	14,400 bps.
USENET News:	Yes. Full feed.
Local File Archives:	Yes. Variety of files for all platforms. Shareware, GIFs, text files.
Domain Registration Service:	No.
Domain Park Service:	Yes.
Consulting Services:	Yes. Full technical support for users.
DNS Service:	Yes. Primary and secondary nameservers.
Commercial Traffic:	Yes.

HOW TO SIGN UP

Internet:
*Telnet to mindlink.bc.ca, login as **guest**. No password required.*

Modem:
*(604) 576-1214, V.32bis, login as **guest**. No password required.*
*(604) 576-1683, HST, login as **guest**. No password required.*
5 hour trial membership is available.

Rates
Basic Membership:
$75/year -or- $48/6 months. 1 hour/day. 40K of free network traffic/day. Internet mail, USENET news.
Internet Membership:
$99/year -or- $66/6 months. 1 hour/day. 100K of free network traffic/day. Internet mail, Telnet, FTP.
Internet Plus Membership:
$159/year -or- $99/6 months. 2 hours/day. 200K of daily free network/traffic. Internet mail, Telnet, FTP, UPI newswire.
UNIX Plus Membership:
$219/year -or- $132/6 months. Same services as Internet Plus Membership, but the user receives an account on a separate UNIX box. No limit on network traffic.
Corporate Membership:
$300/year -or- $174/6 months. 4 hours/day. Same services as an Internet Plus Membership. 300K of daily free network traffic. More than one person can use the account.

For More Information
Telnet:
mindlink.bc.ca
*login: **guest***

Victoria Free-Net
Victoria, British Columbia
freenet.victoria.bc.ca

Victoria Free-Net Association
203-1110 Government Street
Victoria, British Columbia
V8W 1Y2
Voice: (604) 389-6026
Internet: vifa@freenet.victoria.bc.ca

*The Victoria Free-Net is a community-based computer network available
at no cost to residents and visitors of the Greater Victoria region. Our
service goals include: computer-mediated communications among
Victoria Free-Net users; easy access to information posted by
community organizations, individuals, businesses, and government;
community events information; worldwide e-mail; and access to
selected on-line public access resources throughout the world. The
Victoria Free-Net is run by a core of dedicated volunteers belonging to
the Victoria Free-Net Association, a non-for-profit society formed on
June 17, 1992.*

Service Area:	Victoria.
1-800 Service:	No.
PDN Service:	No.
Connection Via:	Camosun College.
Leased Line Service:	No.
Dedicated Dial-Up Service:	No.
Dedicated Line Speeds Supported:	N/A.
SLIP/PPP Service:	No.
UUCP Service:	No.
Interactive Accounts:	Yes. Internet mail, Gopher. Telnet service to other Free-Nets. Permanent disk space. No shell access.
Maximum Casual Dial-Up Speed:	14,400 bps.
USENET News:	Yes.
Local File Archives:	Yes. Community information.
Domain Registration Service:	No.
Domain Park Service:	No.
Consulting Services:	No.
DNS Service:	No.
Commercial Traffic:	No.

HOW TO SIGN UP
Internet:
*Telnet to freenet.victoria.bc.ca, login as **guest**. No password required.*

Modem:
*(604) 595-2300, V.32bis, login as **guest**. No password required.*

Rates
All services provided by the Victoria Free-Net are free to the user.

For More Information
Telnet:	**Gopher:**
freenet.victoria.bc.ca	*freenet.victoria.bc.ca*
login: ***guest***	

Wimsey Information Services
Port Moody, British Columbia
wimsey.com, wimsey.bc.ca

Wimsey Information Services
225B Evergreen Drive
Port Moody, British Columbia
V3H 1S1
Voice: (604) 936-UNIX (8649)
Fax: (604) 937-7718
Internet: admin@wimsey.com

Wimsey Information Services provides dial-up access to a fully configured UNIX host for public access to e-mail and USENET News via a range of access methods including UUCP, SLIP, PPP, Telnet, rlogin, FTP, and interactive sessions. Interactive users have a wide range of of user interfaces including all standard UNIX shells.

Service Area:	Vancouver and the Lower Mainland from Aldergrove to North Vancouver.
1-800 Service:	No.
PDN Service:	No.
Connection Via:	BCnet.
Leased Line Service:	No.
Dedicated Dial-Up Service:	Yes.
Dedicated Line Speeds Supported:	19.2-56 Kbps.
SLIP/PPP Service:	Yes. SLIP and PPP.
UUCP Service:	Yes. Mail and news. UUPC available. Any UUCP package can be installed and customized for a consulting fee. Users can modify their own newsgroup subscriptions once per day.
Interactive Accounts:	Yes. Directly connected to the Internet. 1MB/user permanent storage. Additional storage available for $0.02/MB/day. Telnet, FTP, Gopher, WAIS, WWW, IRC, Archie. Shell access or command menu using SCOshell. E-mail-to-fax gateway for the local calling area.

Maximum Casual Dial-Up Speed:	14,400 bps.
USENET News:	Yes. 3,700+ newsgroups, including Clarinet news .
Local File Archives:	Yes. Public domain software for Macintosh and IBM/PC.
Domain Registration Service:	Yes. Full service.
Domain Park Service:	Yes.
Consulting Services:	Yes. UNIX system administration, specializing in SCO UNIX. UNIX Internet connectivity.
DNS Service:	Yes. Primary and secondary nameservers.
Commercial Traffic:	Yes.

HOW TO SIGN UP
Call or send electronic mail for information.

Rates
Signup Fee (per billing account):
$25 covers up to 4 login ids. Extra login ids are $5 each.
Interactive Dial-Up:
$1.25/hour
Dial-Up SLIP/PPP:
$1.25/hour
Dial-Up UUCP:
$2/hour
Extra login ids over 4:
$5 per id.

For More Information
FTP: **Gopher:**
wimsey.com   *wimsey.com*
directory: /pub/wimsey
file: system.info

ALBERTA

Alberta SuperNet Inc.
Edmonton, Alberta
supernet.ab.ca

#325 Pacific Plaza
10909 Jasper Avenue
Edmonton, Alberta
T5J 3L9
Voice: (403) 441-3663
Fax: (403) 424-0743
Internet: info@tibalt.supernet.ab.ca

Alberta SuperNet is a growing company that is willing to meet the needs of the Alberta public by providing affordable Internet access. We are willing to assist our users in order to provide the highest quality service possible.

Service Area:	Edmonton. Expansion planned to Calgary, Lethbridge, Red Deer, Medicine Hat, and Fort McMurray.
1-800 Service:	No.
PDN Service:	No.
Connection Via:	ARnet.
Leased Line Service:	Yes.
Dedicated Dial-Up Service:	Yes.
Dedicated Line Speeds Supported:	9,600 bps-1.544 Mbps.
SLIP/PPP Service:	Yes. SLIP and PPP.
UUCP Service:	Yes. Mail and news feeds. Newsgroup changes must go through a service person.
Interactive Accounts:	Yes. Direct connection to the Internet. 2.5-10MB of permanent storage/user. Additional storage available for $1.00-$3.00/MB/day. Telnet, FTP, Gopher. Coming soon: WAIS, WWW, IRC, Hytelnet, and Archie. Shell access.
Maximum Casual Dial-Up Speed:	14,400 bps.
USENET News:	Yes. Approximately 3,000 newsgroups. Clarinet news is available.
Local File Archives:	Yes. FAQs. PC and Mac utilities.
Domain Registration Service:	Yes. Full service.
Domain Park Service:	Yes.
Consulting Services:	Yes. Network installation. Network security.
DNS Service:	Yes. Primary and secondary nameservers.
Commercial Traffic:	Call for information.

HOW TO SIGN UP
Call or send electronic mail for information.

Rates
Terminal/Shell Account - Server Plan:
$30 setup fee. $10 month for 7 hours of connect time/month. Additional connect time is $12/hour from 7a.m. to 6p.m. and $6/hour from 6p.m. to 7a.m.
2.5 MB storage/user. Additional storage is $1/MB/day.
Terminal/Shell Account - Gateway Plan
$30 setup fee. $30/month for 15 hours of connect time/month. Additional connect time is $6/hour from 7a.m. to 6p.m. and $3/hour from 6p.m. to 7a.m. 5 MB storage/user. Additional storage is $1/MB/day.
Board Plan - Shared dial-up UUCP
$40 setup fee. $40/month. $0.50/minute for transfer time.

Cooperative Plan - Shared dial-up SLIP/PPP
$40 setup fee. $40/month. $6/hour.
Protocol Plan - Dedicated connection, single IP address
$350 set-up fee. $450/month.
Network Plan - Dedicated connection, up to 10 IP addresses
$750 set-up fee. $550/month for 9600 bps connection, $750/month for
19,200 bps connection.

ARnet
Edmonton, Alberta
arc.ab.ca

Box 8330
Edmonton, Alberta
T6H 5X2
Voice: (403) 450-5179
Fax: (403) 461-2651
Internet: ARnet@arc.ab.ca

ARnet is a non-profit, provincial computer-based communications
network, specifically oriented to meeting the needs of Alberta's research
and education communities in both public and private sectors.

Service Area:	Lethbridge, Calgary, Alberta, Athabasca
1-800 Service:	No.
PDN Service:	No.
Connection Via:	CA*net.
Leased Line Service:	Yes.
Dedicated Dial-Up Service:	Yes.
Dedicated Line Speeds Supported:	9.6-56 Kbps.
SLIP/PPP Service:	Yes. Dedicated service only.
UUCP Service:	No.
Interactive Accounts:	No.
Maximum Casual Dial-Up Speed:	N/A.
USENET News:	Yes. Full feed.
Local File Archives:	No.
Domain Registration Service:	Yes. Full service.
Domain Park Service:	No.
Consulting Services:	No.
DNS Service:	No.
Commercial Traffic:	Yes.

HOW TO SIGN UP
Call or send electronic mail for information.

Rates
Full Membership:
$42,400/year. Some conditions apply.
Associate Membership:
9.6 kbps: $5,000/year.
19.2 kbps: $10,000/year.
56 kbps: $15,000/year.
Some conditions apply.

CCI Networks

Edmonton, Alberta
ccinet.ab.ca

4130 - 95 Street
Edmonton, Alberta
T6E 6H5
Voice: (403) 450-6787
Fax: (403) 450-9143
Internet: info@ccinet.ab.ca

The parent company, Corporate Computers Inc., has been involved in selling, installing, and supporting computer systems and networks for ten years. CCI Networks is a newly-established division within the company with a mandate to provide economical access to the Internet for schools, businesses, and the general public in the Province of Alberta.

Service Area:	Edmonton. Expansion to Calgary is planned for early 1994.
1-800 Service	No.
PDN Service:	Datapac.
Connection Via:	ARnet.
Leased Line Service:	Yes.
Dedicated Dial-Up Service:	Yes.
Dedicated Line Speeds Supported:	9.6-56 Kbps.
SLIP/PPP Service:	Yes. SLIP and PPP.
UUCP Service:	Yes. Mail and News feeds. Newsgroup changes must go through a service person.
Interactive Accounts:	Yes. Permanent storage space. Telnet, FTP, Gopher, WAIS, WWW, IRC, Hytelnet, Archie. Shell access.
Maximum Casual Dial-Up Speed:	14,400 bps.
USENET News:	Yes. Full feed, including Clarinet news.
Local File Archives:	Yes. Software related to Internet access for a number of platforms.
Domain Registration Service:	Yes. Full service.
Domain Park Service:	Yes.

Consulting Services:	Yes. Network connectivity for PCs and Macintosh.
DNS Service:	Yes. Primary and secondary nameservers.
Commercial Traffic:	Yes.

HOW TO SIGN UP

Call or send electronic mail for information.

Rates
Dial-Up Internet account:
$25 setup fee. $20/month plus $5 per hour of connect time.
UUCP:
$25 setup fee. $20/month plus $5 per hour of connect time.
Dial-Up SLIP/PPP:
$40 setup fee. $40/month plus $6 per hour of connect time.
Dedicated SLIP/PPP:
$350 setup fee. $450/month. No time-related charges.
Router to Router Connection:
$750.00 setup plus $550/month (9.6 Kbps) or $750/month (19.2 Kbps).

PUCnet Computer Connections
Edmonton, Alberta
PUCnet.com

10215 - 178 Street
Edmonton, Alberta
T5S 1M3
Voice: (403) 448-1901
Fax: (403) 484-7103
Internet: info@PUCnet.com

PUCnet's mission is to provide the best electronic information access for individuals and small businesses within the system's service area. The future structure of PUCnet is currently under consideration with a view to providing more user direction. Options being considered include a user-owned corporation, and a cooperative.

Service Area:	Edmonton plus extended flat-rate calling area. Possible expansion into other Prairie cities in 1994.
1-800 Service:	No.
PDN Service:	No.
Connection Via:	UUNET Canada.
Leased Line Service:	No. Planned for early 1994.
Dedicated Dial-Up Service:	No. Planned for early 1994.
Dedicated Line Speeds Supported:	56 Kbps planned for 1994.
SLIP/PPP Service:	No. Planned for early 1994.
UUCP Service:	Yes. Mail and News. Newsgroup changes must go through a service person.

Interactive Accounts:	Yes. Direct connection to the Internet. 2MB permanent storage/user. Additional storage available at $0.50/MB/day. Telnet, FTP, IRC, Hytelnet, Archie, IRC, talk, Finger, ntalk. Menu-driven interface or shell access. QWK-compatible readers supported. A locally developed simple batching system is available to enable news and mail batching for users who do not have special software on their own computer.
Maximum Casual Dial-Up Speed:	14,400 bps.
USENET News:	Yes. 2200+ newsgroups, expanding to approximately 7000 in 1994.
Local File Archives:	Yes. Some document files.
Domain Registration Service:	No. Planned for 1994.
Domain Park Service:	Yes.
Consulting Services:	Yes. Software development.
DNS Service:	No. Planned for 1994.
Commercial Traffic:	Yes.

HOW TO SIGN UP
Modem:
(403) 484-5640,V.32bis,login as **guest**. *No password required.*

Rates
E-mail only plan:
$5 for 10 hours per 30-day billing period. Minimum 3 periods prepaid.
$10.00 startup fee.
Plan A (Interactive Account):
Basic connect (E-mail, USENET news, local access). $5/hour with no minimum per 30-day billing period. Interactive Internet services (Telnet/FTP etc.) are $2/hour plus a $10 startup fee.
Plan B (Interactive Account):
Basic connect (E-mail, USENET news, local access). $1/hour. Minimum 20 hours per 30-day billing period. Interactive Internet services (Telnet/FTP etc.) are $2/hour plus a $10 startup fee.
UUCP:
Billed as basic connect time for a Plan B account. A regular interactive Plan B account is included with each UUCP account but the two accounts are billed as one.
Proposed Plan C (Dial-Up SLIP):
$7/hour, minimum 4 hours per 30 day billing period. $20 startup fee. A regular interactive Plan A account is included with each Plan C SLIP account but the two accounts are billed as one.
Proposed Plan D (Dial-Up SLIP):
$3.75/hour, minimum 20 hours per 30 day billing period. $20 startup fee. A regular interactive Plan B account is included with each Plan D SLIP account but the two accounts are billed as one. The first 20 hours of usage of the Plan B account are free.

SASKATCHEWAN

SASK#net
Saskatoon, Saskatchewan
Regina, Saskatchewan
(no domain)

SASK#net
Computing Services
Room 56, Physics Building
University of Saskatchewan
Saskatoon, Saskatchewan
S7N 0W0
Voice: (306) 966-4860
Fax: (306) 966-4938
Internet:
dean.jones@usask.ca
(Dean Jones)

SASK#net
Libraries and Information Services
Administration-Humanities Bldg
University of Regina
Regina, Saskatchewan
S4S 0A2
Voice: (306) 585-4132
Fax: (306) 585-4878
Internet:
wmaes@max.cc.uregina.ca
(William Maes)

*SASK#net is the CA*net regional network which provides access to the
Internet from within Saskatchewan. This access is provided in support of
the research, educational, and technology transfer missions of its
organizations. SASK#net is provided and managed jointly by the
University of Saskatchewan and the University of Regina.*

Service Area:	Prince Albert, Regina, Saskatoon.
1-800 Service:	No.
PDN Service:	Datapac.
Connection Via:	CA*net.
Leased Line Service:	Yes.
Dedicated Dial-Up Service:	Yes.
Dedicated Line Speeds Supported:	9.6-56 Kbps.
SLIP/PPP Service:	Yes. SLIP only. Dedicated service only.
UUCP Service:	Yes. Mail and news feeds. Newsgroup changes must go through a service person.
Interactive Accounts:	Yes. Direct connection to the Internet. 10MB permanent storage/user. Telnet, FTP, Gopher, WAIS, WWW, Hytelnet, Archie. Shell access.
Maximum Casual Dial-Up Speed:	14,400 bps.
USENET News:	Yes. 2500+ newsgroups.
Local File Archives:	Yes. PC Software, Internet usage, Electronic books, texts, and reports. Sun software patches.
Domain Registration Service:	Yes. Full service.

Domain Park Service:	No.
Consulting Services:	Yes. Customer support is limited to assisting with configuration and implementation of of hardware and software required by the connecting organization and diagnosing and solving organizational problems. Organizations are expected to meet their own support and training needs.
DNS Service:	Yes. Primary and secondary nameservers.
Commercial Traffic:	No.

HOW TO SIGN UP
Call or send electronic mail for information.

Rates
The annual membership fee ranges from $3,700-$44,300. Some conditions apply. The fee is based on speed of connection and the size of the organization making the connection. Organizations connecting at a speed of 9.6 Kbps or less pay $200/month regardless of the size of the organization.

For More Information
FTP:
ftp.usask.ca
directory:/pub/net-info/sasknet

Gopher:
gopher.usask.ca
Select: Computing
Select: SASK#net

MANITOBA

MBnet
Winnipeg, Manitoba
MBnet.mb.ca

MBnet
c/o Computer Services
University of Manitoba
15 Gillson Street
Winnipeg, Manitoba
Voice: (204) 474-9590
Fax: (204) 275-5420
Internet: info@MBnet.mb.ca

MBnet is Manitoba's regional data network, supporting education, research and development, and technology transfer. It is currently administered by the University of Manitoba.

Service Area:	Winnipeg. Expansion is planned to Brandon.
1-800 Service:	No.

PDN Service:	Datapac.
Connection Via:	CA*net.
Leased Line Service:	Yes.
Dedicated Dial-Up Service:	Yes.
Dedicated Line Speeds Supported:	9600 bps-1.544 Mbps.
SLIP/PPP Service:	Yes. SLIP and PPP.
UUCP Service:	Yes. Mail feeds only.
Interactive Accounts:	Yes. Direct connection to the Internet. Menu-driven system. 2MB permanent storage/user. Telnet, FTP, Gopher, WAIS, Hytelnet, Archie. IRC and WWW are planned. Shell access.
Maximum Casual Dial-Up Speed:	14,400 bps.
USENET News:	Yes. Full feed.
Local File Archives:	No.
Domain Registration Service:	Yes. Limited.
Domain Park Service:	Yes.
Consulting Services:	No.
DNS Service:	Yes. Primary and secondary nameservers.
Commercial Traffic:	Yes. Some restrictions apply.

HOW TO SIGN UP
Internet:
*Telnet to access.mbnet.mb.ca, login as **guest**. No password required.*
Modem:
*(204) 275-6150, 2400 bps or lower, login as **mbnet**, password is **guest**.*
*(204) 275-6132, V.32bis/V.42bis, login as **mbnet**, password is **guest**.*

Rates
Dial-Up accounts (Individuals):
$25 one-time registration fee — includes 5 hours of connect time for exploration. $50/year for 25 hours of connect time and 2MB of disk space. Additional connect time is $1/hour. Additional disk space is $3/MB.
Dial-Up accounts (Businesses):
$100 one-time charge for domain name setup and all user accounts — includes 20 hours of connect time for exploration. No registration fee. Account charges same as for individual accounts. The initial connect time allocation for each user account is shared among all users. An account may be setup to be polled via uucp.
Leased Line Connection:
Annual fee is (link speed in Kbps/56)*$18,400.
Dial Modem using SLIP/PPP:
$1,150/year for a maximum of 365 connect hours.
$1.00 for each additional hour. $4,600/year for a dedicated modem/port, $2,300/year for each additional load sharing modem/port.

For More Information
FTP: *Telnet:*

ftp.mbnet.mb.ca
directory: /info/

access.mbnet.mb.ca
*login: **guest***

ONTARIO

Data Tech Canada
Hyde Park, Ontario
dt-can.com

1 Routledge Street
Hyde Park, Ontario
N0M 1Z0
Voice: (519) 473-5694
Fax: (519) 645-6639
Internet: info@dt-can.com

We provide commercial Internet services in the Southwest Ontario region as well as value-added features including stock information, news services, and electronic malls. We recognize that education is the key to effective use of these services and we will make every effort to assist our users and potential users through free seminars, second-to-none support, and newsletters containing tips and general information.

Service Area:	London. Planned expansion to Windsor, Sarnia, and Chatam.
1-800 Service:	No.
PDN Service:	No.
Connection Via:	UUNET Canada.
Leased Line Service:	No.
Dedicated Dial-Up Service:	Yes.
Dedicated Line Speeds Supported:	Up to 14,400 bps.
SLIP/PPP Service:	No.
UUCP Service:	Yes. Mail and news feeds. Users can modify their own newsgroup subscriptions.
Interactive Accounts:	Yes. Direct connection to the Internet. 0.5-2MB temporary storage/user. Telnet, FTP, Gopher, WAIS, WWW. Menu-driven with shell access available. First-Reader for DOS supported and supplied at no additional cost.
Maximum Casual Dial-Up Speed:	14,400 bps.
USENET News:	Yes. Approximately 2,000 newsgroups.
Local File Archives:	Yes. Shareware CDs.
Domain Registration Service:	Yes. Full service.

Domain Park Service:	Yes.
Consulting Services:	Yes. On-site training. Needs assessment. Installation of gateway software. Custom software. Free introductory seminars to the general public.
DNS Service:	Yes. Secondary nameserver only.
Commercial Traffic:	Yes.

HOW TO SIGN UP
Internet:
Not Available.
Modem:
(519) 473-7685, V.32bis. Follow prompts for registration. 10 day free trials are available.

Rates
Bronze Personal Account:
$49.95/year. USENET, local files. No Internet mail. Off-peak usage only.
Silver Personal Account:
$79.95/year plus $40.00 for 20 hours telnet or 20 MB FTP. Internet mail, USENET, local files. Off-peak usage only.
Gold Personal Account:
$99.95/year plus $40.00 for 20 hours telnet or 20 MB FTP. Internet mail, USENET, local files. Peak or off-peak usage allowed.
Business Account:
Starting at $295.00/year.

HookUp Communication Corporation
Waterloo, Ontario
hookup.net

HookUp Communication Corporation
50 Westmount Road North, Suite 220
Waterloo, Ontario
N2L 2R5
Voice: Toll-Free: 1-800 363-0400
          Direct Dial: (519) 747-4110
Fax: (519) 746-3521
Internet: info@hookup.net

HookUp Communications provides national commercial access to the Internet. Our committment is to provide low line ratios, low fees, excellent service, and value.

Service Area:	Alma, Ancaster, Ayr, Baden, Binbrook, Bolton, Brantford, Breslau, Bright, Burlington, Caledon East, Caledona, Cambridge, Campville, Castlemore, Clarkson, Cooksville, Drayton, Dundas, Elmira, Elora, Freelton, Grimsby, Guelph, Hagersville, Hamilton, Kitchener, Linwood, Lynden, Malton, Milton, Mississauga, Mount Hope, New Dundee, New Hamburg, Oakville, Plattsville, Port Credit,

	Selkirk, Snelgrove, St. Clements, St. George, St. Jacobs, Stoney Creek, Streetsville, Toronto and surrounding area, Victoria, Waterdown, Waterloo, Wellesley, West Lincoln, Winona. HookUp plans to provide local access in all major urban centres in Canada by the end of 1994.
1-800 Service	Yes.
PDN Service:	No.
Connection Via:	Sprint.
Leased Line Service:	Yes.
Dedicated Dial-Up Service:	Yes.
Dedicated Line Speeds Available:	Up to 1.544 Mbps.
SLIP/PPP Service:	Yes. SLIP and PPP.
UUCP Service:	Yes. Mail and news feeds. Newsgroup changes must go through a service person.
Interactive Accounts:	Yes. Direct connection to the Internet. 1MB permanent storage/user. Additional storage available at $15/MB/yr. Telnet, FTP, Gopher, WAIS, WWW, IRC, Hytelnet, Archie. Shell access.
Maximum Casual Dial-Up Speed:	14,400 bps.
USENET News:	Yes. 2,600+ newsgroups, including Clarinet news.
Local File Archives:	Yes. MS-Windows, SCO, Internet-related files. Mirrors of selected sites.
Domain Registration Service:	Yes. Full service.
Domain Park Service:	Yes.
Consulting Services:	Yes. TCP/IP connectivity. UNIX.
DNS Service:	Yes. Primary and secondary nameservers.
Commercial Traffic:	Yes.

HOW TO SIGN UP

Call or send electronic mail for information.

Rates

Residential Lite Plan:
$35 setup fee. $14.95/month for 5 hours of connect time per month. Additional hours are $3/hour. Line to customer ratio is 1:100.

Residential Plan:
$35.00 setup fee. $34.95/month for 15 hours of connect time per month. Additional hours are $1/hour. Line to customer ratio is 1:15..

Home/Office Plan:
$35.00 setup fee. $299.95/year for 50 hours of connect time per month. Additional hours are $0.50/hour. Line to customer ratio is 1:15..

Corporate Dial-Up:

$50 setup fee. $59.95 for 30 hours of connect time per month.
Additional hours are $0.50/hour. Line to customer ratio is 1:10.
Corporate On-line:
$295 setup fee. $299.95/month (unlimited connection). Line to customer
ratio is 1:1.
Corporate Custom:
Call for consultation. Packages are available for businesses requiring
line speeds of 56K or greater and other custom setups, including custom
applications.

For More Information
Gopher:
gopher.hookup.net

Internex Online Inc.
Toronto, Ontario
io.org

1 Yonge Street, Suite 1801
Toronto, Ontario, Canada
M5E 1W7
Voice: (416) 363-8676
Internet: vid@io.org (David Mason)

Internex has been set up to provide full access to all Internet functions at
an inexpensive cost to experienced and novice users alike.

Service Area:	Toronto.
1-800 Service:	No.
PDN Service:	No.
Connection Via:	UUNET Canada.
Leased Line Service:	No.
Dedicated Dial-Up Service:	Yes.
Dedicated Line Speeds Supported:	N/A.
SLIP/PPP Service:	No.
UUCP Service:	No.
Interactive Accounts:	Yes. Direct connection to the Internet. Permanent storage available for $5/MB/year. Telnet, FTP, Gopher, IRC, Hytelnet, Archie. Menu-driven interface. Shell access. QWK- and HD- compatible off-line mail readers are supported. Other packet formats are supported.
Maximum Casual Dial-Up Speed:	14,400 bps.
USENET News:	Yes. Approximately 7,000 newsgroups.
Local File Archives:	Yes. General files for all computer types.
Domain Registration Service:	No.
Domain Park Service:	No.

Consulting Services:	No.
Nameserver Service:	No.
Commercial Traffic:	Yes.

HOW TO SIGN UP
Internet:
*Telnet to io.org -or- grin.io.org, login as **new**. No password required.*
Modem:
*(416) 363-3783, V.32bis, login as **new**. No password required.*

Rates
$40/year for 1 hour/day. Includes Internet mail, USENET, IRC.
$185/year for 2 hours/day. Includes full Internet access, 4MB of storage.

For More Information
Telnet:
io.org
*login: **new***

Mindemoya Computing and Design
Sudbury, Ontario
MCD.ON.CA

794 Charlotte Street
Sudbury, Ontario
P3E 4C3
Voice: (705) 670-8129
Fax: (705) 522-6402
Internet: info@mcd.on.ca

MCD*Net is an on-line communication service which provides modem users and organizations with access to electronic mail, freely distributable software, and mail and news feeds.

Service Area:	Sudbury. Expansion is planned to Northeastern Ontario including North Bay, Timmins, and Sault Ste. Marie.
1-800 Service:	No.
PDN Service:	No.
Connection Via:	UUNET Canada.
Leased Line Service:	No.
Dedicated Dial-Up Service:	Yes.
Dedicated Line Speeds Supported	14,400-19,200 bps.
SLIP/PPP Service:	Yes. SLIP and PPP.
UUCP Service:	Yes. Mail and news. Customers can modify their own newsgroup subscriptions.

Interactive Accounts:	Yes. Gateway connection to the Internet. 500k permanent storage/user. Each additional 500k is $5.00/month. Full Internet services will be available in mid-1994. Menu-driven interface or shell access if requested. SOUP- and QWK-compatible readers supported. Several off-line mail readers available for downloading. E-mail to fax gateway for the local calling area.
Maximum Casual Dial-Up Speed:	14,400 bps.
USENET News:	Yes. Approximately 3000 newsgroups.
Local File Archives:	Yes. MSDOS, Windows, Macintosh files.
Domain Registration Service:	Yes. Full service.
Domain Park Service:	Yes.
Consulting Services:	No.
DNS Service:	No.
Commercial Traffic:	Yes.

HOW TO SIGN UP
Modem:
*(705) 670-2471, login as **guest**. No password is required.*

Rates
$2.50/hour. Minimum $5.00 month.

National Capital Free-Net
Ottawa, Ontario
freenet.carleton.ca

1125 Colonel By Drive
Ottawa, Ontario
K1S 5B6
Voice: (613) 788-3947
Fax: (613) 788-4448
Internet: ncf@freenet.carleton.ca

The National Capital Free-Net is a computer-based information service designed to meet the present information needs of the people and public agencies in the region, and to prepare the community for full and broadly-based participation in rapidly changing communication environments. The National Capital Free-Net is incorporated as a non-profit community utility that is free to everyone in the community, and will neither charge nor pay for any information or other services it provides.

Service Area:	Ottawa, Hull, and area.
1-800 Service:	No.
PDN Service:	No.

Connection Via:	Carleton University.
Leased Line Service:	No.
Dedicated Dial-Up Service:	No.
Dedicated Line Speeds Supported:	N/A.
SLIP/PPP Service:	No.
UUCP Service:	No.
Interactive Accounts:	Yes. Internet mail. Gopher. Telnet service to other Free-Nets. No shell access.
Maximum Casual Dial-Up Speed:	2,400 bps.
USENET News:	Yes.
Local File Archives:	Yes. Community databases.
Domain Registration Service:	No.
Domain Park Service:	No.
Consulting Services:	No.
DNS Service:	No.
Commercial Traffic:	No.

HOW TO SIGN UP
Internet:
*Telnet to freenet.carleton.ca, login as **guest**. No password required.*
Modem:
*(613) 780-3733, 2400 bps, login as **guest**. No password required.*

Rates:
All services offered by the National Capital Free-Net are free to the user.

For More Information
Telnet:	*Gopher:*
freenet.carleton.ca	*freenet.carleton.ca*
*login: **guest***	

NetAccess Systems Inc.
Hamilton, Ontario
netaccess.on.ca

Suite E
231 Main Street West
Hamilton, Ontario
L8P 1J4
Voice: (905) 524-2544
Fax: (905) 524-3010
Internet: info@netaccess.on.ca

NetAccess was incorporated in May of 1993 to provide Internet access on a subscription basis in the Hamilton-Burlington area. Our primary purpose is to provide high quality access to computer-based communications and information services through the Internet for local area businesses and service organizations. As part of our wider mandate, NetAccess is committed to working with businesses, research, educational, service, and non-profit interests to encourage innovative use of computer technology for the benefit of the whole community.

Service Area:	Hamilton.
1-800 Service:	No.
PDN Service:	No.
Connection Via:	UUNET Canada.
Leased Line Service:	No.
Dedicated Dial-Up Service:	Yes.
Dedicated Line Speeds Supported:	2400 -14,400 bps.
SLIP/PPP Service:	No.
UUCP Service:	Yes. Mail and news feeds. Newsgroup changes must go through a service person. UUCP software is supplied (for a fee, where applicable).
Interactive Accounts:	Yes, Gateway connection to the Internet. 1MB permanent storage/user. Shell access. Telnet and FTP are available as a separate service.
Maximum Casual Dial-Up Speed:	14,400 bps.
USENET News:	Yes. Full feed.
Local File Archives:	Yes. Internet information, public domain software.
Domain Registration Service:	Yes. Full service.
Domain Park Service:	No.
Consulting Services:	Yes. UNIX, LAN and WAN communications, Internet connectivity.
DNS Service:	No.
Commercial Traffic:	Yes.

HOW TO SIGN UP
Call or send electronic mail for information.

Rates
Terminal Access and UUCP access:
$39.99/month.
Electronic mail only:
$19.99/month.
Special group and institutional rates are available.

ONet
Toronto, Ontario
onet.on.ca

University of Toronto Network and Operations Services
c/o Herb Kugel
4 Bancroft Avenue
Toronto, Ontario
M5S 1C1
Voice: (416) 978-4589
Fax: (416) 978-6620
Internet: herb@onet.on.ca (Herb Kugel)

*The ONet Association is a not-for-profit consortium established to
facilitate the communication activities of member organizations in
support of their research and education missions.*

Service Area:	Ontario.
1-800 Service:	No.
PDN Service:	No.
Connection Via:	CA*net.
Leased Line Service:	Yes.
Dedicated Dial-Up Service:	Call for information.
Dedicated Line Speeds Supported:	Call for information.
SLIP/PPP Service:	No. Planned for Toronto, Ottawa, Kitchener-Waterloo. Dial-up POPs will be deployed in Guelph, Hamilton, Kingston, London, North Bay, Peterborough, St.Catharines, Sudbury, Thunder Bay, and Windsor as demand warrants.
UUCP Service:	No.
Interactive Accounts:	No.
Maximum Casual Dial-Up Speed:	N/A.
USENET News:	Yes.
Local File Archives:	Yes. ONet documents.
Domain Registration Service:	Yes.
Domain Park Service:	No.
Consulting Service:	Call for information.
DNS Service:	Call for information.
Commercial Traffic:	No.

HOW TO SIGN UP
Call or send electronic mail for information.

Rates
A+B+Initiation, where:

A=$3,500   if $0M   = < budget < = $50M
* $7,000   if $50M = < budget < = $150M*
* $14,000   if $150M = < budget*

B=$5,000 for a 19,200 bps connection

$10,000 for 56 Kbps connection (=1 DSO)
$7,000 + n * $6,000 for an n*DSO connection (1<n<12)
$79,000 for a 1.544 Mbps connection

For More Information
FTP:
onet.on.ca

RESUDOX Online Services
Nepean, Ontario
Resudox.net

P.O. Box 33067
Nepean, Ontario
K2C 3Y9
Voice: (613) 567-6925
Fax: (613) 567-8289
Internet: info@Resudox.net

We are a locally-owned organization responding to the needs of the high-tech and educational communities. Our mission: To provide an affordable dial-up service for Internet access to individuals and companies in the National Capital Region, to provide an alternative link to the Free-Net community, and to contribute to the development of Internet and Free-Net access in the Ottawa-Carleton region.

Service Area:	Ottawa and area.
1-800 Service:	No.
PDN Service:	No.
Connection Via:	fONOROLA.
Leased Line Service:	No.
Dedicated Dial-Up Service:	Yes.
Dedicated Line Speeds Supported	2400-14,400 bps.
SLIP/PPP Service:	Yes. SLIP and PPP.
UUCP Service:	Yes. Mail and news feeds. Users can modify their own newsgroup subscriptions. UUCP software is supplied.
Interactive Accounts:	Yes. Direct connection to the Internet. 5MB permanent storage/user. Telnet, FTP, Gopher, WAIS, IRC, Hytelnet, Archie, MUDs. Menu-driven interface or shell access. Off-line mail readers supported (qwk, cinetix, qutnet).
Maximum Casual Dial-Up Speed:	14,400 bps.
USENET News:	Yes. Full feed.
Local File Archives:	Yes. Various.
Domain Registration Service:	Yes. Full service.
Domain Park Service:	Yes.

Consulting Services:	Yes. Must be related to hook-up.
DNS Service:	Yes. Primary and secondary nameservers.
Commercial Traffic:	Yes.

HOW TO SIGN UP
Internet:
*Telnet to resudox.net, login as **new**. No password required.*
Modem:
*(613) 567-1714, V.32bis, login as **new**. No password required.*

Rates
Free-Net Access Account:
$17/month plus $1/hour. 10 free hours per month for three months. $2 of each subscriber's monthly subscription fee will be donated to the National Capital Free-Net in Ottawa.
Full Service Account:
$19/month plus $2/hour from 2a.m. to 4p.m. $3/hour from 4p.m. to 2a.m. 10 free hours per month for three months.
Corporate Rates:
$35.00/month plus $2/hour from 5p.m. to 8a.m. $4/hour from 8a.m. to 5p.m.
SLIP/PPP:
$25/month plus $5/hour (dial-up). $450/month (dedicated).
UUCP:
$35/month plus $3.50/hour.

For More Information
FTP:	*Gopher:*	*Telnet:*
resudox.net	*resudox.net*	*resudox.net*
		*login: **guest***

UUISIS
Nepean, Ontario
isis.org

81 Tartan Drive
Nepean Drive
K2J 3V6
Voice: (613) 825-5324
Internet: postmaster@uuisis.isis.isis
rjbeeth@uuisis.isis.org (Rick Beetham)

Our mandate is to deliver affordable access to the Internet for organizations, businesses, and individuals through the use of regular phone lines. Our mission is to remain stable and cost-effective for the customer and to deliver mail in as timely a manner as possible without being directly connected.

Service Area:	Ontario: Ottawa, Nepean, Gloucester, Kanata. Quebec: Hull, Gatineau, Aylmer.
1-800 Service	No..
PDN Service:	No.

Connection Via:	UUNET Canada.
Leased Line Service:	No.
Dedicated Dial-Up Service:	Yes.
Dedicated Line Speeds Supported:	Up to 19,200 bps.
SLIP/PPP Service:	No.
UUCP Service:	Yes. Mail and news feeds. Customers can modify their own newsgroup subscriptions.
Interactive Accounts:	Yes. Gateway connection to the Internet. Internet mail, News. Anonymous FTP by mail via UUNET Canada. Telnet and FTP are planned. Menu-driven Waffle environment. DistNet/ZOOMAIL supported (off-line reader).
Maximum Casual Dial-Up Speed:	19,200 bps.
USENET News:	Yes. Approximately 1,600 newsgroups.
Local File Archives:	Call for information.
Domain Registration Service:	No.
Domain Park Service:	Yes.
Consulting Services:	No.
DNS Service:	No.
Commercial Traffic:	Yes.

HOW TO SIGN UP
Modem:
*(613) 825-6539, V.32/19.2 PEP, login as **bbs**, password is **new**.*

Rates
Premium:
$180/year for 600 minutes/month UUCP or login.
$200/year for 600 minutes/month UUCP and login.
Economy:
$90/year - casual/nonorganizational/nonprofessional users.

UUNorth Incorporated
Willowdale, Ontario
uunorth.north.net

3555 Don Mills Road
Suite 6-304
Willowdale, Ontario
M2H 3N3
Voice: (416) 225-8649
Fax: (416) 225-0525
Internet: uunorth@north.net

Our mission is to provide access to the Internet for individuals and corporations at all levels, with support, training, and application knowhow. We integrate their systems and networks, assist them in developing, learning, and using applications, and manage their network needs.

Service Area:	Toronto. Planned expansion to Montreal, Ottawa, Vancouver, and Windsor in 1994.
1-800 Service:	No.
PDN Service:	No.
Connection Via:	Call for information.
Leased Line Service:	Yes.
Dedicated Dial-Up Service:	Yes.
Dedicated Line Speeds Supported	Dedicated dial-up: 2,400-14,400 bps. Leased Line: 19,200 bps - 1.544 Mbps.
SLIP/PPP Service:	Yes. SLIP and PPP.
UUCP Service:	Yes. Mail and news feeds. Users can modify their own newsgroup subscriptions. Shareware/Freeware UUCP software available.
Interactive Accounts:	Yes. Direct connection to the Internet. Permanent disk space available. Telnet, FTP, Gopher, WWW, WAIS, IRC, Archie, Finger, rlogin, whois. Menu-driven system. Comprehensive manual supplied to all users. Off-line mail readers supported and supplied. E-mail-to-fax gateway planned for 1994. No shell access.
Maximum Casual Dial-Up Speed:	14,400 bps.
USENET News:	Yes. 3,000+ newsgroups.
Local File Archives:	Yes. USENET source newsgroups, FAQs, GNU archives, sources for popular DOS and Macintosh programs.
Domain Registration Service:	Yes. Full service.
Domain Park Service:	Yes.
Consulting Services:	Yes. Network management and network applications. System integration and training, tuning and performance enhancements. Design, implementation, installation, and configuration of LANs.
DNS Service:	Yes. Primary and secondary nameservers.
Commercial Traffic:	Yes.

HOW TO SIGN UP
Internet:
*Telnet to 198.52.32.3, login as **new**. No password required.*
Modem:
*(416) 221-0200, V.32bis, login as **new**. No password required.*

Rates:
Dial-up accounts: $1.25-$3.00/hour. Call for full pricing information.

For More Information

FTP:	**Telnet:**	**Gopher:**
ftp.north.net	*198.52.32.2*	*gopher.north.net*
	login: new	

VRx Incorporated
Toronto, Ontario
vrx.net

VrX Incorporated
87 Seymour Avenue
Toronto, Ontario
M4J 3T6
Voice: (416) 778-5955
Fax: (416) 962-0079

VRx aims to be your one-stop information gateway/provider for home and industry. We are a network service provider that will bring an on-ramp to the information highway right to the door of your home or business.

Service Area:	Opening in 1994: Montreal, Ottawa, Toronto, and Vancouver.
1-800 Service:	Yes.
PDN Service:	Datapac.
Connection Via:	UUNET Canada.
Leased Line Service:	Yes.
Dedicated Dial-Up Service:	Yes.
Dedicated Line Speeds Supported:	Call for information.
SLIP/PPP Service:	Yes. SLIP and PPP.
UUCP Service:	Yes. Mail and news feeds. Users can modify their own newsgroup subscriptions. UUCP software supplied at no charge.
Interactive Accounts:	Yes. Permanent disk space is available. Telnet, FTP, Gopher, WAIS, WWW, IRC, Hytelnet, Archie. Choice of UNIX shell, GUI, or menu-driven interface. Choice of Rosereader or Vrx off-line mail reader. Vrx reader is free. E-mail-to-fax gateway.
Maximum Casual Dial-Up Speed:	14,400 bps.
USENET News:	Yes. Full feed, including Clarinet news.
Local File Archives:	Yes. FAQs and sources.
Domain Registration Service:	Yes. Full service.
Domain Park Service:	Yes.

Consulting Service:	Yes. Installation of mail/news in the home or office. Connectivity of corporate mail. Remote system administration. Training. Local/enterprise newsgroup and mailing list support.
DNS Service:	Yes. Primary and secondary nameservers.
Commercial Traffic:	Yes.

HOW TO SIGN UP
Call for information.

Rates
Call for information.

QUEBEC

Communications Accessibles Montreal
Montreal, Quebec
CAM.ORG

2665 Ste-Cunegonde, Suite 002
Montreal, Quebec
H3J 2X3
Voice: (514) 931-0749
Fax: (514) 931-4105
Internet: info@CAM.ORG

Communications Accessibles Montreal is a non-profit corporation offering affordable Internet connectivity in the 514 (Montreal) area code. Free 15 day trial accounts are available on request.

Service Area:	Montreal, West Island, Laval, South-Shore.
1-800 Service:	No.
PDN Service:	No.
Connection Via:	UUNET Canada.
Leased Line Service:	No.
Dedicated Dial-Up Service:	Yes.
Dedicated Access Speeds Supported:	Up to 14,400 bps.
SLIP/PPP Service:	Yes. SLIP and PPP.
UUCP Service:	Yes. Mail and news feeds. The following UUCP software is supplied free of charge (installation not included): Waffle for DOS customers, UUPC for MAC customers, and Taylor UUCP for UNIX customers. Newsgroup changes must go through a service person.

Interactive Accounts:	Yes. Direct connection to the Internet. 4MB of permanent storage/user. Extra disk space available at $1/MB/month. Telnet, FTP, Gopher, WAIS, WWW, IRC, Archie. Shell access. QWK-compatible readers are supported. E-mail-to-fax gateway for the local calling area.
Maximum Casual Dial-Up Speed:	14,400 bps.
USENET News:	Yes. 7000+ newsgroups available.
Local File Archives:	Yes. Internet materials. UUCP and SLIP/PPP software for PC and Mac users.
Domain Registration Service:	Yes. Full service.
Domain Park Service:	Yes. Non-commercial organizations only.
Consulting Service:	Yes. Electronic mail, news, IP, multiprotocol integration, UNIX.
DNS Service:	Yes. Primary and secondary nameservers.
Commercial Traffic:	Yes.

HOW TO SIGN UP
Call or send electronic mail to register.

Rates
Interactive Shell Access:
$25/month (2400-19200 bps). Limit of 10 hours of connect time per week.
Dial-Up SLIP/PPP + Interactive Account:
$30/month (9600-19200 bps).
Dedicated SLIP/PPP + Interactive Account:
$150/month (9600-19200 bps).
UUCP Mail-only Feed:
$5/month (2400 bps-19200 bps).
Under 1MB/week at 2400 bps or less. Under 4MB/week at 9600 bps and higher.
UUCP Partial Newsfeed with Mail:
$15/month (2400 bps). $10/month (9600-19200 bps).
Under 5MB/week at 2400 bps or less. Under 20MB/week at 9600 bps and higher.
UUCP Full Newsfeed with Mail:
$100/month (9600-19200 bps). Approximately 250MB/week (compressed, average).

For More Information
FTP:	Telnet:	Finger:
ftp.cam.org	cam.org	info@cam.org
file: CAM.ORG-info	login: **info**	

INFOPUQ
Sainte-Foy, Quebec
infopuq.uquebec.ca

INFOPUQ
L'Université du Québec

2875, boul. Laurier
Sainte-Foy, Quebec
G1V 2M3
Voice: (418) 657-4422
Fax: (418) 657-2132
Internet: infopuq@uquebec.ca

INFOPUQ provides dial-up Internet access in several Quebec communities.

Service Area:	Chicoutimi, Hull, Montreal, Quebec City, Rimouski, Rouyn-Noranda, Trois-Rivières.
1-800 Service:	No.
PDN Service:	Datapac.
Connection Via:	RISQ.
Leased Line Service:	No.
Dedicated Dial-Up Service:	No.
Dedicated Access Speeds Supported:	N/A
SLIP/PPP Service:	No.
UUCP Service:	No.
Interactive Accounts:	Yes. Internet mail, Telnet, FTP on request, Gopher. Quarterly newsletter.
Maximum Casual Dial-Up Speed:	14,400 bps.
USENET News:	No. Planned for 1994.
Local File Archives:	No.
Domain Registration Service:	No.
Domain Park Service:	No.
Consulting Service:	No.
DNS Service:	No.
Commercial Traffic:	Yes.

HOW TO SIGN UP

Call or send electronic mail for information.

Rates

$35 setup fee. $5 per month with 30 minutes free connect time each month. Additional hours are $10/hour 7a.m. to 5p.m., $8/hour from 5p.m. to 11p.m., and $6/hour from 11p.m. to 7a.m. System is unavailable between 3a.m. and 4p.m.

Login Informatique

Pierrefonds, Quebec
login.qc.ca

4363 Jacques Bizard
Pierrefonds, Quebec

H9H 4W3
Voice: (514) 626-8086
Internet: infos@login.qc.ca

*The main purpose of Login is to relay news, mail, and data throughout
the Montreal area. Its mission is to provide reliable electronic
communications to individuals and small businesses.*

Service Area:	Montreal.
1-800 Service:	No.
PDN Service:	No.
Connection Via:	RISQ.
Leased Line Service:	No.
Dedicated Dial-Up Service:	No.
Dedicated Line Speeds Supported:	N/A.
SLIP/PPP Service:	Yes. SLIP only.
UUCP Service:	Yes. Mail and news feeds. Customers can modify their own newsgroup subscriptions.
Interactive Accounts:	Yes.
Maximum Casual Dial-Up Speed:	14,400 bps.
USENET News:	Yes. Full feed.
Local File Archives:	No.
Domain Registration Service:	Yes. Full service.
Domain Park Service:	Yes.
Consulting Services:	Yes. Communications and local networking.
DNS Service:	Yes. Primary and secondary nameservers.
Commercial Traffic:	Yes.

HOW TO SIGN UP

Call or send electronic mail for information.

Rates
Basic Service:
*$48 for 4 months. Mail and news via UUCP. Average volume of 2MB of
USENET news per day. Your electronic mail address will be a simple
extension of the domain login.qc.ca.*
MX Service:
*$80 for 4 months. Mail and news via UUCP. Average volume of 2MB of
USENET news per day. Includes an Internet domain name registration.*
PLUS Service:
*$120 for 4 months. Mail, news and FTP. This service entitles you to one
interactive account. Data transferred using FTP will be sent directly to
your site in the directory of your choice. Up to 75 minutes direct Internet
access time in any one day, renewable in increments of 15 minutes per
day. An average of 90 minutes UUCP connect time per day is allowed.*
COMPANY Service:

$300 for 6 months. This service entitles you to four interactive accounts. Data transferred using FTP will be sent directly to your site in the directory of your choice. Up to 105 minutes direct Internet access time in any one day, renewable in increments of 35 minutes per day. An average of 90 minutes UUCP connect time per day is allowed.

For More Information
FTP:
login.qc.ca
directory: /pub/Login
file: tarif.1994

RISQ (Réseau Interordinateurs Scientifique Québécois)

Montreal, Quebec
risq.net

Attention: Centre d'information du RISQ
1801 McGill College Avenue, Suite 800
Montreal, Quebec
H3A 2N4
Voice: (514) 398-1234
Fax: (514) 398-1244
Internet: cirisq@risq.net

Crée en 1989, le RISQ est un réseau provincial de communications informatisies voui la recherche et l'enseignement. Le RISQ relie présentement plusieurs université et centres de recherche publics et privés oeuvrant au Québec.

Fou nded in 1989, RISQ is a provincial, computer-based communications network dedicated to research and education. RISQ presently provides networking for both the public and private research communities operating within Quebec.

Service Area:	Montreal, Quebec City, Sherbrooke.
1-800 Service:	No.
PDN Service:	No.
Connection Via:	CA*net.
Leased Line Service:	Yes.
Dedicated Dial-Up Service:	Yes.
Dedicated Line Speeds Supported:	9,600 bps - 1.544 Mbps.
SLIP/PPP Service:	Yes. SLIP and PPP. Dedicated service only.
UUCP Service:	No.
Interactive Accounts:	No.
Maximum Casual Dial-Up Speed:	N/A.
USENET News:	Yes. Full feed.

Local File Archives:	Yes. Public software. RISQ information.
Domain Registration Service:	Yes. Full service.
Domain Park Service:	No.
Consulting Services:	No.
DNS Service:	Yes. Primary and secondary nameservers.
Commercial Traffic:	No.

HOW TO SIGN UP
Call or send electronic mail for information.

Rates
Enterprises and Associates:
2x56Kbps: $30,000/year (router included)
56Kbps: $20,000/year (router included)
19.2Kbps: $15,000/year (router included)
Enterprises and Associates, Members of CRIM:
2x56Kbps: $27,000 (router included)
56Kbps: $18,000 (router included)
19.2Kbps: $13,000 (router included)
Universities:
56 or 19.2 Kbps: $15,000 (router and communication link included) or
$5,000 (router included)

For more information
FTP: **Gopher:**
risq.net risq.net

NOVA SCOTIA

Nova Scotia Technology Network Inc. (NSTN)
Dartmouth, Nova Scotia
nstn.ns.ca

Administration Offices
900 Windmill Road, Suite 107
Dartmouth, Nova Scotia
B3B 1P7
Voice: (902) 468-NSTN (6786)
Fax: (902) 468-3679
Internet: info@nstn.ns.ca

NSTN's mission is to be the premier computer networking company in Canada specializing in 'interoperability' products and services.

Service Area:	All of Nova Scotia and Points of Presence in Sydney, Antigonish, Truro, Amherst, Halifax, Bridgetown, Bridgewater, Yarmouth, Wolfville, and Ottawa. Expansion is planned to Ottawa and Toronto. NSTN eventually plans to

	have network access points across Canada.
1-800 Service:	No.
PDN Service:	Datapac.
Connection Via:	CA*net.
Leased Line Service:	Yes.
Dedicated Dial-Up Service:	No.
Dedicated Line Speeds Supported:	9.6-56 Kbps.
SLIP/PPP Service:	Yes. SLIP only.
UUCP Service:	No.
Interactive Accounts:	No.
Maximum Casual Dial-Up Speed:	Currently 9,600 bps. 14,400 bps planned for 1994.
USENET News:	Yes. 3000+ newsgroups.
Local File Archives:	Yes. NSTN information. Freeware/shareware.
Domain Registration Service:	Yes. Full service.
Domain Park Service:	Yes.
Consulting Services:	Yes. Network planning, design, and implementation. Network requirements analysis.
DNS Service:	Yes. Primary and secondary nameservers.
Commercial Traffic:	Yes.

HOW TO SIGN UP

Call or send electronic mail for information.

Rates
Individual Connection Service:
$35 startup fee. Minimum $25/month $1/hour from 6p.m. to 8a.m. $5/hour from 8a.m. to 6p.m.
Business Connection Service:
Starts at $250/month plus equipment and line charges.
Internet Librarian Service:
$250 for first four hours. $40 per additional hour.

For More Information
FTP: **Gopher:**
ftp.nstn.ns.ca   nstn.ns.ca
directory:/nstn-documentation/ Select: NSTN Information

NEW BRUNSWICK

NBNet
Saint John, New Brunswick
nbnet.nb.ca

NBTel
One Brunswick Square
P.O. Box 1430
Saint John, New Brunswick
E2L 4K2
Voice: (800) 561-4459 (New Brunswick)
         (506) 458-1690
Internet: NBNHELP@nbnet.nb.ca

NBTel is New Brunswick's local and long distance telephone service provider.

Service Area:	All of New Brunswick.
1-800 Service:	Yes.
PDN Service:	Hyperstream.
Connection Via:	CA*net
Leased Line Service:	Yes.
Dedicated Dial-Up Service:	No.
Dedicated Line Speeds Supported:	56 Kbps to 1.544 Mbps.
SLIP/PPP Service:	Yes. SLIP and PPP. Only to a shared modem pool on a non-dedicated line. POP2 and POP3 are supported.
UUCP Service:	No.
Interactive Accounts:	No.
Maximum Casual Dial-Up Speed:	14,400 bps.
USENET News:	Yes. Approximately 3,000 newsgroups.
Local File Archives:	No.
Domain Registration Service:	Yes. Full service.
Domain Park Service:	Yes.
Consulting Services:	No.
DNS Service:	Yes.
Commercial Traffic:	Yes.

HOW TO SIGN UP
Call or send electronic mail for information.

Rates
SLIP/PPP (Casual Dial-Up):

$0.16/minute to a maximum of $400/month, no minimum. This rate structure includes long distance, so the rate is the same everywhere in New Brunswick.
Dedicated Service:
$0.20/MB plus frame relay service charges.

PRINCE EDWARD ISLAND

PEINet Inc.
Charlottetown, Prince Edward Island
peinet.pe.ca

P.O. Box 3126
Charlottetown, Prince Edward Island
C1A 7N9
Voice: (902) 892-PEINet(7346)
Fax: (902) 368-2446
Internet: admin@peinet.pe.ca

PEInet is Prince Edward Island's Wide Area Network providing connectivity to CA•net and the Internet. Our mission is to provide an information network for PEI to facilitate the connection of users to services. The long-range goal of PEINet is to develop a broad range of network services, to deliver value-added information services and access to external databases, and to provide the environment for the development and promotion of new, local information sources.

Service Area:	All of Prince Edward Island. POPs in Souris, Montague, Charlottetown, Summerside, and Alberton.
1-800 Service:	No.
PDN Service:	No.
Connection Via:	CA•net.
Leased Line Service:	Yes.
Dedicated Dial-Up Service:	Yes.
Dedicated Line Speeds Supported:	Up to 56 Kbps.
SLIP/PPP Service:	Yes. SLIP and PPP.
UUCP Service:	No.
Interactive Accounts:	Yes. Direct connection to the Internet. 2MB permanent storage/user. Additional storage $1/MB/day. Telnet, FTP, Gopher, WWW, Archie. Menu-driven with shell access.
Maximum Casual Dial-Up Speed:	14,400 bps.
USENET News:	Yes. Approximately 2,000 groups.
Local File Archives:	No.

Domain Registration Service:	Yes. Full service.
Domain Park Service:	No.
Consulting Services:	Yes. Connectivity for LANs and WANs.
DNS Service:	Yes. Primary and secondary nameservers.
Commercial Traffic:	Yes.

HOW TO SIGN UP
Call or send electronic mail for information.

Rates
Dial-Up accounts:
$20/month. Includes 20 hours free usage. Additional hours are $5/hour from 6a.m. to 6p.m. and $2/hour from 6p.m. to 6a.m.
Dial-in SLIP:
$50/month. Includes 100 hours free usage. Additional hours are $5/hour from 6a.m. to 6p.m. and $2/hour from 6p.m. to 6a.m.
Dedicated Access:
Cost depends on speed and number of users. Call for consultation.

NEWFOUNDLAND

ACOA/Enterprise Network
St. John's, Newfoundland
entnet.nf.ca

P.O. Box 13670
Station "A"
St. John's, Newfoundland
A1B 4G1
Voice: (709) 729-7038
Fax: (709) 729-7039
Internet: customer_service@mailer.entnet.nf.ca

The Enterprise Network's mandate is to foster innovation and enhanced productivity in small business and economic development agencies by using information technology and data communications systems. We are a network providing communications and information services to the business economic development agencies in Newfoundland and Labrador. We are currently running an Internet service on a very limited basis.

Service Area:	Newfoundland.
1-800 Service:	Yes.
PDN Service	No.
Connection Via:	NLnet.
Leased Line Service:	No.
Dedicated Dial-Up Service:	Yes.

Dedicated Line Speeds Supported:	Up to 14,400 bps.
SLIP/PPP Service:	No.
UUCP Service:	No.
Interactive Accounts:	Yes. Gateway connection to the Internet. Host access is provided for Telnet and FTP, but users do not have accounts on an Internet host. Permanent storage available. Menu-driven interface.
Maximum Casual Dial-Up Speed:	14,400 bps.
USENET News:	No.
Local File Archives:	No.
Domain Registration Service:	No.
Domain Park Service:	No.
Consulting Services:	No.
DNS Service:	No.
Commercial Traffic:	Yes.

HOW TO SIGN UP

Call or send electronic mail for information.

Rates

One-time registration fee:	**$75.00**
25 hour block of time:	**$199.00**
50 hour block of time:	**$379.00**

NLnet (Newfoundland Regional Network)

St. John's, Newfoundland
nlnet.nf.ca

c/o Department of Computing and Communications
Memorial University of Newfoundland
St. John's, Newfoundland
A1C 5S7
Voice: (709) 737-8329
Fax: (709) 737-3514
Internet: admin@nlnet.nf.ca

NLnet is the member-controlled CA*net regional network for Newfoundland and Labrador. NLnet's mission is to provide universal, distance-insensitive connectivity throughout the region.

Service Area:	St. John's, Clarenville, Corner Brook, Grand Falls/Windsor, Labrador City, Stephenville. Nine additional POPs planned in 1994/95.
1-800 Service:	No.

PDN Service:	Datapac.
Connection Via:	CA*net. Currently 112kbps. Moving to 1.544 Mbps by summer 1994.
Leased Line Service:	Yes.
Dedicated Dial-Up Service:	Yes.
Dedicated Line Speeds Supported:	9.6-56 Kbps.
SLIP/PPP Service:	SLIP to be implemented in 1994.
UUCP Service:	No.
Interactive Accounts:	Yes. 2 MB permanent storage/user. Telnet, FTP, Gopher, Hytelnet, Archie. Shell access.
Maximum Casual Dial-Up Speed:	14,400 bps.
USENET News:	Yes. Approximately 1850 newsgroups.
Local File Archives:	No.
Domain Registration Service:	Yes. Full service.
Domain Park Service:	Yes.
Consulting Services:	No.
DNS Service:	Yes. Primary and secondary nameservers.
Commercial Traffic:	Yes.

HOW TO SIGN UP
Call or send electronic mail for information.

Rates
Casual Dial-Up:
$29.00/month for 20 hours connect time per month. Additional hours are $4.20/hour.
PC to Dedicated Modem:
$250/month.
Leased Line Service:
9.6Kbps access:	*$10,000/year.*
19.6Kbps access:	*$12,500/year.*
38,400Kbps access:	*$17,500/year.*
56Kbps access:	*$22,500/year.*

PART 2:
DOMESTIC PROVIDERS WITH OPERATIONS IN MORE THAN ONE PROVINCE

AT&T Mail
Toronto, Ontario
attmail.com

Unitel Electronic Commerce Services
2005 Sheppard Avenue East
Suite 215
Toronto, Ontario
M2J 5B4
Voice: Canada Toll-Free 1-800-567-4671 (2)
Fax-On-Demand: 1-800-354-8800

Whether your business manufactures a product or provides a service, your staff, clients, and vendors exchange dozens of communications each day. By eliminating the traditional obstacles of geography, time and technology, AT&T Mail can help you expand your reach, increase productivity, and dramatically streamline communications — all without purchasing additional hardware equipment. AT&T Mail gives you connectivity options that let you reach over 20 million private and public electronic mail subscribers worldwide, as well as millions of fax machines, telex terminals, and postal addresses — all without leaving your PC.

Service Area:	Local access number in Toronto.
1-800 Service:	No.
PDN Service:	Datapac (no extra charge).
Leased Line Service:	Yes.
Dedicated Dial-Up Service:	Yes.
SLIP/PPP Service:	No.
UUCP Service:	No.
Interactive Accounts:	Yes. Internet mail. Fax, telex, and surface mail delivery services.
Maximum Casual Dial-Up Speed:	9600 bps -or- 2400 bps, depending on your location.
USENET News:	No.
Local File Archives:	No.
Domain Registration Service:	No.
Domain Park Service:	No.
Consulting Services:	No.
DNS Service:	No.
Commercial Traffic:	Yes.

HOW TO SIGN UP
Call for information.

Rates
Message Charges (Within Canada and International):
Up to 1000 characters: $0.70
Up to 2000 characters: $1.00
Up to 3000 characters: $1.30
Each additional 1000 characters (over 3000): $0.15
Fax, Telex, Paper Delivery:
Call for information.

fONOROLA
Ottawa, Ontario
fonorola.net, fonorola.ca

250 Alberta Street, Suite 205
Ottawa, Ontario
K1P 6M1
Voice: (613) 235-3666
Fax: (613) 232-4329
Internet: info@fonorola.net

fONOROLA provides inter-exchange telecommunications in Canada for a full range of voice and data communications services.

Service Area:	Calgary, Montreal, Ottawa, Toronto, Vancouver. Expansion is planned to Edmonton, Halifax, London, Quebec City, and Winnipeg in 1994.
1-800 Service:	Yes. Canadian customers can have 1-800 access in the United States only.
PDN Service:	No.
Connection Via:	ANS.
Leased Line Service:	Yes.
Dedicated Dial-Up Service:	No.
Dedicated Line Speeds Supported:	56 Kbps- 45 Mbps.
SLIP/PPP Service:	Yes. PPP only. Leased line service only.
UUCP Service:	No.
Interactive Accounts:	No.
Maximum Casual Dial-Up Speed:	N/A.
USENET News:	Yes. Full feed, including Clarinet news.
Local File Archives:	Yes. Business-oriented information. RFC archive. "Best of" software files for UNIX, Mac, and PC. Internet publications.
Domain Registration Service:	Yes. Full service.
Domain Park Service:	Yes.

Consulting Service:	Yes. Security. Internet connectivity. Information server setup (e.g. Gopher).
DNS Service:	Yes. Primary and secondary nameservers.
Commercial Traffic:	Yes.

HOW TO SIGN UP
Call or send electronic mail for information.

Rates
From $600.00/month to $10,250.00/month. $350 initial service charge.
Some conditions apply. Call for consultation.

For More Information

FTP:	**Telnet:**	**Gopher:**
nic.fonorola.net	gopher.fonorola.net	gopher.fonorola.net
directory: /pub/	login: **gopher**	

MPACT Immedia
Montreal, Quebec
immedia.ca

1155 bd. Rene-Levesque Ouest/West
Suite 2250
Montreal, Quebec
H3B 4T3
Voice: (514) 397-9747
Fax: (514) 398-0764

Immedia Informatic Corporation provides worldwide electronic
commerce software and services to a variety of industries.   Companies
in manufacturing, transportation, retail, financial services, and
government agencies are using MPACT/Immedia electronic commerce
software, value-added network services, and integration services to
reach their trading partners around the world.

Service Area:	Where TYMNET and Datapac services are available.
1-800 Service:	No.
PDN Service:	Datapac, TYMNET.
Connection Via:	RISQ.
Leased Line Service:	Yes. Call for consultation.
Dedicated Dial-Up Service:	Yes. Call for consultation.
Dedicated Line Speeds Supported:	Call for consultation.
SLIP/PPP Service:	No.
UUCP Service:	No.
Interactive Accounts:	No. Mail access to the Internet is available. It can be composed/read on-line or composed/read off-line using MPACT/Immedia software (software

	supplied at no charge).
Maximum Casual Dial-Up Speed:	9600 bps.
USENET News:	No.
Local File Archives:	No.
Domain Registration Service:	Call for consultation.
Domain Park Service:	No.
Consulting Service:	Yes. Integration services: Electronic commerce planning and cost/benefit analysis, application integration, data mapping, software installation and configuration, systems operations.
DNS Service:	Yes.
Commercial Traffic:	Yes.

HOW TO SIGN UP
Call for information.

Electronic Mail Rates For Basic Services
Service:
One-time service charge: $50.
Monthly organization fee (includes one mailbox): $20.
Monthly charge for additional mailbox: $3.
Monthly charge per gateway: $19.00.
Software:
EXPRESS for the PC and EXPRESS for the Macintosh®: No charge
(One copy of the software is supplied to each client organization, and may be copied for use by other EXPRESS subscribers, members of the organization).
EXPRESS MHS Gateway for LANs: No charge.
Usage:
Charge per 1000 characters sent or received: $0.35.
Communication costs: None.
Telex/Fax: $25.00 monthly charge, communications costs available on request.
Interactive Access Surcharge:
Per minute of interactive mail connection: $0.10.

UUNET Canada
Toronto, Ontario
uunet.ca

1 Yonge Street, Suite 1400
Toronto, Ontario
M5E 1J9
Voice: (416) 368-6621
Fax: (416) 368-1350
Internet: info@uunet.ca

UUNET Canada provides commercial Internet and UUCP networking, wide-area network management, and end-user information services and products. We are Canada's largest commercial IP provider.

UUNET's mission is to provide cost-effective connectivity and services to businesses, government, education, and the home.

Service Area:	Ontario: Hamilton, London, Kitchener-Waterloo, Ottawa, Toronto. Quebec: Montreal, Quebec City. Alberta: Calgary, Edmonton. British Columbia: Vancouver. Nova Scotia: Halifax.
1-800 Service:	Yes.
PDN Service:	Bell ISDN.
Connection Via:	UUNET Canada.
Leased Line Service:	Yes.
Dedicated Dial-Up Service:	Yes.
Dedicated Line Speeds Supported:	Call for consultation.
SLIP/PPP Service:	Yes.
UUCP Service:	Yes.
Interactive Accounts:	No. UUNET Canada has a service called TAC that provides access to Telnet and other interactive Internet services, but customers do not receive accounts on an Internet host, and permanent disk space is not provided.
Maximum Casual Dial-Up Speed:	14,400 bps.
USENET News:	Yes, including Clarinet news.
Local File Archives:	Yes.
Domain Registration Service:	Yes. Full service.
Domain Park Service:	No.
Consulting Services:	Yes.
DNS Service:	Yes. Primary and secondary nameservers.
Commercial Traffic:	Yes.

HOW TO SIGN UP
Call or send electronic mail for information.

Rates
Dial-Up UUCP and Terminal Access:
$20/month plus $6/hour. Shared phone line and modem.
Dial-Up IP (SLIP/PPP):
$50/month plus $6/hour. Shared phone line and modem.
Dedicated Services:
$600/month. V.32bis dial-up to a dedicated phone line and modem. Some conditions apply.
$1200/month. 56 Kbps synchronous serial interface on customer premises. Some conditions apply.

For More Information
FTP:
uunet.ca

WEB
Toronto, Ontario
web.apc.org, web.net

c/o Nirv Community Resource Centre
401 Richmond Street West, Suite 104
Toronto, Ontario
M5V 3A8
Voice: (416) 596-0212
Fax: (416) 596-1374
Internet: support@web.apc.org

*NirvCentre is a nonprofit organization that aims to provide new
information technology and communications resources to organizations
that are not motivated by profit. By doing so, NirvCentre intends to
contribute to building a self-reliant community based on nonprofit
enterprise, cooperation, and mutual aid that, as a community, can
support, maintain, and defend principles of social responsibility, ecology,
and economic justice. In particular, NirvCentre aims to assist those
organizations that advocate, and participate in, making changes to
institutions of all kinds in order to effect a more equal distribution of
wealth and power, and to defend the natural environment.*

*To these ends, NirvCentre operates Web, a nonprofit computer network,
and works to provide and promote affordable global access to
computer and communications technologies and to foster healthy and
productive work environments in nonprofit organizations. WEB provides
electronic communications - e-mail, conferences, fax, and databases to
non-governmental organizations and citizens who are working for the
environment, universal human rights, world peace, and social and
economic justice. A full range of Internet services is expected to be
available in early 1994.*

Service Area:	Toronto, Montreal, Ottawa, Vancouver. Expansion is planned to: Calgary, Edmonton, Guelph, Halifax, Hamilton, London, and Kitchener.
1-800 Service:	No.
PDN Service:	Datapac.
Connection Via:	UUNET Canada.
Leased Line Service:	No.
Dedicated Dial-Up Service:	No.
Dedicated Line Speeds Supported:	N/A.
SLIP/PPP Service:	No.
UUCP Service:	No.

Interactive Accounts:	Yes. Direct connection to the Internet. Currently only mail service is offered. Full Internet services willl be available in 1994. 20Kb permanent storage/user. Unlimited additional mail storage is charged based on the average per month. Menu-driven interface. Custom off-line mail reader (Messenger) supported and supplied for $50 (individual/nonprofit/school user) or $100 (government/corporate users). International e-mail-to-fax gateway. Multi-user accounts. User's manual.
Maximum Casual Dial-Up Speed:	19,200 bps+ (PEP).
USENET News:	Not currently offered. Coming in 1994.
Local File Archives:	Archives of public conferences in the areas of alternative news, environment, international development, human rights, social justice, peace, education, and others.
Domain Registration Service:	No.
Domain Park Service:	Yes.
Consulting Services:	Yes. Online networking, network customization, online group facilitation, international networking (particularly Africa).
DNS Service:	Yes. Primary and secondary nameservers.
Commercial Traffic:	Yes.

HOW TO SIGN UP

Call or send electronic mail for information.

Rates

Individual/Non-profit Organization:

$25 one-time charge for creation of account.
$180/year subscription.
$6/hour for system usage (2 hours/month free).
Datapac (where applicable): $6.50/hour during peak hours (8a.m.. to 8p.m weekdays), $4/hour off-peak (8p.m to 8a.m. and weekends).

Government/Corporate/Industry Association:

$50 one-time charge for creation of account.
$270/year subscription.
$15/hour for system usage.
Datapac (where applicable): $10/hour.

PART 3:
U.S.-BASED PROVIDERS WITH LOCAL ACCESS NUMBERS IN CANADA

America Online Inc.
Vienna, Virginia
aol.com

America Online's corporate mission is to develop "electronic communities" to meet the needs of specific market segments. Focusing on interactive communications, America Online provides its users with a wide variety of features including electronic mail, news/weather/sports, stock quotes, software files, computing support, online classes, and much more. The company has strategic alliances with dozens of leading hardware, software, and media and affinity organizations, including IBM, Apple, Time-Warner, CNN, and Tribune Company, to develop and market online services that appeal to their customers.

8619 Westwood Center Drive
Vienna, Virginia 22182-2285
U.S.A.
Voice: Canada Toll-Free 1-800-827-6364
        Corporate Headquarters: (703) 448-8700

Service Area:	Where TYMNET service is available. There are local access numbers in: Burnaby, Calgary, Dundas, Edmonton, Halifax, Hull, Kitchener, London, Montreal, Ottawa, Quebec City, St. Laurent, Toronto, Vancouver, Winnipeg, Windsor.
Leased Line Service:	No.
Dedicated Dial-Up Service:	No.
SLIP/PPP Service:	No.
UUCP Service:	No.
Interactive Accounts:	Yes. Currently, only Internet mail, but Internet services are scheduled to be introduced throughout 1994.
Maximum Casual Dial-Up Speed:	2400 bps in Burnaby, Dundas, Edmonton, Halifax, Kitchener, London, Quebec City, Windsor. 9600 bps in Calgary, Hull, Montreal, Ottawa, Toronto, St. Laurent, Vancouver, and Winnipeg.
USENET News:	Coming in 1994.
Local File Archives:	Yes.
Domain Registration Service:	No.
Domain Park Service:	No.
Consulting Services:	No.

DNS Service:	No.
Commercial Traffic:	Yes.

HOW TO SIGN UP

Call to register. Software is required (provided at no charge). A merica Online supports all leading platforms including Windows, DOS, Macintosh, and Apple II.

Rates:

US$9.95/month. Includes 5 free hours per month. Additional hours are US$3.50/hour. When you sign up, you receive 10 free hours for your first 30 days.

TYMNET Surcharge:

US$0.20/minute.

Applelink

Herndon, VA
applelink.apple.com

Apple Computer Inc.
P.O. Box 10600
Herndon, Virginia 22070-0600
U.S.A.
Voice: (408) 974-3309
Fax: (703) 318-6701

As Apple's official on-line service, Applelink gives you 24-hour access to Apple and third-party technical support. As well, users have instant, reliable electronic mail service to more than 50,000 Apple users and vendors in 55 countries around the world, and access to late-breaking local, regional, and international news stories about Apple industry and product developments.

Service Area:	Local access numbers in the following cities: Calgary, Edmonton, Halifax, Hamilton, Hespler, London, Montreal, Ottawa, Quebec City, Toronto-Mississauga, Vancouver, Victoria, Winnipeg.
1-800 Service:	No.
PDN Service:	Datapac.
Leased Line Service:	No.
Dedicated Dial-Up Service:	No.
SLIP/PPP Service:	No.
UUCP Service:	No.
Interactive Accounts:	Yes. Internet mail.
Maximum Casual Dial-Up Speed:	9600 bps in Calgary, Montreal, Ottawa, Toronto-Mississauga, Vancouver. 2400 bps in Edmonton, Halifax, Hamilton, Hespler, London, Quebec City, Victoria, Winnipeg.

USENET News:	No.
Local File Archives:	Yes.
Domain Registration Service:	No.
Domain Park Service:	No.
Consulting Services:	No.
DNS Service:	No.
Commercial Traffic:	No.

HOW TO SIGN UP

Call to register.

Rates

$20 setup fee. $35/hour. Minimum billing time of 1 hour/month. Applelink software is required. It will be supplied at no charge upon registration.

BIX

Cambridge, Massachusetts
bix.com

Delphi Internet Services
1030 Massachusetts Avenue
Cambridge, Massachusetts 02138
U.S.A.
Voice: Canada Toll-Free 1-800-695-4775
          Corporate Headquarters: (617) 491-3342
Fax: (617) 491-6642
Internet: info@bix.com

BIX is geared for computing professionals and enthusiasts. While other on-line services cater to computer novices, BIX is the place for knowledgeable people to go for answers to tough questions. You're likely to find many others in similar situations who can offer advice, give technical assistance, or point you in the right direction. BIX is divided into areas called conferences, each devoted to a particular area of interest. Conferences are categorized into groups, usually referred to as "exchanges," so that you can browse through whatever exchange groups interest you and see a list of the conferences they contain.

Service Area:	Where TYMNET service is available. There are local access numbers in: Burnaby, Calgary, Dundas, Edmonton, Halifax, Hull, Kitchener, London, Montreal, Ottawa, Quebec City, St. Laurent, Toronto, Vancouver, Winnipeg, Windsor.
1-800 Service:	No.
PDN Service:	TYMNET.
Leased Line Service:	No.
Dedicated Dial-Up Service:	No.

Dedicated Line Speeds Supported:	Dedicated service is not available.
SLIP/PPP Service:	No.
UUCP Service:	No.
Interactive Accounts:	Yes. Direct connection to the Internet. Internet mail, Telnet, FTP, Finger, WHOIS. Menu-driven. Shell access.
Maximum Casual Dial-Up Speed:	2400 bps in Burnaby, Dundas, Edmonton, Halifax, Kitchener, London, Quebec City, Windsor. 9600 bps in Calgary, Hull, Montreal, Ottawa, Toronto, St. Laurent, Vancouver, and Winnipeg.
USENET News:	Yes.
Local File Archives:	Yes.
Domain Registration Service:	No.
Domain Park Service:	No.
Consulting Services:	No.
DNS Service:	No.
Commercial Traffic:	Yes.

HOW TO SIGN UP
Modem:
*Call your local TYMNET number. Local access numbers are provided at the end of this directory. Type the letter **a** upon connection, but do not press the **<enter>** key. At the "please log in:" prompt, type **bix**. At the "Username" prompt, type **bix.ms** (no password required).*
Internet:
*Telnet to x25.bix.com. At the "Username" prompt, type **bix.ms**.*

Rates
Connect Charges:
CDN$9/hour 6a.m. to 6p.m. on weekdays only. CDN$4/hour on weekends and from 6p.m. to 6a.m. on weekdays. Telnet access: US$1/hour at all times.
Membership:
US$13/month.

CompuServe Incorporated
Columbus, Ohio
compuserve.com

5000 Arlington Centre Blvd.
Columbus, Ohio 43220
U.S.A.
Voice: Canada Toll-Free 1-800-848-8199
        Corporate Headquarters: (614) 457-8600
Fax: (614) 457-0348 (Corporate Office)

CompuServe is committed to being an information industry leader that exceeds customer expectations, challenges its associates with opportunities, provides top-quality products and services, and applies its resources to the betterment of society. With 1.6 million members worldwide, CompuServe is the leading provider of online information services for personal computers worldwide. CompuServe offers nearly 2,000 databases, including information retrieval, communications, and transactional services; an on-line shopping mall featuring merchants selling everything from gourmet food to consumer electronics; and more than 600 interactive forums.

Service Area:	Access is via the CompuServe Packet Network. There are local access numbers in: Calgary, Edmonton, Montreal, Ottawa, Toronto, Vancouver, and Winnipeg.
1-800 Service:	Yes.
PDN Service:	Compuserve Packet Network, Datapac.
Leased Line Service:	No.
Dedicated Dial-Up Service:	No.
SLIP/PPP Service:	No.
UUCP Service:	No.
Interactive Accounts:	Yes. Internet mail.
Maximum Casual Dial-Up Speed:	9600 bps in Calgary, Edmonton, Montreal, Toronto, Vancouver, and Winnipeg. 2400 bps in Ottawa.
USENET News:	No.
Local File Archives:	Yes.
Domain Registration Service:	No.
Domain Park Service:	No.
Consulting Services:	No.
DNS Service:	No.
Commercial Traffic:	Yes.

HOW TO SIGN UP
Call for information.

Rates
Basic Services:
US$8.95/month. Includes US$9.00/month mail allowance, which covers 60 messages of 7500 characters or less sent to or received from Internet, and/or sent to other CompuServe members. Users can only send text messages to the Internet. There is no charge for mail received from other CompuServe members.
Extended Services:
2400 bps: US$8/hour.
9600 bps: US$16/hour.
Datapac Surcharge:
2400 bps: US$8/hour.
9600 bps: US$20/hour.
Access through CompuServe Packet Network:
No surcharge.
1-800 Access:
US$34.70/hour (up to 14,400 bps).

DELPHI

Cambridge, Massachusetts
delphi.com

Delphi Internet Services
1030 Massachusetts Avenue
Cambridge, Massachusetts 02138
Voice: (617) 491-3393
                Corporate Headquarters: (617) 491-3342
Fax: (617) 491-6642
Internet: info@delphi.com

Delphi Internet Services Corporation develops and markets interactive
entertainment and communications services for consumers worldwide.
Delphi's online service has enabled people all over the world to interact,
retrieve information, compete, transact business, and play games in a
friendly, computer-based environment. Delphi's primary goal is to
provide an environment for electronic communities of similarly interested
people to thrive and interact on a global basis.

Service Area:	Where TYMNET service is available. There are local access numbers in: Burnaby, Calgary, Dundas, Edmonton, Halifax, Hull, Kitchener, London, Montreal, Ottawa, Quebec City, St. Laurent, Toronto, Vancouver, Winnipeg, Windsor.
1-800 Service:	No.
PDN Service:	TYMNET and Datapac.
Leased Line Service:	No.
Dedicated Dial-Up Service:	No.
Dedicated Line Speeds Supported:	N/A.
SLIP/PPP Service:	No.
UUCP Service:	No.
Interactive Accounts:	Yes. Telnet, FTP, Gopher, Archie, WWW, IRC, WAIS, WHOIS, Finger, Netfind, Ping, Traceroute. Menu-driven.
Maximum Casual Dial-Up Speed:	2400 bps in Burnaby, Dundas, Edmonton, Halifax, Kitchener, London, Quebec City, Windsor. 9600 bps in Calgary, Hull, Montreal, Ottawa, Toronto, St. Laurent, Vancouver, and Winnipeg.
USENET News:	Yes. Approximately 3,000 newgroups.
Local File Archives:	Yes.
Domain Registration Service:	No.
Domain Park Service:	No.
Consulting Services:	No.
DNS Service:	No.
Commercial Traffic:	Yes.

HOW TO SIGN UP
Internet:
*Telnet to delphi.com, login as **joindelphi**, password is **ZZ2345**.*

Modem:
*Call your local TYMNET number. Local access numbers are provided at the end of this directory. When the connection is established, wait 5 seconds, then type the letter **o**. At the "please log in:" prompt, type **delphi**. When asked for "Username," type **joindelphi**. The password is **ZZ2345**. For general information about Delphi, use the password **info** instead.*

Rates
Membership:
10/4 Plan: US$10.00 month. 4 four hours included. Each additional hour is US$4.00/hour.
20/20 Advantage Plan: US$19.00 enrolment fee. US$20.00/month. 20 free hours included. Each additional hour is US$1.80/hour.
Internet Services Surcharge:
US$3.00/month.
TYMNET Access:
US$9.00/hour from 6a.m. to 6p.m. on weekdays only. US$3.00/hour on weekends and from 6p.m. to 6a.m. on weekdays.
Datapac Access:
US$25.80/hour.

For More Information:
Telnet:
delphi.com
*login: **joindelphi***
*password: **info***

GEnie
Rockville, Maryland
genie.geis.com

GE Information Services
P.O. Box 6403
Rockville, Maryland 20850-1785
U.S.A.
Voice: Canada Toll-Free 1-800-638-9636
Fax: (301) 251-6421

GEnie calls itself "diverse, dynamic, and in-depth." Users can explore over 500 distinct interest areas, ranging from highly technical computer areas dedicated to specific computer platforms, to powerful information tools for business, to sections with broad appeal, such as pets, movies, and music. GEnie offers a wide variety of on-line services, including business and professional services, investment services, real-time multi-player games, and communications services.

Service Area:	Local access numbers in: Calgary, Edmonton, Halifax, Hamilton, Kitchener, London, Mississauga, Montreal, Ottawa, Quebec City, Toronto, Vancouver, Victoria, Winnipeg.
1-800 Service:	No.

PDN Service:	Datapac.
Leased Line Service:	No.
Dedicated Dial-Up Service:	No.
SLIP/PPP Service:	No.
UUCP Service:	No.
Interactive Accounts:	Yes. Internet mail. Gateway connection to the Internet. Worldwide e-mail-to-fax service.
Maximum Casual Dial-Up Speed:	9600 bps in Calgary, Montreal, Mississauga, Vancouver. 2400 bps in Edmonton, Halifax, Hamilton, Kitchener, London, Ottawa, Quebec City, Toronto, Victoria, Winnipeg.
USENET News:	No.
Local File Archives:	Yes. Shareware, freeware.
Domain Registration Service:	No.
Domain Park Service:	No.
Consulting Service:	No.
DNS Service:	No.
Commercial Traffic:	Yes.

HOW TO SIGN UP
Modem:
*Set communications software for half duplex (local echo) at 2400 baud. Set communications software to 8N1 or 7E1 for IBM compatibles. Dial 1-800-387-8330. Immediately upon connection, type **HHH**, then press the <enter> key. When you see the **u#=** prompt, type **signup**, then press the <enter> key and wait about 10 seconds. You will be guided through the registration process, and your password and GEnie id will be generated by the system. Have a major credit card ready. A list of local access telephone numbers will be displayed. Allow 1-2 business days for the account to be activated.*

Rates
CDN$10.95/month for 4 hours connect time during non-peak hours. Additional hours are CDN$4.00/hour during non-peak hours and CDN$16/hour during peak hours. Peak hours are from 8a.m. to 6p.m. on weekdays only. Includes electronic mail, multiplayer games, bulletin boards, chat lines, real-time conferences. There is a surcharge of CDN$8.00/hour for 9600 bps access.
Access Through Datapac:
Surcharge of CDN$6.00/hour.
Access Through A Local Access Number:
No surcharge.

HoloNet
Berkeley, California
holonet.net

Information Access Technologies Inc.

46 Shattuck Square, Suite 11
Berkeley, California
U.S.A.
Voice: (510) 704-0160
Fax: (510) 704-8019
Internet: info@holonet.net

Information Access Technologies provides Internet access for individuals, businesses, e-mail systems, BBSes and more through dial-up access and UUCP accounts.

Service Area:	Local access numbers in: Calgary, Ottawa, Montreal, Toronto, Vancouver.
1-800 Service:	No.
Leased Line Service:	No.
Dedicated Dial-Up Service:	No.
Dedicated Line Speeds Supported:	Dedicated service is not available in Canada.
SLIP/PPP Service:	No.
UUCP Service:	Yes. Mail and news feeds. Users can modify their own newsgroup subscriptions.
Interactive Accounts:	Yes. Direct connection to the Internet. 256K/month permanent disk space. Additional disk space is US$1.00/MB/month. Telnet, FTP, Gopher, WAIS, WWW, IRC, Archie. Menu-driven. QWK-compatible readers supported.
Maximum Casual Dial-Up Speed:	2400 bps in Canada.
USENET News:	Yes. Full feed.
Local File Archives:	Yes. Mac files.
Domain Registration Service:	Yes. Full service.
Domain Park Service:	Yes.
Consulting Service:	No.
DNS Service:	Yes. Primary and secondary nameservers.
Commercial Traffic:	Yes.

HOW TO SIGN UP
Modem:

City	Modem Line	Speed
Toronto	(416) 495-1300	300-2400 bps
Ottawa	(613) 563-9085	300-2400 bps
Vancouver	(604) 669-4040	300-2400 bps
Calgary	(403) 234-7841	300-2400 bps
Montreal	(514) 282-0222	300-2400 bps

Once connected, follow these steps:

Prompt on Screen   What you Type

--	<enter> several times once connected
--	x <enter>
*	set 1:0,7:0,15:0 <enter>
*	31371202020501 <enter>
username	holonet <enter>
password	<enter>
psinet_ts>	terminal download <enter>
psinet_ts>	holonet <enter>

*Once you are connected, login as **guest**.*

*Note: If you do not get a prompt after you type **x <enter>**, try turning off MNP*

Internet:
*Telnet to holonet.net, login as **guest**. No password required.*

Rates:
Membership:
US$6/month or US$60/year. Good for US$6 of credit every month.
Connect Charges:
US$4.50/hour during off-peak hours. US$10/hour during peak hours.

For More Information
FTP:	*Telnet:*
holonet.net	*holonet.net*
directory: info	*login: **guest***

MCI Mail
Washington, D.C.
mcimail.com

1133 19th Street
Washington, D.C. 20036
U.S.A.
Voice: Canada Toll-Free 1-800-444-6245
        Direct Dial: (202) 833-8484
Fax: (202) 416-5858
Internet: 3393527@mcimail.com (MCI Mail Customer Support)

MCI Mail is a premier global electronic mail network with unparalled value-added services. MCI Mail is reachable by MCI Mail Global Access (direct dial to a local in-country number) in 30 countries and is available through packet-switched access in 90 countries, including the 30 countries served by MCI Mail Global Access.

Service Area:	Where Datapac and TYMNET are available.
1-800 Service:	No.
PDN Service:	Datapac and TYMNET.
Leased Line Service:	No.
Dedicated Dial-Up Service:	No.
SLIP/PPP Service:	No.
UUCP Service:	No.

Interactive Accounts:	Yes. Internet mail. Domestic/ international e-mail-to-fax and e-mail-to-telex gateways. E-mail to surface mail service.
Maximum Casual Dial-Up Speed:	9600 bps.
USENET News:	No.
Local File Archives:	No.
Domain Registration Service:	No.
Domain Park Service:	No.
Consulting Service:	No.
DNS Service:	No.
Commercial Traffic:	Yes.

HOW TO SIGN UP
Call to register.

Rates:
Annual mailbox fee: US$35.00.
Message prices:
1st 500 characters: US$0.50.
2nd 500 characters: add US$0.10.
1,001-10,000 characters: add US$0.10/1000 characters.
>10,000 characters: add US$0.05/1000 characters.
Call MCI Mail for pricing on fax, telex, and paper mail services.
Datapac Access:
US$0.15/minute.
TYMNET Access:
US$0.25/minute.

NovaLink
Shrewsbury, Massachusetts
novalink.com

79 Boston Turnpike, Suite 409
Shrewsbury, Massachusetts 01545
U.S.A.
Voice: Canada Toll-Free (800) 274-2814
          DirectDial: (508) 754-9910
Fax: (508) 793-2037
Internet: info@novalink.com

NovaLink is a service for consumers and business people looking for access to the Internet. It is also a major content provider for entertainment and other social-interactive services on the Internet, featuring award-winning games like Legends of Future Past, moderated Special Interest Groups, file libraries, and teleconferencing. Novalink is a friendly outpost on the electronic frontier. Try us - we're fun.

Service Area:	There are local access numbers in the following cities: Calgary, Edmonton, Montreal, Ottawa, Toronto, Vancouver, Winnipeg.
1-800 Service:	No.
PDN Service:	CompuServe Packet Network.
Leased Line Service:	No.
Dedicated Dial-Up Service:	No.
Dedicated Line Speeds Supported:	N/A.
SLIP/PPP Service:	No.
UUCP Service:	No.
Interactive Accounts:	Yes. Direct connection to the Internet. Permanent disk space. Telnet, FTP, Gopher, IRC, Archie, rlogin, tn3270. Menu-driven. Shell access. QWK-compatible off-line mail readers supported and supplied. Local/national/international e-mail-to-fax gateway.
Maximum Casual Dial-Up Speed:	2400 bps in Ottawa. 9600 bps in Calgary, Edmonton, Montreal, Toronto, Vancouver, and Winnipeg.
USENET News:	Yes. Full feed.
Local File Archives:	Yes. IBM PC, Windows software, OS/2, Macintosh, Atari software. Special-interest libraries on subjects such as role-playing games, the occult, music and lyrics, beer/zymurgy, astronomy, and much more.
Domain Registration Service:	No.
Domain Park Service:	No.
Consulting Services:	No.
DNS Service:	No.
Commercial Traffic:	Yes.

HOW TO SIGN UP
Modem:
Set your modem to 7E1. Call your local CompuServe Packet Network number (see the list below). Press **<enter>** *once connected, and enter* **NOVA** *at the "Host Name:" prompt. You will be connected to Novalink. Type* **new** *to register or type* **info** *for information about Novalink.*

City	Modem Number	Speed
Calgary	(403) 294-9155	2400 bps
	(403) 294-9120	9600 bps
Edmonton	(403) 466-5083	2400 bps
	(403) 440-2744	9600 bps
Ottawa	(613) 830-7385	2400 bps

Montreal	(514) 879-8519	2400 bps
	(514) 879-5826	9600 bps
Toronto	(416) 367-1743	2400 bps
	(416) 367-8122	9600 bps
Vancouver	(604) 737-2452	2400 bps
	(604) 739-8194	9600 bps
Winnipeg	(204) 489-9292	2400 bps
	(204) 489-9747	9600 bps

Internet:
*telnet to novalink.com, login as **new***

Rates:
US$12.95 sign-up fee. US$9.95/month membership fee.
US$6.00/hour through CompuServe Packet Network. US$1.80/hour
through the Internet or direct dial.

For More Information
FTP:	Telnet:	Gopher:
ftp.novalink.com	novalink.com	gopher.novalink.com
directory: /info	login: **info**	

Canadian TYMNET Numbers
For Further Information: 1-800-368-3180

ALBERTA
Calgary	(403) 232-6653	2400 bps
Calgary	(403) 264-5472	9600 bps
Edmonton	(403) 484-4404	2400 bps

BRITISH COLUMBIA
Burnaby,Vancouver	(604) 683-7620	2400 bps
Vancouver	(604) 683-7453	9600 bps

MANITOBA
Winnipeg	(204) 654-4041	2400 bps
Winnipeg	(204) 654-0992	9600 bps

NOVA SCOTIA
Halifax	(902) 492-4901	2400 bps

ONTARIO
Dundas	(905) 628-5908	2400 bps
Kitchener	(519) 742-7613	2400 bps
London	(519) 641-8362	2400 bps
Hull, Ottawa	(613) 563-2910	2400 bps
Hull, Ottawa	(613) 563-3777	9600 bps
Toronto	(416) 365-7630	2400 bps
Toronto	(416) 361-3028	9600 bps
Windsor	(519) 977-7256	2400 bps

QUEBEC
Montreal/St. Laurent	(514) 747-2996	2400 bps
Montreal/St. Laurent	(514) 748-8057	9600 bps
Quebec City	(514) 647-1116	2400 bps

How to Access BT TYMNET's Worldwide Information Service

The most recent list of BT TYMNET access numbers and other material about BT TYMNET is available on-line on BT TYMNET's Worldwide Information Service. You can access this information using your computer and your modem:

(1) Call your local TYMNET number.
(2) When the connection is established, type the letter **a**.
(3) At the "please log in:" prompt, type **information**, then press the **<enter>** key.

Datapac
For information about Datapac, call 1-800-267-6574.

THE DIRECTORY OF COMMUNITY NETWORKING ORGANIZATIONS IN CANADA

· ·

© 1994 Rick Broadhead and Jim Carroll

This directory lists Canadian communities which had operational community computer systems or active organizing committees in January 1994. Many of these initiatives involve providing the community with access to the Internet, as well as to local information resources.

If you would like to keep abreast of the community networking movement in Canada, we suggest that you join the **can-freenet** mailing list, which has been established for the discussion of Canadian community networking initiatives. To subscribe to the list, send the message **subscribe can-freenet FIRSTNAME LASTNAME** (replacing FIRSTNAME and LASTNAME with your first and last name), to **listserv@cunews.carleton.ca.** An organization called **Telecommunities Canada** is being incorporated to coordinate Canadian community networking activities on a national level.

A good source of information on community networking is the University of Saskatchewan Gopher server at **gopher.usask.ca,** in **Other/Testing/Freenet_Documents**. There, you'll find papers, reports, and documentation related to community networking. Carleton University also maintains a community networking archive at the anonymous FTP site **alfred.carleton.ca**, in directory **/pub/freenet**.

The **National Public Telecomputing Network** (NPTN) in Cleveland, Ohio is a coordinating body for Free-Net organizations worldwide. The NPTN maintains a list of Free-Nets and organizing committees on their anonymous FTP host, as well as general information about how to start a Free-Net in your city or town. You can retrieve the material by anonymous FTP to **nptn.org**, in the **pub/info.nptn** directory. Send electronic mail to **info@nptn.org** for further information.

BRITISH COLUMBIA

CIAO! Free-Net
Trail, British Columbia
Status: Open

Contact:
Ken McLean
School District #11 (Trail)
2079 Columbia Avenue
Trail, British Columbia
V1R 1K7
Voice: (604) 368-2233
Internet: kmcclean@ciao.trail.bc.ca

Prince George Free-Net
Prince George, British Columbia
Status: Organizing

Contact:
Lynda Williams
210 North Quinn Street
Prince George, British Columbia
V2M 3J5
Voice: (604) 562-2131, local 400
Fax: (604) 562-8463
Internet: williams@cnc.bc.ca

Sea to Sky Free-Net Association
Squamish, British Columbia
Status: Organizing

Contact:
Detlef Rudolph
Box 2539
Squamish, British Columbia
V0N 3G0
Voice: (604) 892-5531
Fax: (604) 892-5227
Internet: drudolph@cue.bc.ca

Vancouver Free-Net
Vancouver, British Columbia
Status: Organizing

Contact:
Brian Campbell
c/o Vancouver Public Library
750 Burrard Street
Vancouver, British Columbia
V6Z 1X5
Voice: (604) 665-3944
Internet: briancam@vpl.vancouver.bc.ca

Victoria Free-Net
Victoria, British Columbia
Status: Open

Contact:
Victoria Free-Net Association
c/o Vancouver Island Advanced Technology Centre
Suite 203-1110 Government Street
Victoria, British Columbia
V8W 1Y2
Voice: (604) 389-6026
Internet: vifa@freenet.victoria.bc.ca

ALBERTA

Calgary Free-Net
Calgary, Alberta
Status: Organizing

Contact:
Shawn Henry
c/o The Canada West Foundation
#810, 400-3rd Avenue SW
Calgary, Alberta
T2P 4H2
Voice: (403) 264-9535
Fax: (403) 269-4776
Internet: henry@acs.ucalgary.ca

Edmonton Free-Net
Edmonton, Alberta
Status: Organizing

Contact:
Doug Poff
Information Technology
4-40 Cameron Library

University of Alberta
Edmonton, Alberta
T6G 2J8
Voice: (403) 492-4770
Fax: (403) 492-8302
Internet: dpoff@library.ualberta.ca

SASKATCHEWAN

Saskatoon Free-Net
Saskatoon, Saskatchewan
Status: Organizing

Contact:
Peter Scott
438 5th Street East
Saskatoon, Saskatchewan
S7H 1E9
Voice: (306) 966-5920
Internet: scottp@herald.usask.ca

MANITOBA

Winnipeg Free-Net
Winnipeg, Manitoba
Status: Organizing

Contact:
Terry Lewycky
c/o Infopak Communications
#7 Killarney
P.O. Box 34027
Winnipeg, Manitoba
Voice: (204) 269-0797
Internet: lewycky@mbnet.mb.ca

ONTARIO

North Shore Free-Net
Elliot Lake, Ontario
Status: Organizing

Contact:
Alan Wilson
81 Central Avenue
Elliot Lake, Ontario

P5A 2G4
Voice: (705) 848-5106
Fax: (705) 848-9225
Internet: alanwils@vef.north.net

Hamilton, Ontario
Status: Organizing

Contact:
Jim Bryce
c/o Computing and Information Services
McMaster University GH-226
1280 Main Street West
Hamilton, Ontario
L8S 4L8
Voice :   (905) 525-9140, ext. 23048
Fax: (905) 528-3773
Internet: bryce@McMaster.CA

HOMEnet
London, Ontario
Status: Organizing

Contact:
Joe Swan
c/o Information London
325 Queens Avenue
London, Ontario
N6B 1X2
Voice :   (519) 432-8887
Fax: (519) 432-1106
Internet: joeswan@julian.uwo.ca

Niagara Free-Net
St. Catharines, Ontario
Status: Organizing

Contact:
Jon Radue
c/o Computer Science Department
Brock University
St. Catharines, Ontario
L2S 3A1
Voice: (905) 688-5550, ext. 3867
Internet: jradue@sandcastle.cosc.brocku.ca

National Capital Free-Net
Ottawa, Ontario
Status: Open

Contact:
National Capital Free-Net
c/o Carleton University
1125 Colonel By Drive
Ottawa, Ontario
K1S 5B6
Voice: (613) 788-3947
Internet: ncf@freenet.carleton.ca

Sudbury Free-Net
Sudbury, Ontario
Status: Organizing

Contact:
Steve Beyon
c/o Computing and Telecommunications Services
Laurentian University
Sudbury, Ontario
P3E 2C6
Voice: (705) 675-1151
Fax: (705) 673-6553
Internet: steve@nickel.laurentian.ca

Thunder Bay Free-Net
Thunder Bay, Ontario
Status: Organizing

Contact:
Don Watson
c/o Computing Services
Lakehead University
Thunder Bay, Ontario
P7B 5E1
Voice :   (807) 343-8354
Fax: (807) 343-8023
Internet: dwatson@flash.lakeheadu.ca

Toronto Free-Net
Toronto, Ontario
Status: Organizing

Contact:
Laine G.M. Ruus
c/o Data Library Service
University of Toronto Library
130 St. George Street
Toronto, Ontario
M5S 1A5
Voice: (416) 978-5365
Internet: laine@vm.utcc.utoronto.ca

QUEBEC

Montreal, Quebec
Status: Organizing

Contact:
Michel Dumais
8965A Berri
Montreal, Quebec
H2M 1P8
Voice: (514) 388-7289
Internet: dumais@cam.org

NOVA SCOTIA

Metro*CAN
Halifax-Dartmouth Metro Area Community Access Network
Halifax, Nova Scotia
Status: Organizing

Contact:
Renee Davis
6234 Summit Street
Halifax, Nova Scotia
B31 1R7
Voice: (902) 424-2862
Fax: (902) 424-0129
Internet: davisr@duncan.alt.ns.ca

NEWFOUNDLAND

Newfoundland and Labrador Community Computer Network
St. John's, Newfoundland
Status: Organizing

Contact:
Randy Dodge
c/o Computing and Communications Department
Memorial University of Newfoundland
St. John's, Newfoundland
A1C 5S7
Voice: (709) 737-4594
Fax: (709) 737-3514
Internet: randy@kean.ucs.mun.ca

THE DIRECTORY OF GOPHER SERVERS AND CAMPUS-WIDE INFORMATION SYSTEMS IN CANADA

....

This is a directory of over 100 Gopher servers and campus-wide information systems (CWIS) in Canada. Entries in this directory are structured like this:

Name of the organization sponsoring the Gopher/CWIS
Name of Department (if applicable)
City where the Gopher/CWIS is located

Brief description of the institution (optional)

ACCESS:	How to access the Gopher/CWIS.
Contains:	Some examples of the type of information that can be found on the Gopher/CWIS.

You can access all the Gopher servers and Campus Wide Information Systems in this directory using either Gopher or telnet. Some organizations give you the choice of using either Gopher or telnet (e.g. the University of Alberta).

Gopher

On most systems where a Gopher client has been installed, you can go directly to a particular Gopher server by typing the word Gopher followed by the domain name of the Gopher server you want to access. For example, to connect to the Gopher server at the University of Alberta, you would type:

gopher cwis.srv.ualberta.ca

A Word About Ports

As you use this directory, you will notice that the addresses of some Gopher servers specify a port. For example, the address of the SchoolNet Gopher server is **ernest.ccs.carleton. ca, port 419**. A port is a way of specifying a specific application at an Internet address. A port number distinguishes applications from each other, so multiple applications can be accessed on the same Internet address. To access a Gopher server that uses a port number, try placing the port number after the address of the Gopher server. For example, to access the SchoolNet Gopher, you would type:

gopher ernest.ccs.carleton.ca 419

This will work on most UNIX systems. VMS systems may require that you specify the port in a different way. On many VMS systems, you have to place **/port=** before the port number. For example:

gopher ernest.ccs.carleton.ca /port=419

Names

Some sites have chosen a special name for their Gopher server or Campus Wide Information System. For example, Lakehead University in Thunder Bay, Ontario calls its Gopher LUCI — an acronym that stands for Lakehead University Campus Information. When the Gopher or CWIS has a name, it will be indicated in brackets after the name of the organization or after the name of the department responsible for the Gopher.

Gopher Clients

To access the Gopher servers in this directory, you will need to have access to a Gopher client. If you are running SLIP/PPP or if you have a dedicated Internet connection, the client will be located on your computer or on your organization's computer system. If you have an Internet account on an Internet Service Provider's machine, the client may be located on the computer that you are dialing into. However, not all Internet Service Providers have installed Gopher clients. If a Gopher client has been installed on your Internet host, you should be able to start it by typing **gopher**. This will connect you to a Gopher server. If your Internet Service

Provider or organization is running a Gopher server, this is Gopher server you will probably be connected to. If a Gopher client isn't installed locally, you can use the public Gopher clients listed below. While these clients are available to anyone on the Internet, only use these clients if you have don't have access to your own Gopher client. A local Gopher client is much faster, and it significantly reduces the drain on overall Internet resources. If a Gopher client isn't available on your Internet host, ask your Internet Service Provider or local computing staff if they can install one.

To access one of these public Gopher clients, telnet to the Internet address indicated, and log in using the userid specified in the table below. Passwords are not required.

Internet Address of Client	Location	Userid
consultant.micro.umn.edu	Minnesota	gopher
ux1.cso.uiuc.edu	Illinois	gopher
panda.uiowa.edu	Iowa	------
gopher.msu.edu	Michigan	gopher
gopher.unc.edu	North Carolina	gopher
gopher.ora.com	California	gopher

For More Information on Gopher

New information is constantly being added to existing Gopher servers, and new Gopher servers are being established every day. For more information about Gopher, we suggest that you monitor the **comp.infosystems.gopher** and alt.gopher newsgroups in USENET. We also recommend a document called *Frequently Asked Questions About Gopher*. It is available by anonymous FTP to **rtfm.mit.edu** in the directory **pub/usenet/news.answers**. The file name is **gopher-faq**. You could also join one of the mailing lists that have been established for the discussion of Gopher, although these discussions can be quite technical at times. To join the Gopher News mailing list, send electronic mail to **gopher-news-request@boombox.micro.umn.edu** with the message **subscribe gopher-news firstname lastname**, replacing firstname and lastname with your first name and last name. To join the Gopher Announce mailing list, send electronic mail to **gopher-announce-request@boombox. micro.umn.edu** with the message **subscribe gopher-announce firstname lastname**, replacing firstname and lastname with your first name and last name. Gopher Announce is a moderated list for the announcement of new or updated Gopher software or services.

Acadia University
Wolfville, Nova Scotia

ACCESS:	Gopher: gopher.acadiau.ca
Contains:	information on the Acadia University Senate (e.g. Senate membership information, Senate committee reports, Senate minutes); information on Faculty Councils and other committees; information from the training and development library; information from the bookstore; student information (e.g. student handbook, information from the Career Planning and Employment Center); Academic information (e.g. academic regulations, calendar dates, course timetables, information from different faculties); information on current events (e.g. news releases, information from the Acadia Art Gallery); information from the library (e.g. library guides, library hours.); Information from the Computer Science Club (e.g. events, directory of faculty and staff in the Computer Science Department).

ACAATO
Ontario, Canada

ACAATIO is the Association of Colleges of Applied Arts and Technology of Ontario.

ACCESS:	Gopher: info.senecac.on.ca, port 2000
Contains:	General information about ACAATO; information about the ACAATO Secretariat; information about the Colleges of Applied Arts and Technology (CAAT) Steering Committee; information from the Council of Governors and the Council of Presidents.

University of Alberta
Edmonton, Alberta

ACCESS:	Telnet: cwis.srv.ualberta.ca, login as "gopherc"
	Gopher: cwis.srv.ualberta.ca
Contains:	Information about campus events and activities (e.g. conferences and conventions, speakers, sports schedules); information about student services (e.g. career and placement services, job postings, workshops, career fairs); information about the library (e.g. access to the library catalogue, telephone numbers, hours, information about the archives).

Bedford Institute of Oceanography (BIOME)
Dartmouth, Nova Scotia

ACCESS:	Gopher: biome.bio.dfo.ca
Contains:	Scientific information related to habitat ecology.

University of British Columbia (View UBC)
Vancouver, British Columbia

ACCESS:	Gopher: gopher.ubc.ca
Contains:	General information about UBC (e.g. facts and figures about the university, policy handbook); information on various departments & faculties; information on construction and renovation projects at UBC; human resources and occupational health & safety newsletters; UBC policy handbook; exam schedules; information on varsity athletic home events; bus schedules for services originating or terminating at UBC; information about the UBC bookstore; information about UBC Press (e.g. lists of books in print, how to order, description of services offered); UBC faculty and staff telephone directory; UBC on-line library catalogue.

British Columbia Electronic Library Network (InfoServ)
Victoria, British Columbia

The Electronic Library Network was established in 1989 to coordinate and support resource sharing among libraries in 24 B.C. colleges, universities, and institutions. ELN's mission is to provide equal, timely, and economic access to information resources beyond institutional library collections and existing services.

ACCESS:	Gopher: infoserv.uvic.ca
Contains:	British Columbia resources with an emphasis on B.C. post-secondary institutions and their libraries.

British Columbia Ministry of Environment, Lands and Parks
Victoria, British Columbia

ACCESS:	Gopher: gopher.env.gov.bc.ca
Contains:	Information about water management: information about water well logs in British Columbia; information about groundwater issues in British Columbia; snow survey bulletins; information about the groundwater observation well network; information about groundwater staff; information about groundwater resources of British Columbia; list of industry contacts in B.C., maps and images;

Brock University
St. Catharines, Ontario

ACCESS:	Gopher: gopher.ac.brocku.ca
Contains:	Information about Brock University (e.g. facts about Brock, direct telephone numbers, emergency telephone numbers, important dates in the university calendar, electronic mail addresses of faculty and staff); information from Administration departments (e.g. External Relations — campus news, research news, media releases); information from the Registrar's office (e.g. undergraduate calendar, undergraduate calendar dates, academic regulations, registrar's office directory), information about student services (e.g. counselling services, health care services, financial aid, monthly student services newsletter, upcoming events); information about the library (e.g. hours, services, staff, library publications).

University of Calgary
Calgary, Alberta

ACCESS:	Gopher: gopher.ucalgary.ca
Contains:	Information about the library (e.g. access to the library catalogue, hours, general information); information from various faculties and departments (e.g. Faculty of Medicine, Department of Computer Science); announcements of events (e.g. athletic events, university events); university documents (e.g. President's address, information on job rotation); electronic campus telephone directory; astronomical information provided by the Royal Astronomical Society (Calgary Chapter).

Camosun College
Victoria, British Columbia

ACCESS:	Gopher: gopher.camosun.bc.ca
Contains:	Electronic campus telephone book; information about the library (e.g. hours, services, connection to the catalogue); committee minutes (e.g. Board of Governors, Faculty Association); notices and announcements; information about community education services; job postings; newsletters (e.g. Computing Services newsletter).

Canadian Climate Centre
Atmospheric Environment Service
Downsview, Ontario

ACCESS:	Gopher: cmits02.dow.on.doe.ca
Contains:	Weather forecasts; weather maps; weather charts; weather satellite images.

Canadian Government X.400 Address Enquiry (via Natural Resources Canada)
Ottawa, Ontario

ACCESS:	Gopher: copper.emr.ca
Contains:	Searchable database of Canadian government X.400 addresses

CANARIE INC.
Ottawa, Ontario

ACCESS:	Gopher: mercure.lacitec.on.ca, port 71
Contains:	Membership application forms; mission; objectives; information on the CANARIE program; CANARIE documents (e.g. vision statement, business plan); selected articles.

Carleton University
Main Gopher
Ottawa, Ontario

ACCESS:	Gopher: gopher.carleton.ca
Contains:	Access to other Carleton Gopher s.

Carleton University
Admissions Gopher
Ottawa, Ontario

ACCESS:	Gopher: admissions.carleton.ca
Contains:	Canadian university calendars; Carleton statistics; Carleton undergraduate calendar.

Carleton University
Computing and Communications Services
Ottawa, Ontario

ACCESS:	Gopher: ernest.carleton.ca
Contains:	General information about computing services at Carleton.

Carleton University
Campus Wide Information System
Ottawa, Ontario

Access:	Telnet: info.carleton.ca. Type decvt100 when prompted for terminal type

Contains:	Academic information (e.g. information about admissions and registration, academic dates, scholarship information, student records information, information about faculties and departments); information about administrative services (e.g. bookings, buildings and grounds information, development and alumni services, parking, public relations, Art Gallery, recycling, information about the Vice-Presidents and President); information about events and entertainment (e.g. pubs, cafeterias, lectures, exhibits, concerts, plays, games room); directory services (e.g. staff directory, electronic mail addresses, fax numbers); schedules (e.g. varsity schedules, class and exam schedules); employment information (e.g. placement and career services, personnel policies, employment opportunities); information about athletics (e.g. facilities and memberships, athletics and recreation programs, sports medicine); student services information (e.g. housing, food services, health, safety, student government); university policies and procedures; information about the library; statistics and facts about Carleton; information about supportive resources (e.g. human rights and equity, daycare, resources for women); information about purchasing (e.g. vehicle rental, courier services).

Carleton University Library
Ottawa, Canada

ACCESS:	**Gopher: library3.library.carleton.ca**
Contains:	Library hours; information about library services; library news; list of library contacts; library guides; information about library tours and orientation; access to the library catalogue.

Carleton University
Media and Community Relations
Ottawa, Ontario

ACCESS:	**Gopher: gsro.carleton.ca, port 413**
Contains:	Directory of experts by academic/administrative unit; searchable database of experts at Carleton; general information about Carleton.

Carleton University
Faculty of Graduate Studies and Research
Ottawa, Ontario

ACCESS:	**Gopher: gsro.carleton.ca**
Contains:	Academic calendar; course schedule; directory of supervisors for graduate programs; funding information for graduate students; research interests and recent publications of faculty members; information about research funding received by faculty members.

Chedoke-McMaster Hospitals
Hamilton, Ontario

ACCESS:	**Gopher: darwin.cmh.mcmaster.ca**
Contains:	General information about the Chedoke-McMaster Hospitals (e.g. services and programs, staff, hospital management, affiliations); electronic telephone book.

La Cité Collegiale (Bilingual Gopher)
Ottawa, Ontario

ACCESS:	**Gopher: mercure.lacitec.on.ca**
Contains:	List of members of the Board of Governors; overview of the College; academic calendar (French only).

Communications Research Centre
Ottawa, Ontario

ACCESS:	**Gopher: debra.doc.ca**
Contains:	General information about the Communications Research Centre; information about Industry Canada; Industry Canada documents (searchable); information about CHAT (Conversational Hypertext Access Technology); CBC radio programs in digital form; list of transcripts available from CBC Radio; list of products available from CBC Radio.

Community Learning Network
Sidney, British Columbia

The Community Learning Network (CLN) is a pilot project of the Education Technology Centre (ETC) and the Ministry of Education in British Columbia. The Community Learning Network provides electronic mail, information services, and conferencing facilities to students and teachers in British Columbia.

ACCESS:	**Gopher: cln.etc.bc.ca**
Contains:	Information about the Community Learning Network (CLN) and the Education Technology Centre (ETC); information from the following B.C. Ministries: Education, Environment, Lands and Parks, Forests, Government Services, Health, Tourism-Culture, and Transportation-Highways; B.C. Government telephone directory; information from B.C. publishers (e.g. catalogues, on-line books); reference materials about the forest.

Conestoga College (CCINFO)
Barrie, Ontario

ACCESS:	**Gopher:** ccinfo.conestogac.on.ca
Contains:	Academic computer lab hardware configurations; information about the software available in each of the academic labs; network server configuration

Confederation of University Faculty Associations of British Columbia (CUFA/BC)
Vancouver, British Columbia

CUFA/BC represents approximately 3500 faculty and professional librarians at Simon Fraser University, University of British Columbia, and University of Victoria.

ACCESS:	**Gopher:** epix.cic.sfu.ca
Contains:	General information about CUFA/BC; information about the CUFA/BC library collection; CUFA/BC newsletters; news releases; Government of British Columbia post-secondary education news releases; electronic CUFA/BC phonebook; B.C. post-secondary legislation; information about post-secondary education in British Columbia.

Dalhousie University(DalInfo)
Halifax, Nova Scotia

ACCESS:	**Gopher:** ac.dal.ca
	Telnet: ac.dal.ca, login as **dalinfo**
Contains:	Campus news; announcements of events and lectures (e.g. Music Department performances, information from the Dalhousie Art Gallery and Dalhousie Arts Centre); information about the library (e.g. hours, loans and fines policy); curriculum and course information (e.g. awards/scholarships, class schedules, university calendar, academic deadlines, admissions deadlines, guide to registration); security and safety information (e.g. safety policies, parking regulations, information about the escort service); sports/athletic information (e.g. varsity schedule, skating schedule, classes/clinical programs); university policies and procedures (e.g. employment equity, smoking, storm closures); university motto; information about student organizations (e.g. Student Union, Dalhousie Christian Fellowship); information on university services and facilities (e.g. financial services, graphics services, research services, student services); information on computer and information technology services (e.g. hours of operation, guide to responsible computing at Dalhousie); information on employment opportunities and job training.

Emergency Preparedness Information Exchange (EPIX)
Vancouver, British Columbia

The purpose of EPIX is to facilitate the exchange of ideas and informa-
tion among Canadian and international public and private sector or-
ganizations about the prevention of, preparation for, recovery from
and/or mitigation of risk associated with natural and socio-technological
disasters.

ACCESS:	Gopher: disaster.cprost.sfu.ca, port 5555
Contains:	Information about emergency/disaster management organizations in Canada and abroad; information on disaster/emergency management topics (e.g. earthquakes, floods, fires, volcanoes); list of upcoming emergency/disaster management conferences and events; connections to other emergency/disaster management organizations; information about B.C. disaster management programs, services, and activities.

Fanshawe College
London, Ontario

ACCESS:	Gopher: gopher.fanshawec.on.ca
Contains:	Electronic campus telephone directory; general information about the college.

fONOROLA
Ottawa, Ontario

ACCESS:	Gopher: gopher.fonorola.net
Contains:	Information about fONORLA's pricing; software archive.

Georgian College
Barrie, Ontario

ACCESS:	Gopher: gc1.georcoll.on.ca
Contains:	Strategic Plan; campus news flashes; information about housing and financial assistance; information on program offerings and application procedures.

Government of Ontario
Ontario, Canada

ACCESS:	Gopher: gov.on.ca
Contains:	Information from several Ontario government ministries.

University of Guelph (Griff)
Guelph, Ontario

ACCESS:	Gopher: griff.uoguelph.ca
Contains:	Academic information (e.g. transcript information, application information, information on awards and scholarships, schedule of dates); administrative announcements; information about campus news and events; athletic information (e.g. arena hours, aquatic information, lifesaving and community service courses); facts about the university (e.g. history, residences, visitor's guide, research facts); entertainment information (e.g. music events); information for staff (e.g. job opportunities); information for faculty (e.g. research and seminar information); information about the library (e.g. hours, borrowing policy, telephone contacts); safety and security information (e.g. health and safety telephone numbers, overnight parking information); information on university services (e.g. Computing and Communications Services, graphics and print services); information for students (e.g. conference information, work/study program information).

HookUp Communication Corporation
Waterloo, Ontario

ACCESS:	Gopher: gopher.hookup.net
Contains:	Information about HookUp's services and pricing.

Humber College
Etobicoke, Ontario

ACCESS:	Gopher: admin.humberc.on.ca
Contains:	Local computer help files

Institute for Fisheries and Marine Technology
St. Johns, Newfoundland

ACCESS:	Gopher: dragger.ifmt.nf.ca
Contains:	Mission statement; information from the Center for Marine Simulation (e.g. reading list for simulator instructors and operators, papers related to marine simulation); Newfoundland and Labrador weather forecasts.

Lakehead University(LUCI)
Thunder Bay, Ontario

ACCESS:	Gopher: flash.lakeheadu.ca

| Contains: | Campus telephone/electronic mail guide; human resources information (e.g. benefits information); access to the library catalogue; library policies and hours; course timetables; exam timetables; university calendar; enrollment history by department; strategic plan; information from the counselling and career centre; information from academic departments; Senate minutes and other information about the Senate; information about Computer Services. |

Université Laval
Main Gopher
Quebec City, Quebec

| ACCESS: | Gopher: genesis.ulaval.ca |
| Contains: | Electronic telephone directory. |

Université Laval
Library
Quebec City, Quebec

| ACCESS: | Gopher: gopher.bibl.ulaval.ca |
| Contains: | Access to the library catalogue; general information about the library. |

University of Lethbridge
Lethbridge, Alberta

| ACCESS: | Gopher: gopher.uleth.ca |
| Contains: | Minutes of university committees and councils; library information (e.g. hours, faculty handbook). |

Malaspina College
Nanaimo, British Columbia

| ACCESS: | Gopher: gopher.mala.bc.ca |
| Contains: | Under construction. |

University of Manitoba (UMINFO)
Winnipeg, Manitoba

The University of Manitoba is home to Canada's first Veronica server. Stop by their Gopher server and sign their guest book!

| ACCESS: | Gopher: gopher.cc.umanitoba.ca |

Contains:	Library information (e.g. hours, services, staff, policies); campus news and public affairs information (e.g. weekly news and events); information provided by faculties and departments (e.g. graduate student awards listing); information about ancillary services (e.g. student parking application, staff and student parking guides); information from Computer Services (e.g. operating hours, computer centre publications, Computer Services newsletter).

McGill University
Campus Wide Information System
Montreal, Quebec

ACCESS:	TN3270: vm1.mcgill.ca
	Press the **<enter>** key at the VM/ESA screen, then type **info**.
Contains:	Montreal weather forecast; history of McGill; registration statistics; library information; directory of Quebec university libraries; campus events calendar; computing information (Code of Ethics, Computing Centre newsletters and documentation); electronic campus telephone book; computer store price list; course timetables; convocation information; registration information; classified ads; calendar of dates; list of student services; information on campus tours; job postings.

McGill University
Main Gopher
Montreal, Quebec

ACCESS:	Gopher: gopher.mcgill.ca
Contains:	Access to other McGill Gopher servers; history of McGill University; history of the McGill Coat of Arms

McGill University
Electrical Engineering Department
Montreal, Quebec

ACCESS:	Gopher: ee470.ee.mcgill.ca
Contains:	Information from student societies (e.g. Engineering Undergraduate Society, Electrical Engineering Graduate Society); course descriptions; department bulletins (e.g. network problems); information about the computer laboratory; course schedule.

McGill University
Microelectronics and Computer Systems Laboratory
Montreal, Quebec

ACCESS:	Gopher: macs.ee.mcgill.ca

Contains:	An overview of the MACS laboratory; announcements of seminars and defences; conference information; access to other McGill Gopher servers.

McGill University
Telecommunications and Signal Processing Laboratory
Montreal, Quebec

ACCESS:	**Gopher: tsp.ee.mcgill.ca**
Contains:	An overview of the TSP lab; announcements of seminars, defences and conferences; access to other McGill Gopher servers.

McGill University
McGill Research Centre For Intelligent Machines
Montreal, Quebec

ACCESS:	**Gopher: gopher.cim.mcgill.ca**
Contains:	Guidelines for the use of computing facilities; technical reports; list of courses; announcements; electronic telephone/e-mail directory; seminar information.

McGill University
Center for the Physics of Materials
Montreal, Quebec

ACCESS:	**Gopher: nazgul.physics.mcgill.ca**
Contains:	under development

McGill University
Photonic Systems Group
Montreal, Quebec

ACCESS:	**Gopher: photon.ee.mcgill.ca**
Contains:	General information about the Photonic Systems Group.

McGill University
Information Network and Systems Lab
Montreal, Quebec

ACCESS:	**Gopher: brahms.insl.mcgill.ca**
Contains:	General information about the INSL, information about the hardware and software facilities at INSL.

McMaster University
Main Gopher
Hamilton, Ontario

ACCESS:	Gopher: goher.mcmaster.ca
Contains:	Code of conduct for computer users; university reports; directory for computing and information services; campus announcements; campus electronic mail directory; library hours; exam timetable.

McMaster University
Bookstore
Hamilton, Ontario

ACCESS:	Gopher: bookstore.services.mcmaster.ca
Contains:	General information about the bookstore (e.g. contact information, electronic ordering information, hours of operation, refund policy, information on special orders, upcoming events).

McMaster University
Computing Services
Hamilton, Ontario

ACCESS:	Gopher: offsv1.cis.mcmaster.ca
Contains:	Mission and goals for Information Technology; information on the instructional computer laboratory; information about research computing; information about software support services; description of helpdesk services; directory of computing services.

McMaster University
Faculty of Health Sciences
Hamilton, Ontario

ACCESS:	Gopher: fhs.csu.mcmaster.ca
Contains:	Facts about the Faculty of Health Sciences (philosophy, history, departments, schools and programs, research accomplishments, faculty and staff, services); NEWSWATCH electronic newsletter (publication of the Faculty of Health Sciences); INFONET electronic newsletter (publication of the Centre for International Health); overview of research activities; information about the Health Sciences Library; overview of the Health Library Network; information about the Health Sciences Bookstore.

Memorial University of Newfoundland
St. John's, Newfoundland

ACCESS:	**Gopher: cwis.ucs.mun.ca**
Contains:	University calendar; registration fees and charges; university diary; undergraduate registration procedures; information from academic departments (e.g. course descriptions); information from the Council of the Students' Union (e.g. by-laws, list of council members, constitution); information about student services (e.g. information about scholarships, food services, housing, health services); electronic telephone directory for student affairs and services; information about campus facilities (e.g. banking, student aid, security and parking); information about orientation; map of St. John's campus (picture); listing of clubs and societies on campus; information about student volunteer organizations; collective agreement between MUN and the Faculty Association; official university documents (e.g. President's address to convocation, emergency procedures, information technology plan, Senate minutes); bus schedules for St. John's; access to the library catalogue; listing of events and seminars; issues of *The Muse* (student newspaper); listing of frequently called telephone numbers on campus; campus postal codes; computing information; information from Sir Wilfred Grenfell College (e.g. information from academic departments, course and program information, information about registration, information about the library, information about student services.

Université de Montréal
Main Gopher
Montreal, Quebec

ACCESS:	**Gopher: gopher.umontreal.ca**
Contains:	Links to other gopher servers at the University of Montreal.

Université de Montréal
Department de Biochimie (MegaGopher)
Montreal, Quebec

ACCESS:	**Gopher: megasun.bch.umontreal.ca**
Contains:	Information on Montreal biology seminars; links to other biology gophers; information on the history of Gopher in biology; archives of the bio-gopher administrators list; information related to organellar genome and molecular evolution research; information related to the MegaSequencing Project at the University of Montreal; information about the Genetic Data Environment (GDE) package.

Université de Montréal
Law Gopher (Bilingual)
Montreal, Quebec

ACCESS:	**Gopher: gopher.droit.umontreal.ca**
Contains:	Searchable Quebec Civil Code; searchable Canadian Unemployment Board decisions; searchable Canadian Supreme Court decisions; student guide book (French), law-related Internet resources.

Université de Montréal
Gopher Litteratures
Montreal, Quebec

ACCESS:	**Gopher: tornade.ere.umontreal.ca, port 7070**
Contains:	Material related to French literature studies.

Université de Montréal (UDEMATIK)
Montreal, Quebec

ACCESS:	**Telnet: udematik.umontreal.ca**
Contains:	Telephone/electronic mail directory for staff; catalogue of courses; program information; admissions information; information about computing resources.

Mount Allison University (MAGS)
Sackville, New Brunswick

ACCESS:	**Gopher: gopher.mta.ca**
Contains:	Staff/student telephone directory; exam schedules; information about the bookstore; research interests of faculty members; union collective agreements; Senate information; information about athletics; information about computing services; announcements of campus events (e.g. Film Society); information about the library (e.g. circulation policies, library hours and telephone numbers); residence constitutions; policies and procedures for student governance; example cases heard by the university judicial committee; classified ads (employment opportunities, buy and sell, lost and found).

Mount Allison University
On Line Learning Centre
Sackville, New Brunswick

The On Line Learning Centre Gopher is part of a project for the TeleEducation Network of New Brunswick. This Gopher will assist in the delivery of TeleEducation materials through the use of the Internet.

ACCESS:	Gopher: pringle.mta.ca
Contains:	Information about computer science and information systems programs at Mount Allison; information on TeleEducation New Brunswick.

National Capital Free-Net
Ottawa, Ontario

ACCESS:	Gopher: freenet.carleton.ca
Contains:	Access to Gopherized resources on the Internet; access to some information from the National Capital Free-Net (under construction).

Natural Resources Canada
Main Gopher
Ottawa, Ontario

ACCESS:	Gopher: gopher.emr.ca
Contains:	NRCan's mandate; employee telephone/electronic mail directory; information about the departmental structure of NRCan; information about each NRCan sector (Canadian Forest Service, Energy, Mining, Geological Survey of Canada, Mineral and Energy Technology Sector, Surveys, Mapping, and Remote Sensing, Corporate Services); list of statutes administered by NRCan; information about the Minister of NRCan.

Natural Resources Canada
Pacific Forestry Centre
Victoria, British Columbia

ACCESS:	Gopher: pfc.pfc.forestry.ca
Contains:	mission of Natural Resources Canada (Forestry sector), mission of the Pacific Forestry Centre

University of New Brunswick (INFO)
Fredericton, New Brunswick

ACCESS:	Gopher: gopher.unb.ca
Contains:	Historical sketch of the University of New Brunswick; mission statement; information for alumni; overview of facilities and services at the University of New Brunswick (e.g. athletics, audio-visual services, banking, bookstore, religious services); information about computing services; telephone/electronic mail directory for faculty/staff; list of faculty/staff; campus newsflashes; list of important academic dates; list of upcoming events; information from Theatre UNB; minutes of the Board of Governors; Senate minutes;

directory of campus recreational facilities; information about intramural sports; access to the library catalogue; general information about the library; course timetables; examination timetables; regulations for undergraduate admissions; graduate awards registrar; information about residence and off-campus housing facilities; information about the UNB Student Union; list of holidays at UNB; New Brunswick weather reports.

University of Northern British Columbia
Prince George, British Columbia

ACCESS:	**Gopher: unbc.edu**
Contains:	Access to the library catalogue.

Northern College
Kirkland Lake, Ontario

ACCESS:	**Gopher: kirk.northernc.on.ca**
Contains:	College calendar; directory of electronic mail addresses for Northern College personnel; Northern Ontario weather; general information about Northern College.

North Island College
Courtenay, British Columbia

ACCESS:	**Gopher: matthew.nic.bc.ca**
Contains:	College calendar; timetables; local weather forecast.

Nova Scotia Technology Network
Dartmouth, Nova Scotia

ACCESS:	**Gopher: nstn.ns.ca**
Contains:	Information about the Nova Scotia Technology Network (e.g. corporate profile, product and service information); access to the NSTN electronic shopping mall; information about some Nova Scotia Associations; access to other Nova Scotia Gopher servers.

Nova Scotia Agricultural College
Truro, Nova Scotia

ACCESS:	**Gopher: ac.nsac.ns.ca**
Contains:	Overview of Nova Scotia Agricultural College; college newsletters (from bee-keeping to strawberry growing!); information about the library; information from the Nova Scotia Department of Agriculture and Marketing (e.g. descriptions of each branch of the department); access to

other agricultural Gopher servers.

Ontario Institute for Studies in Education
Toronto, Ontario

ACCESS:	Gopher: gopher.oise.on.ca
Contains:	Information about graduate study in education at OISE (e.g. admissions information, course offerings by department, staff listing, e-mail/telephone directory of staff, information on fees and financial services).

Ontario Ministry of Education and Training (InfoMET)
Toronto, Ontario

ACCESS:	Gopher: gopher.mcu.gov.on.ca
Contains:	Overview of OMET; information about the organizational structure of OMET; Directory of Education in Ontario.

University of Ottawa
Main Gopher
Ottawa, Ontario

ACCESS:	Gopher: panda1.uottawa.ca
Contains:	Contact information for administrative and academic personnel at the university; campus telephone directory; information about research projects.

University of Ottawa
Department of Epidemiology and Community Medicine
Ottawa, Ontario

ACCESS:	Gopher: zeus.med.uottawa.ca
Contains:	General information about the department; information about the Community Health Research Unit (CHRU); CHRU newsletters; CHRU publications; links to health-related Gopher servers.

University of Prince Edward Island
Charlottetown, Prince Edward Island

ACCESS:	Gopher: gopher.cs.upei.ca
Contains:	General information about UPEI (history, mission, characteristics, governance, structure); faculty handbook; information from the Registrar's Office (e.g. academic dates, academic regulations, admissions information, information about scholarships and awards, class schedule); informa-

tion from the Personnel Office (e.g. hiring policies, staff and student job postings); information from the library (e.g. history of the library, access to the catalogue, hours, location of materials, telephone directory); information about the UPEI Sports Centre (e.g. membership information, hours of operation, rules and regulations, reservations); information about student services (e.g. health services, residence services, counselling services, off-campus housing, Learning Assistance Centre, day care services); information from the Institute of Island Studies (e.g. description, list of publications); list of campus events; weather forecast for PEI; information about Computer Services.

Université du Québec
Sainte Foy, Quebec

ACCESS:	Gopher: gopher.uquebec.ca
Contains:	(In French) Overview of the university; descriptions of the universities that form the University of Quebec; important academic dates; calendars for the University of Quebec; issues of *Réseau*, the university magazine.

Université du Québec à Montréal (INFOPUB)
Montreal, Quebec

ACCESS:	Gopher: infopub.uqam.ca
Contains:	Information about academic programs; information about admissions; information about student services; campus job postings; information about computer services; campus telephone directory; local weather forecast; events calendar; information about the library.

Queen's University (INFOQ)
Kingston, Ontario

ACCESS:	Gopher: gopher.queensu.ca
Contains:	General information about Queen's University; campus publications; information about campus services and facilities; information about computing services; calendars; course timetables; off-campus housing accommodation listings; employment information; information about the Faculty of Law; information about library services; campus phone book and directory; information about scholarship and awards; information about the Graduate Student Society (e.g. constitution, listing of the Executive, policies, by-laws); university policies (e.g. academic, administrative, and personnel policies); conference announcements; events calendar.

Resudox Online Services
Ottawa, Ontario

ACCESS:	**Gopher: resudox.net**
Contains:	Information about Resudox (e.g. prices, services).

Royal Military College
Kingston, Ontario

ACCESS:	**Gopher: gopher.rmc.ca**
Contains:	Under development.

Ryerson Polytechnic University
Toronto, Ontario

ACCESS:	**Gopher: gopher.ryerson.ca**
Contains:	Information about computing services; faculty/ staff telephone directory; information about campus services (e.g. library, bookstore, recreation and athletics); course descriptions.

Saint Mary's University
Halifax, Nova Scotia

ACCESS:	**Gopher: gopher.stmarys.ca**
Contains:	facts about the university

University of Saskatchewan
Saskatoon, Saskatchewan

ACCESS:	**Gopher: gopher.usask.ca**
Contains:	History and mission of the university; campus telephone directory; administrative policies & procedures; course calendar; graduate student awards listing; First and Best Database; information about the library (e.g. hours, floor plans); Computing Services' newsletter; local weather forecasts; SASK#net information.

University of Saskatchewan
College of Engineering
Saskatoon, Saskatchewan

ACCESS:	**Gopher: dvinci.usask.ca**
Contains:	Information from the constituent departments (e.g. exam schedules, faculty lists); information from student societies

(e.g. minutes of meetings, constitutions, phone lists); information about computing services (e.g. policies and procedures); information about the engineering library (e.g. handouts, list of reserve materials); Graduate Student Handbook.

Sault College
Sault Ste. Marie, Ontario

ACCESS:	Gopher: gopher.saultc.on.ca
Contains:	Campus telephone directory.

SchoolNet Gopher
Ottawa, Ontario

ACCESS:	Gopher: ernest.ccs.carleton.ca, port 419
Contains:	Repository for information about Canada's Schoolnet project.

Seneca College
Toronto, Ontario

ACCESS:	Gopher: info.senecac.on.ca
Contains:	Facts and figures about Seneca College; annual report; Strategic Plan; course calendars; student handbook; press releases; electronic mail directory for Ontario Colleges.

Simon Fraser University
Main Gopher
Burnaby, British Columbia

ACCESS:	Gopher: gopher.sfu.ca
Contains:	General information about SFU (e.g. facts, statistics, history, policies and procedures); graduate studies handbook; information about graduate scholarships and awards; undergraduate course descriptions; important academic dates; course timetables; campus telephone directory; information about the library (e.g. services, news, handouts); information about computing services (e.g. policies, procedures, handouts); information about campus services (e.g. dining services, human resources, residence and housing services, traffic and security services, bookstore); research interests of (some) faculty members.

Simon Fraser University
Centre for Experimental and Constructive Mathematics
Burnaby, British Columbia

The Centre for Experimental and Constructive Mathematics is a Simon Fraser University Centre within the Department of Mathematics and Statistics. Its mandate is to explore and promote the interplay of conventional mathematics and modern computation. Part of the mandate of the CECM is to develop the presence of the mathematics community on the Internet.

ACCESS:	Gopher: gopher.cecm.sfu.ca
Contains:	Listing of local events; prospectus for the CECM; CECM telephone directory; directory of CECM members; links to math-related Internet resources.

Sir Sandford Fleming College
Peterborough, Ontario

ACCESS:	Gopher: gopher.flemingc.on.ca
Contains:	Campus telephone directory; approved policies and procedures.

University of Toronto
Main Gopher (UTORinfo)

ACCESS:	Gopher: gopher.utoronto.ca
Contains:	Campus telephone directory.

University of Toronto
VM Gopher
Toronto, Ontario

ACCESS:	Gopher: vm.utcc.utoronto.ca
Contains:	Links to other Gopher servers at the University of Toronto; ONet information; CA*net information.

University of Toronto
Erindale College
Mississauga, Ontario

ACCESS:	Gopher: credit.erin.utoronto.ca
Contains:	List of administrative heads of Erindale College; information about the Career Centre; information about the Computer Centre; information about the library; college calendar and timetable; information about Health Services; information about residence; list of current events.

University of Toronto
Scarborough Campus
Scarborough, Ontario

ACCESS:	**Gopher: wave.scar.utoronto.ca**
Contains:	Academic calendar; campus telephone directory with e-mail addresses; information about the Computer Centre.

University of Toronto
Department of Physics
Toronto, Ontario

ACCESS:	**Gopher: helios.physics.utoronto.ca**
Contains:	Excerpts from the Physics Graduate Studies Handbook.

University of Toronto
Computer Systems Research Institute
Toronto, Ontario

ACCESS:	**Gopher: bathurst.csri.toronto.edu**
Contains:	CSRI technical reports.

Trent University
Peterborough, Ontario

ACCESS:	**Gopher: blaze.trentu.ca**
Contains:	Campus telephone directory; information about academic departments (e.g. registrar, bookstore, president's office); information about administration and service departments; information about the board & Senate; information about computing facilities; announcements of campus events; information about faculty publications; information about the library; information about student organizations (e.g. Trent Student Union, Trent Debating Union).

University of Victoria (UVicINFO)
Victoria, British Columbia

ACCESS:	**Gopher: gopher.uvic.ca**
Contains:	Campus telephone directory; job postings; events calendar; recycling information; hours of campus facilities (e.g. bookstore); off-campus housing registry; campus crime alert; information about administrative departments (e.g. Admissions, Human Resources, Computing Services).

University of Victoria
Child and Youth Care Gopher
Victoria, British Columbia

ACCESS:	Gopher: gopher.cyc.uvic.ca
Contains:	Information about various Child and Youth Care (CYC) programs in B.C., Canada and overseas; information about CYC-related topics and special events; general information about the CYC profession.

University of Victoria
Department of Computer Science
Victoria, British Columbia

ACCESS:	Gopher: gulf.uvic.ca
Contains:	Departmental electronic mail directory; course descriptions; course outlines; faculty biographies and research interests; technical reports; information about computing resources; computing tips.

University of Victoria
Faculty of Fine Arts
Victoria, British Columbia

ACCESS:	Gopher: kafka.uvic.ca
Contains:	Graphic files, theatre database.

University of Waterloo (UWinfo)
Waterloo, Ontario

ACCESS:	Gopher: uwinfo.uwaterloo.ca
Contains:	General information about the university; official documents (e.g. policies and procedures, statistical information); information about university facilities and services (e.g. library, computing services; bookstore, athletics, recycling and waste management, graphic services); information about departments, faculties, associations, and student groups (e.g. Graduate Student Association, Staff Association, Secretariat); varsity sports scores; course and examination schedules; telephone directory for faculty, staff, and students (with e-mail addresses); university-news-of-the-day bulletin; access to the university bookstore; issues of GAZETTE.

University of Western Ontario
Main Gopher
London, Ontario

ACCESS:	Gopher: gopher.uwo.ca
Contains:	Maps (show you how to get to UWO); mission statement; university policies and procedures; information from faculties, departments and associations; information about the library; information about computing; course descriptions; index to the London Free Press (newspaper); campus telephone directory; UWO newsletters.

University of Western Ontario
Faculty of Social Science
London, Ontario

ACCESS:	Gopher: gopher.sscl.uwo.ca
Contains:	Information about the Social Science Computing Laboratory (SSCL) and the Social Science Computing Network; information about SSCL data and information services; course descriptions; departmental research bibliography; access to the SSCL newsletter and other local publications

Wilfrid Laurier University (WLUInfo)
Waterloo. Ontario

ACCESS:	Gopher: mach1.wlu.ca
Contains:	History of the university; university mission; facts and figures about the university; current events calendar; sports news; information from academic departments; class schedules; examination schedules; information about campus facilities and services (e.g. athletics and recreation, Women's Centre); information about Wilfred Laurier Press; description of outreach activities and programs; information about the publications and policies of Computing Services; information about the library (hours, services, regulations); campus telephone directory; financial statements.

University of Windsor (UWINFO)
Windsor, Ontario

ACCESS:	Gopher: gopher.uwindsor.ca
Contains:	Access to the main campus library catalogue; access to the Law Library catalogue; Computing Services newsletter campus newsletter; Registrar's office directory; information about course offerings & course scheduling; schedule and description of courses/seminars offered by Computing Services; information about hardware and software resources of Computing Services; departmental directories for faculties, schools and departments; gopher documentation: security manual and Gopher manual for information

providers.

University of Winnipeg (UWIS)
Winnipeg, Manitoba

ACCESS:	Gopher: gopher.uwinnipeg.ca
Contains:	Campus telephone directory.

UUNORTH Inc.
Toronto, Ontario

ACCESS:	Gopher: gopher.north.net
Contains:	Information about UUNORTH's services.

Victoria Free-Net Association
Victoria, British Columbia

ACCESS:	Gopher: freenet.victoria.bc.ca
Contains:	Information about the Victoria Free-Net; information from the Victoria Free-Net; links to other Free-Net Gopher servers.

York University
Main Gopher
North York, Ontario

ACCESS:	Gopher: gopher.yorku.ca
Contains:	Campus telephone directory; general information about York University; York University Fact Book; York Computing Plan; GIF pictures of the campus; York logo and coat of arms (pictures); information about computing services (e.g. hours, facilities); recent additions to the library catalogue; access to the library catalogue; issues of *Computing News* and *York Bulletin*.

York University
UNICAAT Project
Toronto, Ontario

The UNICAAT Project is concerned with facilitating student transfer, and the sharing of knowledge and resources between Seneca College of Applied Arts and Technology and the Faculty of Pure and Applied Science at York University.

ACCESS:	Gopher: unicaat.yorku.ca

Contains:	Faculty of Pure and Applied Science calendar; Seneca College calendar; information about local hardware and software services; information about UNICAAT administration.

THE DIRECTORY OF INTERNET ACCESSIBLE OPACS IN CANADA

· ·

This is a comprehensive listing of Canadian libraries that have made their Online Public Access Catalogue, or OPAC, available on the Internet. An OPAC allows you to interactively search a library collection for books, authors, and/or subjects that meet your search criteria. Using the Internet, you can search the holdings of almost every university library in Canada. A number of Canadian colleges and public library systems have also connected their electronic catalogue to the Internet. To compile the information for this directory, we surveyed librarians at university, college, and public libraries across the country. Each entry in this directory contains the following information:

(1) Internet Address of the OPAC and Access Method

Each entry will tell you the Internet address of the catalogue, and the access method to be used. The access method will be either telnet, tn3270, or Gopher. Some library catalogues require that you use tn3270, which is a variant of telnet. Telnet may not work with library catalogues that require tn3270, unless your Internet host happens to be an IBM mainframe. To connect to an Internet host using tn3270, a tn3270 client needs to be installed on the Internet host that you are using. To use tn3270, type tn3270 followed by the host name. For example, to connect to McGill University's online catalogue, you would type:

tn3270 mvs.mcgill.ca

(2) Instructions

What to do when you establish a connection. Often you will need to enter a userid, or make a selection off a menu. Because there are so many different types of OPAC software in use across Canada, we do not provide specific instructions on how to use each catalogue. However, every catalogue has online help files that will aid you in performing searches on the catalogue. Often the most common commands are automatically displayed on the screen to help you with your search.

(3) How to Exit

Each entry will have instructions on how to leave the catalogue when you are finished. Occasionally, you will need to use a control sequence like CTRL-Z, CTRL-D, or CTRL-C. To use a control sequence, hold down the control key and press the specified letter at the same time. For example, to use CTRL-Z, press the CTRL key and the letter Z at the same time. If you get stuck in the catalogue at any time, you can use the telnet escape sequence, which is generally **CTRL-]** on UNIX systems (hold down the CTRL key and press the] key). If you are using tn3270, the escape sequence is often **CTRL-C** (hold down the CTRL key and press the letter C). When the "telnet>" or "tn3270>" prompt appears, type **quit** and press <enter>.

(4) OPAC Type

The type of OPAC software the library is using. The commands used to search each catalogue will vary according to the software being used.

(5) Size of the Collection:

Total size of the institution's library collection. Since libraries measure collection sizes in different ways, the collection size estimates in this directory are not standardized.

(6) % Catalogued

The percentage of the library's total collection that is included in the OPAC. We make note of any items in the library collection that are not in the OPAC. While this information is accurate as of January, 1994, it will change as the OPAC is updated.

(7) Subject Strengths

Subject areas in which the library has strong, or notable collections. Special collections are noted, if reported by the library.

(8) Public Databases

Names of any databases on the OPAC that the public has access to. Many libraries have databases on their OPAC that are restricted to local patrons. Databases with restricted access will not be listed.

NAMES

If the library has given a name to its OPAC, the name is indicated in brackets after the name of the institution or organization. For example, Bishop's University in Lennoxville, Quebec, calls its OPAC **Borris**. Trent University in Peterborough, Ontario, calls its OPAC **Topcat**.

Acadia University
Wolfville, Nova Scotia

ACCESS:	**Telnet: auls.acadiau.ca**
Instructions:	At the "login:" prompt, type opac. Type LC to access the library catalogue.
How to Exit:	Type Q to leave the library system. Type X to disconnect.
OPAC Type:	AULS (In-house).
Size of Collection:	> 0.5 million items, including books, serials (2500), microforms, scores, sound recordings, video tapes, films, and educational kits.
% Catalogued:	50%. Not catalogued: special collections, pre-1978 titles, many government documents and archival materials.
Subject Strengths:	Canadiana. Eric R. Dennis Collection of Canadiana, John D. Logan Collection of Canadian Literature, Haliburton Collection of the writings of Thomas Chandler Haliburton, Atlantic Baptist Historical Collection, Mermaid Theatre Collection, Annapolis Valley Regional Collection.
Public Databases:	Planter Database — A bibliography of primary documents about the New England Planters who settled in the Maritime Provinces between 1759 and 1800.

University of Alberta (The GATE)
Edmonton, Alberta

ACCESS:	**Telnet: dra.library.ualberta.ca**
Instructions:	At the "Username:" prompt, type GATE. Type direct to access the library catalogue.
How to Exit:	Press CTRL-Z to return to the main menu. Type quit to disconnect.
OPAC Type:	DRA
Size of Collection:	3,685,000 volumes plus 3,217,000 microforms plus 1,403,000 maps.
% Catalogued:	Majority. Not catalogued: 90% of the Canadian Circumpolar Library, 100% of the map collection, some government publications and large microforms.
Subject Strengths:	Amerindian Anthropology, Geology, Entomology, Law, Sports Medicine, Slavic and German History and Literature, European romanticism, Mathematics, Neuroscience, Nursing, Maps. Library of Faculte Saint-Jean. French language education and French-Canadian studies.
Public Databases:	None.

Athabasca University (AUCAT)
Athabasca, Alberta

ACCESS:	**Telnet: devax.admin.athabascau.ca**
Instructions:	At the "Username:" prompt, type **AUCAT**. At the "Printer Name:" prompt, press **<enter>**. Select option **1** from the menu.
How to Exit:	Type **m** to get back to the main menu. At the main menu, type **q** to disconnect. Type **quit** at any time to disconnect.
OPAC Type:	BUCAT
Size of Collection:	110,051 volumes.
% Catalogued:	95%. Not catalogued: distance education courses from other universities, CD-ROM indexes.
Subject Strengths:	Distance Education, Women's Studies.
Public Databases:	Holdings of the Athabasca University archives, Current Periodical Issues.

Note: The Athabasca University library is totally devoted to distance education librarianship. Most of the circulation is done by mail to students who live in all parts of Canada.

Atlantic School of Theology (Novanet)
Halifax, Nova Scotia

ACCESS:	Telnet: novanet.nstn.ns.ca
Instructions:	A menu appears when the connection is established. Select option **6** to limit the search to the Atlantic School and Theology.
How to Exit:	Type **end**.
OPAC Type:	GEAC
Size of Collection:	69,190 print items, 1,933 non-print items.
% Catalogued:	10%.
Subject Strengths:	Theological and related material. New Hebrides Mission Collection. Hymnody (Hymnology).
Public Databases:	None.

Bishop's University (BORIS)
Lennoxville, Quebec

ACCESS:	Telnet: library.ubishops.ca
Instructions:	At the "login:" prompt, type **lib**. At the "password:" prompt, type **bishops**.
How to Exit:	Type **end** to disconnect.
OPAC Type:	GEAC
Size of Collection:	210,000 titles, 400,000 items.
% Catalogued:	All except government documents and maps.
Subject Strengths:	Humanities and Social Sciences, specifically English, Canadian and Quebec Literature. Religion, specifically Anglican Literature.
Public Databases:	None.

Brandon University (BuCAT)
Brandon, Manitoba

ACCESS:	Telnet: library.brandonu.ca
Instructions:	At the "Username:" prompt, type **libcat**. Select option **1** from the main menu.
How to Exit:	Type **m** to get back to the main menu, type **Q** from the main menu to disconnect.
OPAC Type:	BUCAT
Size of Collection:	1.4 million bibliographic records.
% Catalogued:	100% of print monographs, 100% of non-print materials, 100% of journal titles, 95% of microfiche monographs, 50% of government documents, 15% of journal articles.

Subject Strengths:	Music, Native Studies.
Public Databases:	Course Equivalents Database, BU Serials, BU Films, BU Archives, University and College Calendars held by BU, Annual Reports held by BU, Abstracts of Native Studies, BU Music Programs.

Brandon Public Library
Brandon, Manitoba

ACCESS:	Telnet: library.brandonu.ca
Instructions:	At the "Username:" prompt, login as **libcat**. Select option **5**, "Other Library Catalogues" Select option **1**, "Brandon Area Libraries".
How to Exit:	Type **m** to get back to the main menu, type **Q** from the main menu to disconnect.
OPAC Type:	BUCAT

University of British Columbia (UBCLIB)
Vancouver, British Columbia

ACCESS:	Telnet: library.ubc.ca
Instructions:	Press the **<enter>** key at the "Enter your id:" prompt. Type **LIB** for the library catalogue.
How to Exit:	Type **start** to return to the welcome screen. Type **stop** to disconnect.
OPAC Type:	In-house.
Size of Collection:	9,280,000 items, including 3,347,672 books/serials, 793,798 government publications, 4,106,945 microforms, 242,344 cartographic items, 123,035 audio items, 659,419 photos, 5,420 film and video items.
% Catalogued:	25%. Not catalogued: Government publications, microforms, cartographic materials, photos, and pictures.
Subject Strengths:	All standard academic disciplines. Asian materials, Life Sciences.
Public Databases:	B.C. Archival Union List (description of holdings for B.C. archives), B.C. Newspapers (current and historical B.C. newspapers held by B.C. libraries, museums, and historical societies), Bibliographies (bibliographies compiled and maintained at UBC), Directory of Statistics in Canada (index to statistical publications from Statistics Canada and other governmental and commercial sources, updated annually), B.C. Electronic Library Network media and serials holdings, UBC Recordings, UBC Serials.

Brock University
St. Catharines, Ontario

ACCESS:	Telnet: 139.57.16.2, port 1200
Instructions:	A menu will appear when the connection is established. Press <enter> when asked "Press SEND to begin."
How to Exit:	Press CTRL-D to disconnect. Type START OVER to return to the search menu.
OPAC Type:	GEAC
Size of Collection:	900,000 items.
% Catalogued:	100%.
Subject Strengths:	Niagara Region Collection, specializing in materials about the Niagara region, and containing materials written by local residents.
Public Databases:	None.

Camosun College (CAMCAT)
Victoria, British Columbia

ACCESS:	Telnet: camsrv.camosun.bc.ca
Instructions:	At the "Username:" prompt, type catinq. Select option 1 from the menu.
How to Exit:	Type m to return to the main menu. At the main menu, type Q to disconnect. Type quit at any time to exit the system directly.
OPAC Type:	BUCAT
Size of Collection:	48,000 volumes.
% Catalogued:	100%.
Subject Strengths:	Canadian History. Japan.
Public Databases:	None.

Note: Search outputs from CAMCAT can be e-mailed back to you.

Canada Centre for Mineral and Energy Technology (CMET)
Ottawa, Ontario

ACCESS:	Telnet: canlib.emr.ca
Instructions:	At the "login:" prompt, type opac (lower case only).
How to Exit:	Press the PF1 key until the initial screen is displayed. Use the arrow keys to select Exit from the menu.
OPAC Type:	MULTILIS

Size of Collection:	750,000 volumes.
% Catalogued:	100%.
Subject Strengths:	Mining, Minerals, Metallurgy, Energy Efficiency, Alternative Energy Technology.
Public Databases:	CANMET Technical Publications.

University College of Cape Breton (Novanet)
Sydney, Nova Scotia

ACCESS:	**Telnet: novanet.nstn.ns.ca**
Instructions:	A menu appears when the connection is established. Select option **6** to limit the search to the University College of Cape Breton.
How to Exit:	Type **end** to disconnect. Type **cat** to begin a new search.
OPAC Type:	GEAC
Size of Collection:	275,000 volumes
% Catalogued:	30%. Not catalogued or partially catalogued: Statistics Canada publications, Statutes, Debates, pre-1987 acquisitions.
Subject Strengths:	Environmental Science, Psychology, Sociology, Folklore, History and Culture of Cape Breton. Gaelic Language Collection.
Public Databases:	None.

Carleton University (CUBE)
Carleton University Bibliographic Entry
Ottawa, Ontario

ACCESS:	**Telnet: library.carleton.ca**
Instructions:	A menu appears when the connection is established. Press the **<enter>** key at the "OPTION:" prompt.
How to Exit:	Type **off** to disconnect.
OPAC Type:	In-house.
Size of Collection:	2,601,309 items and volumes.
% Catalogued:	100%.
Subject Strengths:	Social Sciences, German Studies, Canadian Studies, Spanish Studies, Women's Studies, Canadian Government publications, United Nations publications, Batchinsky Collection (Ukrainian politics, 19th-20th Century), Canadian and American and British small-press poetry, French Revolution, Novosti Press Agency Photograph Files, William Blake (Trianon Press).
Public Databases:	None.

Concordia University (CLUES)
Concordia Library Users Enquiry System.
Montreal, Quebec

ACCESS:	Telnet: **mercury.concordia.ca**
Instructions:	At the "login:" prompt, type **clues**.
How to Exit:	Type the letter **D** from the main menu.
OPAC Type:	INNOPAC
Size of Collection:	2,173,451 items.
% Catalogued:	90%. Not catalogued: most government publications, technical standards and codes, uncatalogued technical reports.
Subject Strengths:	Cinema, Building Engineering. Azrieli Holocaust collection (approx. 2,000 titles). Irving Layton collection (manuscripts, letters, memorabilia).
Public Databases:	None.

Dalhousie University (Novanet)
Halifax, Nova Scotia

ACCESS:	Telnet: **novanet.nstn.ns.ca**
Instructions:	A menu appears when the connection is established. Select option **6** to limit the search to Dalhousie University.
How to Exit:	Type **end** to disconnect.
OPAC Type:	GEAC GLIS
Size of Collection:	1,849,000 volumes.
% Catalogued:	37% of all volumes. All current serials and all acquisitions since 1987 (except archival materials) are in the OPAC. Partially catalogued: dead serials, rare books, older special collection items, older maps, scores, micromaterials.
Subject Strengths:	Canadian History and Literature, Sciences, Health Sciences, Law, Oceanography, Kipling materials.
Public Databases:	None.

University of Guelph (searchMe)
Guelph, Ontario

ACCESS:	Telnet: **searchme.uoguelph.ca**
Instructions:	At the "login:" prompt, type **searchme**.
How to Exit:	To disconnect, type the letter **X** from the main menu.
OPAC Type:	In-house.
Size of Collection:	2,000,000 volumes.

% Catalogued:	100%.
Subject Strengths:	Agriculture, Veterinary Medicine, Scottish Studies, Life Sciences, Environmental Sciences, Commonwealth Literature, L.M. Montgomery, Ontario Theatre, Rural Studies.
Public Databases:	None.

Lakehead University
Thunder Bay, Ontario

ACCESS:	Telnet: lib.lakeheadu.ca
Instructions:	At the "Username:" prompt, type **LAKEHEAD**.
How to Exit:	Press the **PF1** key until the initial screen is displayed. Use the arrow keys to select **Exit** from the menu.
OPAC Type:	MULTILIS
Size of Collection:	600,000 books, journals and other documents. 200,000 microform volumes.
% Catalogued:	100%.
Subject Strengths:	Early Canadiana, Northwestern Ontario, Native Studies, Forestry and Outdoor Recreation, Education (41,000 titles).
Public Databases:	Lakehead's Northern Studies Resource Centre, with 21,000 online records.

Laurentian University
Sudbury, Ontario

ACCESS:	Telnet: laulibr.laurentian.ca
Instructions:	At the "Username:" prompt, type **netlib**.
How to Exit:	Press the **PF1** key until the initial screen is displayed. Use the arrow keys to select **Exit** from the menu.
OPAC Type:	MULTILIS
Size of Collection:	500,000 titles.
% Catalogued:	40%.
Subject Strengths:	Franco-Ontario, Land Reclamation, Acid Mine Drainage, Mining Environment, Rock Bursts.
Public Databases:	Mining Environment Database, Rock Burst Database.

Universite Laval (Ariane)
Quebec City, Quebec

ACCESS:	Telnet: ariane.ulaval.ca
Instructions:	At the "Username:" prompt, type **ARIANE**.

How to Exit:	Press the **PF1** key until the initial screen is displayed. Use the arrow keys to select **Exit** from the menu.
OPAC Type:	MULTILIS
Size of Collection:	1,016,000 titles, 50,000 microforms, 16,975 serials.
% Catalogued:	70%. Not catalogued: pre-1975, slides in arts and architecture, maps and aerial photographs .
Subject Strengths:	French Canadian and Quebec Studies, French Canadian Folklore, Quebec Geography, French and French Canadian Literature, Civil Law, 19th century French musical press, Philosophy.
Public Databases:	None.

University of Lethbridge (Eureka!)
Lethbridge, Alberta

ACCESS:	**Telnet: eureka.uleth.ca**
Instructions:	At the "login:" prompt, type **library**.
How to Exit:	Type **D** from the main menu.
OPAC Type:	INNOPAC
Size of Collection:	1,000,000 items.
% Catalogued:	85-90%. Microforms and LPs are not catalogued.
Subject Strengths:	None.
Public Databases:	None.

Lethbridge Community College
Lethbridge, Alberta

ACCESS:	**Gopher: gopher.uleth.ca**
Instructions:	Select **Online Library Catalogues**, then select **LCC Library**.
How to Exit:	Choose **Exit** from the main screen.
OPAC Type:	MULTILIS
Size of Collection:	60,000 titles, 77,000 items. 500 serial subscriptions.
% Catalogued:	100% of books and audiovisuals. Periodical holdings are being added.
Subject Strengths:	Trades such as Electronics and Electronic Drafting, Environmental Science, Criminal Justice, Clinical Nursing, Fashion Design, Communication Arts.
Public Databases:	None.

Malaspina College (MACAT)
Nanaimo, British Columbia

ACCESS:	**Telnet: mala.bc.ca**
Instructions:	At the "Username:" prompt, type **MACAT**. Select option 1 for the library catalogue.
How to Exit:	Type **m** to get to the main menu. At the main menu, type **q** to disconnect. Type **quit** at any time to disconnect from the system without returning to the main menu.
OPAC Type:	TKM
Size of Collection:	113,000 items.
% Catalogued:	100%
Subject Strengths:	Call for information.
Public Databases:	Electronic Libraries Network Media Database (all 16mm films and videorecordings held by post-secondary academic libraries in B.C.), Plays Index, University/College Calendars Collection, ELN Serials Database (periodicals held by post-secondary academic libraries in B.C. and the Vancouver Public Library).

University of Manitoba (Bridge)
Winnipeg, Manitoba

ACCESS:	**Telnet: umopac.umanitoba.ca**
Instructions:	When the "UML=>" prompt appears on the screen, type **be** to display the introductory screen. Type the command **set lib uml** to restrict the search to the University of Manitoba.
How to Exit:	Type **close** to disconnect.
OPAC Type:	PALS
Size of Collection:	1.6 million volumes, 480,000 government publications, 1.2 million microforms and audio-visual materials.
% Catalogued:	Almost 100%. Older government publications, some of the Slavic collection, and several gift collections are not catalogued.
Subject Strengths:	Western Canadian History and Literature, Slavic Studies, Icelandic Studies, Dental collection, slide collection
Public Databases:	None.

McGill University (MUSE)
Montreal, Quebec

ACCESS:	**TN3270: mvs.mcgill.ca**

Instructions:	The "Welcome to McGill University" menu will be displayed. Select **2** for MUSE. When you see the "CICS-VS" screen, press the **<enter>** key.
How to Exit:	Type **stop** to disconnect.
OPAC Type:	NOTIS
Size of Collection:	2,011,480 titles.
% Catalogued:	78%. Not catalogued: many government documents, some maps, music scores and audio room collections from the Music Library.
Subject Strengths:	Canadiana. MUSE contains 60,000 records for the monograph collection of the Canadian Institute for Microreproductions (available at McGill on microfiche).
Public Databases:	None.

McMaster University (MORRIS)
Hamilton, Ontario

ACCESS:	**TN3270: mcmvm1.cis. mcmaster.ca.**
Instructions:	A screen will appear that reads "McMaster University Service Selection Screen." From this screen, choose **F9 — Public Services**. On the next menu, choose "MORRISP" by entering an **s** in the column beside MORRISP.
How to Exit:	Type **= = m** to exit the catalogue, then PF12 to disconnect.
OPAC Type:	NOTIS
Size of Collection:	1,500,000 volumes.
% Catalogued:	Majority. Most government publications and material from archives and research collections are not catalogued.
Subject Strengths:	18th Century Literature, Archives on several Canadian authors, the Bertrand Russell Archives, Canadian government publications, U.S. Government publications, United Nations publications, Health Sciences.
Public Databases:	None.

Memorial University of Newfoundland (FOLIO)
St. John's, Newfoundland

ACCESS:	**Telnet: mungate.library.mun.ca**
Instructions:	At the "login:" prompt, type **mungate**. At the "Please enter terminal type:" prompt, type **vt100**. At the "Your Response:" prompt, type **select**. Select file **2** to access the library catalogue.

How to Exit:	Type **cancel** to leave the library catalogue. Type **end** at the "Your Response:" prompt to return to the welcome screen. Type **logoff** to disconnect.
OPAC Type:	SPIRES
Size of Collection:	960,441 monographs, 80,834 documents/technical reports, 274,064 serial volumes, 9,750 serial subscriptions, 1,694,407 volume equivalents in microform. Marine Institute not included in above figures.
% Catalogued:	100% of post-1979 titles. 100% of journal titles, Centre for Newfoundland Studies, Rare Book Collection, Health Sciences Library, Sir Wilfred Grenfell College, 50% of Marine Institute collection, 50% of pre-1979 titles in main library.
Subject Strengths:	Newfoundland history, Earth Sciences, Biochemistry, Folklore, Linguistics, Irish Studies, Maritime History (trade and commerce).
Public Databases:	Archives of ANSAX-L (Anglo-Saxon Literature/Language Listserv), MUN Library Union Catalogue, Catalogue of Archival Collections in the Centre for Newfoundland Studies, Catalogue of Videotapes produced by MUN extension, Canadian Labour Bibliography, Labrador Institute for Northern Studies Catalogue, Catalogue of MUN Folklore and Language Archives, Catalogue of the Ocean Engineering Information Centre, Bibliography of journal articles concerning Newfoundland and Labrador (40,000 entries), Catalogue of Queen's College (Anglican Seminary), Catalogue of the Collection of Radical Pamphlets (20th Century), Catalogue of the Art Slide Collection at Sir Wilfred Grenfell College.

Université de Moncton (ELOIZE)
Moncton, New Brunswick

ACCESS:	**Telnet: 139.103.2.2.**
Instructions:	at the "Service?" prompt, type **champ**. Follow the instructions.
How to Exit:	Type **fin** to disconnect. Type **REC** to start a new search.
OPAC Type:	GEAC
Size of Collection:	410,000 titles. 55% of the collection is in English, 45% in French.
% Catalogued:	40%.
Subject Strengths:	Acadian people, French and French Canadian Literature.
Public Databases:	None.

Mount Allison University
Sackville, New Brunswick

ACCESS:	**Telnet: bigmac.mta.ca**
Instructions:	At the "Username:" prompt, type **CATALOG**. Follow the on-screen instructions.
How to Exit:	Press **CTRL-Z** to disconnect. Type **st** to start a new search.
OPAC Type:	DRA
Size of Collection:	300,000 volumes.
% Catalogued:	50%. (100% of Government Documents, 30% of the general collection).
Subject Strengths:	Maritime History.
Public Databases:	None.

Mount Saint Vincent University (Novanet)
Halifax, Nova Scotia

ACCESS:	**Telnet: novanet.nstn.ns.ca**
Instructions:	A menu will appear when the connection is established. Select menu option **6** to limit the search to Mount Saint Vincent University.
OPAC Type:	GEAC
How to Exit:	Type **end** to disconnect. Type **cat** to begin a new search.
Size of Collection:	155,000 volumes.
% Catalogued:	80%. Most rare books are not catalogued. Approximately 50% of government documents are not catalogued.
Subject Strengths:	Women's Studies, Tourism and Hospitality, Public Relations. McDonald Rare Book Collection.
Public Databases:	None.

Natural Resources Canada
Headquarters Library
Ottawa, Ontario

ACCESS:	**Telnet: hqlib.emr.ca**
Instructions:	At the "login:" prompt, type **opac**.
OPAC Type:	MULTILIS
How to Exit:	Press **PF1** until the initial screen appears. Select **Exit** from the menu.

University of Northern British Columbia
Prince George, British Columbia

ACCESS:	**Telnet: library.unbc.edu**
Instructions:	At the "Username:" prompt, type **LIBRARY**.
How to Exit:	Select **Quit** from the "Options" item on the menu bar.
OPAC Type:	DRA
Size of Collection:	100,000 items.
% Catalogued:	100%.
Subject Strengths:	First Nations and Northern Literature (collection under development).
Public Databases:	None.

Nova Scotia College of Art and Design (Novanet)
Halifax, Nova Scotia

ACCESS:	**Telnet: novanet.nstn.ns.ca**
Instructions:	A menu will appear when the connection is established. Select option **6** to limit the search to the Nova Scotia College of Art and Design.
How to Exit:	Type **end** to disconnect. Type **cat** to begin a new search.
OPAC Type:	GEAC
Size of Collection:	28,000 volumes.
% Catalogued:	95%.
Subject Strengths:	Environmental Planning, Graphic Communication and Design, Crafts, Fine Arts, Art Education. Exhibition Catalog Collection. Artists Books Collection.
Public Databases:	None.

Ontario Institute for Studies in Education (ELOISE)
Toronto, Ontario

ACCESS:	**Telnet: eloise.oise.on.ca**
Instructions:	At the "login:" prompt, type **eloise**. Follow the instructions, and select option **1** to search the library catalogue.
How to Exit:	Press **PF1** until the initial screen appears, then select **Exit** to leave the catalogue. A menu will appear. Press **PF1** to leave the menu, and press **PF1** again to disconnect.
OPAC Type:	MULTILIS
Size of Collection:	251,723 print volumes, 523,686 microfiche/film, 18,595 multimedia, 30,366 bound journal volumes.
% Catalogued:	100%.

Subject Strengths:	Education and psychology. Unique collection of Ontario historical textbooks and curriculum guidelines.
Public Databases:	Ontario Education Resources Information Service (ONTERIS).

Ottawa Public Library (OTTCAT)
Ottawa, Ontario

ACCESS:	**Telnet: ottlib.carleton.ca**
Instructions:	A menu will appear when the connection is established. Select **1** to search the catalogue.
How to Exit:	Press **CTRL-Z** to return to the main menu. Select option **4** to disconnect. Type **st** to start a new search.
OPAC Type:	DRA
Size of Collection:	325,000 titles, 1,041,894 volumes.
% Catalogued:	90%. Not catalogued: laser discs, paperbacks, telephone books, annual reports, maps, Statistics Canada publications, college and university calendars, pamphlets.
Subject Strengths:	Ottawa Room Collection — books and pamphlets by local authors and publishers, early city directories, local newspapers, maps and briefs, municipal minutes and by-laws.
Public Databases:	None.

University of New Brunswick (PHOENIX)
Fredericton, New Brunswick

ACCESS:	**TN3270: terra.csd.unb.ca**
Instructions:	Choose menu option **8**.
How to Exit:	Type **stop**.
OPAC Type:	In-house.
Size of Collection:	1,045,147 print volumes and 2,002,537 equivalent volumes in microform.
% Catalogued:	Majority. Not catalogued: 20,000 titles from the regular collection, 50% of the government publications, special collections.
Subject Strengths:	Surveying engineering. Canadian history. Loyalist material. Canadian correspondence of Lord Beaverbrook.
Public Databases:	None.

University of Ottawa (ORBIS)
Ottawa, Ontario

ACCESS:	Telnet: lib.uottawa.ca
Instructions:	At the ">>>" prompt, type **pubmrt**. Follow the instructions.
How to Exit:	Type **so** to get back to the main menu, select option 11 to disconnect, and use the telnet escape sequence to disconnect from the ORBIS screen.
OPAC Type:	DYNIX
Size of Collection:	4,122,000 items.
% Catalogued:	85%. Partly catalogued: government publications, microforms, records, musical scores, maps. Uncatalogued collections: slides, air photos, archival material.
Subject Strengths:	Chemistry, Civil Engineering, Physics, Health Sciences, History, French and English literature, Management/Economics, Slavic Studies, Law. Canadian Women's Movement Archives. 600 different titles of feminist periodicals, newspapers, newsletters, and magazines.
Public Databases:	None.

University of Prince Edward Island (BOBCAT)
Charlottetown, Prince Edward Island

ACCESS:	Telnet: lib.cs.upei.ca
Instructions:	At the "Username:" prompt, type **BOBCAT**. Type **pac** to access the library catalogue.
How to Exit:	Press **CTRL-Z** to return to the main menu. From the main menu, select **EXIT** to disconnect.
OPAC Type:	DRA
Size of Collection:	633,000 items
% Catalogued:	65%.
Subject Strengths:	Veterinary Medicine, Nursing, Education.
Public Databases:	None.

Université du Québec (BADADUQ)
Sainte-Foy, Quebec

ACCESS:	Telnet: sigird.uqam.ca
Instructions:	Once connected, choose the number corresponding to your terminal type (usually vt100). Select option **2** to search the library catalogue.
How to Exit:	Press **PF1** until the initial menu appears, then select **1** from the menu to disconnect.

OPAC Type:	SIGIRD.
Size of Collection:	1,190,802 items.
% Catalogued:	42%. Not catalogued or minimally catalogued: 690,125 titles, including 59,000 microforms, 103,000 government documents, 2,400 photographs, 21,000 musical illustrations, 21,000 sound recordings, 50,000 maps, 318,000 aerial photographs, films and videos, computer programs.
Subject Strengths:	Visual Arts, Art slides, Intercultural Education, Thanatology (study of death), Project Management, Real Estate Sciences, Sexology, Sound Archives of Radio-Canada.
Public Databases:	None.

Queen's University (QLINE)
Queen's Library Network
Kingston, Ontario

ACCESS:	**TN3270: qline.queensu.ca**
Instructions:	A menu appears when the connection is established.
	Type **LIB** to search the library catalogue.
How to Exit:	Type **stop**.
OPAC Type:	NOTIS
Size of Collection:	4,000,000 items. 14,000 serials.
% Catalogued:	99%.
Subject Strengths:	Canadiana, Western European History (esp. Britain and France), English and Anglo-Irish Literature, British and French Art and Architecture, Modern South African History, Political Philosophy and Policy Studies, Economics, Mathematics, Geology.
Public Databases:	University Archives.

Regina Public Library
Regina, Saskatchewan

ACCESS:	**Telnet: opc.rpl.regina.sk.ca**
Instructions:	Follow instructions on the screen.
How to Exit:	Type **end** to disconnect.
OPAC Type:	GEAC GLIS
Size of Collection:	265,000 titles.
% Catalogued:	Majority. Not catalogued/partially catalogued: serials, paperbacks, vertical files, small collections (e.g. maps), microforms, professional librarian's material.

Subject Strengths:	Local Saskatchewan history, Genealogical records for Prairie residents, Canadian fiction and poetry.
Public Databases:	None.

University of Regina (MURLIN)
Multi**U**ser **R**egina **L**ibrary **I**nformation **N**etwork
Regina, Saskatchewan

ACCESS:	TN3270: max.cc.uregina.ca
Instructions:	At the MAX logo screen, tab to the command line and type **d vsesp**.
	At the CICS logo screen, clear the screen, and type:
	LUUR to access the University of Regina Library
	LULG to access the Saskatchewan Legislative Library
	LUGD to access the Gabriel Dumont Institute
	LUHL to access the Saskatchewan Department of Health Resource Center, Plains Health Centre Library, and the Regina General Hospital Library
	A MURLIN logo should appear. Press the **<enter>** key at the "NEXT COMMAND:" prompt.
	To change catalogues, clear the screen and type the four letter code of the library catalogue you want to search.
How to Exit:	Clear and screen and type **log**. Type **sta** to start another search.
OPAC Type:	NOTIS
Size of Collection:	830,000 records.
% Catalogued:	Majority. Not catalogued: Department of Health, Plains Health Centre, Gabriel Dumont and Regina General Hospital. Partially catalogued: Legislative Library.
Subject Strengths:	General Arts and Sciences, Education, Administration, Journalism, Social Work, Native Studies.
Public Databases:	None.

Royal Military College of Canada
Kingston, Ontario

ACCESS:	Telnet: pacx.rmc.ca
Instructions:	At the "Enter class" prompt, type **library**. Follow the instructions on the screen.
How to Exit:	Type **so** to start a new search. At the main menu, select option **13** to leave the catalogue. Use your telnet escape sequence to disconnect from the RMC screen.
OPAC Type:	DYNIX

Size of Collection:	363,431 items (March/92).
% Catalogued:	98% of books and serials. Very little catalogued: technical reports, government documents, micro-form, photographs, manuscripts, and prints.
Subject Strengths:	Military studies (45,010 in March/92), first editions of Canadian literature.
Public Databases:	None.

Royal Roads Military College
Victoria, British Columbia

ACCESS:	**Telnet: opac.royalroads.ca**
Instructions:	Press the **<enter>** at the "OPTION:" prompt.
How to Exit:	Type **off** at the "OPTION:" prompt.
OPAC Type:	Carleton's CUBE software.

Ryerson Polytechnic University
Toronto, Ontario

ACCESS:	**Telnet: 141.117.13.1**
Instructions:	At the "Username:" prompt, type **RYERSON**. Select **1** to access the library catalogue.
How to Exit:	Type **stop** to return to the main menu. Type **0** to disconnect.
OPAC Type:	DRA
Size of Collection:	320,898 volumes, 3,239 periodical subscriptions, 1,351,849 microform items, 35,762 audiovisual items, 15,828 maps, 87,786 pamphlets.
% Catalogued:	All books and most audiovisual materials. Not catalogued: pamphlets, maps, annual reports, law reports, theses, some urban planning documents.
Subject Strengths:	Media Arts, Radio and Television, Film and Photography, Fashion, Interior Design, Midwifery, Development Studies.
Public Databases:	None.

Saint Mary's University (Novalink)
Halifax, Nova Scotia

ACCESS:	**Telnet: novalink.nstn.ns.ca**
Instructions:	A menu appears when the connection is established. Select option **6** to limit the search to St. Mary's University.
How to Exit:	Type **end** to disconnect.
OPAC Type:	GEAC

Size of Collection:	301,000 volumes.
% Catalogued:	85%. All currently received periodicals are catalogued. Not catalogued: 25% of the dead titles (periodicals not currently received), government documents collection.
Subject Strengths:	Business, Irish Studies.
Public Databases:	None.

Saskatoon Public Library (HOMER2)
Saskatoon, Saskatchewan

ACCESS:	**Telnet: charly.publib.saskatoon.sk.ca**
Instructions:	At the "Username" prompt, type **PUBLIC**.
	At the "pac>>" prompt, type **pac**. Follow the instructions.
How to Exit:	Type **stop** to return to the "pac>>" prompt. At the "pacc>>" prompt, type **quit** to disconnect.
OPAC Type:	DRA
Size of Collection:	720,000 items.
% Catalogued:	97%. Not catalogued: mass-market paperbacks, audio-cassettes, magazines, vertical file collection.
Subject Strengths:	Local history, English-language literature, History.
Public Databases:	None.

University of Saskatchewan (SONIA)
Saskatoon, Saskatchewan

ACCESS:	**Telnet: sklib.usask.ca**
Instructions:	At the "Username:" prompt, type **SONIA**. Select option **1**, then select option **1** again.
How to Exit:	Type **end**, type **Q**, type **Q** again.
OPAC Type:	GEAC
Size of Collection:	1.53 million print volumes, 2.53 million microform items, 427,500 government publications and pamphlets.
% Catalogued:	97%. Not catalogued: Some older government publications.
Subject Strengths:	Prairie Provinces History and Culture, including the Shortt Library of Western Canadiana. 18th Century History and Enlightenment. International Human Rights. Agriculture and Agrieconomics (including cooperatives). Conrad Aiken published materials. Specialized European Documentation Centre. Russell Green Music Manuscripts.

Public Databases: Saskatoon News Index, Library Hours, Landmarks of Science, University of Saskatchewan Government Publications, University Archives, Special Collections (Canadiana Pamphlets, Manuscripts, Theses), Canadian Institute for Historical Microreproductions, Canadian Education Index, History of Photography (microfilm collection), American Periodical Series — 18th Century (microfilm collection), Saskatchewan Teachers' Federation Library, Native Resource Centre, Saskchewan Theological Libraries Consortium, Rt. Hon. John George Diefenbaker Centre Archive, Film Library, University Archives, ERIC (Resouces in Education and Current Index to Journals in Education).

Université de Sherbrooke (SIBUS)
Sherbrooke, Quebec

ACCESS:	Telnet: catalo.biblio.usherb.ca
Instructions:	At the "login:" prompt, type **qsheru**.
How to Exit:	Press the **PF1** key until the initial screen is displayed. Use the arrow keys to select **Exit** from the menu.
OPAC Type:	MULTILIS
Size of Collection:	457,315 volumes, 232,343 printed periodicals, 5937 periodical subscriptions.
% Catalogued:	Majority. Some categories of maps are not catalogued.
Subject Strengths:	Call for information.
Public Databases:	None.

Simon Fraser University (SFULIB)
Burnaby, British Columbia

ACCESS:	Telnet: library.sfu.ca
Instructions:	At the "Username:" prompt, type **SFULIB**. Follow the instructions.
How to Exit:	Type **end** to disconnect.
OPAC Type:	GEAC
Size of Collection:	2,200,000 items.
% Catalogued:	Not catalogued: slides, microforms, maps, some government documents.
Subject Strengths:	Contemporary Literature, Wordsworth.
Public Databases:	None.

St. Francis Xavier University (Novanet)
Antigonish, Nova Scotia

ACCESS:	Telnet: novanet.nstn.ns.ca
Instructions:	A menu will appear when the connection is established. Select option **6** to limit the search to St. Francis Xavier.
How to Exit:	Type **end** to disconnect.
OPAC Type:	GEAC
Size of Collection:	425,000 volumes.
% Catalogued:	32% by September, 1994.
Subject Strengths:	Celtic History and Gaelic material.
Public Databases:	None.

Technical University of Nova Scotia (Novanet)
Halifax, Nova Scotia

ACCESS:	Telnet: novanet.nstn.ns.ca
Instructions:	A menu will appear when the connection is established. Select option **6** to limit the search to the Technical University of Nova Scotia.
How to Exit:	Type **end** to disconnect.
OPAC Type:	GEAC
Size of Collection:	100,000 volumes, 35,000 monographs, 65,000 serials.
% Catalogued:	70% of all serial titles, 91% of currently received serial titles, 98% of monograph titles including 100% of all TUNS theses.
Subject Strengths:	Architecture, Engineering, Computer Science.
Public Databases:	None.

University of Toronto (UTCAT)
Toronto, Ontario

ACCESS:	Telnet: vax.library.utoronto.ca
Instructions:	At the "Username:" prompt, type **utlink**. Type **e** to skip the bulletins. Press **<enter>** when prompted for a password.
How to Exit:	Select **EXIT/Logoff** the "UTLink Menu" option on the menu bar.
OPAC Type:	DRA
Size of Collection:	7,000,000 volumes.
% Catalogued:	90% of the holdings of the University of Toronto library. Not catalogued: Non-roman titles. 90% of the holdings of the College, Faculty of Department libraries. Not catalogued: some older materials.

Subject Strengths:	All areas.
Public Databases:	None.

Trent University (TOPCAT)
Peterborough, Ontario

ACCESS:	**Telnet: babel.trentu.ca**
Instructions:	At the "Username:" prompt, type **TOPCAT**. Select option **1** from the menu.
How to Exit:	Press **CTRL-Z** to return to the main menu. Type **EX** to disconnect.
OPAC Type:	DRA
Size of Collection:	375,000 titles.
% Catalogued:	>95%. Not catalogued: aerial photos.
Subject Strengths:	Canadiana, local history, archives relating to the Trent Valley Area.
Public Databases:	Trent University Archives. Wilson Social Sciences Index.

University of Victoria (VICTOR)
Victoria, British Columbia

ACCESS:	**Telnet: mpg.uvic.ca**
Instructions:	At "Enter Service Name...", type **victor**.
	Type **vt100** as the terminal type,
	Press **<enter>** when the logon screen appears.
How to Exit:	Type **stop** to disconnect. Type **sta** to return to the welcome screen.
OPAC Type:	NOTIS
Size of Collection:	1.8 million volumes, 1.7 million microforms, 42,000 sound recordings, 28,000 scores, 4,000 films and videos, 170,000 maps and aerial photographs.
% Catalogued:	Not catalogued: pre-1978 holdings of Main Library, pre-1988 holdings of Law Library, 90% of the law serials.
Subject Strengths:	Local History, Modern British Literature.
Public Databases:	None.

University of Waterloo (WATCAT)
Waterloo, Ontario

ACCESS:	**Telnet: watcat.uwaterloo.ca**
Instructions:	Press **<enter>** when the welcome screen is displayed. Follow the instructions.

How to Exit:	Type **end**.
OPAC Type:	GEAC
Size of Collection:	2,968,557 printed materials.
% Catalogued:	100%. Some microforms not catalogued on the OPAC.
Subject Strengths:	Mathematics, Computer Science. Euclid, Dance, Robert Southy, Feminism and Women's Studies, Lady Aberdeen Library, Library of George Santayana, John Herbert, Eric Gill.
Public Databases:	None.

University of Waterloo (WatMedia)
Waterloo, Ontario

ACCESS:	**Gopher: watserv2.uwaterloo.ca**
Instructions:	select **Departments**, then select **Audio Visual Centre**, then select **WATMEDIA Film and Media Holdings Database**.
How to Exit:	Select the **exit** command on your Gopher client.
OPAC Type:	SPIRES. Application software written in-house.
Size of Collection:	5095 items from the University of Waterloo. Over 41,000 items in total.
% Catalogued:	100%.
Subject Strengths:	Art History, History, Computer Science, Engineering, 20th Century Spanish Culture, Anthropology.
Public Databases:	None.

University of Western Ontario
London, Ontario

ACCESS:	**Telnet: library.uwo.ca**
Instructions:	Press the **<enter>** key at the welcome screen. When asked to press "send", press the **<enter>** key.
How to Exit:	Press **CTRL-D** to disconnect. Type **cat** to begin a new search.
OPAC Type:	GEAC
Size of Collection:	2,100,000 volumes, 2,860,000 microforms, 950,000 other items.
% Catalogued:	90-95%. Not catalogued: pamphlets (pre-1993), regional collection, microform analytics.
Subject Strengths:	Canadian, American, and British Government Publications, Canadiana, Medicine, English, American History, Women's Studies, Opera, Milton and Miltoniana, Chemistry, Sciences, Mathematics.
Public Databases:	None.

Wilfrid Laurier University (QCAT)
Waterloo. Ontario

ACCESS:	Telnet: mach1.wlu.ca
Instructions:	At the "Login:" prompt, type **public**. At the first menu, select option 1. At the second menu, select option 1 again.
How to Exit:	Press **CTRL-C** to get back to the menu. Type **E**, then select option **5** on the next menu.
OPAC Type:	In-house.
Size of Collection:	1.2 million.
% Catalogued:	95%. Slides and phone records not catalogued.
Subject Strengths:	Lutheran material, social work, business and economics, post World War II international relations, music.
Public Databases:	Music Ensemble Collection.

University of Windsor (LUIS)
Library User Information System
Windsor, Ontario

ACCESS:	Telnet: library.uwindsor.ca
Instructions:	Select 1 for Main Library or 2 for Law Library, Press the <enter> key twice until you receive the "ENTER TERMINAL TYPE:" prompt. Type **vt100**. When a blank screen appears, press <enter> key several times, and the on-line catalogue will be displayed.
How to Exit:	Type **stop** to disconnect. Type **sta** to start a new search.
OPAC Type:	NOTIS
Size of Collection:	2,375,507 volumes.
% Catalogued:	90-95%. Chinese, Russian, and non-roman alphabet items, newspaper clippings, some archival documents, and some materials in the Curriculum Resource Centre (e.g. posters) are not catalogued.
Subject Strengths:	Asian Studies, Canadian and American Relations, Criminology, International Trade, Labour Economics, Philosophy and Religious Studies, Political Science, Psychology, Theology, Victorian Literature, Sociology, Social Work, the Great Lakes Collection (38,000 documents on the Great Lakes).
Public Databases:	None.

University of Winnipeg (Bridge)
Winnipeg, Manitoba

ACCESS:	Telnet: umopac.umanitoba.ca
Instructions:	Type **be** at the "UML=>" prompt.
	Type **set lib UOW** to restrict the search to the University of Winnipeg.
How to Exit:	Type **close**.
OPAC Type:	PALS.
Size of Collection:	340,000 titles.
% Catalogued:	66%. Includes most bibliographic records since 1976 and almost all records falling between A and H on the Library of Congress Classification.
Subject Strengths:	Theology, Science Fiction, 19th Century Canadian Fiction, Canadian History. Western Canada Pictorial Index (large slide collection of reproductions of photographs dealing with a wide spectrum of western Canadian social history).
Public Databases:	None.

Vancouver Public Library
Vancouver, British Columbia

ACCESS:	Telnet: vpl.vancouver.bc.ca
Instructions:	At the "login:" prompt, type **netpac**. At the "password:" prompt, type **netpac1**.
	When asked to "indicate" which terminal you are using, select option **5**.
How to Exit:	Type **so** to return to the main menu. Select option **17** to exit the catalogue.
OPAC Type:	DYNIX
Size of Collection:	750,000 titles, 2,000,000 items.
% Catalogued:	Serials holdings are partially catalogued.
Subject Strengths:	Business, Northwest History, Photography, Standards.
Public Databases:	Community Organization Directory, Vancouver City Council Minutes, Consumer Index, Community Events Calendar, Quick Reference File.

York University (YORKLINE)
North York, Ontario

ACCESS:	Telnet: yorkline.yorku.ca
Instructions:	Press <enter> several times when the connection is established. At the "ENTER TERMINAL TYPE" prompt, type **vt100**. When the York screen appears, type **YORKLINE**.

ow to Exit:	Type **stop**.
PAC Type:	NOTIS
ize of Collection:	2 million print volumes.
Catalogued:	100%.
ubject Strengths:	Dance, Social Sciences, especially Canadian Studies, Business Administration, Psychology, Sociology, Law.
ublic Databases:	None.

THE DIRECTORY OF WWW SERVERS IN CANADA

· ·

© 1994 Rick Broadhead and Jim Carroll

This directory lists the Canadian World Wide Web serve
that were operational in January, 1994. Directory entries a
structured in the following format:

Name of the Organization Sponsoring the WWW Server
Name of Department (if applicable)
Name of the city where the WWW is located

ACCESS (URL):	The URL of the WWW server.
Contains:	Examples of the type of information that can be found on the WWW server.

BROWSERS

To access the WWW servers in this directory, you will nee
to have access to a WWW client known as a browser. If yo
are running SLIP/PPP or if you have a dedicated Intern
connection, the client will be located on your computer or c
your organization's computer system. If you have an Intern
account on an Internet Service Provider's computer, a WWV
client may be located on the computer that you are dialir
into. If you are not sure if a WWW client has been installe
on your Internet host, ask your Internet Service Provider, o
the local computing staff. Not all Internet Service Provide
have installed WWW clients. If a WWW client isn't installe
locally, you access WWW by using telnet to connect to on
of the public WWW clients listed below. While these clien
are available to anyone on the Internet, only use these clien
if you have don't have access to your own WWW client.
local WWW client is much faster, and it significantly reduce
the drain on Internet resources. WWW clients are availab
by anonymous FTP for a number of different computer pla
forms. If a WWW client is not available on your Intern

ost, ask your Internet Service Provider or local computing
aff if they can install one.

UBLIC WWW CLIENTS

here are two types of public WWW clients:

) **Line Mode Browsers**: You move through the Web by
ying in numbers on a command line. The number you enter
orresponds to the information you want to see.

:) **Full Screen Browsers**: These clients are more powerful
d allow you to move through the Web using your arrow
eys and by selecting highlighted text.

ere are the addresses of some public WWW browsers. Use
e telnet command to connect to them.

Internet Address	Type	Userid
nfo.cern.ch	Line Mode	N/A
ukanaix.cc.ukans.edu	Full Screen	www
www.njit.edu	Full Screen	www

o go directly to the servers listed in the directory below,
ou need to specify the URL (Uniform Resource Locator) of
e server. URLs can be specified for any file or service on
e Internet. URLs look like this:

resource_type://location_of_resource

here:
source_type is the type of Internet resource
cation_of_resource is the physical location of the Internet
source

ll WWW URLs have HTTP as their resource type. HTTP
ands for HyperText Transmission Protocol.

Once connected to a full-screen or line-oriented WWW
owser, use the "Go" command to specify a URL. When
sing a line-oriented browser such as the one at info.cern.ch,
pe **go URL** at the command line, replacing URL with the
ll URL of the WWW server you want to access. For ex-
ple, to connect to the WWW server at the University of
ew Brunswick, type:

go http://degaulle.hil.unb.ca

This command tells the client program to go the WWW server at the address **degaulle.hil.unb.ca**. When using a full screen browser, type the letter **"G"** and the client will prompt you to input the name of the URL.

For More Information
More information about WWW can be found in the Usenet newsgroup **comp.infosystems.www**. We also recommend the document *Frequently Asked Questions About WWW*. This document can be obtained by anonymous FTP at **rtfm.mit.edu** in the directory **pub/usenet/news.answers/www**. The file is **faq**.

To join the WWW discussion list, send an electronic mail message to **listserv@info.cern.ch**. Place the message add **www-announce** on the first line of the body.

University of Alberta
Center for Subatomic Research
Edmonton, Alberta

ACCESS (URL):	http://inuit.phys.ualberta.ca
Contains:	Upcoming conference information.

University of British Columbia
Computer Science Department
Vancouver, British Columbia

ACCESS (URL):	http://www.cs.ubc.ca
Contains:	Database of electronic mail accounts for the computer science department (searchable by login id, host, first name, last name, office#); NHL game schedule; Periodic Table of the Elements; catalogue of locally installed software.

Canadian Astronomy Data Centre
Victoria, British Columbia

ACCESS (URL):	http://ucluelet.dao.nrc.ca
Contains:	Hubble Space Telescope data; information about the Canada-France Hawaii Telescope; information about the Dominion Astrophysical Observatory in Victoria; images from the repaired HST; list of astronomical meetings; mandate and overview of the Centre.

Carleton University
Department of Biology
Ottawa, Ontario

ACCESS (URL):	http://journal.biology.carleton.ca
Contains:	Access to a peer-reviewed journal in conservation biology; general information about the journal (e.g. history, how to make a submission).

Carleton University
Department of Civil and Electronic Engineering
Ottawa, Ontario

ACCESS (URL):	http://www.civeng.carleton.ca
Contains:	Graduate Program information; recent theses; information about faculty members; information about students; information about the Canadian Society for Civil Engineering; pointers to related Civil Engineering and Engineering servers.

Carleton University
School of Architecture
Ottawa, Ontario

ACCESS (URL):	http://thrain.arch.carleton.ca
Contains:	Information about the building; information about facilities and services; information about programs and activities; student resumes

Communications Research Centre
Ottawa, Ontario

ACCESS (URL):	http://debra.dgbt.doc. ca
Contains:	list of CBC Radio products; list of CBC transcripts; CBC Radio programs in digital format; Industry Canada documents

Dalhousie University
Department of Mathematics, Statistics, and Computer Science
Halifax, Nova Scotia

ACCESS (URL):	http://cs.dal.ca/home.html

Contains:	Access to the Metro Halifax Community Access Network (Metro*CAN) Prototype; user guide for local computer systems; access to campus and regional Gopher servers.

Universite Laval
Electrical Engineering Department
Quebec City, Quebec

ACCESS (URL):	http://www.gel.ulaval.ca
Contains:	Information about staff; course listings; information on research laboratories in the department; searchable department telephone directory.

National Research Council of Canada
Knowledge Systems Laboratory
Ottawa, Ontario

The Knowledge Systems Laboratory (KSL) conducts applied research in the field of Artificial Intelligence.

ACCESS (URL):	http://ai.iit.nrc.ca/home-page.html.
Contains:	KSL technical reports; information on KSL staff; links to Internet services related to Artificial Intelligence

Universite de Montreal
Computer Science and Operational Research Department
Montreal, Quebec

ACCESS (URL):	http://www.iro.umontreal.ca
Contains:	(in French) Research papers; information about departmental facilities; information about undergraduate and graduate programs; information about personnel.

University of New Brunswick
Fredericton, New Brunswick

ACCESS (URL):	http://degaulle.hil.unb.ca
Contains:	Information on UNB Chairs, Centres, and Institutes; information about business opportunities in New Brunswick (e.g. information about: quality of life, recreation, research and development); searchable papers of Lord Beaverbrook; information about UNB libraries; information about UNB athletics; information for alumni.

Queens University
Kingston, Ontario

ACCESS (URL):	http://info.queensu.ca
Contains:	Link to Queen's University Campus Wide Information System

THE DIRECTORY OF ARCHIE AND IRC SERVERS IN CANADA

·······································

This directory contains a list of public IRC and Archie servers in Canada.

INTERNET RELAY CHAT (IRC)

To use IRC, you will require access to an IRC client. This will be available on your own system, if you are using SLIP/PPP or if you have a dedicated connection, or on the system of your Internet service provider, if you are dialing into an Internet host. You should check with your Internet Service Provider or local computing staff to determine if an IRC client is installed on your Internet host. If IRC is installed on your system, you should be able to start the client by typing **irc**. This will connect you to a nearby IRC server. IRC clients are available by anonymous FTP for a variety of different platforms. You'll find a complete list of IRC clients in the IRC FAQ, described below. If a local IRC client isn't available, ask your Internet Service Provider or local computing staff if an IRC client can be installed on the system that you are using. Depending on how the IRC client is set up on your Internet host, you may be able to control which server you are connected to.

IRC Servers in Canada

Province	Server Address	Site
Manitoba	castor.cc. umanitoba.ca	University of Manitoba

New Brunswick	degaulle.hil.unb.ca	University of New Brunswick
Nova Scotia	ug.cs.dal.ca	Dalhousie University
Nova Scotia	fox.nstn.ns.ca	Nova Scotia Technology Network
Ontario	green.ariel.cs.yorku.ca	York University
Ontario	clique.cdf.utoronto.ca	University of Toronto
Quebec	pascal.info. polymtl.ca	École Polytechnique de Montréal
Quebec	sifon.cc.mcgill.ca	McGill University

FOR MORE INFORMATION

For more information about IRC, we suggest you monitor the USENET newsgroups **alt.irc**, **alt.irc.ircii**, and **alt.irc. questions**.

Other sources of information on IRC include the IRC FAQ (Frequently Asked Questions About IRC), the IRC Primer, and the IRC Tutorials. They are all available by anonymous FTP, and are strongly recommended if you want to learn how to use IRC.

Description	FTP Site	Directory	File(s)
IRC FAQ	rtfm.mit.edu	pub/usenet/ news.answers	irc.faq
IRC Primer	cs.bu.edu	irc/support	IRCprimer1.1. txt
IRC Tutorials	cs.bu.edu	irc/support	tutorial.*

ARCHIE

In January, 1994, the only public Archie server in Canada was a French-speaking server at the Universite du Québec a Montréal (UQAM). To use this server, telnet to **archie.uqam.ca** and login as **archie**. McGill University, where Archie was originally developed, used to maintain an Archie server at archie.mcgill.ca, but it wasn't returned to service after a hardware failure last year. If you are conversant in French, you can use the Archie server at UQAM. Otherwise, you can try the following Archie servers in the United States. To use these servers, telnet to the server address, and at the "login:" prompt, type **archie**. A password is not required.

Before using these servers, ask your Internet Service Provider or computing staff if an Archie client has been installed on the system that you are using. If an archie client is available on your system, you should be able to start the client by typing **archie**. Archie clients are available by anonymous FTP for a variety of platforms. If an Archie client isn't available on your system, ask your Internet Service Provider or local computing staff if they will install one. You will find that a local Archie client is faster. It also reduces the load on the public archie servers.

Public Archie Servers

Server Address	Location
archie.rutgers.edu	New Jersey
archie.sura.net	Maryland
archie.ans.net	New York
archie.unl.edu	Nebraska
archie.internic.net	Virginia

FOR MORE INFORMATION

If you are interested in Archie, you can subscribe to the Archie-people discussion list. To subscribe, send an electronic mail message to **archie-people-request@bunyip.com** and request that you be added to the list. To send messages to the list, address them to **archie-people@bunyip.com**.

THE DIRECTORY OF CANADIAN USENET NEWSGROUPS

· ·

The attached listing of USENET newsgroups in Canada was compiled by Bruce Becker.

The listing attached is printed in its entirety as compiled by Bruce, with the exception of the exclusion of a count of articles for each newsgroup. No editing changes have been made.

```
Newsgroups:can.general,bc.general,ab.general,
man.general,ont.general,qc.general,ns.general
,nf.general,tor.news,news.groups
Organization: G. T. S., Toronto, Ontario
Subject: A listing of Canadian regional and
university newsgroups
Distribution: can,bc,ab,man,ont,qc,ns,nf,tor
Expires: Sun, 6 Feb 1994 23:59:59 GMT
Archive-name: can-reg-newsgroups
Last-modified: 20 January 1994 by
news@gts.org.
Here's a listing of Canadian regional and
university newsgroups, as it appears from
here. Some of the information is thought to
be reasonably accurate, but some regional
hierarchies are incomplete or perhaps even
missing entirely.
There are 507 groups shown, as well as 32
aliases (indicated by "=" beginning the text
field). Where the text field is merely ".",
no description is known (creative suggestions
are welcomed).
If there are additional such newsgroups on
your system but not in this list, email to
that effect would be appreciated - please
send to "news@gts.org".
Also there is a list of email addresses of
some of the moderators of the moderated
newsgroups, followed by a list of email
addresses of moderated groups for your
"mailpaths" file. These lists are appended
after the end of the newsgroups description
list below.
Thanks to all who send updates, suggestions
and comments - your help is appreciated.
```

```
Bruce Becker News Administration Toronto,
Ont.
Internet: news@gts.org
UUCP: ...!web!gts!news
"We have the technology" - Pere Ubu
```

--------- 8< --------- 8< --------- 8< ----

ab.general	Items of general interest in Alberta, Canada.
ab.jobs	Jobs in Alberta, Canada.
ab.politics	Politics in Alberta, Canada.
acadia.bulletin-board	Acadia University, Wolfville, N.S.
acadia.chat	Acadia University, Wolfville, N.S.
acadia.cs.chat	Acadia University, Wolfville, N.S.
atl.general	Atlantic provinces (conflict with Atlanta newsgroup).
bc.bcnet	British Columbia.
bc.general	British Columbia.
bc.news.stats	British Columbia.
bc.rcbc	British Columbia.
bc.unix	British Columbia.
bc.weather	British Columbia.
calgary.general	Items of general interest in Calgary, Alberta, Canada.
can.ai	Artificial intelligence in Canada.
can.canet.d	An open forum discussing CA*net topics. (Moderated)
can.canet.stats	Usenet statistics from major CA*net NTP sites.
can.domain	Where people re supposed to be able to get even.
can.english	=can.politics
can.forsale	=can.general
can.francais	About the Francophone population (in French).
can.general	Items of general interest to Canadians.
can.jobs	Jobs in Canada.
can.legal	Legal issues in Canada.
can.motss	Gay/Lesbian issues in Canada.
can.newprod	New products for Canada.
can.politics	Canadian politics.
can.schoolnet.biomed.jr	.
can.schoolnet.biomed.sr	.
can.schoolnet.chat.students.jr.	
can.schoolnet.chat.students.sr.	
can.schoolnet.chat.teachers	.
can.schoolnet.chem.jr	.
can.schoolnet.chem.sr	.
can.schoolnet.comp.jr	.

```
can.schoolnet.comp.sr        .
can.schoolnet.earth.jr       .
can.schoolnet.earth.sr       .
can.schoolnet.elecsys.jr     .
can.schoolnet.elecsys.sr     .
can.schoolnet.eng.jr         .
can.schoolnet.eng.sr         .
can.schoolnet.math.jr        .
can.schoolnet.math.sr        .
can.schoolnet.phys.jr        .
can.schoolnet.phys.sr        .
can.schoolnet.problems       .
can.schoolnet.projects.calls .
can.schoolnet.projects.discuss.
can.schoolnet.socsci.jr      .
can.schoolnet.socsci.sr      .
can.schoolnet.space.jr       .
can.schoolnet.space.sr       .
can.sun-stroke       Sun Microsystems Users in
                     Canada.
can.test             Like it sez.
can.usrgroup         /USR/GROUP related
                     information in Canada.
can.uucp             Canadian uucp problems.
can.uucp.maps        Canadian UUCP maps are
                     posted here. (Moderated)
can.vlsi             .
can.wanted.misc      =can.general
carleton.chinese-news Carleton University,
                     Ottawa.
carleton.doe.chat    Carleton University,
                     Ottawa.
carleton.general     Carleton University,
                     Ottawa.
carleton.news        Carleton University,
                     Ottawa.
carleton.scs         Carleton University,
                     Ottawa.
carleton.scs.undergraduate Carleton
                     University, Ottawa.
dal.general          Dalhousie University, Nova
                     Scotia.
dal.test             Dalhousie University, Nova
                     Scotia.
edm.general          Items of general interest
                     in Edmonton, Alberta,
                     Canada.
edm.news.stats       USENET Statistics in
                     Edmonton, Alberta, Canada.
edm.politics         Items of political
                     interest In
                     Edmonton,Alberta, Canada.
edm.usrgrp           Unix Users Group in
                     Edmonton, Alberta, Canada.
hfx.general          Halifax, N.S.
hum.general          Humber College Technology
                     Division, Etobicoke, Ont.
kingston.bbs         The local BBS crowd in
                     Kingston, Ontario,Canada.
```

kingston.eats	Anything dealing with food in Kingston, Ontario, Canada.
kingston.events	Kingston, Ontario, Canada "Happenings".
kingston.forsale	Wanna buy/wanna sell in Kingston, Ontario, Canada.
kingston.general	Miscellaneous discussion in Kingston, Ontario.
kingston.test	1,2,3 ... for Kingston, Ontario, Canada.
kingston.uucp	Discussion of UUCP in Kingston, Ontario, Canada.
kingston.uucp.stats	UUCP statistics in Kingston, Ontario, Canada.
kingston.wanted	Stuff &/or information &/or advice wanted in Kingston.
kw.bb.sale	=kw.forsale
kw.birthdays	Happy birthday in Kitchener-Waterloo, Ontario.
kw.cpsr	KW branch of Computer Professionals for Social Responsibility.
kw.eats	Restaurant reviews.
kw.forsale	Things for sale.
kw.fun	Fun stuff.
kw.general	General information in Kitchener-Waterloo.
kw.housing	Rooms for rent.
kw.internet	=kw.networks
kw.jobs	Job postings.
kw.micro	Microcomputer discussion.
kw.microvax	DEC microvax users.
kw.movies	Film reviews.
kw.networks	Connectivity and networking within the KW community.
kw.news	=kw.news.stats
kw.news.stats	USENET statisitcs in Kitchener-Waterloo, Canada.
kw.stats	=kw.news.stats
kw.theatre	Theatre reviews, etc.
kw.uucp	=kw.networks
mac.test.dant	McMaster University, Burlington, Ontario.
man.general	Manitoba.
mcgill.general	McGill College, Montreal, Quebec.
mcgill.unix	McGill College, Montreal, Quebec.
mtl.general	General stuff in Montreal, Quebec.
mtl.test	USENET Testing in Montreal.
mun.announce	Memorial University of Newfoundland.

```
mun.arts                    .
mun.arts.computing  .
mun.computing           .
mun.cwis                    CampusWide Information
                            System.
mun.general             .
mun.gsu                     Grad Students.
mun.library             .
mun.mac                     Macintosh support.
mun.pc                      General microcomputer.
mun.research            .
mun.safety              .
mun.science             .
mun.seminars            .
mun.sun                     Sun Microsystems.
mun.swgc                    Regional College (Corner
                            Brook).
mun.talk                    .
mun.test                    .
mun.wanted              .
nf.birds                    Newfoundland.
nf.general              Newfoundland.
nf.k12                      Newfoundland.
nf.test                     Newfoundland.
nf.wanted               Newfoundland.
ns.general              Nova Scotia.
ns.nstn.usergroup   Nova Scotia.
ont.archive                 =ont.archives
ont.archives            Archives in Ontario,
                            Canada.
ont.conditions          Road conditions in
                            Ontario, Canada.
ont.events              Ontario, Canada
                            happenings.
ont.events.macwator.ece     =ont.events
ont.followup                =ont.general
ont.forsale                 =ont.general
ont.general             Items of general interest
                            in Ontario, Canada.
ont.jobs                    Jobs in Ontario, Canada.
ont.micro               Microcomputer related
                            postings in Ontario,
                            Canada.
ont.personals.whips.and.rubber.chickens
                            =ont.singles
ont.sf-lovers           Science Fiction Lovers in
                            Ontario, Canada.
ont.singles             Singles in Ontario,
                            Canada.
ont.test                    Testing in Ontario,
                            Canada.
ont.uucp                    UUCP related postings in
                            Ontario, Canada.
ott.events              Seminars and the like at
                            Ottawa, Ontario sites.
ott.for-sale                =ott.forsale
ott.forsale             Things for sale/wanted in
                            Ottawa, Ontario.
ott.general             General news local to
                            Ottawa sites.
```

```
ott.housing              .
ott.ncf                  .
ott.news                  =ott.usenet
ott.online               .
ott.singles              .
ott.usenet               Usenet in Ottawa.
ott.vietnamese           Vietnamese interest group.
ott.weather              Weather forecasts for
                         Ottawa, Ontario.
                         (Moderated)
qc.general               Quebec.
qc.jobs                  Quebec.
qucis.announce           Queens University,
                         Kingston, Ontario.
qucis.chat               Queens University,
                         Kingston, Ontario.
qucis.events             Queens University,
                         Kingston, Ontario.
queens.events            Queens University,
                         Kingston, Ontario.
queens.forsale           Queens University,
                         Kingston, Ontario.
rye.general              Articles of general
                         interest at Ryerson,
                         Toronto.
rye.nets                 Articles on networking at
                         Ryerson.
rye.test                 Group for testing news at
                         Ryerson.
sfu.general              Simon Fraser University,
                         British Columbia.
sfu.grad                 Simon Fraser University,
                         British Columbia.
sj.general               Saint Johns, Newfoundland.
socs.jobs                McGill School of Computer
                         Science,Montreal, Quebec.
socs.misc                McGill School of Computer
                         Science, Montreal, Quebec.
tor.buysell               =tor.general
tor.forsale               =tor.general
tor.general              Items of general interest
                         in Toronto, Canada.
tor.jobs                  =tor.general
tor.news                 USENET in Toronto, Canada.
tor.news.stats           USENET Statistics in
                         Toronto, Canada.
tor.test                 Testing in Toronto,
                         Canada.
tor.uucp                  =tor.general
ualberta.cs.generalUniversity of Alberta.
ualberta.general         .
ualberta.phys.general    .
ubc.events               University of British
                         Columbia.
ubc.forum                University of British
                         Columbia.
ubc.general              University of British
                         Columbia.
```

.bc.help	University of British Columbia.
.bc.unix	University of British Columbia.
.sask.general	University of Saskatchewan.
t.16000k	Discussions on the National Semi series 16000 CPU.
.t.ai	=ut.dcs.ai
.t.biz.sunproducts	.
.t.cdf.announce	UofT Computing Disciplines Facility announcements. (Moderated)
.t.cdf.general	UofT CDF general discussion.
.t.cdf.gripes	UofT CDF complaints.
.t.cdf.student	UofT CDF student talk.
t.cdf.test	UofT CDF testing.
.t.chinese	University of Toronto Chinese community.
t.cquest.general	.
t.cquest.test	.
.t.cslab.problems	.
.t.cslab.system	.
.t.dcs.ai	Artificial Intelligence at the University of Toronto.
.t.dcs.cscw	Computer Supported Cooperative Work.
.t.dcs.dbois	Data Base / Office Information Systems.
.t.dcs.general	General messages from UofT Dept. of Computer Science.
t.dcs.gradnews	Info for Graduates.
t.dcs.graphics	Graphics.
t.dcs.hci	Human-Computer Interaction.
t.dcs.na	Numerical Analysis.
t.dcs.seminars	Seminars.
t.dcs.systems	Systems.
t.dcs.theory	Theory.
t.dcs.vision	Vision Research.
t.ecf.engsci	.
t.ecf.test	.
t.ee	Electrical Engineering.
t.ee.eecg.computer	System-related issues fo the EE Computer Group.
t.ee.eecg.news	EE Computer Group announcements.
t.ee.ieee	IEEE in EE.
t.ee.vlsi	.
t.ee.vlsi.cadence	.
t.ee.vlsi.cmc	.
t.ee.vlsi.cmos4s	.
t.ee.vlsi.electric	.
t.ee.vlsi.test	.
t.eng.gradnews	.
t.general	General messages.
t.mac-users	.
t.na	ut.dcs.na

```
ut.nets.reports        Net connectivity reports.
                       (Moderated)
ut.nonlinear.dynamic-sys    .
ut.org.outing-club Organising indoor &
                       outdoor activities.
ut.org.seta            Students for Ethical
                       Treatment of Animals.
ut.software            .
ut.software.tex        Use of TeX at University
                       of Toronto.
ut.software.x-windows Three guesses.
ut.supercomputer       Pray for the Cray.
ut.ta                  Teaching Assistants.
ut.test                Test messages.
ut.theory                   ut.dcs.theory
ut.unix.sysadmin       System Administration of
                       Unix sites at U. of
                       Toronto.
ut.unix.user           Information for Unix
                       users.
ut.vlsi                Big Iron.
uvic.clubs             University of Victoria,
                       B.C.
uvic.cosi.test         University of Victoria,
                       B.C.
uvic.csc.announce      University of Victoria,
                       B.C.
uvic.csc.coop          University of Victoria,
                       B.C.
uvic.csc.forsale       University of Victoria,
                       B.C.
uvic.csc.general       University of Victoria,
                       B.C.
uvic.csc.mac           University of Victoria,
                       B.C.
uvic.csc.mac.pascalUniversity of Victoria,
                       B.C.
uvic.csc.rigi          University of Victoria,
                       B.C.
uvic.csc.seminar       University of Victoria,
                       B.C.
uvic.csc.system        University of Victoria,
                       B.C.
uvic.csc.system.research University of
                       Victoria, B.C.
uvic.csc.union         University of Victoria,
                       B.C.
uvic.forsale           University of Victoria,
                       B.C.
uvic.general           University of Victoria,
                       B.C.
uvic.jobs              University of Victoria,
                       B.C.
uvic.jobs.adminacadUniversity of Victoria,
                       B.C.
uvic.jobs.confidential University of
                       Victoria, B.C.
uvic.jobs.cupe917      University of Victoria,
                       B.C.
```

vic.jobs.cupe951	University of Victoria, B.C.
vic.jobs.exempt	University of Victoria, B.C.
vic.jobs.external	University of Victoria, B.C.
vic.jobs.notes	University of Victoria, B.C.
vic.jobs.specinstr	University of Victoria, B.C.
vic.lost+found	University of Victoria, B.C.
vic.misc	University of Victoria,B.C.
vic.mlist.apple-ip	University of Victoria, B.C.
vic.mlist.bcnet-info	University of Victoria, B.C.
vic.mlist.framers	University of Victoria, B.C.
vic.mlist.mac-sun	University of Victoria, B.C.
vic.mlist.next-info	University of Victoria, B.C.
vic.mlist.next.next-managers	University of Victoria, B.C.
vic.mlist.next.nextcomm	University of Victoria, B.C.
vic.mlist.next.nug	University of Victoria, B.C.
vic.mlist.offcampus.seminars	University of Victoria, B.C.
vic.mlist.sun-info	University of Victoria, B.C.
vic.mlist.sun-managers	University of Victoria, B.C.
vic.mlist.sunnet-manager	University of Victoria, B.C.
vic.outages	University of Victoria, B.C.
vic.physics.general	University of Victoria, B.C.
vic.physics.seminar	University of Victoria, B.C.
vic.secretariat	University of Victoria, B.C.
vic.secretariat.board	University of Victoria, B.C.
vic.secretariat.senate	University of Victoria, B.C.
vic.seminar	University of Victoria, B.C.
vic.sys.evaluation	University of Victoria, B.C.
vic.sys.mac	University of Victoria, B.C.
vic.sys.next	University of Victoria, B.C.
vic.system	University of Victoria, B.C.

uvic.test	University of Victoria, B.C.
uvic.unix.questions	University of Victoria, B.C.
uw.aco.system	.
uw.ahs.general	.
uw.ahs.system	.
uw.ai.learning	AI stuff at U. of Waterloo, Ontario.
uw.aix.support	Soothing your aix & pains.
uw.archive	.
uw.asplos	.
uw.assignments	for assignment coordination. (Moderated)
uw.campus-news	.
uw.ccng.general	Computer Communications Network Group.
uw.ccng.system	Computer Communications Network Group.
uw.cgl	Computer Graphics Lab.
uw.cgl.software	Computer Graphics Lab.
uw.cgl.system	Computer Graphics Lab.
uw.chinese	(Moderated)
uw.combopt	.
uw.computer-store	(Moderated)
uw.computing.support.staff	Computing Support Staff at U Waterloo.
uw.cong.system	.
uw.cray	nobody uses Crays here, do they?
uw.cs.database	Computer Science.
uw.cs.dept	Computer Science.
uw.cs.eee	Computer Science / Electrical Engineering.
uw.cs.faculty	Computer Science.
uw.cs.general	Computer Science.
uw.cs.grad	Computer Science.
uw.cs.grad.topics	Computer Science.
uw.cs.mdbs	Computer Science.
uw.cs.theory	Computer Science.
uw.cs.ugrad	Computer Science.
uw.csc	Computer Science Club.
uw.csg	.
uw.dcs.changes	Computing Services.
uw.dcs.courses	Computing Services. (Moderated)
uw.dcs.gripe	.
uw.dcs.news	Computing Services. (Moderated)
uw.dcs.operations	Computing Services.
uw.dcs.staff	Computing Services.
uw.dcs.suggestions	Computing Services.
uw.dcs.system	Computing Services.
uw.dcs.trc	Computing Services.
uw.dcs.watserv1	Computing Services.
uw.dcs.watshine	Computing Services.
uw.disspla	.
uw.dp.changes	.
uw.dp.staff	.

w.dsgroup	Data Structures.
w.dsgroup.misc	Data Structures.
w.ee.grad	Electrical Engineering.
w.ee.opt	Electrical Engineering.
w.ee.sunee	Electrical Engineering.
w.engl.phd	.
w.english-usage	.
w.envst.general	.
w.envst.system	.
w.fass	Faculty, Alumnae, Staff, Students amateur theatre.
w.feds	. (Moderated)
w.forsale	Items for sale.
w.general	Whatever.
w.gllow	Gay & Lesbians.
w.gnu	For GNU at WATERLU.
w.grad	.
w.gsa	Graduate Student Association. (Moderated)
w.harmony	Harmony OS.
w.icr	Institute for Computer Research.
w.icr.forum	Institute for Computer Research.
w.icr.hardware	Institute for Computer Research.
w.image-proc	Image Processing.
w.imprint	Imprint, UW student newspaper. (Moderated)
w.jsaw	For Japanese Student Association ofWaterloo.
w.kin	Kinesiology.
w.lang	Languages.
w.laurel	Laurel OS.
w.library	Library.
w.library.journals	Library.
w.library.new-books	Library.
w.logic	Logic programming.
w.lpaig	Linear Programming & Artificial Intelligence Group.
w.lpaig.changes	Linear Programming & Artificial Intelligence Group.
w.lpaig.nlu	Linear Programming & Artificial Intelligence Group.
w.lpaig.system	Linear Programming & Artificial Intelligence Group.
w.mac-users	.
w.mail-list.biomech	mailing list.
w.mail-list.comp-chem	mailing list.
w.mail-list.csnet-forum	mailing list.
w.mail-list.fractals	mailing list.
w.mail-list.s	mailing list.
w.mail-list.sml	mailing list.
w.mail-list.sun-managers	mailing list.
w.maple	Maple symbolic math software.

uw.math.faculty	Math Faculty.
uw.math.grad	Math Faculty.
uw.math.tsa	.
uw.mathcad	.
uw.matlab	.
uw.mech.system	Mechanical Engineering.
uw.mfcf.bugs	Math Faculty Computing Facility.
uw.mfcf.gripe	Math Faculty Computing Facility.
uw.mfcf.hardware	Math Faculty Computing Facility.
uw.mfcf.hardware.mac	Math Faculty Computing Facility.
uw.mfcf.people	Math Faculty Computing Facility.
uw.mfcf.questions	Math Faculty Computing Facility.
uw.mfcf.software	Math Faculty Computing Facility.
uw.mfcf.software.mac	Math Faculty Computing Facility.
uw.mfcf.suggestions	Math Faculty Computing Facility.
uw.mfcf.system	Math Faculty Computing Facility. (Moderated)
uw.mfcf.todo	Math Faculty Computing Facility.
uw.mfcf.updates	Math Faculty Computing Facility.
uw.minos	MINOS project.
uw.msg	Multiprocessor Systems Group.
uw.nag	.
uw.network	Connectivity notices.
uw.network.external	.
uw.network.stats	.
uw.networks	=uw.network
uw.neural-nets	.
uw.newsgroups	.
uw.opinion	Blather.
uw.os.research	OS research.
uw.os2-users	
uw.outers	UW Outers Club: events, activities and discussions.
uw.pami	Pattern Analysis & Machine Intelligence.
uw.pami.bsd	Pattern Analysis & Machine Intelligence.
uw.pami.gripe	Pattern Analysis & Machine Intelligence.
uw.pami.system	Pattern Analysis & Machine Intelligence.
uw.pmc	Pure Math and C&O club.
uw.psychology	.
uw.recycling	.
uw.sas	.

ıw.scicom	Scientific Computing.
ıw.science.computing	.
ıw.sd.grad	Systems Design.
ıw.sd.smsg	Systems Design.
ıw.shoshin	Shoshin project.
ıw.shoshin.changes	Shoshin project.
ıw.shoshin.system	Shoshin project.
ıw.stats	Statistics department.
ıw.stats.grad	Statistics department.
ıw.stats.s	=uw.mail-list.s
ıw.sun-owners	for people who have Suns.
ıw.sylvan	Sylvan project.
ıw.sylvan.os	Sylvan project.
ıw.sys.amiga	for people with Amigas.
ıw.sys.apollo	for people with Apollos.
ıw.sys.atari	for people with Ataris.
ıw.sytek	Sytek communication system.
ıw.talks	upcoming seminars.
ıw.test	testing.
ıw.test.xxx	=uw.test
ıw.test.yyy	=uw.test
ıw.test.zzz	=uw.test
ıw.tex	TEX text formatting.
ıw.ucc.fortrade	University Computing Committee.
ıw.ugrad.cs	Undergrads.
ıw.unix	arguments about Unix.
ıw.unix.sysadmin	.
ıw.usystem	u-kernel and u-system.
ıw.uwinfo	UWinfo discussion, comments, feedback, etc.
ıw.virtual-worlds	Exploring virtual reality at U Waterloo.
ıw.visualization	.
ıw.vlsi	VLSI group.
ıw.vlsi.ate	VLSI group.
ıw.vlsi.cadence	VLSI group.
ıw.vlsi.cmc	VLSI group.
ıw.vlsi.electric	VLSI group.
ıw.vlsi.industry	VLSI group.
ıw.vlsi.software	VLSI group.
ıw.vlsi.system	VLSI group.
ıw.vlsi.vlsiic	VLSI group.
ıw.vlsi.works	VLSI group.
ıw.vm-migration	.
ıw.vms	people who have to use VMS.
ıw.watserv	=uw.dcs.watserv1
ıw.watshine	=uw.dcs.watshine
ıw.watstar	.
ıw.wira	.
ıw.wpirg	.
ıw.x-hints	how to use X windows.
ıw.x-windows	how to use X windows.
ıwo.biomed.engrg	Biomedical Engineering Research.
ıwo.biomed.inroads	Rehabilitation Engineering Research and Development.
ıwo.ccs.changes	.

```
uwo.ccs.talk              .
uwo.chinese               University of Western
                          Ontario.
uwo.comp.epix             .
uwo.comp.helpdesk         .
uwo.comp.ibm.announce     .
uwo.comp.net-status       University of Western
                          Ontario.
uwo.comp.next             .
uwo.comp.nupop            University of Western
                          Ontario.
uwo.comp.packet           .
uwo.comp.pine             University of Western
                          Ontario.
uwo.comp.security         Computer security issues
                          and policy.
uwo.comp.sgi.announce     .
uwo.comp.snmp             University of Western
                          Ontario.
uwo.comp.sun-managers     University of
                          Western Ontario.
uwo.comp.sun.announce     .
uwo.comp.wais             .
uwo.comp.x500             .
uwo.csd                   University of Western
                          Ontario.
uwo.events                .
uwo.forsale               University of Western
                          Ontario.
uwo.general               University of Western
                          Ontario.
uwo.iaa.research          .
uwo.library               .
uwo.med.research          .
uwo.news.config           University of Western
                          Ontario.
uwo.newsletters           University of Western
                          Ontario.
uwo.physics.optics        Applied optics, University
                          of Western Ontario.
uwo.rri.ctrg              .
uwo.slis                  .
uwo.ssc.network           Social Sciences Computing
                          Centre Network.
uwo.sscl.network           =uwo.ssc.network
uwo.test                  .
van.chatter               Vancouver, British
                          Columbia.
van.general               Vancouver, British
                          Columbia.
van.test                  Vancouver, British
                          Columbia.
wpg.general               Winnipeg, Manitoba.
york.announce             Announcements at York
                          University, Toronto.
york.ariel                .
york.calumet              .
york.canet-status-reports =york.ml.canet-
                          status-reports
```

```
york.doc                   .
york.email                 .
york.general               Postings of general
                           interest at York
                           University.
york.ml.big-lan            Big-lan mailing list.
york.ml.bind               Bind mailing list.
york.ml.canet-status-reports Canet-status-
                           reports mailing list.
york.ml.cmutcp             CMUtcp mailing list.
york.ml.decstation-managers Decstation-
                           managers mailing list.
york.ml.future             Future mailing list.
york.ml.info-pmdf          Info-pmdf mailing list.
york.ml.namedroppers          Namedroppers
                           mailing list.
york.ml.nn                 NN mailing list.
york.ml.onet-status-reports Onet-status-
                           reports mailing list.
york.ml.openbook           Openbook mailing list.
york.ml.pcm-dev            PCM-dev mailing list.
york.ml.sun-managers Sun-managers mailing
                           list.
york.ml.texhax             Texhax mailing list.
york.onet-status-reports
                           =york.ml.onet-status-
                           reports
```

--------- < --------- < --------- < --------
              - <

Here is a list of email addresses for
contacting the moderators of some of the
moderated newsgroups in the Canadian regional
news hierarchies:

```
can.uucp.maps Ed Hew
                      pathadmin@cs.toronto.edu
```

Here is a list of email addresses for
submitting articles to moderated newsgroups
in the Canadian regional news hierarchies:

```
can.canet.d            canet-d@canet.ca
can.uucp.maps          pathadmin@cs.toronto.edu
ott.weather

                       weather@aficom.ocunix.on.c
                       a
ut.cdf.announce        clarke@csri.toronto.edu
uw.assignments

                       cagillin@watmath.waterloo.
                       edu

uw.chinese

                       jshen@watdragon.waterloo.e
                       du
uw.computer-store

                       jwdodd@watserv1.waterloo.e
                       du
```

```
uw.dcs.courses
                        editor@watserv1.waterloo.e
                        du
uw.dcs.news
                        editor@watserv1.waterloo.e
                        du
uw.feds  feds@watserv1.waterloo.edu
uw.imprint  imprint@watmath.waterloo.edu
uw.gsa   broberts@kingcong.waterloo.edu
uw.mfcf.system   operator@watmath.waterloo.edu
```

THE DIRECTORY OF CANADIAN INTERNET RESOURCES

· ·

© 1994 Rick Broadhead and Jim Carroll

This is a directory of Internet resources that pertain to Canada. Each entry in this directory contains the name of the resource, a brief description of the resource, and instructions that describe how you can access the resource using the Internet.

We welcome additions to the list for the next edition of this book. If you are aware of a Canadian Internet resource that doesn't appear in this directory, please contact the authors at **handbook@uunet.ca.**

CANADIAN UFO SURVEY, 1992

This document, published by Ufology Research of Manitoba, documents and analyzes UFO sightings across Canada in 1992.

HOW TO ACCESS:
Gopher: **wiretap.spies.com.** Select: /Wiretap Online Library/Fringes of Reason/UFOs and Mysterious Abductions.

1992 REPORT ON CROP CIRCLES AND RELATED TRACES

This document, published by the North American Institute for Crop Circle Research in Winnipeg, documents and analyzes reports of unusual ground markings (UGMs) in North America in 1992.

HOW TO ACCESS:
Gopher: wiretap.spies.com. Select: /Wiretap Online Library/Fringes of Reason/UFOs and Mysterious Abductions.

BOTANICAL ELECTRONIC NEWS MAILING LIST

Botanical Electronic News is a newsletter distributed on electronic mail. It covers the botany and plant ecology of predominantly British Columbia, Canada, and the Pacific

Northwest with broader reference to planet Earth. It is published approximately once every two weeks. The newsletter is also distributed in the USENET newsgroup **bio.plants**.

HOW TO ACCESS:
Requests for subscription should be sent to the owner:
Adolf Ceska, **aceska@cue.bc.ca**.

CANADA GAZETTE MAILING LIST

This mailing list distributes excerpts from the Canada Gazette that are relevant to the Communications sector of Industry Canada.

HOW TO ACCESS:
To subscribe to the mailing list, send an electronic mail message to **listserv@debra.dgbt.doc.ca**, and put the following command on the first line of the body of the message:
subscribe gazette-list <First Name> <Last Name>
e.g. subscribe gazette-list John Smith
Archives of the Gazette notices are available by anonymous FTP to **debra.dgbt.doc.ca** in the directory **/pub/isc/gazette**.

CA DOMAIN DOCUMENTS

Here you will find a complete list of organizations registered in the CA Domain (organized by name and by subdomain), a list of members on the CA Domain Committee, CA Domain Statistics, an overview and history of the CA Domain, and a CA Domain application form.

HOW TO ACCESS:
Anonymous FTP: **ftp.cdnnet.ca**
Directory: **ca-domain**

CBC RADIO INFORMATION

The Canadian Broadcasting Corporation, in cooperation with the Communications Research Centre in Ottawa, is making programming information available over the Internet. The following items are currently available: a selection of CBC Radio programs in "au" format, (including daily news broadcasts), program schedules for CBC Radio Ottawa, a list of transcripts available from CBC Radio, and a list of CBC Radio products.

HOW TO ACCESS:
Gopher: **debra.dgbt.doc.ca**. Select: /CBC Radio Trial
Anonymous FTP: **debra.dgbt.doc.ca**, Directory: **/pub/cbc**

WWW: **http://debra.dgbt.doc.ca/cbc/cbc.html**
Comments about this service can be sent to:
cbc@debra.dgbt.doc.ca.

CANADIAN BUSINESS AND THE INTERNET

A mailing list has been established to discuss how Canadian businesses can make effective use of the Internet.

HOW TO ACCESS:

To subscribe to the mailing list, send an electronic mail message to **listserv@nstn.ns.ca**, and put the following command in the body of the message:
subscribe enterprise-l <First Name> <Last Name>
e.g. subscribe enterprise-l John Smith

CANADIAN CLIMATIC PERSPECTIVES

This is a weekly publication prepared by the Canadian Meteorological Centre, Atmospheric Environment Service. It shows temperature, precipitation, and wind statistics for 225 weather stations across Canada.

HOW TO ACCESS:

Gopher: cmits02.dow.on.doe.ca. Select: /Climatic Information/Climatic Perspectives/Current Issue Climatic Perspectives.

CANADIAN GOVERNMENT DOCUMENTS

This archive contains the text of the Canadian Constitution Act , Meech Lake Accord, Charlottetown Constitutional Agreement, and excerpts from Canada's Constitutional Act.

HOW TO ACCESS:

Gopher: wiretap.spies.com. Select: /Government Documents (U.S. and World)/Canadian Documents.

CANADIAN EDUCATION LIBRARY ISSUES MAILING LIST

For the discussion of issues affecting Canadian education libraries.

HOW TO ACCESS:

Send an electronic mail message to **listserv@dewey.ed.brocku.ca**, and put the following command on the first line of the body of the message:
subscribe OTELA-L <First Name> <Last Name>
e.g. subscribe otela-l John Smith

CANADIAN FOOTBALL - FREQUENTLY ASKED QUESTIONS

This document answers common questions about Canadian Football, such as "Why do we have a team called the Ottawa Rough Riders and another team called the Roughriders?" This document also looks at the history of the CFL and provides a directory of CFL teams, including mailing addresses and Grey Cup wins. It is updated periodically, and posted to the USENET group **rec.sport.football.canadian**. The maintainer of this document is Michael Burger. He can be reached at mmb@lamar.colostate.edu.

HOW TO ACCESS:
Anonymous FTP: **rtfm.mit.edu**
Directory: **/pub/usenet/news.answers**
File: **canadian-football**

CANADIAN GRADUATE COUNCIL MAILING LIST

The Canadian Graduate Council provides graduate students with an independent forum to express, and lobby for, their concerns. The priority of the organization is to represent graduate students in their roles as researchers, students, and teachers. The CGC represents over 17,000 graduate students from the University of Alberta, University of Calgary, Carleton, McMaster, Memorial, Queen's, University of Saskatchewan, University of Waterloo, and the University of Windsor. Canadian Graduate Students are invited to join the CGC mailing list.

HOW TO ACCESS:
To subscribe to the mailing list, send an electronic mail message to **listserver@morgan.ucs.mun.ca**, and put the following command on the first line of the body of the message: **subscribe cgc**

CANADIAN ISSUES FORUM

This is a mailing list for the discussion of political, social, cultural, and economic issues in Canada.

HOW TO ACCESS:
To subscribe to this mailing list, send an electronic mail message to **listserv@vm1.mcgill.ca**, and put the following command on the first line of the body of the message:
subscribe canada-l <First Name> <Last Name>
e.g. subscribe canada-l John Smith

CANADIAN SUPREME COURT DECISIONS

The University of Montreal Law Gopher contains the full text of Canadian Supreme Court decisions, from January 1993 onward. Supreme Court decisions will be made available on this server within 24 hours of the decision being announced.

HOW TO ACCESS:

Gopher: gopher.droit.umontreal.ca. **Select:**

/Law:Primary Documents/Case Law/Canadian Supreme Court Decisions.

CANADIAN WEATHER FORECASTS

Current weather forecasts for all the provinces and territories.

HOW TO ACCESS:

Gopher: nstn.ns.ca. **Select: /Canadian Weather Forecasts.**

DIRTY LINEN FOLK MUSIC CALENDAR

This is a list of folk music concerts in Canada and the United States, updated monthly. Canadian listings are organized by province.

HOW TO ACCESS:

Anonymous FTP: nysernet.org

Directory: /folk_music/dirty_linen

File: DLCALxxx.TXT

where XXX **is the monthly abbreviation**

e.g. DLCALFEB.TXT

EARTHQUAKES IN CANADA

What was the largest Earthquake in Canada this century? How many earthquakes are recorded in Canada each year? What is the most active Earthquake region in Canada? This document, prepared by the Geological Survey of Canada, answers these questions and more.

HOW TO ACCESS:

Gopher: gopher.emr.ca. Select: /NRCan-Info/Geological Survey of Canada/Earthquakes in Canada.

FALCON LAKE CASE

This is a survey of the research and literature surrounding the Falcon Lake Case, an incident which occurred on May 20, 1967. A person claimed to have been burned by a strange craft, just north of the town of Falcon Lake, Manitoba. A recreation of this story was broadcast on Unsolved Mysteries in 1992 and 1993. According to the author of this research paper, "although largely unknown, the case may be the most significant in North America because of the intense investigation by the United States Air Force, the Royal Canadian Air Force, the Royal Canadian Mounted Police, and civilian groups, and because of the amount of physical evidence and physiological effects on the witness."

HOW TO ACCESS:
Anonymous FTP: **ftp.rutgers.edu**
Directory: **/pub/ufo**
File: **falcon-lake.1967.Z**
(you need to uncompress this file)

FREQUENTLY ASKED QUESTIONS ABOUT CANADA

This document is regularly posted on the USENET group **soc.culture.canada**. It contains questions and answers on such topics as Canadian History (e.g. When was Canada discovered?), Canadian Politics (e.g. Who were Canada's Prime Ministers?), Canadian Society and Culture (e.g. Do Canadians use British or American Spelling?, Why isn't the Canadian Thanksgiving the same day as the American Thanksgiving?), Canadian Education (e.g. What Canadian universities offer programs in Canadian Studies), and Canadian Business (e.g. How can I start a business in Canada?). This document is maintained by Martin Savard (ag656@freenet.carleton.ca).

HOW TO ACCESS:
Anonymous FTP: **rtfm.mit.edu**
Directory: **/pub/usenet/news.answers/canada-faq**
Files: **part1, part2**

GUIDE TO VEGETARIANISM IN CANADA

This guide contains a list of vegetarian restaurants, vegetarian-friendly restaurants, natural food stores, and vegetarian organizations, and other items of interest to Canadian vegetarians.

OW TO ACCESS:
nonymous FTP: **rtfm.mit.edu**
irectory: **/pub/usenet/news.answers/vegetarian/guide**
les: **canada1, canada2**

EALTHNET MAILING LIST

EALTHNET is an Internet forum for the discussion of is-
es surrounding high speed networking initiatives focusing
1 (but not specific to) Canadian health care. Potential uses
* HEALTHNET include the discussion of the use of net-
orks for health care applications (e.g. Medical Electronic
ata Interchange), and announcements of programs involv-
g computer networks and Canadian health care facilities.

OW TO ACCESS:
o subscribe to the list, send an electronic mail message to
tserv@debra.dgbt.doc.ca, and put the following com-
and on the first line of the body of the message:
bscribe healthnet <First Name> <Last Name>
g. subscribe healthnet John Smith

ORTICULTURE INFORMATION SERVICE

he Department of Horticulture at the University of Sas-
tchewan has produced over 40 fact sheets on horticultural
pics. Topics include: "Earthworms: Friend or Foe?"
'acts about Potatoes," and "Saskatchewan's Edible Wild
uits and Nuts."

OW TO ACCESS:
opher: **gopher.usask.ca**. Select: /Other/Horticulture In-
rmation.

IDUSTRY CANADA NEWS

dustry Canada News is a mailing list for the distribution of
ews Releases and Fact Sheets issued to the pubic by the
ommunications Canada branch of Industry Canada. The
ews Releases are for announcements concerning Canadian
mmunications policy. The Fact Sheets are for the an-
ouncement of developments in communications technology
d related applications in Canada.

OW TO ACCESS:
o subscribe to this list, send an electronic mail message to
tserv@debra.dgbt.doc.ca, and put the following com-
and on the first line of the body of the message:

subscribe iscnews <First Name> <Last Name>
e.g. subscribe iscnews John Smirth
Archives of the ISCNEWS are available by anonymous F⁻
to **debra.dgbt.doc.ca**, in the directory **/pub/isc/iscnews**.

LIBRARY JOBS IN ATLANTIC CANADA MAILING LIST

For the announcement of job openings for graduates in t
field of library and information studies. All postings will
for the announcements for such positions within Atlan
Canada. Job listings received electronically, or by mail
fax directed to the School of Library and Information Studi
at Dalhousie University, will be posted on the list as soon
they are received.

HOW TO ACCESS:
To subscribe to this list, send an electronic mail message
mailserv@ac.dal.ca, and put the following command on t
first line of the body of the message: **subscribe lis-joblist**

MEMORIAL UNIVERSITY OF NEWFOUNDLAND ONLINE BOOKSTORE

Allows users to search the holdings of the MUN booksto
Searches can be made by author, title, course, and ISBN.

HOW TO ACCESS:
Telnet: bkstore.ubs.mun.ca, **login as** bkinq

METEORITES IN CANADA

How much will the Geological Survey of Canada pay you
you find the first specimen of a Canadian meteorite? Th
document, prepared by the Geological Survey of Canad
gives an overview of meteorites and their importance, a
tells you what to do if you happen to find one in Canada.

HOW TO ACCESS:
Gopher: gopher.emr.ca. Select: /NRCan-Info/Geologic
Survey of Canada/Meteorites-Identification Services.

MONTREAL FAX SERVICE

A public e-mail-to-fax gateway for the city of Montre
courtesy of Communications Accessibles Montreal, an Inte
net Service Provider in Montreal. This service allows you
send an electronic mail message from an Internet accou
and have it delivered to any fax machine within local calli
distance of downtown Montreal.

OW TO ACCESS:

o send a message to a fax machine in Montreal, use the
ollowing address format:

irstname_Lastname@5551212.FAX.CAM.ORG

g. an e-mail message sent to Rick_Broadhead@555-
212.FAX.CAM.ORG will be faxed to Rick Broadhead at
55-1212.

ANAIMO SCHOOLSNET

free, open-access computer system developed by the
anaimo School District in Nanaimo, British Columbia.

OW TO ACCESS:

elnet: crc.sd68.nanaimo.bc.ca, login as guest

EWS FROM CANADA

ews From Canada is a daily summary of major Canadian
ws items, intended for Canadians and others living abroad.
ources include the *Globe and Mail* and CBC News, with
ccasional other sources such as MuchMusic. The TSE and
anadian Dollar are reported on regularly, and there are oc-
sional reports from the fields of entertainment and sports.
ews From Canada is posted regularly on the USENET
oup **soc.culture.canada**, and it is also echoed on the Well
San Francisco. It can also be received by electronic mail
on request.

OW TO ACCESS:

he Editor of News From Canada is Stephanie Fysh. She
n be reached at **sfysh@epas.utoronto.ca**.

ORTH AMERICAN FREE TRADE AGREEMENT

he text of the North American Free Trade Agreement.

OW TO ACCESS:

opher: wiretap.spies.com. Select: /Government Docu-
ents (US and World)/North American Free Trade Agree-
ent.

ORTH PACIFIC MARINE SCIENCE ORGANIZATION
PICES) MAILING LIST

he Convention for the establishment of the North Pacific
arine Science Organization came into force on March 24,
992. Canada is one of the four contracting countries. The
ganization is concerned with marine scientific research in

the North Pacific Ocean and adjacent seas, especially nor
of 30 degrees north. Messages from the organization's bull
tin board are periodically sent out to Internet users via tl
mailing list.

HOW TO ACCESS
To be added to the mailing list, send a request by electron
mail to the PISCES Secretariat at **PICES@ios.bc.ca**.

ONET/INTERNET INSTRUCTION MANUAL

A description of the Internet using Computer Interactive Te
(CIT). Developed by Doug van Vianen at Northern Colleg
in Kirkland Lake, Ontario.

HOW TO ACCESS:
Telnet: kirk.northernc.on.ca, **login as** vianen

POLYGRAM RECORDS OF CANADA MAILING LIST

The list is for press releases, concert announcements, ar
announcements of release dates for new albums in Canad
Recently the list has featured information on new albums ar
tour dates of Canadian acts such as Bootsauce, Lost and Pr
found, Crash Vegas, The Pursuit of Happiness, Martine S
Claire, Cindy Church, and others. Questions about any po
jazz, or classical release by PolyGram Records of Cana
can be directed here. The list does not accept special orde
for albums. In addition, information cannot be provide
about releases in other countries.

HOW TO ACCESS:
To subscribe to the mailing list, send an electronic mail me
sage to **listserv@canrem.com**, and put the following co
mand on the first line of the body of the message:
subscribe polygram-l <First Name> <Last Name>
e.g. subscribe polygram-l John Smith
Submissions to the list can be sent to **polygra
l@canrem.com**.

PRINCE EDWARD ISLAND CRAFTS INFORMATION
SERVICE

The PEI Crafts Information Service is a service of the no
profit PEI Crafts Council. It offers solutions to crafts pr
ducers looking for information about sources of supplie
equipment, services, and expertise. The organization mai
tains a database of some 4,000 suppliers located across Nor

America. They can provide references to craftspeople looking for particular products (e.g. "Where can I buy a flexishaft in Manitoba") or general supplier lists (e.g. Who sells weaving supplies in Canada?). The organization can also provide information about crafts experts who offer training, education, or advice. They also track consumer experiences with suppliers. Service is only available by electronic mail, with direct Internet-accessible searching capabilities in the planning stages. The PEI Crafts Information Service is only a locating service — actual contact with suppliers for information and ordering is left to the craftspersons.

HOW TO ACCESS:

Craftspersons looking for information on sources of supplies, materials, or equipment should send electronic mail to **INFO@crafts-council.pe.ca**. Please put **WANTED** at the beginning of the subject line.

If you have information to add to the Craft Council's database, send it to: **LISTME@crafts-council.pe.ca**.

ROSWELL ELECTRONIC COMPUTER BOOKSTORE

This is a searchable database of all the titles carried by Roswell Computer Books in Halifax. While the bookstore specializes in computer books, they will order any book in print for you. Users can search the bookstore holdings by partial author, title, or ISBN. Roswell's will ship anywhere in Canada. Orders can be placed by electronic mail.

HOW TO ACCESS:

Gopher: nstn.ns.ca. Select: /NSTN's Cybermall/Roswell Electronic Computer Bookstore.

RUSH MAILING LIST

This mailing list is for the discussion of the Canadian musical group Rush.

HOW TO ACCESS:

Subscription requests should be sent to:
rush-request@syrinx.umd.edu.

STATISTICS CANADA DAILY REPORTS

Statistical reports and publication announcements issued daily from Statistics Canada.

HOW TO ACCESS:
Telnet: info.carleton.ca.   At the "Enter Terminal Type
prompt, enter **decvt100**.   Follow the instructions on th
screen, and select option **16** (Statistics Canada Daily R
ports) from the menu.

TORONTO BLUE JAYS MAILING LIST

This is a mailing list for the discussion of the Toronto Blu
Jays. There are over 240 subscribers.

HOW TO ACCESS:
Subscriptions and requests for information should be sent t
jays-request@hivnet.ubc.ca.

TRAVEL INFORMATION FOR CANADA

Travel guides for British Columbia, Ontario, Quebec, Ne
Brunswick, Nova Scotia, and Newfoundland, compiled b
people on the Internet.

HOW TO ACCESS:
Anonymous FTP: ftp.cc.umanitoba.ca
Directory: /rec-travel/north_america/canada

UNIVERSITY OF TORONTO SCHOOLS MAILING LIST

This is an electronic mailing list for use by students, staf
and alumni of the University of Toronto Schools, a Toront
high school.

HOW TO ACCESS:
Subscription requests should be sent to:
uts-request@mit.edu.

UNIVERSITY OF WATERLOO ONLINE BOOKSTORE
INQUIRY (WITH BUILT-IN GEOGRAPHIC INFORMATION SYSTEM!)

Users can search the inventory of the bookstore by titl
author, instructor, course, or ISBN number. The system w
tell you how many copies of the book are in stock, and pre
ent all the standard bibliographic information. What's nift
about this system is that you can call up a map of the boo
store on the screen, and a blinking symbol will indicat
where the book is located.

HOW TO ACCESS:

Telnet: bg1.uwaterloo.ca, login as booklook

VANCOUVER CANUCKS MAILING LIST

The Vancouver Canucks Mailing list is devoted to the discussion of the Vancouver Canucks, Vancouver's NHL team. Discussion topics include trade talks and criticism/praise of players. The list also serves as a medium to organize trips, hockey pools, and hockey games. Canuck statistics are usually posted after every game, and league/player statistics are posted on a monthly basis.

HOW TO ACCESS:

To subscribe to the mailing list, send an electronic mail message to the list owner at **boora@sfu.ca.** Put **SUBSCRIBE CANUCKS** on the subject line, and put your name and electronic mail address on the first line of the body of the message.

VIRTUAL RECORD STORE

The Virtual Record Store (VRS) is an on-line service offering a selection of over 5000 CD titles, searchable by artist, title, or product code. While VRS specializes in imports and alternative music, they can order almost any CD in the world for you. Orders can be placed by electronic mail. For more information, send electronic mail to **vrs@nstn.ns.ca**.

HOW TO ACCESS:

Gopher: nstn.ns.ca.   Select: /NSTN's Cybermall/Virtual Record Store.

YUKON MAILING LIST

For people interested in information and/or gossip about the Yukon. A cool mailing list!

HOW TO ACCESS:

Send your e-mail address to yukon-request@cs.concordia.ca.

THE DIRECTORY OF ORGANIZATIONS REGISTERED IN THE .CA DOMAIN

....

This is a directory of Canadian organizations that have registered subdomains within the .ca (Canada) top-level domain, a
of January, 1994. The most recent version of this list may b
obtained by anonymous FTP to **ftp.cdnnet.ca** in the ca
domain directory. The file is **index-by-organization**. Th
same list, ordered by subdomain, is in the **file index-by-
subdomain**. These files are maintained by John Demco, th
CA Domain Registrar. A searchable database of organization
registered in the .CA domain can be found on the NSTN In
Gopher at **nstn.ns.ca** under the menu **White Pages/Canadia
Organizations Search.**

The list below does not include every organization that ha
registered an Internet domain. As discussed in Chapter 4, som
organizations have chosen to register in the **.com**, **.edu**. **.or**
or **.net** domains, rather than register in the .CA domain. The
organizations register through InterNIC in the United State
and they do not appear in the list below. You should als
recognize that the presence of an organization in the list belo
does not mean that the organization is using the Internet, n
does it mean that all personnel in the organization have acce
to the Internet. Organizations often register an Internet doma
in advance of connecting to the Internet. For example, a
organization may register an Internet domain in January, b
not connect to the Internet until May. Many organizations th
are connected to the Internet use their connection for speci
projects or purposes, and access is restricted to certa
individuals in the organization, usually technical personnel.

HOW TO RETRIEVE INFORMATION ON A SUBDOMAIN

The CA Domain Registrar maintains a file for eve
organization that registers a subdomain. This file contai
information about the organization, such as: the date th

main application was approved, a description of the
ganization, technical and administrative contacts for the
ganization, and the name of the organization's Internet
rvice Provider. These files are available by anonymous FTP
ftp.cdnnet.ca in the directory **/ca-domain/registrations-
t.** The file names are the same as the domain names, but the
bdomain components have been reversed. For example, to
t the file for Air Canada, whose domain is **aircanada.ca**,
u have to ask for the file **ca.aircanada.**

me of Organization	Subdomain
. Ozrout Consultants	ozrout.qc.ca
Dunn Systems Corporation	adscorp.on.ca
J. Lill Consultants	ajlc.waterloo.on.ca
.I. Technologies Ltd.	ali.bc.ca
L Canada Inc.	abl.ca
adia University	acadiau.ca
quired Intelligence Inc.	aiinc.bc.ca
TC Technologies Inc.	actc.ab.ca
umen Computers Inc.	acumen.ca
Technologies Inc.	adtech.ca
aptive Answers, Inc.	adaptive.mb.ca
vanced Cultural Technologies Inc.	actinc.bc.ca
vanced Radiodata Research ntre	arrc.ca
vanced Technology Centre	atc.edmonton.ab.ca
GO Consulting Inc	aego.ca
fa Canada Inc.	agfa.ca
riculture Canada	agr.ca
T Ltd.	agt.ab.ca
Л Systems	aim-systems.on.ca
Canada	aircanada.ca
Ontario Inc.	airontario.ca
erta Cancer Board	cancerboard.ab.ca
erta College	abcollege.ab.ca
erta Educational Communications rporation	accessnet.ab.ca
erta General Provincial Children's spital	child-hosp.ab.ca
erta Packet Radio Network	ampr.ab.ca
erta Provincial Government	gov.ab.ca
erta Public Safety Services	apss.ab.ca
erta Regional Network	arnet.ab.ca
erta Research Council	arc.ab.ca
erta SuperNet Incorporated	supernet.ab.ca
erta Vocational College--Calgary	avc.calgary.ab.ca
can Aluminium Ltd.	alcan.ca
catel Canada Wire, Inc.	alcatel.ca
ex Informatique Inc.	alex.qc.ca
gonquin College of Applied Arts and chnology	algonquinc.on.ca

Allan Crawford Associates Ltd	aca.ca
Almanac User's Group	almanac.bc.ca
Alphen International Inc.	alphen.on.ca
Amiga Mail Service BBS	amsbbs.bc.ca
Amiga Users Of Victoria	amusers.victoria.bc.ca
AMT Solutions Group Inc.	amtsgi.bc.ca
Analog Services Informatiques (1993) Inc.	analog.ca
Analysis Synthesis Consulting Incorporated	analsyn.on.ca
Andyne Computing Limited	andyne.on.ca
Antel Optronics Inc.	antel.on.ca
Apotex Inc.	apotex.ca
Applied Microelectronics Institute	appliedmicro.ns.ca
Arcane Computer Consulting	arcane.calgary.ab.ca
Architech Microsystems Inc.	architech.on.ca
Arete Software Inc.	arete.ca
Armstrong/Spallumcheen School District	schdist21.bc.ca
Array Systems Computing Inc.	array.ca
Arris Design and Development Limited	arris.on.ca
Ascom Timeplex Canada	ascom-timeplex.ca
Ashlin Computer Corporation	ashlin.on.ca
ASL Analytical Service Laboratories Ltd.	asl-labs.bc.ca
Assiniboine Community College	assiniboinec.mb.ca
Association of Universities and Colleges of Canada	aucc.ca
Astra Pharma Inc.	astrapharma.on.ca
AT&T Canada Inc.	att.ca
Athabasca University	athabascau.ca
ATI Technologies Inc.	atitech.ca
Atlantic Canada Opportunity Agency	acoa.ca
Atlantic Centre for Remote Sensing of the Oceans	acrso.ns.ca
Atlantic Computer Institute	aci.ns.ca
Atomic Energy Control Board	atomcon.ca
Atomic Energy of Canada Limited	aecl.ca
ATS Aerospace	ats.qc.ca
Attic Enterprise	attic.bc.ca
Augustana University College	augustana.ab.ca
Automated Systems Group	autosysgr.nb.ca
B.C. Children's Hospital	childhosp.bc.ca
Bank of Canada	bank-banque-canada.ca
BC Provincial Government	gov.bc.ca
BCnet	bcnet.bc.ca
Beame and Whiteside Software, Ltd.	bw-software.on.ca
Bedford Institute of Oceanography	bio.ns.ca
Bell Canada	bell.ca
Bell-Northern Research	bnr.ca
Bishop's University	ubishops.ca
Bombardier/Canadair	canadair.ca
Bomem Inc.	bomem.qc.ca

ulet Fermat Associates	bouletfermat.ab.ca
Resources Canada Limited	bprc.ab.ca
andon University	brandonu.ca
stol Aerospace Ltd.	bristol.ca
tish Columbia Automobile sociation	bcaa.bc.ca
tish Columbia Drug and Poison formation Centre (DPIC)	dpic.bc.ca
tish Columbia Hydro and Power uthority	bchydro.bc.ca
tish Columbia Institute of Technology	bcit.bc.ca
tish Columbia Research Corporation	bcr.bc.ca
tish Columbia Teachers' Federation	bctf.bc.ca
ck University	brocku.ca
OH Enterprises	bsoh.bc.ca
ll HN Information Systems Limited	bull.ca
rchill Communications Research oup	burchill.ns.ca
A*net	canet.ca
abot Institute of Applied Arts and chnology	cabot.nf.ca
AE Electronics Ltd	cae.ca
algary Board of Education	cbe.ab.ca
algary Unix Connect	cuc.ab.ca
algary Unix User Group	cuug.ab.ca
ALIAN Technology Ltd.	calian.ca
ambrian College of Applied Arts and chnology	cambrianc.on.ca
amosun College	camosun.bc.ca
anada Centre for Inland Waters	cciw.ca
anada Post Corporation	canpost.ca
anadian Airlines International Ltd.	cdnair.ca
anadian Bacterial Diseases Network	cbdn.ca
anadian Broadcasting Corporation	cbc.ca
anadian Centre for Architecture	cca.qc.ca
anadian Council of Ministers of the vironment Inc.	ccme.ca
anadian Genetic Diseases Network	generes.ca
anadian International Development gency	devcan.ca
anadian Language Technology stitute - Institut Canadien De chnologie Linguistique	clti-ictl.nb.ca
anadian Marconi Company	marconi.ca
anadian Market Images	cmi.on.ca
anadian Medical Association	canmed.ca
anadian Mennonite Bible College	cmbiblecoll.mb.ca
anadian Microelectronics orporation/Societe Canadienne de icro-Electronique	cmc.ca
anadian Musical Reproduction Rights gency Ltd	cmrra.ca

Canadian National Railways - CN Rail	cn.ca
Canadian Nazarene College	cnaz.mb.ca
Canadian Occidental Petroleum Ltd.	canoxy.ab.ca
Canadian Plastics Institute	plasticsinstitute.ca
Canadian Regional Airlines Ltd.	cral.ca
Canadian Space Agency	sp-agency.ca
Canadian Union College	cauc.ab.ca
Canadian Utilities Limited	cul.ca
Canadian Wheat Board	canwheatbrd.ca
Canadore College of Applied Arts and Technology	canadorec.on.ca
CANARIE Inc.	canarie.ca
Capilano College	capcollege.bc.ca
Caravan Consultants	caravan-con.toronto.on.ca
Cariboo College	cariboo.bc.ca
Caritas Health Care Institute	caritas.ab.ca
Carleton Board of Education	carletonbe.ottawa.on.ca
Carleton University	carleton.ca
Carlton Cards Limited	carltoncards.ca
Carp Systems International CSI Inc.	csi.on.ca
CCI Networks, a division of Corporate Computers Incorporated	ccinet.ab.ca
CDNnet	cdnnet.ca
Cegep de Levis-Lauzon	clevislauzon.qc.ca
Centennial College of Applied Arts and Technology	cencol.on.ca
Centre de Recherche Informatique de Montreal	crim.ca
Centre for Image and Sound Research	cisr.bc.ca
Centre universitaire de Shippagan	cus.ca
Centre universitaire Saint-Louis-Maillet	cuslm.ca
Champlain Regional College	champlaincollege.qc.c
Chedoke-McMaster Hospitals	cmh.on.ca
Cherniak Giblon	cherniak.on.ca
Chernoff Thompson Architects	cta.bc.ca
Chi Systems, Inc.	chisystemsinc.ca
Children's Hospital of Eastern Ontario	cheo.on.ca
Choreo Systems Inc.	choreo.ca
City of Edmonton	gov.edmonton.ab.ca
City of Mississauga	city.mississauga.on.ca
City of Toronto	gov.toronto.on.ca
Clarke Institute of Psychiatry	clarke-inst.on.ca
Coast Peripherals and Systems Inc.	coast-peripherals.bc.c
Coffyn Communications	ccom.mb.ca
CoGenTex Inc.	cogentex.qc.ca
College Militaire Royal de St-Jean	cmr.ca
College of New Caledonia	cnc.bc.ca
College universitaire de Saint-Boniface	ustboniface.mb.ca
Combyne Data Inc.	combyne.qc.ca
ComDev	comdev.ca

ommunaute urbaine de Montreal (CUM)	cum.qc.ca
ommunications Accessibles Montreal nc.)	cam.qc.ca
ommunications Babylonne	babylon.montreal.qc.ca
ommunications Canada he Federal Department f Communications)	doc.ca
ommunity Information Access rganization	ciao.trail.bc.ca
ompudyn Systems Ltd.	compudyn.on.ca
ompuSoft	compus.ca
ompusult Limited	compusult.nf.ca
omputerActive Inc.	computeractive.on.ca
omputerland	computerland.ca
oncordia University	concordia.ca
onestoga College	conestogac.on.ca
onfederation College	confederationc.on.ca
onsumers Software Inc.	consumers.bc.ca
onxsys Inc.	conxsys.on.ca
oopers & Lybrand	cooperslybrand.ca
orel Corporation	corel.ca
OSKA Information Service	coska.bc.ca
ouncil of Ontario Universities	cou.on.ca
P Limited	cp.ca
reo Products Inc.	creo.bc.ca
rosfield Canada Inc.	crosfield.ca
UE Here BBS, Commodore Users of dmonton	cuehere.edmonton. ab.ca
umberland Computer Group Ltd	ccg.bc.ca
ybernetic Control Incorporated	cybercon.nb.ca
yberstore Online Information Systems nc.	cyberstore.ca
.H. Kumka & Associates	dhka.bc.ca
alhousie University	dal.ca
ata Terminal Mart	dtm.bc.ca
ataCorp Distributions	datacorp.montreal. qc.ca
ATAP Systems	datap.ca
atapanik Design	panik.vancouver.bc.ca
ataSpace Insight Inc.	dataspace.ca
awson College	dawsoncollege.qc.ca
e Havilland Inc.	dehavilland.ca
ECUS Canada, Digital Equipment omputer Users ociety	decus.ca
epartment of Energy, Mines, and esources	emr.ca
epartment of Environment	doe.ca
epartment of Fisheries and Oceans isheries Canada)	dfo.ca
epartment of National Defence	dnd.ca
exotek Canada Corp.	dexotek.ca

Dilltech Systems	dilltech.vancouver.bc.ca
Discovery Training Network	dtn.bc.ca
Discreet Logic IncG	discreet.qc.ca
District of Coquitlam	gov.coquitlam.bc.ca
DMR Group Inc.	dmr.ca
Dofasco Inc.	dofasco.ca
Dominion Textile Inc.	domtex.ca
Douglas College	douglas.bc.ca
Driver Design Labs, a division of Clarendon Datex Ltd.	driver-design-labs.bc.cc
Durham College of Applied Arts and Technology	durhamc.on.ca
Dymaxion Research Limited	dymaxion.ns.ca
Dynamis Productivity Software Limited	dynamis.bc.ca
Dynapro Systems Inc.	dsi.bc.ca
Dynatek Automation Systems Inc.	dynatek.ca
East Kootenay Community College	ekcc.bc.ca
Ecole de technologie superieure	etsmtl.ca
Ecole des Hautes Etudes Commerciales de Montreal	hec.ca
Ecole Polytechnique de Montreal	polymtl.ca
Economic Innovation and Technology Council	eitc.mb.ca
ED-NET Educational Electronic Information Service	ednet.bc.ca
EdgeWays! InfoLink Online Services	edgeways.vancouver.bc.ca
Edmonton Public School Board, District No. 7	epsb.edmonton.ab.ca
Edmonton Remote Systems	ersys.edmonton.ab.ca
Edmonton Telephones	edtel.ab.ca
Education Technology Centre of British Columbia	etc.bc.ca
Eicon Technology Corporation	eicon.qc.ca
Electronic Library Network	eln.bc.ca
Electronic Mail Pathways (1003662 Ontario Inc.)	empath.on.ca
ELSAG Bailey Canada Inc.	bailey.ca
EmGee Products International	emgee.on.ca
Emily Carr College of Art and Design	eccad.bc.ca
EMJ Data Systems	emj.ca
Enhance Systems Inc.	enhance.ca
Enhanced Systems Inc.	enhanced.ca
Enterprise Network Inc.	entnet.nf.ca
ESSO Chemical Canada	esso.ca
Etobicoke Board of Education	bdofed.etobicoke.on.c
Expert Technology Corporation	extec.mb.ca
Eye Research Institute of Canada	eric.on.ca
Eyepoint Inc.	eyepoint.on.ca
Fairview College	fairviewc.ab.ca
Fanshawe College	fanshawec.on.ca
Faxon Canada Ltd.	faxon.ca

ederated Insurance Company f Canada	fed-ins.ca
G Commodity Electronics Inc.	fgcom.qc.ca
irstClass Systems Corp.	firstclass.ca
ocus Automation Systems Inc.	focus-systems.on.ca
olkstone Design Inc.	folkstone.bc.ca
onds FCAR	fcar.qc.ca
ONOROLA Inc.	fonorola.ca
oothills Provincial Hospital	fhhosp.ab.ca
orest Heights Collegiate Institute	fhci.kitchener.on.ca
orestry Canada	forestry.ca
orintek Canada Ltd.	forintek.ca
raser and Beatty	fraserbeatty.ca
raser Valley College	fvc.bc.ca
reedman Sharp and Associates Inc.	fsa.ca
ujitsu Canada, Inc.	fujitsu.ca
uturetron Software Services	futuretron.on.ca
Gandalf Data Ltd.	gandalf.ca
Gemini Group, Inc.	gemini.ca
Genesis Microchip Incorporated	genesis-microchip.on.ca
Geological Survey of Newfoundland	geosurv.gov.nf.ca
Geomatics International Inc.	geomatics.on.ca
George Brown College	gbrownc.on.ca
George Weston Ltd.	weston.ca
Georgian College	georcoll.on.ca
Geoterrex Ltd.	geoterrex.ca
Global DataFlux Ltd.	dataflux.bc.ca
Global Travel Computer Services	global-travel.on.ca
Goal Electronics Inc.	goal.waterloo.on.ca
Godin London Inc.	godin.on.ca
Golem Consulting Services	golem.waterloo.on.ca
Gouvernement du Quebec (Ministere des Communications)	gouv.qc.ca
Government of Manitoba	gov.mb.ca
Government of the Northwest erritories	gov.nt.ca
Government of the Province of Ontario	gov.on.ca
Grafnetix Systems Inc.	grafnetix.qc.ca
Grande Prairie Regional College	gprc.ab.ca
Grant MacEwan Community College	gmcc.ab.ca
Grass Root Systems	grassys.bc.ca
Gray Beverage Inc.	gray-beverage.ca
Gray Sage Holdings, Ltd.	graysage.edmonton.ab.ca
Great-West Life Assurance Company	gwl.ca
Groupe Environnement Shooner inc.	shooner.qc.ca
GWR Human Resource Services	gwresource.mb.ca
H.C.S. Health Care Systems Inc.	hcs.ca
Harris Computer Service	harriscs.on.ca
Health and Welfare, Canada	hwc.ca
Health Sciences Centre	hsc.mb.ca
HealthVISION Corporation	healthvision.ca

HexaCom Info Services	hexacom.montreal.qc.ca
HiBiTek	hibitek.on.ca
Holland College	hollandc.pe.ca
Holt Software Associates Inc.	hsa.on.ca
Honeywell Limited	honeywell.ca
Hospital for Sick Children	sickkids.on.ca
Humber College of Applied Arts and Technology	Humberc.on.ca
Husky Injection Molding Systems Ltd.	husky.on.ca
Hutchison Avenue Software Corporation	hasc.ca
Hydro-Quebec	hydro.qc.ca
Hypercomp, An Organization for High Performance Computing	hypercomp.ns.ca
Hyprotech Ltd.	hyprotech.ab.ca
I.C.E. Online Services	ice.bc.ca
IBM Canada	ibm.ca
Idon Corporation	idon.ottawa.on.ca
Imagen Communications Inc.	imagen.bc.ca
Immedia Infomatic Inc.	immedia.ca
Imperial Oil Limited	iol.ca
InContext Corp.	incontext.ca
INDE Electronics	inde.bc.ca
Industry Science & Technology Canada	istc.ca
Infobase Consultants Inc.	infobase.on.ca
Infolytica Corporation	infolytica.qc.ca
InfoMagnetics Technologies Corporation	infomag.mb.ca
Information Systems Management Corporation	ism.ca
Information Technology Research Centre (ITRC)	itrc.on.ca
InfoWare Canada Inc	infoware.ca
Innovus Inc.	innovus.on.ca
Institute for Space and Terrestrial Science	ists.ca
Institute of Ocean Sciences	ios.bc.ca
InStore Focus	instore.ca
Integral Investments Incorporated	integral.on.ca
Integrated Engineering Software	Integrated.mb.ca
Integrated Systems Applications Corporation	isac.ca
Intera Information Technologies	intera.ca
InterAccess Technology Corp.	interaccess.ca
InterLink On-line Services Inc.	interlink.bc.ca
International Centre for Ocean Development	icod.ns.ca
International Development Research Centre	idrc.ca
International Institute for Sustainable Development	iisd.ca

erprovincial Pipe Line Inc.	ipl.ca
repid Information Systems Inc.	intrepid.on.ca
estors Group	igroup.ca
ek Inc.	iotek.ns.ca
Systems Inc.	iris.mb.ca
Corporation	itncorp.ca
ak Walton Killam Hospital for ildren	iwkhosp.ns.ca
. Conklin Communications	jjconklin.mb.ca
de Simulations International rporation	jade.ab.ca
f Voskamp	voskamp.waterloo.on.ca
Library Automation	jeslacs.bc.ca
natek Technologies	kanatek.ca
sten Chase Applied Research	kasten.on.ca
A Systems Ltd.	kea.bc.ca
yano College	keyanoc.ab.ca
g's College	kingsu.ab.ca
gston General Hospital	kgh.on.ca
ilano Network Research	kitsnet.vancouver.bc.ca
ift General Foods Canada	kraft.ca
industries Ltd.	ktindustries.mb.ca
Networks	kwnet.on.ca
antlen College	kwantlen.bc.ca
Business Solutions Inc.	li-business.ab.ca
Cite College	lacitec.on.ca
kehead University	lakeheadu.ca
keland College	lakelandc.ab.ca
nbton College of Applied Arts & chnology	lambton.on.ca
RG-Net	larg-net.london.on.ca
urentian University	laurentian.ca
vy and Associates, Ltd.	lavy.mb.ca
v Society of Upper Canada	lsuc.on.ca
arnix Ltd.	learnix.ca
nman Computer Group, Inc. o/a Wollongong Group Canada	lehman.on.ca
Conseillers INRO Consultants inc.	inro.ca
Entreprises Videoway Ltee	videoway.qc.ca
Services Informatiques BRS Inc.	brs.qc.ca
Services NPK+ inc.	npkservices.qc.ca
hbridge Community College	lethbridgec.ab.ca
S Group Inc.	lgs.ca
net Graphics International Inc.	linnet.ca
co Systems Inc.	litcosys.ca
co Systems Inc.	litcosys.on.ca
ckheed Canada Inc.	lockheed.on.ca
giciels et Applications Scientifiques	lasinc.qc.ca
GIN: Logiciel Interactif/ eractive software JMP/SDA Inc.	login.qc.ca
oking Glass Software Limited	looking.on.ca
us Development Canada Ltd.	lotus.ca

Loyalist College of Applied Arts and Technology	loyalistc.on.ca
LV Software Canada Inc.	lvsoftware.ca
M3i Systems Inc.	m3isystems.qc.ca
MacDonald Dettwiler and Associates	mda.ca
Maclean Hunter Communications Inc.	maclean-hunter.ca
MacMillan Bloedel Ltd.	macblo.ca
MAI Canada Ltd	mai.ca
Malaspina College	mala.bc.ca
Manitoba Cancer Treatment and Research Foundation	mctrf.mb.ca
Manitoba Go Association	goassoc.mb.ca
Manitoba Museum of Man and Nature	museummannature.mb.ca
Manitoba Organization of Faculty Associations	mofa.mb.ca
Manitoba Public Insurance Corporation	mpic.mb.ca
Manitoba Regional Network (MBnet)	mbnet.mb.ca
Manitoba UNIX User Group	muug.mb.ca
Maritime Tel & Tel	maritime-tel.ns.ca
Market Connections, Inc.	marketcon.mb.ca
Matrox Electronics Systems Ltd.	matrox.qc.ca
Maxon Services	maxon.ca
MAYA heat transfer technologies, ltd	mayahtt.ca
MBnet UUCP User Group	bison.mb.ca
McCullough Computer Consulting	mcc.ab.ca
McGill University	mcgill.ca
McMaster University	mcmaster.ca
MD Computer Consulting	mdcomp.toronto.on.ca
Mediaworks Magazine	mediaworks.toronto.on.ca
Medicine Hat College	mhc.ab.ca
Melchior Management Systems Inc.	melchior.ca
Memorial University of Newfoundland	mun.ca
Merlin Systems	merlin-systems.on.ca
MetaLink Communications Inc.	metalink.ca
Metalogic Software	metalogic.bc.ca
Metropolis Graphics Ltd.	metropolis.qc.ca
Metrowerks Inc.	metrowerks.ca
Microsoft Workgroup Canada	msworkgroup.bc.ca
Microtel Pacific Research Ltd.	mpr.ca
Midland Walwyn Capital Inc.	midwal.ca
Milliken Mills High School	milliken-mills.markham.on.ca
Mind Computer Products	mind.mb.ca
MIND LINK!	mindlink.bc.ca
Mindemoya Computing and Design	mcd.on.ca
Minerva Technology Inc.	minerva.ca
Mirus International Inc.	mirus.on.ca
Mitel Corporation	mitel.ca
Mitra Imaging Corporation	mitra.on.ca
Mitsubishi Electric Sales Canada, Inc.	mesca.ca

S Informatique	mksinfo.qc.ca
hawk College of Applied Arts and chnology	mohawkc.on.ca
li Energy Ltd.	molienergy.bc.ca
nenco Agra	monenco.ca
unt Allison University	mta.ca
unt Royal College	mtroyal.ab.ca
unt Saint Vincent University	msvu.ca
unt Sinai Hospital	mtsinai.on.ca
B Technologies Inc.	mpbtech.qc.ca
M Steel Ltd.	mrm.mb.ca
ltiprocessor Toolsmiths Inc.	toolsmiths.on.ca
nicipality of Metropolitan Toronto	metrotor.on.ca
rias Computer Technologies orporated	myrias.ab.ca
nometrics, Inc.	nanometrics.on.ca
tional Archives of Canada	archives.ca
tional Library of Canada	nlc-bnc.ca
tional Optics Institute	ino.qc.ca
tional Research Council Canada	nrc.ca
tive Education Centre	native-ed.bc.ca
tural Sciences and Engineering search Council	nserc.ca
'net	nbnet.nb.ca
R Canada Limited	ncr.ca
oText SophtWear International, Inc.	neotext.ca
otec Design Group	neptec.on.ca
Access Systems Inc.	netaccess.on.ca
Link Online Information Services	netlink.on.ca
North Consortium	netnorth.ca
trix Incorporated	netrix.on.ca
w Brunswick Provincial Government	gov.nb.ca
w Brunswick Telephone Co. Ltd.	nbtel.nb.ca
w Democratic Party of Canada	ndp.ca
w Era Systems Limited	newera.ab.ca
wfoundland and Labrador mputer Services	nlcs.nf.ca
wfoundland and Labrador Institute isheries and	marine technology
wfoundland and Labrador Institute isheries and Marine Technology	ifmt.nf.ca
wfoundland Regional Network	nlnet.nf.ca
XT User Group Yukon Territory	nugyt.yk.ca
xus Computing, Inc.	nexus.ca
gara College of Applied Arts and chnology	niagarac.on.ca
issing University	unipissing.ca
bis	nobis.ottawa.on.ca
rth Island College	nic.bc.ca
rth York Board of Education	nybe.north-york.on.ca
rthern Alberta Institute of chnology	nait.ab.ca

Northern College of Applied Arts and Technology	northernc.on.ca
Northwest Atlantic Fisheries Centre	nwafc.nf.ca
Northwest Community College	nwcc.bc.ca
Northwood Pulp & Timber Ltd.	northwood.ca
NOVA Corporation of Alberta	nova.ca
Nova Scotia Advanced Technology Centre	nsatc.ns.ca
Nova Scotia Agricultural College	nsac.ns.ca
Nova Scotia Association of Health Organizations	nsaho.ns.ca
Nova Scotia Community College, Burridge Campus	burridgec.ns.ca
Nova Scotia Department of Industry, Trade & Technology	ditt.ns.ca
Nova Scotia Government	gov.ns.ca
Nova Scotia Research Foundation Corporation	nsrfc.ns.ca
Novasys Inc.	novasys.qc.ca
Novatel Communications Limited	novatel.ca
NR/NS Inc.	nrnsinc.on.ca
NSTN Inc.	nstn.ca
NSTN Inc.	nstn.ns.ca
Object Technology International Inc.	oti.on.ca
ObjecTime Limited	objectime.on.ca
Oceanroutes Canada Incorporated	oceanroutes.ns.ca
Odyssey Research Associates Inc.	ora.on.ca
Okanagan College	okanagan.bc.ca
Okanagan University College	ouc.bc.ca
Olds College	oldscollege.ab.ca
ONet	onet.on.ca
Ontario Blue Cross	bluecross.on.ca
Ontario Cancer Treatment and Research Foundation	octrf.on.ca
Ontario College Application Service	ocas.on.ca
Ontario Hydro	hydro.on.ca
Ontario Inst. for Studies in Education	oise.on.ca
Ontario Library Service - North	olsn.on.ca
Ontario Universities' Application Centre	ouac.on.ca
Open Learning Agency	ola.bc.ca
OpenSys Inc.	opensys.on.ca
Oracle Communications Inc.	oci.bc.ca
Ordinox Network Inc.	ordinox.qc.ca
Ortech International Inc	ortech.on.ca
Oshawa General Hospital	hospital.oshawa.on.cc
OSIWARE Inc.	osiware.bc.ca
Ottawa Carleton Unix Group	ocunix.on.ca
P.E.I. Farm Centre	farmctr.pe.ca
Pacific Geoscience Centre	pgc.bc.ca
Pacific Visualization Systems	pvs.montreal.qc.ca
Pamap Technologies Corporation	pamap.bc.ca
PanCanadian Petroleum Limited	pcp.ca

nix Support Services	panix.surrey.bc.ca
prican	paprican.ca
rkridge Computer Technology	parkridge.on.ca
rkview Education Centre	pvec.bridgewater.ns.ca
I, Inc.	pci.on.ca
ace River North School District	schdist60.bc.ca
Crafts Council, Inc.	crafts-council.pe.ca
Net Incorporated	peinet.pe.ca
aedra V	phaedrav.on.ca
ilips Electronics Limited (TDS - ontreal)	philips
oenix Systems Synectics Inc.	phoenix.ca
anon Telexpertise Inc.	planon.qc.ca
MC-Sierra Inc.	pmc-sierra.bc.ca
IT Video Inc.	pmt.qc.ca
lar Bear Heaven	polarbear.rankin-inlet.nt.ca
tash Corporation of skatchewan Inc.	pcsinc.ca
ecise Systems Corporation	precise.ab.ca
nce of Wales Secondary School	pwss.vancouver.bc.ca
or Data Sciences	prior.ca
odigy Technologies Corp.	prodigy.bc.ca
gressive Solutions Inc.	psi.bc.ca
ject CUE	cue.bc.ca
otocols Standards and ommunication Inc.	pscinc.ca
ovigo Distribution Inc.	provigo.ca
blic Works Canada	pwc-tpc.ca
bNIX Montreal	pubnix.qc.ca
rchaseMaster Science Inc.	purchasemaster.qc.ca
& P Semiconductor Technology inc.	qpstech.ca
CC Communications Corporation	qcc.sk.ca
Systems, Ltd.	qlsys.ca
netix Computer Consultants Inc.	qnetix.ca
NX Software Systems, Ltd.	qnx.ca
antic Laboratories Inc.	quantic.mb.ca
antum Software Systems, Ltd.	quantum.on.ca
een Elizabeth II Hospital	qeiihosp.ab.ca
een's University at Kingston	queensu.ca
O.T. Recherche Operationelle en ecommunication	rot.qc.ca
dio Free Nyongwa	nyongwa.montreal.qc.ca
nmar Business Systems Ltd.	ranmar.qc.ca
ytheon Canada Limited	raytheon.ca
CO Consultants Inc.	rco.qc.ca
alTime Consulting Ltd.	realtime.ab.ca
d Deer College	rdc.ab.ca
gina Public Library	rpl.regina.sk.ca
gistered Nurses Association of ish Columbia	rnabc.bc.ca
iter Software Inc.	rsoft.bc.ca

Remuera Corp.	remuera.ca
Research In Motion Limited	rmotion.on.ca
Revenue Canada, Taxation	rct.ca
RGD Communications	rgdc.ottawa.on.ca
Richmond Public Library	rpl.richmond.bc.ca
Royal Military College of Canada at Kingston	rmc.ca
Royal Ontario Museum	rom.on.ca
Royal Roads Military College	royalroads.ca
Ryerson Polytechnical Institute	ryerson.ca
S-MOS Systems Vancouver Design Centre	smos.bc.ca
S-S Technologies Inc.	sstech.on.ca
Saint Francis Xavier University	stfx.ca
Saint Mary's University	stmarys.ca
Samuel Lunenfeld Research Institute of Mt. Sinai Hospital	mshri.on.ca
Saskatchewan Government	gov.sk.ca
Saskatchewan Institute of Applied Science and Technology	siast.sk.ca
Saskatchewan Oil Co.	saskoil.sk.ca
Saskatchewan Research Council	src.sk.ca
Saskatchewan Telecommunications	sasktel.sk.ca
Saskatoon Public Library	publib.saskatoon.sk.ca
Sault College of Applied Arts and Technology	saultc.on.ca
Scarborough Board of Education (Computers in Education)	sbe.scarborough.on.ca
Scheduled Solutions Inc.	scheduledsolutions.on.ca
School District # 36 (Surrey)	sd36.surrey.bc.ca
School District # 42 (Maple Ridge - Pitt Meadows)	schdist42.bc.ca
School District # 42 (Maple Ridge - Pitt Meadows)	sd42.mapleridge.bc.ca
School District # 43 (Coquitlam)	schdist43.bc.ca
School District #28 (Quesnel)	sd28.quesnel.bc.ca
School District #44 North Vancouver	schdist44.bc.ca
School District No. 68 (Nanaimo)	sd68.nanaimo.bc.ca
Science World of British Columbia	scienceworld.bc.ca
Scott Paper Ltd.	scottpaper.ca
SEAC Software Engineering	seac.bc.ca
Securiplex Technologies Inc.	spxtech.qc.ca
SED Systems, Inc.	sedsystems.ca
Selkirk College	selkirk.bc.ca
Seneca College of Applied Arts and Technology	senecac.on.ca
Sensors & Software Inc.	sensoft.on.ca
Servacom America Inc.	servacom.ca
Shell Canada Corporation	shell.ca
Sheridan College	sheridanc.on.ca

Sherritt Gordon Limited	sherritt.ca
Shoppers Drug Mart, National Office, Canada	shoppersdrugmart.ca
Shoreline Communications, Inc.	shoreline.ca
SIDOCI Enr.	sidoci.qc.ca
Sidus Systems Inc.	sidus.ca
Siemens Nixdorf Information Systems Limited	sni.ca
Sierra Wireless Inc.	sierrawireless.ca
Signal Path Designs	signalpath.on.ca
Simon Fraser University	sfu.ca
Sir Sandford Fleming College of Applied Arts and Technology	flemingc.on.ca
Sirius Solutions Limited	sirius.ns.ca
Sloth	sloth.bc.ca
Smegheads Appreciation Society	smegheads.montreal.qc.ca
Sobeco Inc.	sobeco.ca
Social Science and Humanities Research Council	sshrc.ca
Societe GRICS (Reseau EDUPAC)	edupac.qc.ca
Soden Software Corporation	soden.toronto.on.ca
Softimage Inc.	softimage.qc.ca
Software Alberta Society	sas.ab.ca
Software Industry Association of Nova Scotia	sians.ns.ca
Software Kinetics Ltd.	sofkin.ca
Softwords, A Division of Press Porcepic Limited	softwords.bc.ca
Solucorp	solucorp.qc.ca
Sorbus Canada Limited	sorbus.on.ca
South Winnipeg Technical Centre	swtc.mb.ca
Southam Newspaper Group	southam.ca
Southern Alberta Institute of Technology	sait.ab.ca
Southport Technologies Inc.	southport.on.ca
SPAR Aerospace Limited	spar.ca
Spectrum Signal Processing Inc	spectrumsignal.bc.ca
Spindrift Software Inc.	spindrift.qc.ca
SportsWorld Bulletin Board System Inc.	sportsworld.bc.ca
St. Clair College of Applied Arts and Technology	stclairc.on.ca
St. Joseph's Health Centre Hospital and Research Institution	stjosephs.london.on.ca
St. Lawrence College	stlawrencec.on.ca
St. Thomas University	stthomasu.ca
Statistics Canada	statcan.ca
Steinberg Inc.	steinberg.ca
Stem-net of Newfoundland and Labrador	stemnet.nf.ca
Stentor Canadian Network Management Corporation	stentor.ca
Strategic Focus	stratfocus.ottawa.on.ca

Strategic Unix Networks Corporation	strategic.victoria.bc.ca
Strategy First Inc	strategy.qc.ca
STS SYSTEMS LTD.	sts-systems.ca
Sun Microsystems Of Canada, Inc.	sun.ca
Sutherland-Schultz, Ltd.	schultz.on.ca
Synamics Inc.	synamics.on.ca
Synectic Advice Inc.	synectic.on.ca
System Telly	telly.on.ca
Taarna System Inc.	taarna.qc.ca
Tanda and Associates	tanda.on.ca
TDK Consulting Services	tdkcs.waterloo.on.ca
Technical University of Nova Scotia	tuns.ca
Technologies Lyre Inc.	lyre.qc.ca
Telco Consulting	telco.waterloo.on.ca
Telecommunications Research Laboratories	trlabs.ca
TELERIDE SAGE Ltd.	teleride.on.ca
Telesat Canada	telesat.ca
Tesuji Software	tesuji.qc.ca
Tetres Consultants, Inc.	tetres.ca
Texxen Consulting Limited	texxen.richmond.bc.ca
The Alt Society	alt.ns.ca
The Banff Centre for Continuing Education	banffcentre.ab.ca
The City of Calgary	gov.calgary.ab.ca
The College of Geographic Sciences	cogs.ns.ca
The GameMaster / Le Maitre de Jeu (enr.)	gamemaster.qc.ca
The Globe and Mail	globeandmail.ca
The Joymarmon Group Inc.	joymrmn.on.ca
The Land of the Darkside BBS	lotds.waterloo.on.ca
The MacLawran Group Inc.	maclawran.ca
The Manitoba Institute of Management, Inc.	maninstmgt.mb.ca
The Nova Scotia Provincial Library System	library.ns.ca
The Object People	objectpeople.on.ca
The PEER Group Inc.	peer.on.ca
The Princess Margaret Hospital	pmh.toronto.on.ca
The Proteus Group, Montreal Canada	proteus.qc.ca
The Salvation Army Grace Maternity Hospital	gracehosp.ns.ca
The WATCOM Group Inc.	watcom.on.ca
Think+ Computer Resources Inc.	thinkplus.on.ca
Thinkage Ltd.	thinkage.on.ca
Thomas Haney Secondary	ths.mapleridge.bc.ca
Thought Technology Ltd.	thought.ca
Timberline Forest Inventory Consultants	tfic.bc.ca
TM Software Associates Inc.	tmsoftware.ca
Totem Building Supplies Ltd.	totem.ab.ca
Tradart	tradart.ottawa.on.ca
TransAlta Utilities Corporation	transalta.ab.ca
Tremar Virtual	tremarvirtual.mb.ca

nt University	trentu.ca
University Meson Facility	triumf.ca
um Sound Research Inc.	trillium.ab.ca
ity Western University	twu.ca
OS Training Centres Ltd.	trios.ca
le S Business Development rporation	triplesbdc.mb.ca
M Technologies Inc.	trm-technologies.on.ca
nica Computer Centre	tronica.mb.ca
ger Technologies Inc.	truger.ca
International Inc.	tsb-intl.ca
Ontario	tvo.on.ca
G The Westrheim Group	twg.bc.ca
trex Corporation	ubitrex.mb.ca
C Consulting Ltd.	ugc.ab.ca
SSES Systems	ulysses.bc.ca
base Telecom Ltd.	unibase.sk.ca
fax Communiations Inc.	unifax.bc.ca
Forum Canada	uniforum.ca
Forum Quebec	uniforum.qc.ca
ted Grain Growers, Ltd.	unitedgrain.ca
versite de Moncton	umoncton.ca
versite de Montreal	umontreal.ca
versite de Sherbrooke	usherb.ca
versite du Quebec (C.S.C.Q.)	uquebec.ca
versite du Quebec a Montreal	uqam.ca
versite Laval	ulaval.ca
versity College of Cape Breton	uccb.ns.ca
versity College of the Fraser Valley	ucfv.bc.ca
versity of Alberta	ualberta.ca
versity of British Columbia	ubc.ca
versity of Calgary	ucalgary.ca
versity of Guelph	uoguelph.ca
versity of Lethbridge	uleth.ca
versity of Manitoba	umanitoba.ca
versity of New Brunswick, Saint John mpus	unbsj.ca
versity of New Brunswick	unb.ca
versity of Ottawa	uottawa.ca
versity of Prince Edward Island	upei.ca
versity of Regina	uregina.ca
versity of Saskatchewan	usask.ca
versity of Toronto	utoronto.ca
versity of Victoria	uvic.ca
versity of Waterloo	uwaterloo.ca
versity of Western Ontario	uwo.ca
versity of Windsor	uwindsor.ca
versity of Winnipeg	uwinnipeg.ca
R/GROUP Edmonton	ugedm.ab.ca
as International, Canada	utlas.ca
MH - Unix Users of Medicine Hat	uumh.ab.ca
NET Canada Inc.	uunet.ca
NORTH Incorporated	uunorth.on.ca

uuserve&	uuserve.on.ca
V-COM Computer Warehouse	vcom.ca
Van den Heede Computing	vdhcomp.on.ca
Vancouver Community College	vcc.bc.ca
Vancouver NeXT Users Society	vnus.bc.ca
Vancouver Public Library	vpl.vancouver.bc.ca
Vansco Electronics Ltd.	vansco.mb.ca
Vernon Rentals and Leasing	vernonrentals.ca
Victoria Digital Information Service	victoriadigital.bc.ca
Victoria Free-Net Association	freenet.victoria.bc.ca
Victoria General Hospital	victoriahosp.winnipeg.b.ca
Victoria Online -- Victoria Digital Information Service	victoriaonline.bc.ca
Ville de Sherbrooke	ville.sherbrooke.qc.ca
Virtual Prototypes Inc	virtualprototypes.ca
Vital Technologies Corporation	vitaltech.on.ca
Waterloo Engineering Software	wes.on.ca
Waterloo Maple Software Inc.	maplesoft.on.ca
Waterloo Regional Domain Park	waterloo-rdp.on.ca
West Fraser Mills Ltd.	westfraser.ca
West-Net Consulting Services Ltd.	west-net.bc.ca
Whitman Benn Group Inc.	whitmanbenn.ns.ca
Wilfrid Laurier University	wlu.ca
William M. Mercer Limited	wm-mercer.ca
WILLOW Information Systems Inc.	willow.on.ca
Willowglen Systems Ltd.	willowglen.ab.ca
Wilson King & Company	wilsonking.bc.ca
Wimsey Associates	wimsey.bc.ca
Winnipeg PC User Group, Inc.	wpcusrgrp.mb.ca
Wiz Zone Computers for Kids Incorporated	wizzone.vancouver.bc.a
Wor-Ker Window Technology Inc.	wor-ker.ca
Wordcraft Systems Corporation	wcraft.bc.ca
WordDancer Systems Inc.	worddancer.ca
XBR Communications Inc.	xbrcom.qc.ca
XeniTec Consulting Services	xenitec.on.ca
York University	yorku.ca
ZED Data Systems	zed.ca
Zentronics	zentronics.ca
ZIFTech Computer Systems Inc.	ziftech.on.ca

A P P E N D I X   B

....

INTERNET FORMS

CA SUBDOMAIN APPLICATION INSTRUCTIONS

CA Subdomain Application Instructions
(Updated 1994 January 15)

This document describes the CA subdomain
application form. To apply for a subdomain,
please fill out an application form and
submit it to the appropriate liaison from
the list below. It is recommended that you
edit the sample form included below and
change the information as appropriate for
your organization.

Your liaison may charge a fee for the registration service, and may also require
further information. Unaffiliated organizations wishing to reserve a name for future
or internal use may register directly with
the CA Registrar for an annual fee of $50.
Currently the registrar cannot accept telephone requests.

Please note that your application is being
made on behalf of your entire organization.
As such, it is important that you are
authorized to speak for your entire organization in this matter and that you obtain
the agreement of all interested parties
within your organization prior to submis-
sion.

See below for instructions on how to obtain
more information on the CA domain, such as
an introduction to the domain and a list of
current subdomain registrations.

Here is a description of each field of the application form:

Subdomain:

The name of the subdomain applied for.

Since the CA domain is structured according to Canadian political geography, this will be of the form "yourorg.CA", or "yourorg.province-or-territory.CA", or "yourorg.locality.province-or-territory.CA".

"province-or-territory" is one of the following provincial and territorial abbreviations, as recommended by the Department of the Secretary of State: AB, BC, MB, NB, NF, NS, NT, ON, PE, QC, SK, and YK. "locality" is the full name of a city, town, or village.

Hyphens are used to replace spaces, e.g., Niagara-Falls, New-Westminster.

Here are requirements and guidelines to help determine the appropriate level of subdomain name for your organization:

(1) second (national) level - To qualify for a second level domain, your organization must have offices or other points of presence (such as computer hosts or dial-up facilities) in more than one province or territory, or be incorporated or chartered nationally.

(2) third (provincial or territorial) level - To qualify for a third level domain, your organization must have offices or other points of presence (such as computer hosts or dial-up facilities) in more than one locality, or be incorporated or registered provincially or territorially. Universities, colleges, referral hospitals, and provincial and territorial governments should have third level subdomain names.

   Municipality names are reserved.

(3) fourth (municipal) level - Small organizations such as companies which do most of their business in one locality and bulletin board systems should apply for a fourth level or municipal subdomain name, as should organiza-

tions such as local hospitals, libraries, municipal governments, and
schools.

When applying for anything other than a
fourth level subdomain name, please provide
supporting information such as your incor-
poration number, office locations, etc.

"yourorg" is a string that encodes the
proper name of your organization. Determin-
ing the string is a matter of establishing
the "corporate electronic identity" of your
organization for years to come. This is
something you should discuss with the individual in your organization whose authority
includes the "corporate image". If the appropriate string is not immediately obvious
to this person, then we suggest that you
use the following steps to determine the
string for which you are applying.

(1) Start with the full proper name by
    which your organization conducts its
    business.

    e.g.: "AB Systems Incorporated",
    "University of Waterloo"

(2) Remove all the blanks.

    e.g.: "ABSystemsIncorporated",
    "UniversityofWaterloo"

(3) Remove truly extraneous components, if
    there are any.

    e.g.: "ABSystems",
    "UniversityWaterloo"

(4) If it is excessively long, abbreviate
    by trimming the parts whose removal
    will result in the least loss of rec-
    ognizability outside the sphere in
    which your organization is already
    well known.

    e.g.: "ABSystems", "UWaterloo"

(5) Please try to avoid a cryptic abbre-
    viation that defeats the objective of
    step (4) above. In particular, please
    use an acronym only if it conveys your
    organization's corporate electronic
    identity. Otherwise, please choose a
    more descriptive abbreviation of your
    organization's name. If you are in
    doubt, ask your CA Domain Committee

> member to offer an opinion before you
> submit the application.

It is your responsibility to ensure that
you have the right to use the name you have
chosen.

Obscene names are not permitted.

Legal characters are letters, digits, and
the hyphen. You may mix upper and lower
case, or use all upper or all lower case.
Software will ignore case, and users can
type in whatever case they like.

You should capitalize your subdomain name
as you wish it to appear in machine generated lists, such as the return address generated in your outgoing electronic mail.
Hyphens may be used to separate words if
necessary or consistent with normal references to the proper name of your organization.

The CA domain registrar is the final
authority on all matters relating to registration and subsequent use of your subdomain name.

Your subdomain name must be approved by the
CA domain registrar before it is used in
network communications. If you devise further subdomains of your domain name, then
you in turn will have final authority on
matters relating to the use of those subdomains.

Since the CA domain was first created, the
requirements and guidelines have been modi-
fied from time to time. Although all existing registrations remain in effect, some
registered subdomain names might not be
permitted if applied for today. New applications and voluntary applications for re-
registration will be considered using the
current guidelines.

Examples:

MegaCo.CA National company.

WidgetCo.PE.CA Provincial Company.

CityAutoLtd.Melville.SK.CA Small business.

AlphaBetaU.MB.CA University.

Organization:

> The full name of your organization.

Type:

>   Type of organization.

>   For example:

>   For-Profit Corporation

>   Non-Profit Corporation

>   For-Profit Partnership

>   Proprietorship

>   Ph.D. granting university

>   High School

>   Federal Government Branch

>   Provincial Government

>   Military Branch

Description:

A short paragraph describing your organization. Please include any appropriate justification for your choice of subdomain level. For example, please state whether your corporation is federally or provincially incorporated, and whether your corporation has offices in more than one province.

Admin-Name:

Admin-Title:

Admin-Postal:

Admin-Phone:

Admin-Fax:

Admin-Mailbox:

The name, title, full mailing address, phone number, facsimile number, and electronic address of an administrative contact for the organization. This person is within the subdomain's organization and is the contact point for administrative and policy questions about the subdomain. This person is responsible for this application and for any future changes. We recommend that you choose a person who is expected to be around and in a position of authority for many years, and that you use a properly-maintained generic electronic address.

For example:

```
Admin-Name: John Smith
Admin-Title: Administrative Assistant
Admin-Postal: Alpa Beta University
Dept. of Computer Science
1234 Main St.
Hoople, Manitoba
M1B 2C3
Admin-Phone: +1 (204) 555 1511
Admin-Fax: +1 (204) 555 9095
Admin-Mailbox: admin@AlphaBetaU.MB.CA
```

```
Tech-Name:
Tech-Title:
Tech-Postal:
Tech-Phone:
Tech-Fax:
Tech-Mailbox:
```

The name, title, full mailing address,
telephone number, facsimile number, and
electronic address of two or more technical
contacts. This is the contact point for
problems with the subdomain and for updat-
ing information about the subdomain. The
registrar will verify changes by sending
the current registration information back
to the submitter and to the administrative
contact. We recommend that you use a prop-
erly maintained generic electronic address.

Don't list people who hate to get electronic mail. One or more of the contacts
must read their mail often enough to respond quickly, should a problem arise. For
very small organizations, it is permissible
to have only one technical contact. It is
appropriate to have at least one contact
corresponding to each of the forwarders
within the organization. Forwarders are described below.

For example:

```
Tech-Name: Jean Smith
Tech-Title: Researcher
Tech-Postal: Alpha Beta University
Dept. of Computer Science
1234 Main St.
Hoople, Manitoba
M1B 2C3
Tech-Phone: +1 (204) 555 1512
Tech-Name: Fred Rogers
Tech-Title: Computing Staff
Tech-Postal: Alpha Beta University
Dept. of Computer Science
1234 Main St.
```

Hoople, Manitoba
M1B 2C3
Tech-Phone: +1 (204) 555 1513
Tech-Fax: +1 (204) 555 9099
Tech-Mailbox: tech@AlphaBetaU.MB.CA

Location:

The latitude and longitude of the subdomain. (This can be taken as the location of
the main organizational machine, or the
headquarters, or the contact persons; usually the machine is used.)

Give as much precision as you know; if you
can determine the location only to the
nearest minute, or the nearest few minutes,
that's satisfactory. Include "city" only if
you are using the location of your city
center, for which information is often
available in an atlas, at a library, City
Hall, or a nearby airport. At a minimum,
please provide the location of your city
center. This field is used to draw maps.

For example:

52 04 05 N / 97 37 46 W

or

52 04 N / 97 37 W city

Net-Provider:

The name of your primary network provider.
Your network provider is the organization
which provides your IP connectivity to the
Internet. Here is a list of network providers:

ARnet
BC Systems
BCnet
DREnet
fONOROLA
GTA
HookUp
MBnet
NB*net
NLnet
NSTN
ONet
PEInet
RISQ
SASK#net
UUNET Canada

If you have no IP connectivity to the Internet but do have UUCP connectivity, spec
ify "UUCP" as your provider. If you have n
connectivity but wish to apply for a subdo
main name anyway, specify "none" as your
provider.

The list above will be expanded as needed.
If your network provider is not on the
list, have them contact the CA Registrar
directly before proceeding with your appli
cation.

Forwarder:

The forwarder fields describe how your organization can be reached FROM specified
networks. This information is used to guid
tasks such as the routing of electronic
mail to your organization. (They do not de
scribe how your organization sends traffic
TO any network.) For the purposes of your
application, there are two kinds of forwarders:

Organization-Internal Forwarder. Your organization has one or more computing systems that have direct Internet or UUCP con
nections. Also, all computing systems
within your organization are internally
connected. Please see the examples below
for what to do in the case of a forwarder
that cannot reach all recipients within
your organization.

Organization-External Forwarder. Your organization is directly connected to networ
A; another organization is directly connected to both networks A and B, and has
agreed to provide a forwarder that will ac
cept mail from network B and forward it to
your organization-internal forwarder in
network A.

Within the application form, each forwarde
specification appears as follows:

Forwarder: networkname: forwarder_address
(comment) <reference_address>;

or

Forwarder: networkname: none;

or:

Forwarder: Internet: DNS;

where "networkname" is the name of the network, "forwarder_address" is the network-
specific electronic address of the forwarder, "(comment)" is optional explanatory
text, and "reference_address" is the electronic address of an individual to whom
questions

regarding the use of that forwarder may be
sent. For an organization-internal forwarder, the reference will be some entity
within your organization subdomain; for an
organization-external forwarder, it will be
the entity external to your organization
that has authorized your organization to
use that forwarder.

 Specify forwarder fields for both the Internet and UUCP, even if you do not have
access to both. For historical reasons, existing registrations may have forwarder
fields for CDNnet and NetNorth.

Example 1 -- Internet and UUCP connections

>   In this case, the organization can be
>   reached directly from both networks.

>   Forwarder: Internet: DNS;

>   Forwarder: UUCP: abunix
>   <rob@AlphaBetaU.MB.CA>;

>   When DNS (Domain Name System) is
>   specified, please provide as supple-
>   mentary information the subdomain
>   names and IP addresses of at least two
>   nameserver hosts (one primary and at
>   least one secondary) for the new sub-
>   domain. See the sample application
>   form below for an example.

Example 2 -- Internet-only

>   Here are the forwarder specifications
>   for an organization which is directly
>   connected to the Internet, but which
>   has no direct UUCP connection.

>   Forwarder: Internet: DNS;

>   Forwarder: UUCP: none;

>   Example 3 -- External Internet for-
>   warder

>   Forwarder: Internet: relay.otherorg.ca
>   <joe@otherorg.ca>;

> Forwarder: UUCP: abunix
> <rob@AlphaBetaU.MB.CA>;
>
> Here the organization does not have
> direct Internet connectivity, but
> joe@otherorg.ca (whose organization i
> on the Internet) has agreed to forwar
> mail from the Internet to the organi-
> zation. In this case the CA nameserve
> administrator will put the appropriat
> MX records into the CA nameservers to
> make this work.

Example 4 -- UUCP-only

> Here is an example of the forwarder
> specification for an organization wit
> a direct UUCP connection, but with no
> access to the Internet.
>
> Forwarder: Internet: none;
>
> Forwarder: UUCP: abunix
> <rob@AlphaBetaU.MB.CA>;
>
> Note that in this case, your organiza
> tion will not be directly addressable
> from the Internet. That is, your sub-
> domain name will not appear in the
> DNS.

Example 5 -- No connectivity

> When applying for a subdomain name fo
> your organization's future use, spec-
> ify "none" for the forwarders.
>
> Forwarder: Internet: none;
>
> Forwarder: UUCP: none;

Once you establish forwarders, resubmit th
application with the updated information.

NOTES:

(1) In the case of direct connection to a
    network but lack of full organization
    internal connectivity, please do not
    omit the forwarder specification. If
    you can arrange full connectivity wit
    the help of an external organization,
    specify the forwarder as above. Other
    wise, specify:

    Forwarder: networkname: none;

(2) Each network-administration body may
    have specific regulations covering
    the valid uses of its network. The ac

ceptance of an application for a CA
subdomain in no way alters or elimi-
nates your obligations to adhere to
the regulations for the uses of those
networks.

Here is a sample application form:

Subdomain: AlphaBetaU.MB.CA
Organization: Alpha Beta University
Type: Ph.D. granting university
Description: Alpha Beta University is a de-
gree granting academic organization widely
known for its program in Greek studies.
Admin-Name: Jean Smith
Admin-Title: Associate Director
Admin-Postal: Alpha Beta University
Computing Services
1234 Main St.
Hoople, Manitoba
M1B 2C3
Admin-Phone: +1 (204) 555 1511
Admin-Fax: +1 (204) 555 9095
Admin-Mailbox: admin@AlphaBetaU.MB.CA
Tech-Name: John Smith
Tech-Title: Systems Manager
Tech-Postal: Alpha Beta University
Dept. of Computer Science
1234 Main St.
Hoople, Manitoba
M1B 2C3
Tech-Phone: +1 (204) 555 1512
Tech-Fax: +1 (204) 555 9099
Tech-Name: Fred Rogers
Tech-Title: Computing Staff
Tech-Postal: Alpha Beta University
Dept. of Computer Science
1234 Main St.
Hoople, Manitoba
M1B 2C3
Tech-Phone: +1 (204) 555 1513
Tech-Fax: +1 (204) 555 9098
Tech-Mailbox: tech@AlphaBetaU.MB.CA
Location: 52 04 05 N / 97 37 46 W
Net-Provider: MBnet
Forwarder: Internet: DNS;
Forwarder: UUCP: abunix
<rob@AlphaBetaU.MB.CA>;
Nameserver information:
hub.alphabetau.mb.ca 199.3.2.1
relay.otherorg.ca 200.1.2.3

Applications and updates may be submitted
to the following contacts:

UUCP sites:
 CA Registry
 c/o XeniTec Consulting Services,
 199 Silver Aspen Cr.
 Kitchener, Ontario
 N2N 1H5
 E-mail: registry@ai.toronto.edu, regis-
try@utai.uucp

UUNET Canada:
 Lynda Fincham
 UUNET Canada Inc.
 1 Yonge St., Suite 1400
 Toronto, ON
 Canada M5E 1J9
 E-mail: support@uunet.ca

BCnet and British Columbia:
 Darren Kinley
 BCnet Headquarters
 413 - 6356 Agricultural Road
 Vancouver, B.C.
 V6T 1Z2
 E-mail: Darren.Kinley@BCnet.BC.CA

ARnet and Alberta:
 Chris Thierman
 University Of Alberta
 Computing and Network Services
 352 General Services Building
 Edmonton, Alberta
 Canada T6G 2H1
 E-mail: thierman@namao.ucs.ualberta.ca
 Fax: +1 (403) 492 1729
 Phone: +1 (403) 492 9318

MBnet and Manitoba:
 Gary Mills
 Networking Group, Computer Services
 Room 603, Engineering Building
 University of Manitoba
 Winnipeg, Manitoba
 R3T 2N2
 E-mail: mills@ccu.umanitoba.ca

ONet and Ontario:
 Herb Kugel
 ONET Registrar
 Univ of Toronto Network Operating Services
 255 Huron Street
 Toronto, Ontario,
 M5S 1A1
 E-mail: herb@gpu.utcc.utoronto.ca

RISQ and Quebec:
  Francois Robitaille
  Centre de recherche informatique de
      Montreal (CRIM)
  1801, McGill College Avenue
  Suite 800
  Montreal (Quebec) Canada
  H3A 2N4
  E-mail: f_robita@crim.ca

NBnet and New Brunswick:
  Brian Kaye
  Computing Services
  University of New Brunswick
  P.O. Box 4400
  Fredericton, N.B.
  E3B 5A3
  E-mail: bdk@unb.ca

NSTN and Nova Scotia
  Daniel MacKay
  Communications Services
  Dalhousie University
  Halifax, N.S.
  B3H 4H8
  E-mail: daniel@nstn.ns.ca

fONOROLA:
  Hung Vu
  Network Engineering
  fONOROLA
  250 Albert Street, Suite 205
  Ottawa, Ontario
  Canada K1P 6M1
  E-mail: hungv@fonorola.com
  Fax: +1 (613) 232 4329
  Phone: +1 (613) 235 3666

British Columbia Systems Corporation:
  Russ Forster
  Interconnect Services
  British Columbia Systems Corporation
  4000 Seymour Place
  Victoria, B.C.
  Canada V8X 4S8
  E-Mail: RForster@Galaxy.GOV.BC.CA
  Fax: +1 (604) 389-3412
  Phone: +1 (604) 389-3186

Other organizations:
  CA Domain Registrar
  c/o John Demco
  Department of Computer Science
  University of British Columbia

Vancouver, British Columbia
V6T 1Z2
E-mail: ca-registrar@CDNnet.CA

Information about the CA domain is available via electronic mail,
anonymous FTP, and gopher.

1. To retrieve CA domain information via electronic mail, specify a line of the following form:

    index ca-domain

    or

    send ca-domain <filename> [<filename>]

    in the subject line or body of an electronic mail message to the CDNnet archive server. Send this message to:

    archive-server@relay.CDNnet.CA

    or in X.400 format:

    S=archive-server; OU=relay; O=CDNnet; P=cdn; A=telecom.canada; c=CA;

    or use this UUCP path:

    !ubc-cs!relay.cdnnet.ca!archive-server

    Example:

    To: archive-server@relay.CDNnet.CA

    Subject: send ca-domain Introduction Application-form

2. CA domain information is available from a number of FTP sites. Use a service such as "archie" to find them, or use ftp.cdnnet.ca as follows. Establish an FTP connection to ftp.cdnnet.ca, log in with the username "anonymous", and specify your e-mail address as the password. When logged in, change to the "ca-domain" directory with the following command:

    cd ca-domain

    Individual files can then be retrieved using the "get" command:

    get <remote filename>

    For example:

    get Index

get Introduction

get Application-form

3. CA domain information is available for
    searching and browsing via the Nova
    Scotia Technology Network (NSTN) go-
    pher. Point your gopher at

    nstn.ns.ca

    and select

    White Pages

    from the main menu. Then browse
    through organizations in the _Canadian
    Organizations_ directory or search on
    full words (e.g."macmillan") using the
    search menu item. There are keywords
    for cities, people, organizations, and
    a little paragraph on each entity,so
    you may be able to do some creative
    searching.

CANADIAN INTERNET PROTOCOL NETWORK NUMBER APPLICATION FOR CLASS C NETWORK NUMBER(S)

Template [8/23/93/hck]

This template is to be used to obtain a TCP-IP number from CA*net.It obsoletes Form [1/3/tjm] which should no longer be used.

This template is in two parts. The first part is a sample template and the second part is the template itself which should be filled out carefully, using the guidelines in the sample template, and returned as indicated below.

Please fill in the template in EXACTLY the same format as shown in the sample. This information is scanned by software and any errors WILL result in delays in the issuance of the number(s) to you. In this situation, EXACTLY means EXACTLY as shown, line by line, item by item, field by field. The NIC software designed to parse the application can accept no other format. Please do not change this format in any way. Do not combine fields that are on different lines and separate them with a semicolon; the NIC software will not handle this. Please, in this case, EXACTLY really does mean EXACTLY.

Please note that the network name is not the domain name of the network. The network name may contain dashes but no other special characters and must be less then or equal to twelve characters. This name is used as an identifier for the network in the Network Information Center (NIC) 'WHOIS' database and will be changed by the Network Registrar if the name is already in use.

Applications may be sent by e.mail to: IPregist@CAnet.Ca or by fax to:

CA*Net IP Registry

(416) 978 6620

If possible, send your request by e.mail. E.mail submissions allow us to automatically process the application and will therefore result in the request being processed in a shorter time than if the request is submitted by fax.

Please do not send requests to the NIC in the USA. They will be forwarded by the NIC to the Canadian IP Registry office who will then process the number. You will lose a considerable amount of time if you send your request to the NIC.

Replies will be via e.mail if the request was received through e.mail and via telephone if the request was received by fax

In the following, the 'Type of Organization' should be either 'government,' 'educational,' or 'commercial' while the fifth item deals with the actual number of networks being requested.

In the case of Class C addresses, IP numbers are assigned in blocks to CA*net and then reassigned to specific organizations through this template. Enter the number of Class C addresses you desire here. If you wish a class B address, contact the IP registrar BEFORE submitting this form.

Item 6 is required for installations who are currently connected to or planning to be connected to one of the provincial networks such as MBnet, ARCnet, etc. It is used strictly to gather statistical information for CA*net and is not used for routing or any other technical purpose whatsoever. As this form is to be used by any organization in Canada to obtain an IP number or numbers, it should be left blank by those organizations not planning to join a regional network.

Thus, in the following example, the Pooh Software Company is requesting two Class C networks and planning to connect to ONet.

```
------------------Sample Template---------
1a.  Technical Contact name (Lastname,
     Firstname): Smith, John
1b.  Technical Contact title: Sr. Program-
     mer
1c.  Mail address:
     1230 Main Street
     Toronto, Ontario; M5S 1A1
     Canada
```

```
1d.   Phone: +1 (604) 432-8711
1e.   Net Mailbox: smith@pooh.on.ca
2.    Network name: pooh-on-ca
3a.   Postal address for main/headquarters
      network site:
      1280 Main Street
      Toronto, Ontario; M5S 1A1
      Canada
3b.   Name of Organization: Pooh Software
      Company
4.    Type of Organization: Commercial
5.    Quantity of network numbers being re-
      quested: 2
6.    Regional Network Affiliation: ONet
```
+++
Please fill out the following carefully us-
ing the above as as a guide line.
-------------Application Template----------

```
1a.   Technical Contact name (Lastname,
      Firstname):
1b.   Technical Contact title:
1c.   Mail address:
1d.   Phone:
1e.   Net Mailbox:
2.    Network name:
3a.   Postal address for main/headquarters
      network site:
3b.   Name of Organization:
4.    Type of Organization:
5.    Quantity of Networks being requested:
6.    Regional Network Affiliation:
```

A P P E N D I X   C

. . . .

SCHOOLNET

The following is a summary concerning SchoolNet, obtained directly from the Internet.

CANADA'S NATIONAL EDUCATIONAL NETWORKING
INITIATIVE

What is SchoolNet?

SchoolNet is a cooperative federal/ provincial /territorial and industry initiative announced by the Federal Government in August
1993. The objective of SchoolNet is to enhance educational opportunities and achievements in elementary and secondary schools
across Canada by electronically linking them
and by making national and international resources available to Canadian teachers and
students.

Who Funds SchoolNet?
The Federal Government has committed $1.6
million to SchoolNet beginning in 1994-95.
Canada's full service telephone companies
have invested $100 000 dollars in this ven-
ture through the Stentor Alliance. SchoolNet
has also received significant contributions
from Apple Canada Inc., Sun Microsystems of
Canada Inc., The Globe and Mail, Southam
News, and KAO Infosystems Company.

How were offical SchoolNet schools selected?
Provincial/territorrial selection committees were responsible for selecting official
SchoolNet schools. Interested schools submitted applications listing their computer hard-

ware and software inventory (they had to have the ability to connect ie., computers, modems, communication software and a phone line) and a description of an interactive project that they would develop and run. The most technologically intensive schools along with those that had the best project were selected. It is anticipated that a new selection process will be used to choose official participants for the 1994-95 school year. Previous participants are welcome to apply again.

How many schools are involved?

For the initial phase of SchoolNet (Sept. 1993 - Sept. 1994), it was anticipated to connect the 300 schools selected to participate in the project. However, due to the large membership of British Columbia's CLN, Nova Scotia's NSTN and Newfoundland's STEM-NET, and the fact that some schools already have Internet access, the number of schools accessing SchoolNet far exceeds the original target.

How are schools connecting to SchoolNet?

Schools are accessing SchoolNet in a variety of ways. One of them is through various commercial and non-commercial regional networks that exist in British Columbia (Community Learning Network [CLN]), Saskatchewan (SaskNet), Manitoba (Manitoba Information Network [MINET]), Nova Scotia (Nova Scotia Technology Network [NSTN]), New Brunswick (New Brunswick Education Network [NEWBED]) and Newfoundland (Science & Technology Education and Mathematics Network [STEM-NET]). Schools in Alberta will be accessing SchoolNet and the Internet through Universities and the Alberta Research Network (ARNET) . Schools in the Northwest Territories will also be accessing through ARNET. Various Universities and Community Colleges are providing Internet access for schools in Ontario and Quebec. Freenets in Ottawa, Ont., Trail and Victoria, BC., are also providing access to SchoolNet. Freenet organizing committees are present in many communties across Canada, and when operational, these Freenets will also provide SchoolNet access. SchoolNet is also currently investigating the feasibility of providing Internet access to Schools via CATV and ISDN technologies.

Who can use SchoolNet?

We welcome anyone with Internet access to make use of SchoolNet resources and services. We do however ask that all schools using SchoolNet register with us, as this will give them access to our SchoolNet Whitepages and other protected databases which will be secured for privacy reasons.

Where is SchoolNet?

SchoolNet services are provided on a Gopher server. The address of the English language gopher is ERNEST. CCS.CARLETON.CA 419. The address for the French language gopher is ERNEST.CCS.CARLETON.CA.415. SchoolNet can also be found on the National Capital Freenet (telnet freenet.carleton.ca) in the Science and Engineering Technology Centre (#8) and in the Schools, Colleges and Universities section under Academy One (#1).

What services and resources does SchoolNet offer?

1)   A guide to the 100 best Internet science and technology related resources.

2)   Over 400 scientists, engineers and other advisors from around the world are available through the Electronic Innovators program; Electronic Innovators are available in the following capacities:

-        School Advisors - this role will involve advising teachers and students on areas of curriculum and-project development. In this respect they can also act as role models to students;

- Discussion Leaders - this role involves monitoring subject-specific USENET newsgroups and answering questions posted by students and teachers;

and,

- In-Class Visitors - this role will involve visits to classroom.

3)   On-line network training through School-Net/Internet Scavenger Hunts and a SchoolNet Navigator.

4)   Career selection guide.

5)   Subject-specific USENET newsgroups for teachers and students (can.schoolnet.*).

6)   Electronic Classroom Edition of The
     Globe and Mail and an electronic Na-
     tional Press newsfeeds from Southam
     News.

7)   Access to institutional and university
     on-line library catalogues from across
     Canada and around the world.

8)   Access to databases from around the
     world.

9)   Innovative teacher designed networking
     projects.

10) On-line technical support.

For more information of SchoolNet, please
contact:

National SchoolNet Office or Freenet Science
and Engineering
Industry Canada Consulting Group
Room 805F (SchoolNet Support and Development)
235 Queen Street e-mail: schoolnet-
admin@carleton.ca
Ottawa, Ontario
Canada
K1A 0H5

For service in:
English

tel: (613) 991-6057
fax: (613) 941-2811
e-mail: charlton@sci.istc.ca

French

tel: (613) 998-7166
fax: (613) 941-2811
e-mail: boisjoly@sci.istc.ca

A P P E N D I X   D

....

INTERNET-RELATED
PUBLICATIONS

In this section, we provide you with information on eight
publications that cover the Internet. For each publication, we
list the frequency of publication, format, contact information,
and subscription rates in Canada. We also indicate if the
publication is sold at newsstands, or only available by mail
subscription.

Connect: The Modem User's Resource
Frequency: Bimonthly.
Format: Colour glossy.
Available at newsstands.

Connect has regular columns on bulletin board systems, the Internet,
and the major commercial online services such as America Online, BIX,
CompuServe, Delphi, and GEnie. All varieties of computer platforms
(IBM/Apple Macintosh, Commodore/Amiga, Atari) are covered, and
hardware/software reviews and industry news briefs appear regularly.
Recent articles include "Riding the Wild Internet," "Online Investing,"
"Conferencing 101," and "Getting Online with a High Speed Modem".

Pegasus Press, Inc.
3487 Braeburn Circle
Ann Arbor, Michigan 48108
U.S.A.
Voice: (313) 973-8825
Fax: (313) 973-0411
Internet: pegasus@cyberspace.org

Canadian residents: US$30.00 per year (surface).

The Internet Business Journal
Frequency: Monthly.

Format: Paper.
Available by mail only.

The *Internet Business Journal* was established to help businesses use the Internet. It provides regular coverage of commercial services and products on the Internet, and documents how large and small businesses are using the Internet for competitive advantage. Recent articles include "Advertising on the Internet," "Direct Marketing By E-mail," "Partnering on the Internet," and "Creating a Corporate Presence on the Net."

Strangelove Internet Enterprises
208 Somerset Street East
Suite A
Ottawa, Ontario, Canada
K1N 6V2
Voice: (613) 565-0982
Fax: (613) 569-4432
Internet: mstrange@fonorola.net

Regular Rate: CDN$179.00 (plus GST) per year.
Educational Libraries, Small Businesses, and Individuals:
CDN$89.00 (plus GST) per year.

The Internet Letter
Frequency: Monthly.
Format: Paper.
Available by mail only.

The Internet Letter covers the businesses that use the Internet, the political forces that shape it, and the information that flows across it.

Jayne Levin
Editor, The Internet Letter
220 National Press Building
Washington, D.C. 20045
U.S.A.
Voice: (202) 638-6020
Fax: (202) 638-6019
Internet: netweek@access.digex.net

Subscription: US$249.00 per year.

Internet Society News
Frequency: Quarterly.
Format: B&W glossy.
Available by mail only.

The *Internet Society News* provides an international forum for the exchange of information about the evolution and use of Internet technology, further growth of the global Internet and related private networks, the activities of the Internet Society and its members, and events significant to Internet Society constituents. Each issue features networking reports from around the world.   Recent articles include "Internet Debut into the World of Publishing," Electronic Mail and the University of Zimbabwe," "The Icelandic Educational Network," Toward the Haitian Research Network," and "Changing Eras: Evolution of the NSFNET." *Internet Society News* is free with membership in the Internet Society.

Internet Society
1895 Preston White Drive, Suite 100
Reston, VA 22091
U.S.A.
Voice: (703) 648-9888
Fax: (703) 620-0913
Internet: isoc@isoc.org

Regular membership: US$70.00 per year.
Student membership: US$25.00 per year.

Internet World
Frequency: Bimonthly.
Format: Colour glossy.
Available at newsstands.

Meckler Corporation
11 Ferry Lane West
Westport, Connecticut T 06880
U.S.A.
Voice: (203) 226-6967
Internet: meckler@jvnc.net

Internet World is a magazine for and about the Internet user community...the primary audience is the extended user community — end-users, and people like librarians and MIS managers and system administrators who are responsible for providing services to these users, plus the information and service providers and the developers who develop the business and educational resources users use." Internet World's mission statement is "Information for the Connected and Outreach for the Interested.   Recent articles include "What's My Motivation - Why Businesses Are Turning to the Internet," "Exploring Library Resources on the Internet," "Internet Libel — Is The Provider Responsible?" "Teens for Telnet — K-12 and the Internet," and "How To Be a Supported User." *Internet World* will begin publishing on a monthly basis in May 1994.

Institutions (Canada): US$77.00 per year.
Individual subscription (Canada): US$47.00 per year.

Matrix News
Frequency: Monthly.
Format: Paper.
Available by mail only.

Matrix Information and Directory Services
1106 Clayton Lane
Suite 500W
Austin, Texas 78723
Voice: (512) 451-7602
Internet: mids@tic.com

Matrix News is a newsletter about cross-network issues in the Matrix — all
computer networks worldwide that exchange electronic mail. Networks
covered include USENET, UUCP, FidoNet, BITNET, Internet, and
conferencing systems such as the WELL and CompuServe. Recent
articles include "The Uruguayan Academic Network," "Global Growth
Rates: The Matrix and the Internet," "The Matrix in East Asia: FidoNet,
UUCP, BITNET and the Internet," and "Networking in Baltic Countries: The
Growing Matrix."

**Online version: US$25/year ($15 for students). Paper version:
US$30/year ($20 for students). Both online and paper:
US$35/year ($25 for students).**

Online Access
Frequency: 10 times a year.
Format: Colour glossy.
Available at newsstands.

Online Access
900 North Franklin Street
Suite 310
Chicago, Illinois 60610
U.S.A.
Voice: (312) 573-1700
Fax: (312) 573-0520
Internet: 70324.343@CompuServe.com

Online Access' mission is "to educate our readers about online services
and how these services can benefit both their professional and personel
lives". Online Access covers the full spectrum of online services from
major online vendors and corporate databases to bulletin board
services and the Internet.

Recent articles include: "How to Telecommute," "News You Can Usenet," "5.5 Things Everyone Should Know About the Internet," and "Making the Most of E-Mail."

US$29.70 for a one-year subscription.

3W - The Internet With A Human Face
Frequency: Bi-monthly.
Format: Paper glossy.
Available by mail only.

461 West 49th Street
Suite 338
New York, New York 10019
U.S.A.
Voice: (212) 388-2830
Fax: (212) 399-0577
Internet: 3W@ukartnet.demon.co.uk
UK Editorial Office:
+44 81 533 0818 Voice and Fax

"**3W** is the paper-based magazine that covers all the global networks from a user perspective. The magazine avoids technical jargon and concentrates on providing information, advice, news, and ideas and references about the new global networks."

US$45 for a one-year subscription.

INDEX

....

Internet Society

Application for Membership

To: Internet Society

Please enroll me as a member of the Internet Society. I understand that membership entitles me to receive the quarterly Internet Society News, reduced fees for attendance at Internet Society conferences and other benefits. Membership privileges will be for twelve months from the receipt of payment. I am applying for

❑ regular membership at $70.00
❑ student membership at $25.00
(please send proof of status)

NAME: _____

POSTAL ADDRESS: _____

_____

_____

_____

INTERNET ADDRESS: _____

❑ Please bill me.

❑ Payment is included with this application as below.

PAYMENT INFORMATION:
Payment of Internet Society annual dues may be made via cheque, money order, credit card or wire transfer.

For **credit card** payments:

❑ AMEX ❑ VISA ❑ MC
❑ DINERS ❑ CARTE BLANCHE

Card Number: _____

Expiration Date: _____

Signature: _____

Send **wire transfers** to:

Bank: Riggs Bank of Virginia
Merrifield Office
8315 Lee Highway
Fairfax, VA 22031 USA

Bank ABA Number:
056001260

Account Number: Internet Society 14838710

Send via **e-mail** to:
isoc@isoc.org
File headers will be
accepted as signatures.

or **mail** to:
Internet Society
Suite 100
1895 Preston White Drive
Reston, VA 22091 USA

or **fax** to: 1 703 620 0913